GMAT VERBAL BIBLE

POWERSCORE
TEST PREPARATION

Published by
PowerScore Publishing, a division of PowerScore Incorporated
57 Hasell Street
Charleston, SC 29401

Authors: David M. Killoran, Steven G. Stein, Victoria Wood

Manufactured in Canada
February 2009

ISBN: 978-0-9801782-6-5

Need More Help?
We Offer Live GMAT Courses Nationwide.

Live GMAT Preparation Courses

Our test professionals have designed the PowerScore courses to provide you with the maximum exposure to the concepts that appear on the GMAT, access to the best possible instructors and classroom material, and the best support system to augment your studies. All of our instructors have scored in the 99th percentile on a real GMAT (administered by GMAC), and are GMAT experts. Whether you take our 30-hour Full-Length Course, or our 16-hour Weekend Course, you will find that we offer the best classes and instruction for your valuable time and money. For more information, please visit www.powerscore.com.

Full-Length GMAT Course—————————————————$995

This comprehensive course is best if you prefer the energy and motivation of a small group setting, have 6 weeks to prepare, and like a structured study environment.

- 30 hours of live, in-class instruction
- Free GMAT Hotline and Online Student Center
- Extensive Course Materials and Homework, including access to 7 Computer Adaptive Tests

Weekend GMAT Course—————————————————$395

For some students, time, location, and budget will dictate that they take the Weekend Course. The Weekend course is best if you need a quick jumpstart into your GMAT preparation, need to refine your GMAT techniques and approaches, or don't have much time to prepare.

- 16 hours of live, in-class instruction on one weekend
- Free Email Assistance and Online Student Center
- Extensive Course Materials and Homework, including access to 7 Computer Adaptive Tests
- Repeat the course for free within a year, no strings attached

Student Testimonials:

"**I got so much out of the PowerScore GMAT preparation class**, which I attribute to two things: the energy and personality of the teacher and the organization of the material. The instructor let us know that the class is designed to give us techniques to apply to our continuous studies and it did just that. **I now feel that I have a solid foundation for the test and will be confident going in to take it in three weeks!**" –J.L. Wisneski, New York City, NY

"I was skeptical about the PowerScore Weekend GMAT Prep Course because PowerScore wasn't as popular as the Kaplan or Princeton review courses. The price of the course was also unbelievable in comparison to the hours being offered. **This course was powerful! The instructor was superb! I would recommend PowerScore over any other prep course program on the market!**"–T. L. Taylor, New York City, NY

"I am writing to let you know that with the help of your course, I raised my GMAT score from a 470 to a 610! **Now, I can go to the school I want to go to.** Mark, the instructor, was encouraging, knowledgeable and interesting. **I highly recommend this course to anyone trying to increase their GMAT score.**" –S. Nelson, Nashville, TN

Also Available...

PowerScore GMAT Critical Reasoning Bible

The PowerScore GMAT Critical Reasoning Bible is a comprehensive how-to manual that teaches you how to solve every type of GMAT Critical Reasoning question. Featuring dozens of questions with detailed explanations, the Bible is the ultimate resource for improving your GMAT Critical Reasoning performance.

Available on the PowerScore website for $19.99.
Website: www.powerscore.com/pubs.htm

PowerScore GMAT Sentence Correction Bible

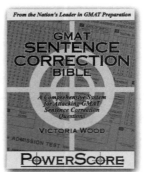

The PowerScore GMAT Sentence Correction Bible™ is a complete guide that teaches the grammar, style, and diction required to successfully attack GMAT Sentence Correction questions. The book is teeming with tips and tricks and includes an entire section on strategy. With dozens of examples, over 140 practice questions, and detailed explanations, the *Sentence Correction Bible™* is the absolute resource for gaining an the edge on the GMAT.

Available on the PowerScore website for $29.99.
Website: www.powerscore.com/pubs.htm

PowerScore GMAT Private and Telephone Tutoring

Tutoring is ideal for students unable to enroll in one of our preparation courses, or who need assistance with a specific area. Whether you need personalized lesson plans designed for you, or you just need to work on a few concepts, we can create a tutoring experience that will address all of your LSAT difficulties. Since both you and the instructor work off the same materials, describing the correct approach and appropriate diagramming is easy.

Our tutors are the same people that teach our classes, and every tutor has scored in the 99th percentile on a GMAC-administered GMAT. We offer in-person tutoring or telephone tutoring, with multiple price points and package rates. Please visit www.powerscore.com for more information.

PowerScore MBAdmissions Counseling

For the past five years, the number of students and professionals applying to business school has increased at a record-breaking pace. As more and more students apply to business school, acceptance into the school of your choice becomes more difficult. While your GMAT score and GPA will undeniably be major factors in admissions, you can separate yourself from the rest of the applicant pool by assembling the most powerful application folder possible. To do this you must have perfect admissions essays, top-notch letters of recommendation, superior oral interviews, and flawless overall presentation. PowerScore has gathered a team of admissions experts—including former business school admissions board members, top executives, and students from top ten business schools—to address your admissions counseling and admissions essay needs.

CONTENTS

CHAPTER ONE: INTRODUCTION

Introduction 1
A Brief Overview of the GMAT 3
Experimental Questions 5
The GMAT CAT Format 6
Special GMAT CAT Considerations 7
Computers and Scratch Paper 10
The GMAT Scoring Scale 11
The GMAT Percentile Table 11
The Use of the GMAT 12

SECTION ONE: CRITICAL REASONING

CHAPTER TWO: THE BASICS OF CRITICAL REASONING

Critical Reasoning 13
GMAT Critical Reasoning 15
Analyzing the Stimulus 18
Complex Arguments 31
Truth versus Validity 34

CHAPTER THREE: THE QUESTION STEM AND ANSWER CHOICES

The Question Stem 44
The Answer Choices 64
Question Approach Review 67
Final Chapter Note 68

CHAPTER FOUR: MUST BE TRUE QUESTIONS

Must Be True Questions 69
Must Be True Question Problem Set 86

CHAPTER FIVE: WEAKEN QUESTIONS

Weaken Questions 93
Weaken Question Problem Set 104

CHAPTER SIX: CAUSE AND EFFECT REASONING

What is Causality? 113
Causal Reasoning Problem Set 123

CHAPTER SEVEN: STRENGTHEN AND ASSUMPTION QUESTIONS

The Second Family 129
Strengthen Questions 131
Strengthen Question Problem Set 142
Assumption Questions 148
Assumption—Fill in the Blank Questions 164
Assumption Question Problem Set 167

CHAPTER EIGHT: RESOLVE THE PARADOX QUESTIONS

Resolve the Paradox Questions 173
Resolve the Paradox Question Problem Set 180

CHAPTER NINE: NUMBERS AND PERCENTAGES

Numbers and Percentages 185
Markets and Market Share 194
Numbers and Percentages Problem Set 199

SECTION TWO: READING COMPREHENSION

CHAPTER TEN: THE BASICS OF READING COMPREHENSION

Reading Comprehension 205
The Reading Comprehension Passages 207
Approaching the Passages 209
Analyzing the Passage Using VIEWSTAMP 218
    1. Viewpoint Identification and Analysis 218
    2. Tone/Attitude 222
    3. Passage Argumentation 230
    4. The Main Point 230
    5. Passage Structure 231
A Sample Passage Analyzed 236

CHAPTER ELEVEN: PASSAGE ELEMENTS AND FORMATIONS

Chapter Preview 240
Sources of Difficulty: The Test Makers' Arsenal 240
Passage Elements That Generate Questions 242
Viewpoint-Specific Elements 242
Text-based Questions 243
Two Broad Reasoning Structures 248
Pitfalls to Avoid 250

Chapter Twelve: The Questions and Answers

The Questions..258
The Location Element 259
Reading Comprehension Question Types 264
Reading Comprehension Question Types Examined in Detail 272
Must Be True/Most Supported Questions 272
Must Be True Question Subtypes 273
Correct Answers in Must Be True Questions 278
Incorrect Answers in Must Be True Questions 278
Non-Must Be True Question Types 281
Strengthen Questions 281
Weaken Questions 283
Parallel Reasoning Questions 284
Cannot Be True Questions 284
Question Modifiers and Overlays 285
Question Type Variety 288
Prephrasing Answers 295
The Answer Choices 296
Tricks of the Trade 298
Practicing With Time 299
Final Chapter Note 299

Chapter Thirteen: Putting It All Together

Chapter Preview 300
Reading Approach Review 300
Two Passages Analyzed..303

Section Three: Sentence Correction

Chapter Fourteen: The Basics of Sentence Correction

Sentence Correction 315
Grammar Review...317
Sentence Correction Question Directions 317
The Parts of a Sentence Correction Question 318
Tested Curriculum 318

Chapter Fifteen: Errors Involving Verbs

Subject and Verb Agreement 319
Verb Tense 333
Verb Voice...344

CHAPTER SIXTEEN: ERRORS WITH NOUNS AND PRONOUNS

Noun Agreement...349
Pronouns...350
Pronoun and Antecedent Agreement 351
Relative Pronouns...358
Ambiguous and Implied Pronouns 363

CHAPTER SEVENTEEN: ERRORS INVOLVING MODIFIERS

Adjectives Versus Adverbs 369
Quantifiers 370
Modifier Placement 376
Verb Forms as Modifiers 381

CHAPTER EIGHTEEN: ERRORS INVOLVING CONJUNCTIONS

Coordinating Conjunctions 385
Subordinating Conjunctions...387
"Like" Versus "As" 389

CHAPTER NINETEEN: ERRORS IN CONSTRUCTION

Comparisons..393
Parallel Structure..399
Semicolons 410
Idiom 413

CHAPTER TWENTY: ERRORS INVOLVING STYLE

Wordy Language 421
Redundant Expressions 423

CHAPTER TWENTY-ONE: MULTIPLE ERRORS

Double and Triple Errors..427

CHAPTER TWENTY-TWO: SENTENCE CORRECTION STRATEGIES

Look for Error Indicators 435
Analyze the Answer Choices... 438
Eliminate Answer Choices 440
Substitute with New Words and Phrases 440
Rearrange the Phrase, Clause, or Sentence 443
Use Miscellaneous Strategies... 444
Practice 444

CHAPTER TWENTY-THREE: TEST READINESS

The day of the test.. 451
The morning of the test 451
At the test center 452
After the test 452
Afterword 453

COMPLETE CHAPTER ANSWER KEY

Notes.. 455
Critical Reasoning Section Answer Key 455
Reading Comprehension Section Answer Key...................................... 457
Sentence Correction Section Answer Key... 458

Contacting PowerScore 462

About PowerScore

PowerScore is one of the world's fastest growing test preparation companies. Headquarted in Charleston, South Carolina, PowerScore offers GMAT, GRE, LSAT, and SAT preparation courses in over 75 locations in the U.S. and abroad. For more information, please visit our website at www.powerscore.com.

CHAPTER ONE: INTRODUCTION

Introduction

Welcome to the PowerScore GMAT Verbal Bible. The purpose of this book is to provide you with a thorough review of the concepts, strategies, and techniques necessary for attacking the three types of questions on Verbal section of the Graduate Management Admission Test (GMAT). By carefully studying and correctly applying the techniques we employ, we are certain that you will increase your GMAT Verbal score.

The concepts and techniques discussed herein are drawn from our live GMAT courses, which we feel are the most effective in the world. In order to apply our methods effectively and efficiently, we strongly recommend that you carefully read and re-read each of the discussions regarding question theory. We also suggest that as you finish each question you look at both the explanation for the correct answer choice and the explanations for the incorrect answer choices. Closely examine each problem and determine which elements led to the correct answer, and then study the analyses provided in the book and check them against your own work. By doing so you will greatly increase your chances of recognizing the patterns present in all Verbal questions.

This book also contains a variety of drills and exercises that supplement the discussion of techniques and question analysis. The drills help strengthen specific skills that are critical for GMAT excellence, and for this reason they are as important as the questions. In the answer keys to these drills we will often introduce and discuss important GMAT points, so we strongly advise you to read through all explanations.

Because the GMAT Verbal section contains three types of questions—Critical Reasoning, Reading Comprehension, and Sentence Correction—this book is divided into three sections that discuss each type. Each question type is addressed in its entirety, separate from the other types.

On page 455 there is a complete quick-reference answer key to all problems in this book. The answer key contains a legend of question identifiers, as well as chapter-by-chapter answer keys.

Because access to accurate and up-to-date information is critical, we have devoted a section of our website to GMAT Verbal Bible students. This free online resource area offers supplements to the book material, answers questions posed by students, offers study plans, and provides updates as needed. There is also an official book evaluation form that we strongly encourage you to use.

The exclusive GMAT Verbal Bible online area can be accessed at:

www.powerscore.com/gvbible

If we can assist you in your GMAT preparation in any way, or if you have any questions or comments, please do not hesitate to contact us via e-mail at gvbible@powerscore.com. Additional contact information is provided at the end of this book. We look forward to hearing from you!

The Graduate Management Admission Test is required for admission at over 1000 business schools worldwide. According to the Graduate Management Admission Council (GMAC), the makers of the test, "The GMAT is specifically designed to measure the verbal, quantitative, and writing skills of applicants for graduate study in business. It does not, however, presuppose any specific knowledge of business or other specific content areas, nor does it measure achievement in any particular subject areas." The GMAT is given in English, and consists of the following four separately timed sections:

When you take an actual GMAT, you must present an ID. This is done in case of test security problems..

- **Analytical Writing Assessment.** 2 essays, 30 minutes each; one essay asks for an analysis of an issue, the other asks for an analysis of an argument.

- **Quantitative Section.** 37 multiple-choice questions, 75 minutes; two question types: Problem Solving and Data Sufficiency.

- **Verbal Section.** 41 multiple-choice questions, 75 minutes; three question types: Reading Comprehension, Critical Reasoning, and Sentence Correction.

An optional break of 5 minutes is allowed between each section, and so the order of the test sections is always identical:

Analytical Writing Assessment

Analysis of an Issue	30 minutes	1 question
Analysis of an Argument	30 minutes	1 question
Break	5 minutes	

Quantitative Section

Data Sufficiency Problem Solving	75 minutes	37 questions
Break	5 minutes	

Although the 5-minute breaks are optional, you should always take the entire break time in order to avoid fatigue.

Verbal Section

Critical Reasoning Reading Comprehension Sentence Correction	75 minutes	41 questions

The Analytical Writing Assessment

The Analytical Writing Assessment (AWA) appears at the beginning of the GMAT, immediately after the computer tutorial. The AWA consists of two essays, and you have thirty minutes to complete each essay. There is no break between the two sections. The two essay topics are Analysis of an Argument and Analysis of an Issue.

The AWA was developed in 1994 in response to requests from business schools to add a writing component to the GMAT. Studies had shown that strong writing and communication abilities are critical for strong business performance, and business schools wanted to have a means of assessing candidates' communication abilities. According to GMAC, "The AWA is designed as a direct measure of your ability to think critically and to communicate your ideas. More specifically, the Analysis of an Issue task tests your ability to explore the complexities of an issue or opinion and, if appropriate, to take a position informed by your understanding of those complexities. The Analysis of an Argument task tests your ability to formulate an appropriate and constructive critique of a specific conclusion based upon a specific line of thinking."

At the conclusion of the GMAT you have the option to cancel your score. Unfortunately, there is no way to determine exactly what your score would be before cancelling.

If you choose to accept your score, the results of your test (excluding the Writing scores) are available immediately.

Each Analytical Writing Assessment essay is initially scored on a 0 to 6 scale in half-point increments by two readers—one human reader, and one machine reader, the "e-rater." The two scores are averaged to produce a final score for each essay. The final score of each essay are then averaged together to create an overall score on a scale from 0 to 6, in half-point increments.

The Quantitative Section

The Quantitative section of the GMAT is comprised of questions that cover mathematical subjects such as arithmetic, algebra, and geometry. There are two question types—Problem Solving and Data Sufficiency.

Problem Solving questions contain five separate answer choices, each of which offers a different solution to the problem. Approximately 22 of the 37 Quantitative section questions will be in the Problem Solving format.

Data Sufficiency questions consist of a question followed by two numbered statements. You must determine if the numbered statements contain sufficient information to solve the problem—individually, together, or not at all. Each Quantitative section contains approximately 15 Data Sufficiency questions, and this type of problem is unique to the GMAT and can be exceptionally challenging.

The Verbal Section

The GMAT Verbal section is a test of your ability to read for content, analyze argumentation, and to recognize and correct written errors. Accordingly, there are three types of problems—Reading Comprehension, Critical Reasoning, and Sentence Correction. The remaining chapters of this book address each section in detail, starting with Critical Reasoning.

Critical Reasoning questions present a short argument followed by a question such as: "Which of the following weakens the argument?" "Which of the following parallels the argument?" or "Which of the following must be true according to the argument?" The key to these questions is understanding the reasoning types and question types that frequently appear. Within the Verbal Section you will encounter approximately 10 to 14 Critical Reasoning questions.

Reading Comprehension questions examine your ability to analyze large amounts of material for content and understanding. Passages range up to 350 words in length, and each passage is accompanied by 3 to 8 questions. Passage topics are drawn from a variety of areas, including business, science, politics, law, and history.

Each Sentence Correction problem presents a sentence containing an underlined section. Five answer choices follow the problem, and each suggests a possible phrasing of the underlined section. The first answer choice is a repeat of the underlined section, and the remaining four answers are different than the original. Your task is to analyze the underlined section and determine which of the answers offers the best phrasing.

Experimental Questions

During the GMAT you will encounter questions that will not contribute to your score. These questions, known as "experimental" questions, are used on future version of the GMAT. Unfortunately, you will not be informed during the test as to which questions do not count, so you must give your best performance on each question.

About 1/4 of the questions on the GMAT are experimental, with the questions roughly split between the Quantitative and Verbal sections.

As opposed to the traditional paper-and-pencil format used by many other tests, the GMAT is administered on a computer. Consequently, only one question at a time is presented, the order of questions is not predetermined, and the test actually responds to your answers and shapes the exam in order to most efficiently arrive at your proper score. This format is known as a Computer Adaptive Test, or CAT.

For example, the first question in the Verbal or Quantitative section will be a medium difficulty question. If answered correctly, the computer will supply a somewhat harder question on the assumption that your score is somewhere above that level. If this next question is answered correctly, the following question will again be more difficult. This process continues until a question is missed. At that point, the test will supply a somewhat easier question as it tries to determine if you have reached your score "ceiling." By increasing or decreasing the difficulty of the questions based on prior response, the test attempts to quickly pinpoint your appropriate score level and then confirm that level. Consequently, the first several questions are used to broadly establish your general scoring range:

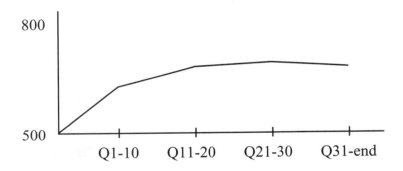

In the diagram above, correct responses to the first several questions lead to significant jumps in score, whereas later questions make smaller adjustments. A strong beginning followed by a weak finish will produce a higher score than a weak beginning followed by a strong finish. For this reason it is essential that your performance early in the section be as strong as possible, even if this requires using more than the average time allotted per question.

The CAT format has certain features that appreciably alter the testing experience:

- The CAT format does not allow you to "skip" a question; that is, you cannot leave a question blank nor can you come back to a question. In order to move forward in the test you *must* answer the question on the screen. If you do not know the answer, you must make an educated guess. And since the test adapts to your previous responses, once you complete a question, you cannot return to that question.

- You cannot write on the computer screen, but scratch paper is available and should be used (more on this in a moment).

- Facility with a computer is clearly an advantage; fast typing is also an advantage in the Analytical Writing Sections where your response must be typed into the computer.

- The test penalizes examinees who do not finish all the questions in the section. Thus, since the number of questions answered is incorporated into the calculation of scores, it is essential that you complete every question in each section. There is a strong penalty for leaving questions unanswered, and so it is better to miss a question than to leave it unanswered.

- The results of your test (excluding the Writing scores) are available at the conclusion of the exam.

Question Difficulty Matters

Complicating the GMAT CAT scoring system is that question difficulty affects your overall score. Each question is assigned a predetermined "weight," and more difficult question have a greater weight. Consequently, it is important that you answer difficult questions and not just "skip" any question that appears difficult. Answering fifteen easy questions will produce a lower score than answering fifteen difficult questions.

General Pacing

Since completing every question in a section is critical, pacing is equally important. Based purely on the number of questions and the total time per section, the following lists the the average amount of time you can spend per question:

Quantitative Section: 37 questions, 75 minutes
Average time per question: *2 minutes, 1 second*

Verbal Section: 41 questions, 75 minutes
Average time per question: *1 minute, 49 seconds*

Score-Specific Pacing

The following references provide alternate pacing strategies depending on desired score.

Basic Quantitative Strategy for various scoring ranges:

700-800: Complete every question, average of just under 2 minutes per question

600-690: Attempt to complete every question, average of 2 minutes, 15 seconds per question, keep enough time to guess on uncompleted questions

500-590: Attempt to complete at least 75% of questions, average of 2 minutes, 35 seconds per question, keep enough time to guess on uncompleted questions

Basic Verbal Strategy for various scoring ranges:

700-800: Complete every question, average of 1 minute, 45 seconds per question

600-690: Attempt to complete every question, average of 2 minutes per question, keep enough time to guess on uncompleted questions

500-590: Attempt to complete at least 75% of questions, average of 2 minutes, 20 seconds per question, keep enough time to guess on uncompleted questions

However, since the questions at the start of each section are more critical than later questions, a greater amount of time than the average can be allotted to the early questions, and then the pace can be accelerated as the sections proceeds.

Timing Your Practice Sessions

One of the most important tools for test success is a timer. When working with paper tests or the *Official GMAT Review,* your timer should be a constant companion during your GMAT preparation.

Although not all of your practice needs to be timed, you should attempt to do as many questions as possible under timed conditions. Time pressure is the top concern cited by test takers, and practicing with a timer will help acquaint you with the challenges of the test. After all, if the GMAT were a take-home test, no one would be too worried about it.

When practicing with a timer, keep notes about how many questions you complete in a given amount of time. You should vary your approach so that practice does not become boring. For example, you could track how long it takes to complete 3, 5, or 8 questions. Or you could see how many questions you can complete in 6 or 10 minutes. Trying different approaches will help you get the best sense of how fast you can go while still maintaining a high degree of accuracy.

Silent countdown timers can be purchased through our website at www. powerscore.com

A timer is invaluable because it is both an odometer and speedometer for your practice. With sufficient practice you will begin to establish a comfortable Verbal section speed, and the timer allows you to make sure you are maintaining this pace. Whether you use a watch, stopwatch, or kitchen timer is irrelevant; just make sure you time yourself rigorously.

Computers and Scratch Paper

Taking a standardized test on a computer is an unusual experience. The natural tendency to mark up the page is thwarted since you cannot write on the computer screen. Consequently, using noteboards, laminated pages provided in place of scratch paper by the test administrator, is an important aid to smooth test performance. A special marker and a spiral-bound booklet of five noteboards will be supplied by the test administrator, and more noteboards can be requested during the exam.

During the pre-test tutorial, use part of one noteboard to quickly draw out the following chart:

A									
B									
C									
D									
E									

As you progress though each question, you can use the chart to keep track of eliminated answer choices as is necessary. For example, if you are certain answer choices (A) and (C) are incorrect in problem #2, simply "X" them out on the chart:

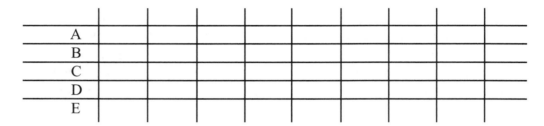

	2								
A	X								
B									
C	X								
D									
E									

In this fashion you can overcome the inability to physically mark out answer choices on the computer screen.

You should also familiarize yourself with GMAT CAT computer controls since computer aptitude is clearly an advantage. Although the test is given on standard computers, the GMAT CAT program does not allow the use of certain keys, such as the "tab" key. *The Official Guide for GMAT Review* contains a detailed explanation of the GMAT CAT computer controls, and the free GMATPrep Software contains test tutorials to help you gain experience with the computer controls. Additionally, in the Analytical Writing Sections, your typing ability affects overall performance, and thus you must have at least basic typing skills.

The GMAT Scoring Scale

Every GMAT score report contains four sections:

- A Quantitative Score—on a scale of 0 to 60
- A Verbal Score—on a scale of 0 to 60
- A Total Score—on a scale of 200 to 800
- An Analytical Writing Assessment Score—on a scale of 0 to 6

The Quantitative and Verbal scores are section scores, and these two section scores are combined to create the Total Score. The Total Score is the one most familiar to GMAT test takers and is given on the famous 200 to 800 scale, with 200 being the lowest score and 800 the highest score.

Each Analytical Writing Assessment essay is initially scored on a 0 to 6 scale by two readers—one human reader and one machine reader, the "E-rater." The two scores are averaged to produce a final score for each essay. The final scores of each essay are then averaged together to create an overall score. Approximately 90% of all test takers receive a score of 3 or higher. Your AWA score has no effect on your Total Score.

The GMAT Percentile Table

It is important not to lose sight of what the GMAT Total Score actually represents. The 200 to 800 test scale contains 61 different possible scores. Each score places a student in a certain relative position compared to other test takers. These relative positions are represented through a percentile that correlates to each score. The percentile indicates where the test taker ranks in the overall pool of test takers. For example, a score of 680 represents the 90th percentile, meaning a student with a score of 680 scored better than 90 percent of the people who have taken the test in the last two years. The percentile is critical since it is a true indicator of your positioning relative to other test takers, and thus business school applicants.

Charting out the entire percentage table yields a rough "bell curve." The number of test takers in the 200s and 700s is very low (only 7% of all test takers receive a score in the 700s; only 2% in the 200s), and most test takers are bunched in the middle, comprising the "top" of the bell. In fact, approximately 30% of all test takers score between 450 and 550 inclusive, and about 60% of all test takers score between 400 and 600 inclusive.

The median score on the GMAT scale is 540. The median, or middle, score is the score at which approximately 50% of test takers have a lower score and 50% of test takers have a higher score.

It is important to remember that you do not have to answer every question correctly in order to receive an excellent GMAT score. There is room for error, and accordingly you should never let any single question occupy an inordinate amount of your time.

The use of the GMAT in business school admissions is not without controversy. Experts agree that your GMAT score is one of the most important determinants of the type of school you can attend. At many business schools an "admissions index" consisting of your GMAT score and your undergraduate grade point average is used to help determine the relative standing of applicants, and at some schools a sufficiently high admissions index virtually guarantees your admission.

For all the importance of the GMAT, the exam is not without flaws. As a standardized test currently given in the computer adaptive format there are a number of skills that the GMAT cannot measure, including listening skills, note-taking ability, perseverance, etc. GMAC is aware of these limitations and on a regular basis they warn all business school admission offices about using the GMAT scores as the sole admission criterion. Still, because the test ultimately returns a number for each student, the tendency to rank applicants is strong. Fortunately, once you get to business school the GMAT is forgotten. For the time being consider the test a temporary hurdle you must leap in order to reach the ultimate goal.

For more information on the GMAT, or to register for the test, contact the Graduate Management Admission Council at (800) 717-GMAT or at their website at www.mba.com.

SECTION ONE:

CRITICAL REASONING

CHAPTER TWO: THE BASICS OF CRITICAL REASONING

GMAT Critical Reasoning

On average, you have 1 minute and 45 seconds to complete each question.

The focus of this section is on Critical Reasoning, and each Verbal section contains a total of 10 to 14 Critical Reasoning questions. When the total time allotted is weighed against the total number of questions in the Verbal section, you have an average of approximately one minute and forty-five seconds to complete each question. Of course, the amount of time you spend on each question will vary with the difficulty of each question. For virtually all students the time constraint is a major obstacle, and as we progress through this book we will discuss time-saving techniques that you can employ within the section.

Critical Reasoning Question Directions

The directions for Critical Reasoning problems are short and seemingly simple:

> "For this question type, select the best of the given answer choices."

Because these directions always precede first Critical Reasoning question in a Verbal section, you should familiarize yourself with them now. Once the GMAT begins, *never* waste time reading the question directions in any section.

Always read each of the five answer choices before deciding which answer is correct.

Let's examine the directions more closely. Consider the following phrase: "select the best of the answer choices given." By stating up front that answers have comparative value and some are better than others, the makers of the test compel you to read every single answer choice before making a selection. If you read only one or two answer choices and then decide you have the correct one, you could end up choosing an answer that has some merit but is not as good as a later answer. One of the test makers' favorite tricks is to place a highly attractive wrong answer choice immediately before the correct answer choice in the hopes that you will pick the wrong answer choice and then move to the next question without reading any of the other answers.

What is notable about the directions is what is *not* stated. No mention is made of whether to accept all statements as true, nor is any comment made about what you should assume about each question. A bit later in this chapter we will address the truth of the statements in each passage, but let's take a moment to talk about the assumptions that underlie each problem. In general, standardized tests such as the GMAT operate on "commonsense" grounds; that is, you should only assume things that would be considered common sense or widely known to the general public. The implication is that you can make some assumptions when working with questions, but not other assumptions. Of course, the GMAC does not hand out a list of what constitutes a reasonable assumption! Even outside of the GMAT, the test makers do not clearly state what assumptions are acceptable or unacceptable for you to make, mainly because such a list would be almost infinite. For GMAT purposes, approaching each question you can take as true any statement or idea that an average person would be expected to believe on the basis of generally known and accepted facts. For example, in a question you can assume that the sky sometimes becomes cloudy, but you cannot assume that the sky is always cloudy (unless stated explicitly by the question). GMAT questions will *not* require you to make assumptions based on extreme ideas (such as that it always rains in Seattle) or ideas not in the general domain of knowledge (such as the per capita income of residents of France). Please note that this does not mean that the GMAT cannot set up scenarios where they discuss ideas that are extreme or outside the bounds of common knowledge. Within a Critical Reasoning question, the test makers can and do discuss complex or extreme ideas; in these cases, they will give you context for the situation by providing additional information. However, be careful about assuming something to be true (unless you believe it is a widely accepted fact or the test makers indicate you should believe it to be true). This last idea is one we will discuss in much more detail as we look at individual question types.

The Parts of a Critical Reasoning Question

Every Critical Reasoning question contains three separate parts: the stimulus, the question stem, and the five answer choices. The following diagram identifies each part:

1. Most serious students are happy students, and most serious students go to graduate school. Furthermore, ————— Stimulus all students who go to graduate school are overworked.

    Which one of the following can be properly inferred ————— Question Stem from the statements above?

    (A) Most overworked students are happy students.
    (B) Some happy students are overworked.
    (C) All overworked students are serious students. ————— Answer Choices
    (D) Some unhappy students go to graduate school.
    (E) All serious students are overworked.

As a technical note, on the GMAT CAT an empty answer bubble appears next to each answer, and there is no letter in the bubble. However, for identification purposes and the convenience of discussion, throughout this book we will present problems with the answer choices lettered (A) through (E).

Approaching the Questions

When examining the three parts, students sometimes wonder about the best strategy for attacking a question: should I read the question stem first? Should I preview the five answer choices? The correct answer is *Read the parts in the order given*. That is, first read the stimulus, then read the question stem, and finally read each of the five answer choices. Although this may seem like a reasonable, even obvious, approach we mention it here because some GMAT texts advocate reading the question stem before reading the stimulus. We are certain that these texts are seriously mistaken, and here are a few reasons why:

1. Understanding the stimulus is the key to answering any question, and reading the question stem first tends to undermine the ability of students to fully comprehend the information in the stimulus. On easy questions this distraction tends not to have a significant negative impact, but on more difficult questions the student often is forced to read the stimulus twice in order to get full comprehension, thus wasting valuable time. Literally, by reading the question stem first, students are forced to juggle two things at once: the question stem and the information in the stimulus. That is a difficult task when under time pressure. The bottom line is that any viable strategy must be effective for questions at all difficulty levels, but when you read the question stem first you cannot perform optimally. True, the approach works with the easy questions, but those questions could have been answered correctly regardless of the approach used.

2. Reading the question stem first often wastes valuable time since the typical student will read the stem, then read the stimulus, and then read the stem again. Unfortunately, there simply is not enough time to read every question stem twice.

3. Some question stems refer to information given in the stimulus, or add new conditions to the stimulus information. Thus, reading the stem first is of little value and often confuses or distracts the student when he or she goes to read the stimulus.

4. On stimuli with two questions, reading one stem biases the reader to look for that specific information, possibly causing problems while doing the second question, and reading both stems before reading the stimulus wastes entirely too much time and leads to confusion.

5. For truly knowledgeable test takers there are situations that arise where the question stem is fairly predictable. One example—and there are others—is with a question type called Resolve the Paradox. Usually, when you read the stimulus that accompanies these questions, an obvious paradox or discrepancy is presented. Reading the question stem beforehand does not add anything to what you would have known just from reading the stimulus. In later chapters we will discuss this situation and others where you can predict the question stem with some success.

The correct answer to the problem on the previous page is answer choice (B).

In our experience, the vast majority of high-scoring GMAT takers read the stimulus first.

6. Finally, we believe that one of the main principles underlying the read-the-question-stem-first approach is flawed. Many advocates of the approach claim that it helps the test taker identify and skip (by simply guessing instead of doing the question) the "harder" question types such as Parallel Reasoning or Method of Reasoning. However, test data show that questions of any type can be hard or easy. Some Parallel Reasoning questions are phenomenally easy whereas some Parallel Reasoning questions are extremely difficult. In short, the question stem is a poor indicator of difficulty because question difficulty is more directly related to the complexity of the stimulus and the corresponding answer choices.

Understandably, reading the question stem before the stimulus sounds like a good idea at first, but for the majority of students (especially those trying to score in the 600s and above), the approach is a hindrance, not a help. Solid test performance depends on your ability to quickly comprehend complex argumentation; do not make your task harder by reading the question stem first.

Analyzing the Stimulus

As you read the stimulus, initially focus on making a quick analysis of the topic under discussion. What area has the author chosen to write about? You will be more familiar with some topics than with others, but do not assume that everything you know "outside" of the stimulus regarding the topic is true and applies to the stimulus. For example, say you work in a real estate office and you come across a GMAT question about property sales. You can use your work experience and knowledge of real estate to help you better understand what the author is discussing, but do not assume that things will operate in the stimulus exactly as they do at your workplace. Perhaps property transactions in your state are different from those in other states, or perhaps protocols followed in your office differ from those elsewhere. In a GMAT question, look carefully at what the author says about the topic at hand; statements presented as facts on the GMAT can and do vary from what occurs in the "real world." This discrepancy between the "GMAT world" and the "real world" is one you must always be aware of: although the two worlds overlap, things in the GMAT world are often very different from what you expect. From our earlier discussion of commonsense assumptions we know that you can assume that basic, widely-held facts will hold true in the GMAT world, but by the same token, you cannot assume that specialized information that you have learned in the real world will hold true on the GMAT. We will discuss "outside information" in more detail when we discuss GMAT question types.

Next, make sure to read the entire stimulus very carefully. The makers of the GMAT have extraordinarily high expectations about the level of detail you should retain when you read a stimulus. Many questions will test your knowledge of small, seemingly nitpicky variations in phrasing, and reading carelessly is GMAT suicide. In many respects, the requirement forced upon you

Reading closely is a critical GMAT skill.

to read carefully is what makes the time constraint so difficult to handle. Every test taker is placed at the nexus of two competing elements: the need for speed (caused by the timed element) and the need for patience (caused by the detailed reading requirement). How well you manage these two elements strongly determines how well you perform. In the previous chapter we discussed how to practice using time elements, so make sure to use those ideas as you work through practice questions both in this book and in your other test materials.

Finally, analyze the structure of the stimulus: what pieces are present and how do those pieces relate to each other? In short, you are tasked with knowing as much as possible about the statements made by the author, and in order to do so, you must understand how the test makers create GMAT arguments. We will discuss argumentation in more detail in a moment.

GMAT argumentation is one of the main topics of this section, and will be discussed in every chapter.

Stimulus Topics

The spectrum of topics covered by Critical Reasoning stimuli is quite broad. Previous stimuli topics have ranged from art to business to medicine and science. According to the makers of the test, "Questions are based on materials from a variety of sources. No familiarity with the specific subject matter is needed."

Despite the previous statement, many GMAT students come from a humanities background and these test takers often worry about stimuli containing scientific or medical topics. Remember, the topic of a stimulus does not affect the underlying logical relationship of the argument parts. And, the GMAT will not assume that you know anything about advanced technical or scientific ideas. For example, while the GMAT may discuss mathematicians or the existence of a difficult problem in math, you will not be asked to make calculations nor will you be assumed to understand esoteric terminology. Any element beyond the domain of general public knowledge will be explained for you, as in the following example:

Some specific topics do recur, and we will note those in future chapters.

> Scientist: Isaac Newton's *Principia*, the seventeenth-century work that served as the cornerstone of physics for over two centuries, could at first be understood by only a handful of people, but a basic understanding of Newton's ideas eventually spread throughout the world. This shows that the barriers to communication between scientists...

The stimulus above, although reproduced only in part, is a good example of how the test makers will supply information they feel is essential to understanding the question. In this case, the reader is not expected to understand either the content or historical importance of *Principia*, and so the test makers conveniently furnish that information. Thus, although on occasion you will see a stimulus that references an ominous looking word or idea (examples include *high-density lipoprotein* and *pironoma*, you will not need to know or be assumed to know anything more about those elements than what you are told by the test makers.

When you read a science-based stimulus, focus on understanding the relationship of the ideas and do not be intimidated by the terminology used by the author. As we will ultimately find, reading a GMAT stimulus is about seeing past the topic to analyze the structural relationships present in the stimulus. Once you are able to see these relationships, the topic will become less important.

Arguments versus Fact Sets

There are many books on logic and argumentation. In this book we attempt to concisely spell out what you need to know to succeed on the GMAT. This is different from philosophical logic, and therefore this section will not teach you argumentation as it is taught in a university.

GMAT stimuli fall into two distinct categories: those containing an argument and those that are just a set of facts. Logically speaking, an argument can be defined as a set of statements wherein one statement is claimed to follow from or be derived from the others. Consider the following short example of an argument:

> All professors are ethical. Mason is a professor. So Mason is ethical.

The first two statements in this argument give the reasons (or "premises") for accepting the third statement, which is the conclusion of the argument.

Fact sets, on the other hand, are a collection of statements without a conclusion, as in the following example:

Fact sets rarely cause a strong reaction in the reader because no persuasion is being used. When an author attempts to persuade you to believe a certain conclusion, there tends to be a noticeable reaction.

> "The Jacksonville area has just over one million residents. The Cincinnati area has almost two million residents. The New York area has almost twenty million residents."

The three sentences above do *not* constitute an argument because no conclusion is present and an argument, by definition, requires a conclusion. The three sentences merely make a series of assertions without making a judgment. Notice that reading these sentences does not cause much of a reaction in most readers. Really, who cares about the city sizes? This lack of a strong reaction is often an indication that you are not reading an argument and are instead reading just a set of facts.

When reading Critical Reasoning stimuli, you should seek to make several key determinations, which we call the Critical Reasoning Primary Objectives™. Your first task is to determine if you are reading an argument or a fact set.

Primary Objective #1: Determine whether the stimulus contains an argument or if it is only a set of factual statements.

To achieve this objective, you must recognize whether a conclusion is present. Let us talk about how to do this next.

Identifying Premises and Conclusions

For GMAT purposes, a premise can be defined as:

> "A fact, proposition, or statement from which a conclusion is made."

Premises support and explain the conclusion. Literally, the premises give the reasons why the conclusion should be accepted. To identify premises, ask yourself, *"What reasons has the author used to persuade me? Why should I believe this argument? What evidence exists?"*

A premise gives a reason why something should be believed.

A conclusion can be defined as:

> "A statement or judgment that follows from one or more reasons."

Conclusions, as summary statements, are supposed to be drawn from and rest on the premises. To identify conclusions, ask yourself, *"What is the author driving at? What does the author want me to believe? What point follows from the others?"*

A conclusion is the point the author tries to prove by using another statement.

Because language is the test maker's weapon of choice, you must learn to recognize the words that indicate when a premise or conclusion is present. In expressing arguments, authors often use the following words or phrases to introduce premises and conclusions:

Premise Indicators	Conclusion Indicators
because	thus
since	therefore
for	hence
for example	consequently
for the reason that	as a result
in that	so
given that	accordingly
as indicated by	clearly
due to	must be that
owing to	shows that
this can be seen from	conclude that
we know this by	follows that
	for this reason

Make sure to memorize these word lists. Recognizing argument elements is critical!

Because there are so many variations in the English language, these lists cannot be comprehensive, but they do capture many of the premise and conclusion indicators used by GMAT authors. As for frequency of appearance, the top two words in each list are used more than any of the other words in the list.

Arguments can contain more than one premise and more than one conclusion.

When you are reading, always be aware of the presence of the words listed above. These words are like road signs; they tell you what is coming next. Consider the following example:

> Humans cannot live on Venus because the surface temperature is too high.

As you read the first portion of the sentence, "Humans cannot live on Venus," you cannot be sure if you are reading a premise or conclusion. But, as soon as you see the word "because"—a premise indicator—you know that a premise will follow, and at that point you know that the first portion of the sentence is a conclusion. In the argument above, the author wants you to believe that humans cannot live on Venus, and the reason is that the surface temperature is too high.

In our daily lives, we make and hear many arguments. However, unlike on the GMAT, the majority of these arguments occur in the form of conversations (and when we say "argument," we do not mean a fight!). Any GMAT argument can be seen as an artificial conversation, even the basic example above:

> Author: "Humans cannot live on Venus."
> Respondent: "Really? Why is that?"
> Author: "The surface temperature of Venus is too high."

If at first you struggle to identify the pieces of an argument, you can always resort to thinking about the argument as an artificial conversation and that may assist you in locating the conclusion.

Here are more examples of premise and conclusion indicators in use:

1. "The economy is in tatters. Therefore, we must end this war."

   "Therefore" introduces a conclusion; the first sentence is a premise.

2. "We must reduce our budget due to the significant cost overruns we experienced during production."

   "due to" introduces a premise; "We must reduce our budget" is the conclusion.

3. "Fraud has cost the insurance industry millions of dollars in lost revenue. Thus, congress will pass a stricter fraud control bill since the insurance industry has one of the most powerful lobbies."

   This argument contains two premises: the first premise is the first sentence and the second premise follows the word "since" in the second sentence; the conclusion is "congress will pass a stricter fraud control bill."

Notice that premises and conclusions can be presented in any order—the conclusion can be first or last, and the relationship between the premises and the conclusion remains the same regardless of the order of presentation. For example, if the order of the premise(s) and conclusion was switched in any of the examples above, the logical structure of the argument would not change.

Also notable is that the premises and the conclusion can appear in the same sentence, or be separated out into multiple sentences. Whether the ideas are together or separated has no effect on the logical structure of the argument.

If a conclusion is present, you *must* identify the conclusion prior to proceeding on to the question stem. Often, the reason students miss questions is because they have failed to fully and accurately identify the conclusion of the argument.

Primary Objective #2: If the stimulus contains an argument, identify the conclusion of the argument. If the stimulus contains a fact set, examine each fact.

One Confusing Form

Because the job of the test makers is to determine how well you can interpret information, they will sometimes arrange premise and conclusion indicators in a way that is designed to be confusing. One of their most confusing forms places a conclusion indicator and premise indicator back-to-back, separated by a comma, as in the following examples:

> "Therefore, since..."
> "Thus, because..."
> "Hence, due to..."

A quick glance would seemingly indicate that what will follow is both a premise and a conclusion. In this instance, however, the presence of the comma creates a clause that, due to the premise indicator, contains a premise. The end of that premise clause will be closed with a second comma, and then what follows will be the conclusion, as in the following:

> "Therefore, since higher debt has forced consumers to lower their savings, banks now have less money to loan."

"Higher debt has forced consumers to lower their savings" is the premise; "banks now have less money to loan" is the conclusion. So, in this instance "therefore" still introduces a conclusion, but the appearance of the conclusion is interrupted by a clause that contains a premise.

Order of presentation has no effect on the logical structure of the argument. The conclusion can appear at the beginning, the middle, or the end of the argument.

CR

Remember, a fact set does not contain a conclusion; an argument must contain a conclusion.

This form is called the "conclusion/ premise indicator form."

Premise and Conclusion Recognition Mini-Drill

Each of the following problems contains a short argument. For each argument, identify the conclusion and the premise(s). Answers on the next page.

1. "Given that the price of steel is rising, we will no longer be able to offer discounts on our car parts."

2. "The political situation in Somalia is unstable owing to the ability of individual warlords to maintain powerful armed forces."

3. "Since we need to have many different interests to sustain us, the scientists' belief must be incorrect."

4. "So, as indicated by the newly released data, we should push forward with our efforts to recolonize the forest with snowy tree crickets."

5. "Television has a harmful effect on society. This can be seen from the poor school performance of children who watch significant amounts of television and from the fact that children who watch more than six hours of television a day tend to read less than non-television watching children."

6. "The rapid diminishment of the ecosystem of the Amazon threatens the entire planet. Consequently, we must take immediate steps to convince the Brazilian government that planned development projects need to be curtailed for the simple reason that these development projects will greatly accelerate the loss of currently protected land."

Premise and Conclusion Recognition Mini-Drill Answer Key

1. Features the premise indicator "given that."
     Premise: "Given that the price of steel is rising,"
     Conclusion: "we will no longer be able to offer discounts on our car parts."

2. Features the premise indicator "owing to."
     Premise: "owing to the ability of individual warlords to maintain powerful armed forces."
     Conclusion: "The political situation in Somalia is unstable"

3. Features the premise indicator "since."
     Premise: "Since we need to have many different interests to sustain us,"
     Conclusion: "the scientists' belief must be incorrect."

4. Features the conclusion/premise form indicator "So, as indicated by."
     Premise: "as indicated by the newly released data"
     Conclusion: "we should push forward with our efforts to recolonize the forest with snowy tree crickets."

5. Features the premise indicator "this can be seen from." The second sentence contains two premises.
     Premise 1: "This can be seen from the poor school performance of children who watch significant amounts of television"
     Premise 2: "and from the fact that children who watch more than six hours of television a day tend to read less than non-television watching children."
     Conclusion: "Television has a harmful effect on society." Note how this sentence does not contain a conclusion indicator. Yet, we can determine that this is the conclusion because the other sentence contains two premises.

6. Features the conclusion indicator "consequently" and the premise indicator "for the simple reason that." There are also two premises present.
     Premise 1: "The rapid diminishment of the ecosystem of the Amazon threatens the entire planet."
     Premise 2: "for the simple reason that these development projects will greatly accelerate the loss of currently protected land."
     Conclusion: "we must take immediate steps to convince the Brazilian government that planned development projects need to be curtailed"

Additional Premise Indicators

Additional premises are still, of course, premises. They may be central to the argument or they may be secondary. To determine the importance of the premise, examine the remainder of the argument.

Aside from previously listed premise and conclusions indicators, there are other argument indicator words you should learn to recognize. First, in argument forms, sometimes the author will make an argument and then for good measure add another premise that supports the conclusion but is sometimes non-essential to the conclusion. These are known as *additional premises*:

Additional Premise Indicators

Furthermore
Moreover
Besides
In addition
What's more

Following are two examples of additional premise indicators in use:

1. "Every professor at Fillmore University teaches exactly one class per semester. Fillmore's Professor Jackson, therefore, is teaching exactly one class this semester. Moreover, I heard Professor Jackson say she was teaching only a single class."

   The first sentence is a premise. The second sentence contains the conclusion indicator "therefore" and is the conclusion of the argument. The first sentence is the main proof offered by the author for the conclusion. The third sentence begins with the additional premise indicator "moreover." The premise in this sentence is non-essential to the argument, but provides additional proof for the conclusion and could be, if needed, used to help prove the conclusion separately (this would occur if an objection was raised to the first premise).

2. "The city council ought to ease restrictions on outdoor advertising because the city's economy is currently in a slump. Furthermore, the city should not place restrictions on forms of speech such as advertising."

   The first sentence contains both the conclusion of the argument and the main premise of the argument (introduced by the premise indicator "because"). The last sentence contains the additional premise indicator "furthermore." As with the previous example, the additional premise in this sentence is non-essential to the argument but provides additional proof for the conclusion.

Counter-Premise Indicators

When creating an argument, an author will sometimes bring up a counter-premise—a premise that actually contains an idea that is counter to the argument. At first glance, this might seem like an odd thing for an author to do. But by raising the counter-premise and then addressing the complaint in a direct fashion, the author can minimize the damage that would be done by the objection if it were raised elsewhere.

Counter-premises, also called adversatives, bring up points of opposition or comparison.

Counter-premises can also be ideas that compare and contrast with the argument, or work against a previously raised point. In this sense, the general counter-premise concept discusses an idea that is in some way different from another part of the argument.

<u>Counter-premise Indicators</u>

But
Yet
However
On the other hand
Admittedly
In contrast
Although
Even though
Still
Whereas
In spite of
Despite
After all

Note that some terms, such as "After all," could appear on multiple indicator lists because the phrase can be used in a variety of ways. As a savvy GMAT taker, it is up to you to identify the exact role that the phrase is playing in the argument.

Following is an example of a counter-premise indicator in use:

1. "The United States prison population is the world's largest and consequently we must take steps to reduce crime in this country. Although other countries have higher rates of incarceration, their statistics have no bearing on the dilemma we currently face."

> The first sentence contains a premise and the conclusion (which is introduced by the conclusion indicator "consequently"). The third sentence offers up a counter-premise as indicated by the word "although."

Additional Premise and Counter-Premise Recognition Mini-Drill

Each of the following problems contains a short argument. For each argument, identify the conclusion, the premise(s), and any additional premises or counter-premises. Answers on the next page.

1. Wine is made by crushing grapes and eventually separating the juice from the grape skins. However, the separated juice contains impurities and many wineries do not filter the juice. These wineries claim the unfiltered juice ultimately produces a more flavorful and intense wine. Since these wine makers are experts, we should trust their judgment and not shy away from unfiltered wine.

2. Phenylketonurics are people who cannot metabolize the amino acid phenylalanine. There are dangers associated with phenylketonuria, and products containing phenylalanine must carry a warning label that states, "Phenylketonurics: contains phenylalanine." In addition, all children in developed societies receive a phenylketonuria test at birth. Hence, at the moment, we are doing as much as possible to protect against this condition.

3. During last night's robbery, the thief was unable to open the safe. Thus, last night's robbery was unsuccessful despite the fact that the thief stole several documents. After all, nothing in those documents was as valuable as the money in the safe.

Additional Premise and Counter-Premise Recognition Mini-Drill Answer Key

1. Features the counter-premise indicator "however" and the premise indicator "since."

> Premise: "Wine is made by crushing grapes and eventually separating the juice from the grape skins."
> Counter-premise: "However, the separated juice contains impurities and many wineries do not filter the juice."
> Premise: "These wineries claim the unfiltered juice ultimately produces a more flavorful and intense wine."
> Premise: "Since these wine makers are experts,"
> Conclusion: "we should trust their judgment and not shy away from unfiltered wine."

2. Features the additional premise indicator "in addition" and the conclusion indicator "hence." In this problem the additional premise is central to supporting the conclusion.

> Premise: "Phenylketonurics are people who cannot metabolize the amino acid phenylalanine."
> Premise: "There are dangers associated with phenylketonuria, and products containing phenylalanine must carry a warning label that states, 'Phenylketonurics: contains phenylalanine.' "
> Additional Premise: "In addition, all children in developed societies received a phenylketonuria test at birth."
> Conclusion: "Hence, at the moment, we are doing as much as possible to protect against this condition."

3. Features the counter-premise indicator "despite"; the additional premise indicator "after all"; and the conclusion indicator "thus." The additional premise serves to downplay the counter-premise.

> Premise: "During last night's robbery, the thief was unable to open the safe."
> Counter-premise: "despite the fact that the thief stole several documents."
> Additional Premise: "After all, nothing in those documents was as valuable as the money in the safe."
> Conclusion: "Thus, last night's robbery was unsuccessful "

Recognizing Conclusions Without Indicators

Many of the arguments we have encountered up until this point have had conclusion indicators to help you recognize the conclusion. And, many of the arguments you will see on the GMAT will also have conclusion indicators. But you will encounter arguments that do not contain conclusion indicators. Following is an example:

> The best way of eliminating traffic congestion will not be easily found. There are so many competing possibilities that it will take millions of dollars to study every option, and implementation of most options carries an exorbitant price tag.

An argument such as the above can be difficult to analyze because no indicator words are present. How then, would you go about determining if a conclusion is present, and if so, how would you identify that conclusion? Fortunately, there is a fairly simple trick that can be used to handle this situation, and any situation where you are uncertain of the conclusion (even those with multiple conclusions, as will be discussed next).

GMAC says you are expected to possess, in their words, "a college-level understanding of widely used concepts such as argument, premise, assumption, and conclusion."

Aside from the questions you can use to identify premises and conclusions (described earlier in this chapter), the easiest way to determine the conclusion in an argument is to use the Conclusion Identification Method™:

> Take the statements under consideration for the conclusion and place them in an arrangement that forces one to be the conclusion and the other(s) to be the premise(s). Use premise and conclusion indicators to achieve this end. Once the pieces are arranged, determine if the arrangement makes logical sense. If so, you have made the correct identification. If not, reverse the arrangement and examine the relationship again. Continue until you find an arrangement that is logical.

Let us apply this method to the argument at the top of this page. For our first arrangement we will make the first sentence the premise and the second sentence the conclusion, and supply indicators (in italics):

> *Because* the best way of eliminating traffic congestion will not be easily found, *we can conclude that* there are so many competing possibilities that it will take millions of dollars to study every option, and implementation of most options carries an exorbitant price tag.

Does that sound right? No. Let us try again, this time making the first sentence the conclusion and the second sentence the premise:

> *Because* there are so many competing possibilities that it will take millions of dollars to study every option, and implementation of most options carries an exorbitant price tag, *we can conclude that* the best

way of eliminating traffic congestion will not be easily found.

Clearly, the second arrangement is far superior because it makes sense. In most cases when you have the conclusion and premise backward, the arrangement will be confusing. The correct arrangement always sounds more logical.

Complex Arguments

Up until this point, we have only discussed simple arguments. Simple arguments contain a single conclusion. While many of the arguments that appear on the GMAT are simple arguments, there are also a fair number of complex arguments. Complex arguments contain more than one conclusion. In these instances, one of the conclusions is the main conclusion, and the other conclusions are subsidiary conclusions (also known as sub-conclusions).

While complex argumentation may sound daunting at first, you make and encounter complex argumentation every day in your life. In basic terms, a complex argument makes an initial conclusion based on a premise. The author then uses that conclusion as the foundation (or premise) for another conclusion, thus building a chain with several levels. Let us take a look at the two types of arguments in diagram form:

In abstract terms, a simple argument appears as follows:

Conclusion

↑

Premise

As discussed previously, the premise supports the conclusion, hence the arrow from the premise to the conclusion. By comparison, a complex argument takes an initial conclusion and then uses it as a premise for another conclusion:

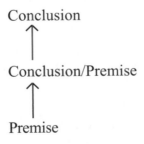

Conclusion

↑

Conclusion/Premise

↑

Premise

Thus, a statement can be both a conclusion for one argument and a premise for another. In this sense, a complex argument can appear somewhat like a ladder, where each level or "rung" is used to build the next level. Given enough time you could build an argument with hundreds of levels. On the GMAT, however,

A simple argument does not mean that the argument is easy to understand! Simple in this context means that the argument contains only a single conclusion.

there are typically three or four levels at most. Let us look at an example of a complex argument:

> Because the Colts have the best quarterback in football, they therefore have the best offense in football. Because they have the best offense in football, they will win the Super Bowl next year.

In this argument, the first sentence contains a premise followed by a conclusion. This initial conclusion is then used in the second sentence as a premise to make a larger conclusion:

> Premise: "Because the Colts have the best quarterback in football,"
> Sub-Conclusion (conclusion of the previous premise/Premise for the following conclusion): "they therefore have the best offense in football."
> Main Conclusion: "they will win the Super Bowl next year."

One of the most commonly used complex argument forms is to place the main conclusion in the first sentence of the argument, and then to place the sub-conclusion in the last sentence of the argument, preceded by a conclusion indicator. This form is quite useful since it tends to trick students into thinking the last sentence is the main conclusion.

Another form of complex argumentation occurs with two-speaker stimuli. In these questions, two separate speakers are identified, and each presents his or her own argument or comment. Here is an example:

> Anne: Halley's Comet, now in a part of its orbit relatively far from the Sun, recently flared brightly enough to be seen by telescope. No comet has ever been observed to flare so far from the Sun before, so such a flare must be highly unusual.
>
> Sue: Nonsense. Usually no one bothers to try to observe comets when they are so far from the Sun. This flare was observed only because an observatory was tracking Halley's Comet very carefully.

In the argument above, each speaker presents premises and a conclusion. As often occurs with this form of question, the two speakers disagree.

One of the benefits of a two-speaker stimulus is that the test makers can introduce multiple viewpoints on the same subject. As you might imagine, the presence of multiple viewpoints tends to be confusing, and the extra viewpoints offer the test makers the opportunity to ask a wider variety of questions.

CR

A Commonly Used Construction

Even within a single-speaker stimulus the test makers can raise alternate viewpoints. One of the most frequently used constructions is to raise a viewpoint at the beginning of the stimulus and then disagree with it immediately thereafter. This efficiently raises two opposing views in a very short paragraph. These stimuli are recognizable because they often begin with the phrase, "Some people claim..." or one of the many variations on this theme, including but not limited to the following:

"Some people propose..."
"Many people believe..."
"Some argue that..." or "Some people argue that..."
"Some critics claim..."
"Some critics maintain..."
"Some scientists believe..."

The structure of this opening sentence is remarkably consistent in form, and adheres to the following formula:

A *number* (some, many, etc.) of *people* (critics, students, teachers, legislators, vegetarians, psychologists etc.) *believe* (claim, propose, argue, etc.) that...

Of course, there are exceptions, as with these opening sentences:

"Although some people claim..."   (starts with "although")
"It has been claimed that..."   (drops the *number* and *people*)
"Cigarette companies claim that..."   (drops the *number*)

The author can also break up the idea, by inserting contextual information, as in the following example:

"*Some critics* of space exploration programs *claim* that..."

The use of this device to begin a stimulus almost always leads to the introduction of the opposing view, as in the following partial stimulus:

Editorialist: Some people propose that, to raise revenues and encourage conservation, our country's taxes on oil, gasoline, and coal should be increased. Such a tax, however, would do more harm than good.

The editorialist uses the "Some people propose" device to introduce one opinion of taxes and then in the following sentence counters the idea with the view that turns out to be the editorialist's main point ("Such a tax, however..."). The remainder of the problem went on to explain the reasoning behind the editorialist's view.

Given the frequency with which this construction appears at the beginning of stimuli, you should learn to begin recognizing it now. We will again discuss this device in the Main Point section.

Truth versus Validity

So far, we have only identified the parts that are used to construct arguments. We have not made an analysis of the reasonableness or soundness of an argument. But, before moving on to argument analysis, you must be able to distinguish between two commonly confused concepts: validity and truth.

When we evaluate GMAT arguments, we are primarily concerned with validity. That is, what is the logical relationship of the pieces of the argument and how well do the premises, if accepted, prove the conclusion? We are less concerned with the absolute, real world truthfulness of either the premises or the conclusion. Some students will at first try to analyze every single GMAT statement on the basis of whether it is an absolutely true statement (does it happen as stated in the real world). For the most part, that is wasted effort. GMAT Critical Reasoning is primarily focused on whether the conclusion follows logically from a set of given premises. In many cases, the GMAT makers will let you work under a framework where the premises are simply accepted as factually accurate, and then you must focus solely on the method used to reach the conclusion. In a sense this could be called relative truthfulness—you are only concerned about whether the conclusion is true relative to the premises, not whether the conclusion is true in an absolute, real world sense. This is obviously a critical point, and one we will analyze later as we discuss different question types.

Argument Analysis

Once you have determined that an argument is present and you have identified the conclusion, you must determine if the argument is a good one or a bad one. This leads to the third Primary Objective:

Primary Objective #3: If the stimulus contains an argument, determine whether the argument is strong or weak.

To determine the strength of the argument, consider the relationship between the premises and the conclusion—do the premises strongly suggest that the conclusion would be true? Does the conclusion feel like an inevitable result of

Logicians spend a great deal of time discussing validity and truth, even going so far as to create complex truth tables that analyze the validity of arguments. We are not concerned with such methods because they do not apply to the GMAT.

In logic, the terms "strong/weak," "good/bad," "valid/invalid," and "sound/unsound" are used to evaluate arguments. For our purposes, "strong," "good," "valid," and "sound" will be interchangeable and all terms refer to the logical structure of the argument. The same holds true for "weak," "bad," "invalid," and "unsound."

the premises? Or does the conclusion seem to go beyond the scope of the information in the premises? How persuasive does the argument seem to you? When evaluating argument validity, the question you must always ask yourself is: Do the given facts support the conclusion?

To better understand this concept we will examine two sample arguments. The following argument uses the fact set we used before, with the addition of a conclusion:

> "The Jacksonville area has just over one million residents. Cincinnati has almost two million residents. The New York area has almost twenty million residents. Therefore, we should move to Jacksonville."

The last sentence contains the conclusion, and makes this an argument. Notice how the presence of the conclusion causes you to react more strongly to the stimulus. Now, instead of just reading a set of cold facts, you are forced to consider whether the premises have proven the given conclusion. In this case the author asks you to accept that a move to Jacksonville is in order based on the population of the city. Do you think the author has proven this point?

When considering the above argument, most people simply accept the premises as factually accurate. There is nothing wrong with this (and indeed in the real world they are true). As mentioned moments ago, in GMAT argumentation the makers of the test largely allow authors to put forth their premises unchallenged. The test makers are far more concerned about whether those premises lead to the conclusion presented. In the argument above, there is no reason to doubt the accuracy of the premises, but even if we accept the premises as accurate, we still do not have to accept the conclusion.

Most people reading the argument above would agree that the reasoning is weak. Even though the premises are perfectly acceptable, by themselves they do not prove that "we should move to Jacksonville." The typical reader will experience a host of reactions to the conclusion: Why Jacksonville—why not a city that is even smaller? What about a larger city? What is so important about population? What about considerations other than population size? Because questions of this nature point to flaws in the argument, we would classify the argument as a poor one. That is, the premises do not prove the conclusion. As shown by this example, the acceptability of the premises does not automatically make the conclusion acceptable. The reverse is also true—the acceptability of the conclusion does not automatically make the premises acceptable.

The following is an example of a strong argument:

> "Trees that shed their foliage annually are deciduous trees. Black Oak trees shed their leaves every year. Therefore, Black Oak trees are deciduous."

CR

An argument can be valid without being true. For example, the following has a valid argument structure but is not "true" in a real world sense:

"All birds can fly. An ostrich is a bird. Therefore, an ostrich can fly."

Questions such as the ones posed in this paragraph suggest that the author has made unwarranted assumptions while constructing the argument. We will discuss assumptions in more detail later.

In this argument, the two premises lead directly to the conclusion. Unlike the previous argument, the author's conclusion seems reasonable and inevitable based on the two premises. Note that the strength of this argument is based solely on the degree to which the premises prove the conclusion. The truth of the premises themselves is not an issue in determining whether the argument is valid or invalid.

Inferences and Assumptions

When glancing through GMAT questions, you will frequently see the words *inference* and *assumption*. Let us take a moment to define the meaning of each term in the context of GMAT argumentation.

Most people have come to believe that the word *inference* means probably true or likely to be true. Indeed, in common usage *infer* is often used in the same manner as *imply*. On the GMAT these uses are incorrect. In logic, an inference can be defined as something that *must be true*. Thus, if you are asked to identify an inference of the argument, you must find an item that must be true based on the information presented in the argument.

Earlier we discussed assumptions in the context of commonsense assumptions that you can bring into each problem. In argumentation, an assumption is simply the same as an *unstated* premise—what must be true in order for the argument to be true. Assumptions can often have a great effect on the validity of the argument.

Assumptions are a part of every argument, and we will discuss them in a later chapter.

Separating an inference from an assumption can be difficult because the definition of each refers to what "must be true." The difference is simple: an inference is what follows from an argument (in other words, a conclusion) whereas an assumption is what is taken for granted while making an argument. In one sense, an assumption occurs "before" the argument, that is, while the argument is being made. An inference is made "after" the argument is complete, and follows from the argument. Both concepts will be discussed in more detail in later chapters, but for the time being you should note that all authors make assumptions when creating their arguments, and all arguments have inferences that can be derived from the argument.

The Mind of a GMAT Author

Actually, the GMAC is just the "producer" of the GMAT. The actual question construction is done by outside companies such as Pearson VUE and ACT, Inc.

Let us take a moment to differentiate the makers of the test from the author of each stimulus. The maker of the test is the GMAC, the organization that oversees the protocols under which the GMAT is constructed, administers the test, and processes and distributes the results. The stated purpose of the test makers is to examine your ability to analyze arguments, in an attempt to assess your suitability for business school. The author of the stimulus is the person from whose point of view each piece is written or the source from which the piece is drawn. Sometimes the persona of the author is made abundantly clear to you because the stimulus is prefaced by a short identifier, such as *Division Manager* or *Reviewer*, or even a proper name such as *Roland* or *Sharon*. The source of a stimulus can also be made clear by similar identifiers, such as *Advertisement* or *Editorial*.

GMAT students sometimes confuse the aim of the test makers with the way those aims are executed. We know that the GMAC has an active interest in testing your ability to discern both good and bad reasoning. The makers of the exam intentionally present flawed arguments because they want to test whether you are easily confused or prone to be swayed by illogical arguments. This often raises situations where you are presented with arguments that are false or seemingly deceptive in nature. This does not mean that the *author* of the piece is part of the deception. The role of a GMAT author is simply to present an argument or fact set. GMAT authors (as separated from the test makers) do *not* try to deceive you with lies. Although GMAT authors may end up making claims that are incorrect, this is not done out of a willful intention to deceive. Deception on the *author's* part is too sophisticated for the GMAT—it is beyond the scope of GMAT stimuli, which are too short to have the level of complexity necessary for you to detect deception if it was intended. So, you need not feel as if the author is attempting to trick you in the making of the argument. This is especially true when premises are created. For example, when a GMAT author makes a premise statement such as, "19 percent of all research projects are privately funded," this statement is likely to be accurate. A GMAT author would not *knowingly* create a false premise, and so, when examining arguments the likelihood is that the premises are not going to be in error and you should not look at them as a likely source of weakness in the argument. This does not mean that authors are infallible. GMAT authors make plenty of errors, but most of those mistakes are errors of reasoning that occur in the process of making the conclusion.

Not only do GMAT authors not attempt to deceive you, they believe (in their GMAT-world way) that the arguments they make are reasonable and solid. *When you read a GMAT argument from the perspective of the author, he or she believes that their argument is sound.* In other words, they do not knowingly make errors of reasoning. This is a fascinating point because it means that GMAT authors, as part of the GMAT world, function as if the points they raise and the conclusions they make have been well-considered and are airtight. This point will be immensely useful when we begin to look at certain forms of reasoning.

Consider the following argument: "My mail was delivered yesterday, so it will also be delivered today."

Although this argument is flawed (it could be Sunday and the mail will not be delivered), the author has not intentionally made this error. Rather, the author has made the conclusion without realizing that he has committed an error.

Read the Fine Print

One of the aims of the GMAT is to test how closely you read. This is obviously an important skill for anyone in business (who wants an employee who makes a critical mistake in a big negotiation?). One of the ways the GMAT tests whether you have this skill is to probe your knowledge of exactly what the author said. Because of this, you must read all parts of a problem incredibly closely, and you must pay special attention to words that describe the relationships under discussion. For example, if an author concludes, "Therefore, the refinery can achieve a greater operating efficiency," do not make the mistake of thinking the author implied that greater operating efficiency *will* or *must* be achieved. The GMAT makers love to examine your comprehension of the exact words used by the author, and that leads to the fourth Primary Objective:

Primary Objective #4: Read closely and know precisely what the author said. Do not generalize!

When it comes to relationships, the makers of the GMAT have a wide variety of modifiers in their arsenal. The following are two lists of words that should be noted when they appear, regardless of whether they appear in the premises or conclusion.

These word lists do not require memorization. They are presented to give you a broad idea of the type of words that can take on an added importance in GMAT questions.

Quantity Indicators	Probability Indicators
all	must
every	will
most	always
many	not always
some	probably
several	likely
few	would
sole	not necessarily
only	could
not all	rarely
none	never

Quantity indicators refer to the amount or quantity in the relationship, such as "some people" or "many of the laws." Probability indicators refer to the likelihood of occurrence, or the obligation present, as in "The Mayor should resign" or "The law will never pass." Many of the terms fit with negatives to form an opposing idea, for example, "some are not" or "would not."

Words such as the Quantity and Probability Indicators are critical because they are a ripe area for the GMAT makers to exploit. There are numerous examples of incorrect answer choices that attempt to capitalize on the meaning of a single word in the stimulus, and thus you must commit yourself to a careful examination of every word on the test.

Scope

One topic you often hear mentioned in relation to argumentation is scope. The scope of an argument is the range to which the premises and conclusion encompass certain ideas. For example, consider an argument discussing a new surgical technique. The ideas of surgery and medicine are within the scope of the argument. The idea of federal monetary policy, on the other hand, would not be within the scope of the argument.

Arguments are sometimes described as having a narrow (or limited) scope or a wide (or broad) scope. An argument with a narrow scope is definite in its statements, whereas a wide scope argument is less definite and allows for a greater range of possibility. When we begin to examine individual questions, we will return to this idea and show how it can be used to help consider answer choices in certain situations.

Scope can be a useful idea to consider when examining answer choices, because some answer choices go beyond the bounds of what the author has established in the argument. However, scope is also a concept that is overused in modern test preparation. One test preparation company used to tell instructors that if they could not answer a student's question, they should just say that the answer was out of the scope of the argument! As we will see, there are always definite, identifiable reasons that can be used to eliminate incorrect answer choices.

Final Chapter Note

The discussion of argumentation in this chapter is, by design, not comprehensive. The purpose of this chapter is to give you a broad overview of the theory underlying GMAT arguments. In future chapters we will apply those theories to specific questions and continue to expand upon the discussion in this chapter. The vast majority of students learn best by examining the application of ideas, and we believe the great bulk of your learning will come by seeing these ideas in action.

CR

Premise and Conclusion Analysis Drill

For each stimulus, identify the conclusion(s) and supporting premise(s), if any. The answer key will identify the conclusion and premises of each argument, the logical validity of each argument, and also comment on how to identify argument structure. *Answers on Page 42*

Answers on Page 42

1. Every year, new reports appear concerning the health risks posed by certain substances, such as coffee and sugar. One year an article claimed that coffee is dangerous to one's health. The next year, another article argued that coffee has some benefits for one's health. From these contradictory opinions, we see that experts are useless for guiding one's decisions about one's health.

   A. What is the conclusion of the argument, if any?

   B. What premises are given in support of this conclusion?

   C. Is the argument strong or weak? If you think that the argument is weak, please explain why.

2. Some teachers claim that students would not learn curricular content without the incentive of grades. But students with intense interest in the material would learn it without this incentive, while the behavior of students lacking all interest in the material is unaffected by such an incentive. The incentive of grades, therefore, serves no essential academic purpose.

   A. What is the conclusion of the argument, if any?

   B. What premises are given in support of this conclusion?

   C. Is the argument strong or weak? If you think that the argument is weak, please explain why.

Premise and Conclusion Analysis Drill

3. Damming the Merv River would provide irrigation for the dry land in its upstream areas; unfortunately, a dam would reduce agricultural productivity in the fertile land downstream by reducing the availability and quality of water there. The productivity loss in the downstream area would be greater than the productivity gain upstream, so building a dam would yield no overall gain in agricultural productivity in the region as a whole.

A. What is the conclusion of the argument, if any?

B. What premises are given in support of this conclusion?

C. Is the argument strong or weak? If you think that the argument is weak, please explain why.

4. In a study, infant monkeys given a choice between two surrogate mothers—a bare wire structure equipped with a milk bottle, or a soft, suede-covered wire structure equipped with a milk bottle—unhesitatingly chose the latter. When given a choice between a bare wire structure equipped with a milk bottle and a soft, suede-covered wire structure lacking a milk bottle, they unhesitatingly chose the former.

A. What is the conclusion of the argument, if any?

B. What premises are given in support of this conclusion?

C. Is the argument strong or weak? If you think that the argument is weak, please explain why.

Premise and Conclusion Analysis Drill Answer Key

Question #1.

> Conclusion: From these contradictory opinions, we see that experts are useless for guiding one's decisions about one's health.
>
> Premise: Every year, new reports appear concerning the health risks posed by certain substances, such as coffee and sugar.
>
> Premise: One year an article claimed that coffee is dangerous to one's health.
>
> Premise: The next year, another article argued that coffee has some benefits for one's health.

The conclusion is introduced by the phrase "we see that."

The argument is weak. The conclusion is far too strong in saying that "experts are useless." Just because the different articles about substances disagree does not prove that experts cannot help you with your *health* (a much broader field than the substances cover). In addition, the articles about coffee could have covered differing aspects of coffee, some of which are beneficial and some of which are detrimental.

Question #2.

> Conclusion: The incentive of grades, therefore, serves no essential academic purpose.
>
> Premise: Some teachers claim that students would not learn curricular content without the incentive of grades.
>
> Premise: But students with intense interest in the material would learn it without this incentive, while the behavior of students lacking all interest in the material is unaffected by such an incentive.

The conclusion contains the conclusion indicator, "therefore." Note also the use of the "Some teachers claim..." device discussed earlier in the chapter. This construction raises a viewpoint that the author eventually argues against.

The argument is weak. When discussing the students, the author makes the mistake of discussing only the extremes—those with intense interest and those lacking all interest. No effort is made to address the students who fall between these extremes.

Premise and Conclusion Analysis Drill Answer Key

Question #3.

> Conclusion: Building a dam would yield no overall gain in agricultural productivity in the region as a whole.
>
> Premise: Damming the Merv River would provide irrigation for the dry land in its upstream areas.
>
> Premise: Unfortunately, a dam would reduce agricultural productivity in the fertile land downstream by reducing the availability and quality of water there.
>
> Premise: The productivity loss in the downstream area would be greater than the productivity gain upstream.

The conclusion is introduced in the last sentence by the indicator "so."

The argument is strong. The author discusses both the upstream and downstream areas, showing that the gain from the dam in the upstream area would not offset the loss of productivity in the downstream area. In fact, it appears an even stronger conclusion would be warranted, such as "building a dam would yield an overall loss of productivity. Since the author directly addresses overall productivity, possible objections about acreage and volume produced are rendered moot. The author even goes so far as to indicate that the downstream land is fertile, deflecting another possible objection about the work involved in making the land productive.

Note that this is a good example of a fantasy stimulus, one that is based on a scenario that does not exist in the real world. There is no "Merv River" anywhere in the world (although there was an ancient city of Merv in Turkmenistan). Stimuli like this one are often created to portray a certain reasoning form or situation. While fantasy stimuli are often obvious (containing fake countries, etc.), you should not approach them any differently than real-world, fact-based stimuli because Critical Reasoning is about argumentation, and argumentation can be portrayed equally well in real world or fantasy stimuli.

Question #4.

> Premise: In a study, infant monkeys given a choice between two surrogate mothers—a bare wire structure equipped with a milk bottle, or a soft, suede-covered wire structure equipped with a milk bottle—unhesitatingly chose the latter.
>
> Premise: When given a choice between a bare wire structure equipped with a milk bottle and a soft, suede-covered wire structure lacking a milk bottle, they unhesitatingly chose the former.

Careful! The stimulus is only a fact set and does not contain a conclusion. Therefore, there is no argument present and no evaluation of argument validity can be made.

CHAPTER THREE: THE QUESTION STEM AND ANSWER CHOICES

The Question Stem

The question stem follows the stimulus and poses a question directed at the stimulus. In some ways the question stem is the most important part of each problem because it specifies the task you must perform in order to get credit for the problem.

GMAT question stems cover a wide range of tasks, and will variously ask you to:

- identify details of the stimulus

- describe the structure of the argument

- strengthen or weaken the argument

- identify inferences, main points, and assumptions

- recognize errors of reasoning

- reconcile conflicts

- find arguments that are identical in structure

Analyzing the Question Stem

When examining a typical Critical Reasoning section, you may come to the conclusion that there are dozens of different types of question stems. The test makers create this impression by varying the words used in each question stem. As we will see shortly, even though they use different words, many of these question stems are identical in terms of what they ask you to do.

In order to easily handle the different questions, we categorize the question stems that appear on the GMAT. Fortunately, every question stem can be defined as a certain type, and the more familiar you are with the question types, the faster you can respond when faced with individual questions. Thus, one of your tasks is to learn each question type and become familiar with the characteristics that define each type. We will help you accomplish this goal by including a variety of question type identification drills, and by examining each type of question in detail. This leads to the fifth Primary Objective:

Primary Objective #5: Carefully read and identify the question stem. Do not assume that certain words are automatically associated with certain question types.

Make sure to read the question stem very carefully. Some stems direct you to focus on certain aspects of the stimulus and if you miss these clues you make the problem much more difficult.

You must correctly analyze and classify every question stem because the question stem ultimately determines the nature of the correct answer choice. A mistake in analyzing the question stem almost invariably leads to a missed question. As we will see, the test makers love to use certain words—such as "support"—in different ways because they know some test takers will automatically assume these words imply a certain type of question. Properly identifying the question stem type will allow you to proceed quickly and with confidence, and in some cases it will help you determine the correct answer before you read any of the five answer choices.

The Ten Critical Reasoning Question Types

Each question stem that appears in the Critical Reasoning section of the GMAT can be classified into one of ten different types:

1. Must Be True/Most Supported
2. Main Point
3. Assumption
4. Strengthen/Support
5. Resolve the Paradox
6. Weaken
7. Method of Reasoning
8. Flaw in the Reasoning
9. Parallel Reasoning
10. Evaluate the Argument

Question stems contain criteria that must be met. The task could be to weaken the argument, find the method of reasoning, etc.

Occasionally, students ask if we refer to the question types by number or by name. We always refer to the questions by name as that is an easier and more efficient approach. Numerical question type classification systems force you to add two unnecessary levels of abstraction to your thinking process. For example, consider a question that asks you to "weaken" the argument. In a numerical question classification system, you must first recognize that the question asks you to weaken the argument, then you must classify that question into a numerical category (say, Type 6), and then you must translate Type 6 to mean "Weaken." Literally, numerical classification systems force you to perform an abstract, circular translation of the meaning of the question, and the translation process is both time-consuming and valueless.

In the following pages we will discuss each question type in brief. Later we will examine the major question types.

1. Must Be True/Most Supported

   This category is simply known as "Must Be True." Must Be True questions ask you to identify the answer choice that is best proven by the information in the stimulus. Question stem examples:

   "If the statements above are true, which one of the following must also be true?"

   "Which one of the following can be properly inferred from the passage?"

2. Main Point

   Main Point questions are a variant of Must Be True questions. As you might expect, a Main Point question asks you to find the primary conclusion made by the author. Question stem example:

   "The main point of the argument is that"

3. Assumption

   These questions ask you to identify an assumption of the author's argument. Question stem example:

   "Which one of the following is an assumption required by the argument above?"

4. Strengthen/Support

   These questions ask you to select the answer choice that provides support for the author's argument or strengthens it in some way. Question stem examples:

   "Which one of the following, if true, most strengthens the argument?"

   "Which one of the following, if true, most strongly supports the statement above?"

5. Resolve the Paradox

    Every Resolve the Paradox stimulus contains a discrepancy or seeming contradiction. You must find the answer choice that best resolves the situation. Question stem example:

    "Which one of the following, if true, would most effectively resolve the apparent paradox above?"

6. Weaken

    Weaken questions ask you to attack or undermine the author's argument. Question stem example:

    "Which one of the following, if true, most seriously weakens the argument?"

7. Method of Reasoning

    Method of Reasoning questions ask you to describe, in abstract terms, the way in which the author made his or her argument. Question stem example:

    "Which one of the following describes the technique of reasoning used above?"

8. Flaw in the Reasoning

    Flaw in the Reasoning questions ask you to describe, in abstract terms, the error of reasoning committed by the author. Question stem example:

    "The reasoning in the astronomer's argument is flawed because this argument"

9. Parallel Reasoning

    Parallel Reasoning questions ask you to identify the answer choice that contains reasoning most similar in structure to the reasoning presented in the stimulus. Question stem example:

    "Which one of the following arguments is most similar in its pattern of reasoning to the argument above?"

In the answer key to this book, all questions are classified as one of these ten types. There are also additional indicators designating reasoning type, etc.

10. Evaluate the Argument

With Evaluate the Argument questions you must decide which answer choice will allow you to determine the logical validity of the argument. Question stem example:

"The answer to which one of the following questions would contribute most to an evaluation of the argument?"

Other question type elements will be discussed, most notably question variants (such as Argument Part questions). Those will be discussed in later chapters.

> **Important Note**: Although there are ten separate question types on the GMAT, each question type does *not* appear with the same frequency. The most popular question types are Weaken, Must Be True, Assumption, Strengthen, and Resolve. If your GMAT test date is approaching quickly and you have little time to study, go directly to those chapters and study those question types first.

Although each of these question types is distinct, they are related in terms of the root function you are asked to perform. Questions that appear dissimilar, such as Must Be True and Method of Reasoning, are actually quite similar when considered in terms of how you work with the question. All question types are variations of three main question "families," and each family is comprised of question types that are similar to each other.

On the next page, we delineate the three families using box-and-arrow diagrams that reflect the flow of information between the stimulus and the answer choices.

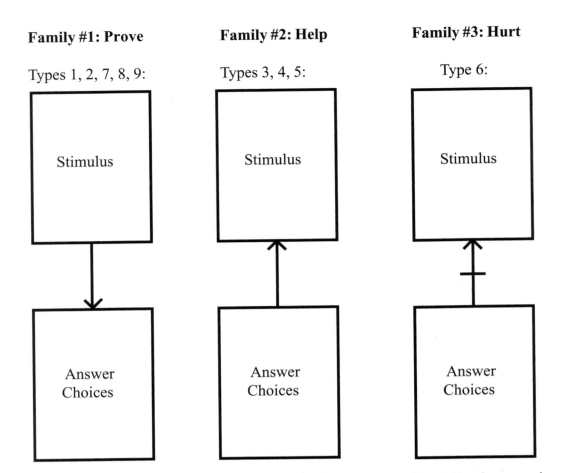

Family #1: Prove

Types 1, 2, 7, 8, 9:

Stimulus

Answer Choices

Family #2: Help

Types 3, 4, 5:

Stimulus

Answer Choices

Family #3: Hurt

Type 6:

Stimulus

Answer Choices

Family #1, also known as the Must Be or Prove Family, consists of the following question types:

(1) Must Be True
(2) Main Point
(7) Method of Reasoning
(8) Flaw in the Reasoning
(9) Parallel Reasoning

Family #2, also known as the Help Family, consists of the following question types:

(3) Assumption
(4) Strengthen/Support
(5) Resolve the Paradox

Family #3, also known as the Hurt Family, consists of the following question type:

(6) Weaken

The boxes on the preceding page represent the stimulus and answer choices for any given Critical Reasoning question. The arrows represent the flow of information; one part of the problem is simply accepted and the other part is affected. There are two basic rules to follow when analyzing the diagrams:

1. The part (stimulus or answer choices) at the start of the arrow is accepted as is, and no additional information (aside from general domain assumptions) can be brought in.

2. The part (stimulus or answer choices) at the end of the arrow is what is affected or determined (for example, are you asked to Weaken the argument or determine which answer Must Be True?).

One of the signature features of the three question families is that they define the parameters of what you can do with the information in each question.

In very rough terms, the part at the start of the arrow is taken for granted and the part at the end of the arrow is under suspicion. While this characterization may sound a bit vague, this occurs because there are three different types of relationships, and the details vary from type to type.

Part of the purpose of classifying questions into these three categories is to understand the fundamental structure of Critical Reasoning problems. Many students ask the following two questions upon seeing Critical Reasoning questions for the first time:

1. Should I simply accept every statement in the stimulus as true?

2. Can the answer choices bring in information that is off-the-page, that is, ideas and concepts not stated in the stimulus?

The answer to both questions depends on the question stem and corresponding question family. Let us examine each question family and address these questions in more detail.

The First Question Family

The First Question Family is based on the principle of using the information in the stimulus to prove that one of the answer choices must be true.

In the First Family diagram, the arrow points downward from the stimulus to the answer choices. Hence, the stimulus is at the start of the arrow, and the answer choices are at the end of the arrow. According to the rules above, whatever is stated in the stimulus is simply accepted as given, with no additional information being added. And, because the arrow points to the answer choices, the answer choices are "under suspicion," and the information in the stimulus is used to prove one of the answer choices correct.

Because the stimulus is accepted as stated (even if it contains an error of reasoning), you cannot bring in additional information off the page—you can only use what is stated in the stimulus. Thus, in a Must Be True question, only what the author states in the stimulus can be used to prove one of the answer choices. This reveals the way the arrow works: you start at the stimulus and then use only that information to separate the answers. If an answer choice references something that is not included or encompassed by the stimulus, it will be incorrect. In a Method of Reasoning question, for example, the process works the same. If one of the answers references some method of argumentation that did not occur in the stimulus, then the answer is automatically incorrect. The test makers do not hide this relationship. Most question stems in this family (especially Must Be True) will contain a phrase similar to, "The information above, *if true...*" (italics added). In this way the test makers are able to indicate that you should accept the statements in the stimulus as given and then use them to prove one of the answer choices.

The following rules apply to the First Question Family:

1. You must accept the stimulus information—even if it contains an error of reasoning—and use it to prove that one of the answer choices must be true.

2. Any information in an answer choice that does not appear either directly in the stimulus or as a combination of items in the stimulus will be incorrect.

These rules will be revisited in more detail once we begin analyzing individual Critical Reasoning questions.

<u>The Second Question Family</u>

The Second Question Family is based on the principle of assisting or helping the author's argument or statement in some way, whether by revealing an assumption of the argument, by resolving a paradox, or in some other fashion.

As opposed to the First Family, in this family the arrow points upward to the stimulus. This reverses the flow of information: the answer choices are at the start of the arrow, and the stimulus is at the end of the arrow. Functionally, this means you must accept the answer choices as given, and the stimulus is under suspicion. Accepting the answer choices as given means you cannot dispute their factual basis, even if they include elements not mentioned in the stimulus (we often call this "new" or "outside" information). The test makers make this principle clear because most question stems in this family contain a phrase similar to, "Which of the following, *if true,...*" (italics added). By including this phrase, the test makers indicate that they wish you to treat each answer choice as factually correct. Your task is to examine each answer choice and see which one best fits the exact criteria stated in the question stem (strengthen, resolve, etc.).

In this question grouping, the stimulus is under suspicion. Often there are errors of reasoning present, or leaps in logic, and you are asked to find an answer choice that closes the hole. When you encounter a question of this category, immediately consider the stimulus—were there any obvious holes or gaps in the argument that could be filled by one of the answer choices? Often you will find that the author has made an error of reasoning and you will be asked to eliminate that error.

The following rules apply to the Second Question Family:

1. The information in the stimulus is suspect. There are often reasoning errors present, and depending on the question, you will help shore up the argument in some way.

2. The answer choices are accepted as given, even if they include "new" information. Your task is to determine which answer choice best meets the question posed in the stem.

The Third Question Family

The Third Question Family consists of only one question type—Weaken. Accordingly, you are asked to attack the author's argument.

Compared to the Second Question Family, the only difference between the diagrams is that the third family diagram has a bar across the arrow. This bar signifies a negative: instead of strengthening or helping the argument, you attack or hurt the argument. In this sense the third family is the polar opposite of the second family; otherwise the two question families are identical.

For the Third Question Family, the following rules apply:

1. The information in the stimulus is suspect. There are often reasoning errors present, and you will further weaken the argument in some way.

2. The answer choices are accepted as given, even if they include "new" information. Your task is to determine which answer choice best attacks the argument in the stimulus.

As you might expect, there are deeper relationships between the individual question types and the question families. As we discuss the mechanics of individual questions we will further explore these relationships.

Those of you reading closely may have noticed that one of the question types was not listed among the Families. Evaluate the Argument questions are a combination of the second and third question families, and thus cannot be diagrammed easily.

Question Type Notes

The following is a collection of notes regarding the Ten Question Types. These notes help clear up some questions that typically arise when students are learning to identify the question types. In the chapters that discuss each question type we will reintroduce each of these points.

- Must Be True and Resolve the Paradox questions are generally connected to stimuli that do *not* contain conclusions. All remaining question types must be connected to stimuli with conclusions (unless a conclusion is added by the question stem, as sometimes occurs). Hence, when a stimulus without a conclusion appears on the GMAT, only two types of questions can be posed to you: Must Be True or Resolve the Paradox. Question types such as Weaken or Method of Reasoning do not generally appear because no argument or reasoning is present, and those question types ask you to address reasoning. Generally, Resolve the Paradox questions are easy to spot because they contain a paradox or discrepancy. Thus, if you encounter a stimulus without a conclusion and without a paradox, you are most likely about to see a Must Be True question stem.

- Weaken and Strengthen are polar opposite question types, and both are often based on flawed or weak arguments that contain holes that must be closed or opened further.

- Method of Reasoning and Flaw in the Reasoning questions are a brother/sister pair. The only difference between the two is that Flaw in the Reasoning question stems explicitly note that the stimulus contains an error of reasoning. In a Method of Reasoning question the stimulus contains valid or invalid reasoning.

- Parallel Reasoning questions are a one-step extension of Method of Reasoning questions in that you must first identify the type of reasoning used and then parallel it. Method of Reasoning and Parallel Reasoning questions both have a strong Must Be True element.

- Main Point, Method of Reasoning, Flaw in the Reasoning, Parallel Reasoning, and Evaluate the Argument appear the *least* frequently on the GMAT.

Question Type Variety

One of the aims of the test makers is to keep you off-balance. An unsettled, frustrated test taker is prone to making mistakes. By mixing up the types of questions you face, the makers of the test can keep you from getting into a rhythm. Imagine how much easier the Critical Reasoning questions would be if you faced only Must Be True questions. For this reason, you will always see a spread of question types among the Critical Reasoning questions, and you will rarely see the same question type twice in a row. Since this situation is a fact of the GMAT, before the test begins prepare yourself mentally for the quick shifting of mental gears that is required to move from question to question.

"Most" in Question Stems

Many question stems—especially Strengthen and Weaken stems—contain the qualifier "most." For example, a typical question stem will state, "Which one of the following, if true, most weakens the argument above?" Astute test takers realize that the presence of "most" opens up a Pandora's box of sorts: by including "most," there is a possibility that other answer choices will also meet the criteria of the question stem (Strengthen, Weaken, etc.), albeit to a lesser extent. In other words, if a question stem says "most weakens," the possibility is that every answer choice weakens the argument and you would be in the unenviable task of having to choose the best of a bunch of good answer choices. *Fortunately, this is not how it works*. Even though "most" will appear in many stems, you can rest assured that only one answer choice will meet the criteria. So, if you see a "most weakens" question stem, only one of the answers will weaken the argument. So, then, why does "most" appear in so many question stems? Because in order to maintain test integrity the test makers need to make sure their credited answer choice is as airtight and defensible as possible. Imagine what would occur if a question stem, let us say a Weaken question, did not include a "most" qualifier: any answer choice that weakened the argument, even if only very slightly, could then be argued to meet the criteria of the question stem. A situation like this would make constructing the test exceedingly difficult because any given problem might have multiple correct answer choices. To eliminate this predicament, the test makers insert "most" into the question stem, and then they can always claim there is one and only one correct answer choice.

Of course, every once in a while two answer choices achieve the desired goal; in those cases you simply choose the better of the two answers. Normally, the difference between the two answers is significant enough for you to make a clear distinction as to which one is superior.

Identify the Question Stem Drill

Each of the following items contains a question stem. In the space provided, categorize each stem into one of the ten Critical Reasoning Question Types: Must Be True, Main Point, Assumption, Strengthen, Resolve the Paradox, Weaken, Method of Reasoning, Flaw in the Reasoning, Parallel Reasoning, or Evaluate the Argument. While we realize that you have not yet worked directly with each question type, by considering the relationships now you will have an advantage as you attack future questions. In later chapters we will present more Identify the Question Stem drills to further strengthen your abilities. *Answers on Page 58*

1. Question Stem: "Which of the following, if true, most helps to explain the viewpoint described above?"

   Question Type: _____

2. Question Stem: "Which of the following can be properly inferred from the historian's statement?"

   Question Type: _____

3. Question Stem: "Which of the following, if true, most seriously weakens the reasoning above?"

   Question Type: _____

4. Question Stem: "Which of the following is an assumption required by the argument above?"

   Question Type: _____

5. Question Stem: "Which of the following is most like the argument above in its logical structure?

   Question Type: _____

6. Question Stem: "Of the following, which one most accurately expresses the main point of the argument?"

   Question Type: _____

7. Question Stem: "Which of the following statements, if true, would provide the most support for the scientists' assertion?"

    Question Type: _____

8. Question Stem: "The argument is flawed because it"

    Question Type: _____

9. Question Stem: "The advertisement proceeds by"

    Question Type: _____

10. Question Stem: "The answer to which of the following questions would most help in evaluating the columnist's argument?"

    Question Type: _____

11. Question Stem: "Mary challenges Shaun's reasoning by"

    Question Type: _____

12. Question Stem: "The statements above, if true, most strongly support which of the following?"

    Question Type: _____

CR

Identify the Question Stem Drill Answer Key

The typical student misses about half of the questions in this drill. Do not worry about how many you miss; the point of this drill is to acquaint you with the different question stems. As you see more examples of each type of question, your ability to correctly identify each stem will improve.

1. Question Type: Resolve the Paradox

The presence of the phrase "Which of the following, if true," indicates that this question stem must be from either the second or third question family. Because the third family is Weaken, and the question stem asks you to "explain," the question cannot be from the third family. Thus, the question must be from the second family and can only be an Assumption, Strengthen, or Resolve question. The idea of explaining is most closely aligned with Resolving the Paradox.

2. Question Type: Must Be True

The word "inferred" means "must be true," hence that is the classification of this question.

3. Question Type: Weaken

The presence of the phrase "Which of the following, if true," indicates that this question stem must be from either the second or third question family. The presence of the word "weakens" indicates that this is a Weaken question.

4. Question Type: Assumption

The key words in this stem are "required" and "assumption," making this an Assumption question.

5. Question Type: Parallel

The key phrases in this stem are "most like...in logical structure" and "the argument above." Because the argument in the stimulus is used as a model for one of the answers, this is a Parallel Reasoning question.

6. Question Type: Main Point

Because the stem asks you to find the main point, this question is categorized as Main Point.

7. Question Type: Strengthen

The presence of the phrase "Which one of the following, if true," indicates that this question stem must be from either the second or third question family. Because the third family is Weaken, and the question stem asks you to "support," the question cannot be from the third family. Thus, the question must be from the second family and can only be an Assumption, Strengthen, or Resolve question. The idea of supporting is the same as Strengthening.

8. Question Type: Flaw

The presence of the word "flawed" could indicate either a Weaken question or a Flaw in the Reasoning question. In this case, the stem requests you to identify the flaw in the argument (or reasoning), hence this question is a Flaw in the Reasoning question.

9. Question Type: Method

By asking how the advertisement "proceeds," the test makers wish to know the way in which the argument is made, in other words, the method of the reasoning.

10. Question Type: Evaluate

The key phrase is "evaluating the columnist's argument," which indicates that the test makers require you to find the question that would best help in evaluating the author's argument. Thus, the question is classified as Evaluate the Argument.

11. Question Type: Method

Although the question stem uses the word "challenges," this is not a Weaken question because the stem asks for a description of the way Anne's reasoning was challenged. Thus, you are asked to identify Mary's method of reasoning.

12. Question Type: Must Be True

The phrase "The statements above, if true," indicates that this question must come from either the first or fourth question family. In this case, the "most strongly support" is used with the intent of proving one of the answers as correct. Hence, this is a Must Be True question. Note how the use of the word "support" in this question stem differs from the usage in problem #7.

"Except" and "Least" in Question Stems

The true effect of "except" is to logically negate the question stem. We will discuss Logical Negation in more detail in the Assumption question chapter.

The word "except" has a dramatic impact when it appears in a question stem. Because "except" means "other than," when "except" is placed in a question it negates the logical quality of the answer choice you seek. Literally, it turns the intent of the question stem upside down. For example, if a question asks you to weaken the argument, the one correct answer weakens the argument and the other four answers do not weaken the argument. If "except" is added to the question stem, as in "Each of the following weakens the argument EXCEPT," the stem is turned around and instead of the correct answer weakening the argument, the four incorrect answers weaken the argument and the one correct answer does not weaken the argument.

Many students, upon encountering "except" in a question stem, make the mistake of assuming that the "except" charges you with seeking the polar opposite. For example, if a question stem asks you to weaken the argument, some students believe that a "Weaken EXCEPT" question stem actually asks you to strengthen the argument. This is incorrect. Although weaken and strengthen are polar opposites, because except means "other than," when a "Weaken EXCEPT" question stem appears, you are asked to find any answer choice other than Weaken. While this could include a strengthening answer choice, it could also include an answer choice that has no effect on the argument. Thus, in a "Weaken EXCEPT" question, the four incorrect answers Weaken the argument and the one correct answer does not weaken the argument (could strengthen or have no effect). Here are some other examples:

1. "Which of the following, if true, strengthens the argument above?"

    One correct answer: Strengthen
    Four incorrect answers: Do not Strengthen

    "Each of the following, if true, strengthens the argument above EXCEPT:"

    One correct answer: Does not Strengthen
    Four incorrect answers: Strengthen

2. "Which of the following, if true, would help to resolve the apparent discrepancy above?"

> One correct answer: Resolves the Paradox
> Four incorrect answers: Do not Resolve the Paradox

"Each of the following, if true, would help to resolve the apparent discrepancy above EXCEPT:"

> One correct answer: Does not Resolve the Paradox
> Four incorrect answers: Resolve the Paradox

Some GMAT Critical Reasoning sections feature "except" questions very heavily, especially as you encounter higher-difficulty problems.

As you can see from the two examples, the presence of except has a profound impact upon the meaning of the question stem. Because "except" has this powerful effect, it always appears in all capital letters whenever it is used in a GMAT question stem.

The word "least" has a similar effect to "except" when it appears in a question stem. Although "least" and "except" do not generally have the same meaning, when "least" appears in a question stem you should treat it *exactly the same* as "except." Note: this advice holds true only when this word appears in the question stem! If you see the word "least" elsewhere on the GMAT, consider it to have its usual meaning of "in the lowest or smallest degree."

Let us look more closely at how and why "least" functions identically to "except." Compare the following two question stems:

"Which of the following, if true, would help to resolve the apparent discrepancy above?"

> One correct answer: Resolves the Paradox
> Four incorrect answers: Do not Resolve the Paradox

"Which of the following, if true, helps LEAST to resolve the apparent discrepancy described above?"

> One correct answer: Does not Resolve the Paradox
> Four incorrect answers: Resolve the Paradox

"Except" is used far more frequently in GMAT question stems than "least."

By asking for the question stem that "least" helps resolve the paradox, the test makers indicate that the four incorrect answers will more strongly help resolve the paradox. But, in practice, when "least" is used, all five answer choices do *not* resolve the paradox to varying degrees. Instead, four answers resolve the paradox and the one correct answer does *not* resolve the paradox. Why do the test makers do this? Because the test makers cannot afford to introduce uncertainty into the correctness of the answers. If all five answer choices resolve the paradox, then reasonable minds could come to a disagreement about which one "least" resolves the paradox. In order to avoid this type of controversy, the test makers simply make sure that exactly one answer choice does not resolve the paradox (and, because that answer choice does not resolve the paradox it automatically has the "least" effect possible). In this way, the test makers can present a seemingly difficult and confusing task while at the same time avoiding a test construction problem. Because of this situation, any time you encounter "least" in a question stem, simply recognize that four of the answers will meet the stated criteria (weaken, strengthen, resolve, etc.) and the one correct answer will not. Thus, you will not have to make an assessment based on degree of correctness.

Here is another example comparing the use of the word "least:"

> "Which one of the following, if true, would most strengthen the argument above?"
>
>> One correct answer: Strengthen
>> Four incorrect answers: Do not Strengthen
>
> "Which one of the following, if true, LEAST strengthens the argument above?"
>
>> One correct answer: Does not Strengthen
>> Four incorrect answers: Strengthen

Because "least," like "except," has such a strong impact on the meaning of a question stem, the test makers kindly place "least" in all capital letters when it appears in a question stem.

In the answer keys to this book, we will designate questions that contain "except" or "least" by placing an "X" at the end of the question stem classification. For example, a "Weaken EXCEPT" question stem would be classified as "WeakenX." A "Strengthen EXCEPT" question stem would be classified as "StrengthenX" and so on.

Prephrasing Answers

Most students tend to simply read the question stem and then move on to the answer choices without further thought. This is disadvantageous because these students run a greater risk of being tempted by the expertly constructed incorrect answer choices. One of the most effective techniques for quickly finding correct answer choices and avoiding incorrect answer choices is prephrasing. Prephrasing an answer involves quickly speculating on what you expect the correct answer will be based on the information in the stimulus.

Although every answer you prephrase may not be correct, there is great value in considering for a moment what elements could appear in the correct answer choice. Students who regularly prephrase find that they are more readily able to eliminate incorrect answer choices, and of course, many times their prephrased answer is correct. And, as we will see in later chapters, there are certain stimulus and question stem combinations on the GMAT that yield predictable answers, making prephrasing even more valuable. In part, prephrasing puts you in an attacking mindset: if you look ahead and consider a possible answer choice, you are forced to involve yourself in the problem. This process helps keep you alert and in touch with the elements of the problem.

Primary Objective #6: Prephrase: after reading the question stem, take a moment to mentally formulate your answer to the question stem.

Keep in mind that prephrasing is directly related to attacking the stimulus; typically, students who closely analyze the stimulus can more easily prephrase an answer.

Prephrasing is the GMAT version of the old adage, "An ounce of prevention is worth a pound of cure."

All high-scoring test takers are active and aggressive. Passive test takers tend to be less involved in the exam and therefore more prone to make errors.

When we speak of opposites on the GMAT, we mean logical opposites. For example, what is the opposite of "wet?" Most people would say "dry." But, that is the polar opposite, not the logical opposite. The logical opposite of "wet" is "not wet." Logical opposites break the topic under discussion into two parts. In this case, everything in the spectrum of moisture would be classified as either "wet" or "not wet."

The Answer Choices

All GMAT questions have five answer choices and each question has only one correct, or "credited," response. As with other sections, the correct answer in a Critical Reasoning question must meet the Uniqueness Rule of Answer Choices™, which states that "Every correct answer has a unique logical quality that meets the criteria in the question stem. Every incorrect answer has the opposite logical quality." The correctness of the answer choices themselves conforms to this rule: there is one correct answer choice; the other four answer choices are the opposite of correct, or incorrect. Consider the following specific examples:

1. Logical Quality of the Correct Answer: Must Be True
   Logical Quality of the Four Incorrect Answers:
   the opposite of Must Be True = Not Necessarily True (could be not necessarily the case or never the case)

2. Logical Quality of the Correct Answer: Strengthen
   Logical Quality of the Four Incorrect Answers:
   the opposite of Strengthen = not Strengthen (could be neutral or weaken)

3. Logical Quality of the Correct Answer: Weaken
   Logical Quality of the Four Incorrect Answers:
   the opposite of Weaken = not Weaken (could be neutral or strengthen)

Even though there is only one correct answer choice and this answer choice is unique, you still are faced with a difficult task when attempting to determine the correct answer. The test makers have the advantage of time and language on their side. Because identifying the correct answer at first glance can be quite hard, you must always read all five of the answer choices. Students who fail to read all five answer choices open themselves up to missing questions without ever having read the correct answer. There are many classic examples of GMAC placing highly attractive wrong answer choices just before the correct answer. If you are going to make the time investment of analyzing the stimulus and the question stem, you should also make the wise investment of considering each answer choice.

Primary Objective #7: Always read each of the five answer choices.

There may be times when you would not read all five answer choices, for example, if you only a short amount of time left in the section and you determine that answer choice (B) is clearly correct. In that case, you would choose answer choice (B) and then move on to the next question.

As you read through each answer choice, sort them into contenders and losers. If an answer choice appears somewhat attractive, interesting, or even confusing, keep it as a contender and move on to the next answer choice. You do not want to spend time debating the merits of an answer choice only to find that the next answer choice is superior. However, if an answer choice immediately strikes you as incorrect, classify it as a loser and move on. Once you have evaluated all five answer choices, return to the answer choices that strike you as most likely to be correct and decide which one is correct.

Primary Objective #8: Separate the answer choices into Contenders and Losers. After completing this process, review the contenders and decide which answer is the correct one.

The Contender/Loser separation process is exceedingly important, primarily because it saves time. Consider two students—1 and 2—who each approach the same question, one of whom uses the Contender/Loser approach and the other who does not. Answer choice (D) is correct:

Student 1 (using Contender/Loser)

> Answer choice A: considers this answer for 15 seconds, keeps it as a Contender.
> Answer choice B: considers this answer for 10 seconds, eliminates it as a Loser.
> Answer choice C: considers this answer for 20 seconds, eliminates it as a Loser.
> Answer choice D: considers this answer for 20 seconds, keeps it as a Contender, and mentally notes that this answer is preferable to (A).
> Answer choice E: considers this answer for 15 seconds, would normally keep as a contender, but determines answer choice (D) is superior.

> After a quick review, Student 1 selects answer choice (D) and moves to the next question. Total time spent on the answer choices: 1 minute, 20 seconds (irrespective of the time spent on the stimulus).

Student 2 (considering each answer choice in its entirety)

> Answer choice A: considers this answer for 15 seconds, is not sure if the answer is correct or incorrect. Returns to stimulus and spends another 20 seconds proving the answer is wrong.
> Answer choice B: considers this answer for 10 seconds, eliminates it.
> Answer choice C: considers this answer for 20 seconds, eliminates it.
> Answer choice D: considers this answer for 20 seconds, notes this a good answer, then spends an additional 10 seconds returning to the stimulus to prove the answer correct.
> Answer choice E: considers this answer for 15 seconds, but determines answer choice (D) is superior.

> After a quick review, Student 2 selects answer choice (D) and moves to

Some companies assert that only two of the five answer choices have merit. This type of "rule" is valueless because only one answer choice can be correct; the other four answers can be eliminated for concrete and identifiable reasons.

the next question. Total time spent on the answer choices: 1 minute, 50 seconds.

Comparison: both students answer the problem correctly, but Student 2 takes 30 more seconds to answer the question than Student 1.

Some students, on reading this comparison, note that both students answered the problem correctly and that the time difference was small, only 30 seconds more for Student 2 to complete the problem. Doesn't sound like that big a difference, does it? But, the extra 30 seconds was for just one problem. Imagine if that same thing occurred on every single Critical Reasoning problem in the section: that extra 30 seconds per question would translate to a loss of 5 to 7 minutes when multiplied across 10 to 14 questions in the section! And that lost time would mean that student 2 would get to several questions than Student 1 in this section. This example underscores an essential GMAT truth: little things make a big difference, and every single second counts. If you can save even five seconds by employing a certain method, then do so!

Occasionally, students will read and eliminate all five of the answer choices. If this occurs, return to the stimulus and re-evaluate the argument. Remember— the information needed to answer the question always resides in the stimulus, either implicitly or explicitly. If none of the answers are attractive, then you must have missed something key in the stimulus.

Primary Objective #9: If all five answer choices appear to be Losers, return to the stimulus and re-evaluate the argument.

Take a moment to review the methods discussed in Chapters Two and Three. Together, these recommendations form a cohesive strategy for attacking any Critical Reasoning question. Let us start by reviewing the Primary Objectives™:

Primary Objective #1: Determine whether the stimulus contains an argument or if it is only a set of factual statements.

Primary Objective #2: If the stimulus contains an argument, identify the conclusion of the argument. If the stimulus contains a fact set, examine each fact.

Primary Objective #3: If the stimulus contains an argument, determine if the argument is strong or weak.

Primary Objective #4: Read closely and know precisely what the author said. Do not generalize!

Primary Objective #5: Carefully read and identify the question stem. Do not assume that certain words are automatically associated with certain question types.

Primary Objective #6: Prephrase: after reading the question stem, take a moment to mentally formulate your answer to the question stem.

Primary Objective #7: Always read each of the five answer choices.

Primary Objective #8: Separate the answer choices into Contenders and Losers. After you complete this process, review the Contenders and decide which answer is the correct one.

Primary Objective #9: If all five answer choices appear to be Losers, return to the stimulus and re-evaluate the argument.

> Memorize this process and make it second nature! These steps constitute the basic approach you must use to attack each question.

As you attack each problem, remember that each question stem governs the flow of information within the problem:

- The First family uses the stimulus to prove one of the answer choices must be true. No information outside the sphere of the stimulus is allowed in the correct answer choice.

- The Second Family takes the answer choices as true and uses them to help the stimulus. Information outside the sphere of the stimulus is allowed in the correct answer choice.

- The Third Family takes the answer choices as true and uses them to hurt the stimulus. Information outside the sphere of the stimulus is allowed in the correct answer choice.

By consistently applying the points above, you give yourself the best opportunity to succeed on each question.

Final Chapter Note

The individuals who construct standardized tests are called *psychometricians*. Although this job title sounds ominous, breaking this word into its two parts reveals a great deal about the nature of the GMAT. Although we could make a number of jokes about the *psycho* part, this portion of the word refers to psychology; the *metrician* portion relates to metrics or measurement. Thus, the purpose of these individuals is to create a test that measures you in a precise, psychological way. As part of this process, the makers of the GMAT carefully analyze reams of data from every test administration in order to assess the tendencies of test takers. As Sherlock Holmes observed, "You can, for example, never foretell what any one man will do, but you can say with precision what an average number will be up to." By studying the actions of all past test takers, the makers of the exam can reliably predict where you will be most likely to make errors. Throughout this book we will reference those pitfalls as they relate to specific question and reasoning types. For the moment, we would like to highlight one mental trap you must avoid at all times in any GMAT section: the tendency to dwell on past problems. Many students fall prey to "answering" a problem, and then continuing to think about it as they start the next problem. Obviously, this is distracting and creates an environment where missing the next problem is more likely. When you finish a problem, you must immediately put it out of your mind and move to the next problem with 100% focus. If you let your mind wander back to previous problems, you fall into a deadly trap.

This concludes our general discussion of Critical Reasoning questions. In subsequent chapters we will deconstruct each major question type and some of the reasoning types frequently used by the test makers. At all times we will use the principles presented in these early chapters. If, in the future, you find yourself unclear about some of these ideas, please return to these chapters and re-read them.

If you feel as if you are still hazy on some of the ideas discussed so far, do not worry. When discussing the theory that underlies all questions, the points can sometimes be a bit abstract and dry. In the remaining chapters we will discuss the application of these ideas to real questions, and working with actual questions often helps a heretofore confusing idea become clear.

Chapter Four: Must Be True Questions

Must Be True Questions

Must Be True questions require you to select an answer choice that is proven by the information presented in the stimulus. The correct answer choice can be a paraphrase of part of the stimulus or it can be a logical consequence of one or more parts of the stimulus. However, when selecting an answer choice, you must find the proof that supports your answer in the stimulus. We call this the Fact Test™:

> The correct answer to a Must Be True question can always be proven by referring to the facts stated in the stimulus.

The test makers will try to entice you by creating incorrect answer choices that could possibly occur or are likely to occur, but are not certain to occur. You must avoid those answers and select the answer choice that is most clearly supported by what you read. Do not bring in information from outside the stimulus (aside from commonsense assumptions); all of the information necessary to answer the question resides in the stimulus.

Must Be True question stems appear in a variety of formats, but one or both of the features described below appear consistently:

1. The stem often indicates the information in the stimulus should be taken as true, as in:

   "If the statements above are true..."
   "The statements above, if true..."
   "If the information above is correct..."

   This type of phrase helps indicate that you are dealing with a First Family question type.

2. The stem asks you to identify a single answer choice that is proven or supported, as in:

   "...which of the following must also be true?"
   "...which of the following conclusions can be properly drawn on the basis of it?"
   "...most strongly support which of the following?"
   "Which of the following can be properly inferred..."

First Family Information Model:

Because Must Be True is the first question type under discussion, we will make test-taking comments that relate to other question types as well.

In each case, the question stem indicates that one of the answer choices is proven by the information in the stimulus.

Here are several Must Be True question stem examples:

"If the statements above are true, which of the following must be true?"

"Which of the following conclusions is best supported by the statements above?"

"The statements above, if true, best support which of the following assertions?"

"Which of the following can be correctly inferred from the statements above?"

"Which of the following is most strongly supported by the information above?"

Remember, if a point can be "correctly inferred," it means it "must be true."

Although difficult questions can appear under any type, Must Be True questions are often considered one of the easier question types.

Must Be True questions are considered the foundation of the GMAT because the skill required to answer a Must Be True question is also required for every other GMAT Critical Reasoning question. Must Be True questions require you to read text and understand the facts and details that logically follow. To Weaken or Strengthen an argument, for example, you first need to be able to ascertain the facts and details. The same goes for every other type of question. Because every question type relies on the fact-finding skill used to answer Must Be True questions, your performance on Must Be True questions is often a predictor of your overall Critical Reasoning score. For this reason you must lock down the understanding required of this question category: what did you read in the stimulus and what do you know on the basis of that reading?

Prephrasing with Must Be True Questions

When you read an argument, you are forced to evaluate the validity of a conclusive statement generated by a framework designed to be persuasive (that is, after all, what argumentation is all about). When judging an argument, people tend to react with agreement or disagreement depending on the persuasiveness of the conclusion. Fact sets do not engender that same level of response because no argument is present, and, as mentioned in Chapter Two, most Must Be True stimuli are fact sets. Because prephrasing relies in part on your reaction to what you read, prephrasing Must Be True questions can often be difficult. There are exceptions, but if you find yourself having difficulty prephrasing an answer to a Must Be True question, do not worry.

The following question will be used to further discuss prephrasing. Please take a moment to read through the problem and corresponding answer choices:

1. Flavonoids are a common component of almost all plants, but a specific variety of flavonoid in apples has been found to be an antioxidant. Antioxidants are known to be a factor in the prevention of heart disease.

    Which one of the following can be properly inferred from the passage?

    (A) A diet composed largely of fruits and vegetables will help to prevent heart disease.
    (B) Flavonoids are essential to preventing heart disease.
    (C) Eating at least one apple each day will prevent heart disease.
    (D) At least one type of flavonoid helps to prevent heart disease.
    (E) A diet deficient in antioxidants is a common cause of heart disease.

Do not worry if you have never heard of a flavonoid. The question does not depend on your knowledge, or lack thereof, of flavonoids.

Applying Primary Objective #1 we can make the determination that since there is no conclusion in the stimulus, this is a fact set and not an argument. In this case the stimulus is short, and according to Primary Objective #2 can be broken down into three components:

First Statement: Flavonoids are a common component of almost all plants,

Second Statement: a specific variety of flavonoid in apples has been found to be an antioxidant.

Third Statement: Antioxidants are known to be a factor in the prevention of heart disease.

Remember, you can often predict the occurrence of Must Be True questions because the stimulus of most Must Be True questions does not contain a conclusion.

The question stem is obviously a Must Be True, and to prephrase (Primary Objective #6), take a moment to consider what the elements in the stimulus add up to. To do so, consider the premises together, and look for the connection between the elements: the first and second premises have "flavonoid" in common, and the second and third premises have "antioxidant" in common. Take a moment to examine each connection.

Review the Primary Objectives on page 67!

The flavonoid connection between the first two premises proves to be non-informative. The first premise indicates flavonoids appear frequently in plants and the second premise cites a specific instance in apples.

The antioxidant connection in the last two premises is more revealing. The second premise indicates that a flavonoid in apples is an antioxidant, and the third premise states that antioxidants are a factor in preventing heart disease.

Adding these two points together, we can deduce that the specific flavonoid in apples is a factor in preventing heart disease. Since that statement must be true based on the premises, we can attack the five answer choices with this prephrase in mind. Note that if you did not see that connection between the premises, you would simply move on and attack each answer choice with the facts at hand.

Answer choice (A): This is an interesting answer choice, and most people take a moment before categorizing this as a Loser. The answer choice *could be true*, but it is too broad to be supported by the facts: nowhere are we told that a *diet* of fruits and vegetables will help prevent heart disease (and in this sense the answer fails the Fact Test). Perhaps apples are the only fruit with the antioxidant flavonoid and there is nothing beneficial about other fruits and vegetables. And, eating a diet of fruits and vegetables is no guarantee that the diet includes apples. Regardless, this answer choice can be especially attractive because it plays on the general perception that fruits and vegetables are good for you.

Answer choice (B): This answer is also a Loser. Nothing in the stimulus supports the rather strong statement that flavonoids are *essential* to preventing heart disease.

Answer choice (C): Many people hold this answer as a Contender and then move on to answer choice (D). As it will turn out, this answer is incorrect because the language is too strong: the stimulus only stated that apples contain an element that was a *factor* in preventing heart disease, not that they definitely *will* prevent heart disease.

Answer choice (D): This answer is the closest to our prephrase, and this is the correct answer choice. Notice how the language of this answer choice— "helps to prevent"—matches the stimulus language—"factor in the prevention."

Answer choice (E): This answer choice also could be true, but it cannot be correct because the stimulus makes no mention of the causes of heart disease. Just because an antioxidant can help prevent heart disease does not mean that a lack of antioxidants causes heart disease.

Notice how the scope of the stimulus plays a role in how we attack the answer choices. The language of the stimulus is relatively broad—"almost all," "factor in the prevention,"—and the author shies away from making definite statements. Because the stimulus does not contain much in the way of direct, absolute information, selecting an answer choice that contains a direct, absolute statement is difficult to justify. This reasoning helps us eliminate answer choices (B) and (C), both of which contain strong statements that are ultimately unsupportable (literally, they both fail the Fact Test because they are too strong).

Returning to the Stimulus

As you attack the answer choices, do not be afraid to return to the stimulus to re-read and confirm your perceptions. Most GMAT stimuli contain a large amount of tricky, detailed information, and it is difficult to gain a perfect understanding of many of the stimuli you encounter. There is nothing wrong with quickly looking back at the stimulus, especially when deciding between two or more answer choices.

This advice also holds true for Reading Comprehension questions.

Please note that there is a difference between returning to the stimulus and re-reading the entire stimulus. On occasion, you will find yourself with no other option but to re-read the entire passage, but this should not be your normal mode of operation.

Primary Objective #4 and Modifier Words Revisited

Primary Objective #4 states: "Read closely and know precisely what the author said. Do not generalize!" This is especially important in Must Be True questions because the details are all the test makers have to test you on. Consider the following stimulus:

2. The importance of the ozone layer to terrestrial animals is that it entirely filters out some wavelengths of light but lets others through. Holes in the ozone layer and the dangers associated with these holes are well documented. However, one danger that has not been given sufficient attention is that these holes could lead to severe eye damage for animals of many species.

In Must Be True questions you are like the detective Sherlock Holmes, looking for clues in the stimulus and then matching those clues to the answer choices.

When reading the stimulus, your eye should be drawn to the modifier and indicator words, which are underlined below:

The importance of the ozone layer to terrestrial animals is that it <u>entirely</u> filters out <u>some</u> wavelengths of light <u>but</u> lets others through. Holes in the ozone layer and the dangers associated with these holes are well documented. However, one danger that has <u>not</u> been given sufficient attention is that these holes <u>could lead to</u> severe eye damage for animals of <u>many</u> species.

The scope of the stimulus is relatively broad, and aside from the word "entirely," most of the modifiers are not absolute.

Words like "some," "could," and "many" encompass many different possibilities and are broad scope indicators. Words like "must" and "none" indicate a narrow scope.

Now, look at the rest of the problem and see how several of the answer choices attempt to prey upon those who did not read the stimulus closely. Here are the question stem and corresponding answer choices for the stimulus above:

2. The importance of the ozone layer to terrestrial animals is that it entirely filters out some wavelengths of light but lets others through. Holes in the ozone layer and the dangers associated with these holes are well documented. However, one danger that has not been given sufficient attention is that these holes could lead to severe eye damage for animals of many species.

Which one of the following is most strongly supported by the statements above, if they are true?

(A) All wavelengths of sunlight that can cause eye damage are filtered out by the ozone layer where it is intact.

(B) Few species of animals live on a part of the earth's surface that is not threatened by holes in the ozone layer.

(C) Some species of animals have eyes that will not suffer any damage when exposed to unfiltered sunlight.

(D) A single wavelength of sunlight can cause severe damage to the eyes of most species of animals.

(E) Some wavelengths of sunlight that cause eye damage are more likely to reach the earth's surface where there are holes in the ozone layer than where there are not.

With the previous discussion in mind, let us analyze the answer choices:

Answer choice (A): The very first word—"all"—should be a red flag. Nowhere in the stimulus do we have support for stating that *all* damaging wavelengths are filtered out by the ozone layer. The stimulus only states that the ozone layer filters "some" wavelengths and lets others through. Some of those that are filtered are dangerous, as indicated by the last sentence. Surprisingly, about 10% of all test takers select this answer choice.

Answer choice (B): We know that many animal species could suffer severe eye damage, and from this we can infer that some of them live in areas threatened by the ozone layer. We do *not* know that few of the species live in non-threatened areas. Do not forget the Fact Test—it will eliminate any answer choice without support.

Answer choice (C): Nothing in the passage proves this answer choice. If you selected this answer thinking that "many" implied "not all," then you made a simple, correctable mistake. From a pure logic standpoint, "many" can include "all."

Answer choice (D): Again, watch those modifiers! One reason the answer choice is incorrect is because it references "most" species when the stimulus only discusses "many" species.

Answer choice (E): This is the correct answer choice. We can follow the chain of connections in the stimulus to prove this answer: the ozone layer filters some wavelengths of light; holes in the ozone layer are dangerous, but one previously overlooked danger of the holes is possible eye damage for many species. From these two statements we can infer that the holes must be letting some damaging wavelengths of light through. This is essentially what answer choice (E) states.

The lesson from this question is simple: read closely and pay strict attention to the modifiers used by the author. Even though you must read quickly, the test makers expect you to know exactly what was said, and they will include answer choices specifically designed to test whether you understood the details.

Correct Answers in Must Be True Questions Reviewed

Let us take a moment to review two types of answers that will always be correct in a Must Be True question.

1. Paraphrased Answers

   Paraphrased Answers are answers that restate a portion of the stimulus in different terms. Because the language is not exactly the same as in the stimulus, Paraphrased Answers can be easy to miss. Paraphrased Answers are designed to test your ability to discern the author's exact meaning. Sometimes the answer can appear to be almost too obvious since it is drawn directly from the stimulus.

2. Answers that are the sum of two or more stimulus statements (Combination Answers)

   Any answer choice that would result from combining two or more statements in the stimulus will be correct. The correct answer to the flavonoid question earlier in this chapter is an excellent example of this idea in action.

Should you encounter either of the above as answer choices in a Must Be True question, go ahead and select the answer with confidence.

Paraphrased answers occur primarily in Must Be True and Main Point questions. Some students have said they missed paraphrased answer choices because they did not feel the test makers would simply change the language of the text. They will!

There are other classic GMAT tricks that we will discuss in this and future chapters.

Incorrect Answers in Must Be True Questions

There are several types of answers that appear in Must Be True questions that are incorrect. These answers appear frequently enough that we have provided a review of the major types below. Each answer category below is designed to attract you to an incorrect answer choice, and after this brief review we will examine several GMAT questions and analyze actual instances of these types of answers.

1. Could Be True or Likely to Be True Answers

   Because the criteria in the question stem requires you to find an answer choice that Must Be True, answers that only could be true or are even likely to be true are incorrect. These answers are attractive because there is nothing demonstrably wrong with them (for example, they do not contain statements that are counter to the stimulus). Regardless, like all incorrect answers these answers fail the Fact Test. Remember, you must select an answer choice that must occur based on what you have read.

   This category of incorrect answer is very broad, and some of the types mentioned below will fall under this general idea but place an emphasis on a specific aspect of the answer.

2. Exaggerated Answers

   Exaggerated Answers take information from the stimulus and then stretch that information to make a broader statement that is not supported by the stimulus. In that sense, this form of answer is a variation of a could be true answer since the exaggeration is possible, but not proven based on the information. Here is an example:

   > If the stimulus states, "*Some* software vendors recently implemented more rigorous licensing procedures."

   > An incorrect answer would exaggerate one or more of the elements: "*Most* software vendors recently implemented more rigorous licensing procedures." In this example, *some* is exaggerated to *most*. While it could be true that most software vendors made the change, the stimulus does not prove that it must be true. This type of answer is often paraphrased, creating a deadly combination where the language is similar enough to be attractive but different enough to be incorrect.

   Here is another example:

   > If the stimulus states, "Recent advances in the field of molecular biology make it *likely* that many school textbooks will be rewritten."

The exaggerated and paraphrased version would be: "Many school textbooks about molecular biology will be re-written." In this example, *likely* has been dropped, and this omission exaggerates the certainty of the change. The paraphrase also is problematic because the stimulus referenced school textbooks whereas the paraphrased answer refers to school textbooks *about molecular biology*.

3. "New" Information Answers

Because correct Must Be True answers must be based on information in the stimulus or the direct result of combining statements in the stimulus, be wary of answers that present so-called new information—that is, information not mentioned explicitly in the stimulus. Although these answers can be correct when they fall under the umbrella of a statement made in the stimulus, they are often incorrect. For example, if a stimulus discusses the economic policies of Japan, be careful with an answer that mentions U.S. economic policy. Look closely at the stimulus—does the information about Japanese economic policy apply to the U.S., or are the test makers trying to get you to fall for an answer that sounds logical but is not directly supported? To avoid incorrectly eliminating a New Information answer, take the following two steps:

1. Examine the scope of the argument to make sure the "new" information does not fall within the sphere of a term or concept in the stimulus.

2. Examine the answer to make sure it is not the consequence of combining stimulus elements.

4. The Shell Game

The GMAT makers have a variety of psychological tricks they use to entice test takers to select an answer choice. One of their favorites is one we call the Shell Game: an idea or concept is raised in the stimulus, and then a very similar idea appears in the answer choice, but the idea is changed just enough to be incorrect but still attractive. This trick is called the Shell Game because it abstractly resembles those street corner gambling games where a person hides a small object underneath one of three shells, and then scrambles them on a flat surface while a bettor tries to guess which shell the object is under (similar to three-card Monte). The object of a Shell Game is to trick the bettor into guessing incorrectly by mixing up the shells so quickly and deceptively that the bettor mistakenly selects the wrong shell. The intent of the GMAT makers is the same.

Shell Game answers occur in all GMAT question types, not just Must Be True.

As we will see in later chapters, the Shell Game can also be played with elements in a stimulus.

Reverse Answers
can occur in any
type of question.

5. The Opposite Answer

    As the name suggests, the Opposite Answer provides an answer that is
    completely opposite of the stated facts of the stimulus. Opposite Answers
    are very attractive to students who are reading too quickly or carelessly.
    Because Opposite Answers appear quite frequently in Strengthen and
    Weaken questions, we will discuss them in more detail when we cover
    those question types.

6. The Reverse Answer

    Here is a simplified example of how a Reverse Answer works, using
    italics to indicate the reversed parts:

    > The stimulus might state, "*Many* people have *some* type of security
    > system in their home."

    > An incorrect answer then reverses the elements: "*Some* people have
    > *many* types of security systems in their home."

    The Reverse Answer is attractive because it contains familiar elements
    from the stimulus, but the reversed statement is incorrect because it
    rearranges those elements to create a new, unsupported statement.

Idea Application: An Analysis of Correct and Incorrect Answers

In this section we analyze three Critical Reasoning questions. We will use the examples to discuss the various answer types you learned in the previous section.

Please take a moment to complete the following problem:

3. In an experiment, two-year-old boys and their fathers made pie dough together using rolling pins and other utensils. Each father-son pair used a rolling pin that was distinctively different from those used by the other father-son pairs, and each father repeated the phrase "rolling pin" each time his son used it. But when the children were asked to identify all of the rolling pins among a group of kitchen utensils that included several rolling pins, each child picked only the one that he had used.

    Which one of the following inferences is most supported by the information above?

    (A)   The children did not grasp the function of a rolling pin.
    (B)   No two children understood the name "rolling pin" to apply to the same object.
    (C)   The children understood that all rolling pins have the same general shape.
    (D)   Each child was able to identify correctly only the utensils that he had used.
    (E)   The children were not able to distinguish the rolling pins they used from other rolling pins.

The "rolling pin" problem above lured many people to incorrectly select answer choice (D), a Shell Game answer. Answer choice (D) looks perfect at first glance, but the author never indicated that the children could identify only the *utensils* that they used. Rolling pins, yes; utensils, no. The correct answer choice is (B), which many test takers quickly pass over. Let's examine each answer:

Answer choice (A): From the text, it seems possible that the children did understand the function of a rolling pin; certainly, they were able to identify the rolling pin they used.

Answer choice (B): This is the correct answer choice. The answer must be true because we know that despite being asked to identify all the rolling pins, each child selected *only* the rolling pin he had used. No two children picked the same rolling pin and therefore no two children understood the name "rolling pin" to apply to the same object.

Answer choice (C): Apparently not, otherwise logic would say the children

Shell Game answers are exceedingly dangerous because, when selected, not only do you miss the question but you walk away thinking you got it right. This misperception makes it difficult to accurately assess your performance after the test.

would pick other rolling pins aside from the one they used.

Answer choice (D): Do not be concerned if you fell into this trap, but consider it a lesson for the future. The test makers smoothly slip "utensils" into the answer choice, and most students make the mistake of equating utensils with rolling pins. Yes, a rolling pin is a utensil, but there are other utensils as well, and the stimulus does not give us information about whether the children could identify those utensils. This is the essence of the Shell Game: you expect one thing and the test makers slip something quite similar but essentially different into its place.

Answer choice (E): This is an Opposite Answer. As indicated by the final sentence of the stimulus, the children were able to distinguish the rolling pin they used from the other rolling pins. This circumstance is exactly opposite of that stated in answer choice (E), which declares, "The children were *not* able to distinguish..." In this case, if you miss the "not," this answer choice is very attractive.

Let's continue looking at the way answers are constructed. Please take a moment to complete the following problem:

4. The increasing complexity of scientific inquiry has led to a proliferation of multiauthored technical articles. Reports of clinical trials involving patients from several hospitals are usually coauthored by physicians from each participating hospital. Likewise, physics papers reporting results from experiments using subsystems developed at various laboratories generally have authors from each laboratory.

    If all of the statements above are true, which one of the following must be true?

    (A) Clinical trials involving patients from several hospitals are never conducted solely by physicians from just one hospital.
    (B) Most reports of clinical trials involving patients from several hospitals have multiple authors.
    (C) When a technical article has multiple authors, they are usually from different institutions.
    (D) Physics papers authored by researchers from multiple laboratories usually report results from experiments using subsystems developed at each laboratory.
    (E) Most technical articles are authored solely by the researchers who conducted the experiments these articles report.

Answer choice (A): The stimulus never discusses who *conducts* the studies, only who authors the reports. Thus, there is no proof for this answer choice and it fails the Fact Test. Even if you mistook "conducted" for "reported," the answer choice is still incorrect because the stimulus indicates that reports involving patients from several hospitals are *usually* coauthored by physicians from each hospital. Although "usually" could mean "always," it does not have to, and hence it is possible that a clinical trial could be reported by physicians from just one hospital.

Answer choice (B): This is the correct answer choice. This answer choice is a direct paraphrase of the second sentence. The second sentence states, "Reports of clinical trials involving patients from several hospitals are usually coauthored by physicians from each participating hospital." Answer choice (B) translates "usually" into "most," and "coauthored by physicians from each participating hospital" into "multiple authors." Thus, the answer choice passes the Fact Test and is correct.

Answer choice (C): This is a Shell Game answer choice. Although the stimulus says there has been a proliferation of multiauthored technical articles, no comment is made about the frequency of multiauthored technical articles. In the next sentence, a frequency—"usually"—is given, but only for multiauthored clinical trial reports. The test makers give you hard data about the clinical trial reports, and then try to entice you into picking a broader answer involving technical reports.

Answer choice (C) shows how the Shell Game can occur in the stimulus as well as in the answer choices. The stimulus of this problem switches from "technical articles" to "reports of clinical trials." Answer choice (C) plays on that substitution.

Answer choice (D): This is a Reverse answer that contains a complex pair of reversed elements when matched against the stimulus. Let us compare the stimulus and the answer choice, using italics to indicate the reversed parts:

The stimulus states, "physics papers reporting results from experiments using *subsystems developed at various laboratories* generally have *authors from each laboratory*."

Answer choice (D) states, "Physics papers authored by *researchers from multiple laboratories* usually report results from experiments using *subsystems developed at each laboratory*."

The reversed pair has two notable features:

1. The numbers are reversed—authors from *each* laboratory have become researchers (authors) from *multiple* laboratories, and subsystems from *various* laboratories have become subsystems from *each* laboratory. In a nutshell, the "various" and "each" elements have been reversed in the sentences.

2. The pair also reverses logical position within the argument, as the stimulus states that the experiments generally have authors from each

laboratory and the answer choice states that the researchers usually report experiments from each laboratory.

Answer choice (E): As with answer choice (C), we do not know enough about technical articles to support this answer choice.

Stimulus Opinions versus Assertions

Please take a moment to complete the following problem:

5. Some environmentalists question the prudence of exploiting features of the environment, arguing that there are no economic benefits to be gained from forests, mountains, or wetlands that no longer exist. Many environmentalists claim that because nature has intrinsic value it would be wrong to destroy such features of the environment, even if the economic costs of doing so were outweighed by the economic costs of not doing so.

   Which one of the following can be logically inferred from the passage?

   (A) It is economically imprudent to exploit features of the environment.
   (B) Some environmentalists appeal to a noneconomic justification in questioning the defensibility of exploiting features of the environment.
   (C) Most environmentalists appeal to economic reasons in questioning the defensibility of exploiting features of the environment.
   (D) Many environmentalists provide only a noneconomic justification in questioning the defensibility of exploiting features of the environment.
   (E) Even if there is no economic reason for protecting the environment, there is a sound noneconomic justification for doing so.

The "Some environmentalists question..." construction at the start of the stimulus does not lead to the usual counter-conclusion because the stimulus does not contain an argument.

This is a very interesting stimulus because the author repeats the opinions of others and never makes an assertion of his or her own. When a stimulus contains only the opinions of others, then in a Must Be True question you can eliminate any answer choice that makes a flat assertion without reference to those opinions. For example, answer choice (A) makes a factual assertion ("It is...") that cannot be backed up by the author's survey of opinions in the stimulus—the opinions do not let us know the actual facts of the situation. Answer choice (E) can be eliminated for the very same reason.

Answer choices (B), (C), and (D) each address the environmentalists, and thus each is initially a Contender.

Answer choice (B): This is the correct answer choice. The second sentence references the views of many environmentalists, who claim that "nature has intrinsic value" (for example, beauty). This view is the noneconomic justification cited by the answer choice.

With the analysis of these three questions, examples of each of the incorrect answer categories have been presented.

This answer can be a bit tricky because of the convoluted language the test makers use. "Questioning the defensibility of exploiting features of the environment" is a needlessly complex phrase. A more direct manner of writing that phrase would be "attacking the exploitation of the environment."

To increase the difficulty of this problem, this language was then repeated in answer choices (C) and (D).

Answer choice (C): We only know the opinions of "some" and "many" environmentalists, and these numbers do not provide enough information to discern the views of "most" environmentalists, which is the term used in the answer choice ("many" is not the same as "most").

Answer choice (D): This answer choice cannot be proven. While we know that many environmentalists claim a noneconomic justification, we do not know that that is the *only* justification they provide.

When you are reading a stimulus, keep a careful watch on the statements the author offers as fact, and those that the author offers as the opinion of others. In a Must Be True question, the difference between the two can sometimes be used to eliminate answer choices.

Final Note

This chapter is only the start of our question analysis. The ideas discussed so far represent a fraction of what you will learn from this book. Future chapters will build on the ideas discussed herein, and present new concepts that will help you attack all types of questions.

On the following page is a review of some of the key points from this chapter. After the review, there is a short problem set to help you test your knowledge of some of the ideas. An answer key follows with explanations. Good luck!

Must Be True Question Type Review

Must Be True questions require you to select an answer choice that is proven by the information presented in the stimulus. The question format can be reduced to, "What did you read in the stimulus, and what do you know on the basis of that reading?"

You cannot bring in information from outside the stimulus to answer the questions; all of the information necessary to answer the question resides in the stimulus.

All Must Be True answer choices must pass the Fact Test™:

> The correct answer to a Must Be True question can always be proven by referring to the facts stated in the stimulus.

If you find yourself having difficulty prephrasing an answer to a Must Be True question, do not be concerned.

The scope of the stimulus—especially if that scope is broad—often helps eliminate one or more of the answer choices.

You can often predict the occurrence of Must Be True questions because the stimulus of most Must Be True questions does not contain a conclusion.

Correct Answer Types:

> Paraphrased answers are answers that restate a portion of the stimulus in different terms. When these answers mirror the stimulus, they are correct.

> Combination answers result from combining two or more statements in the stimulus.

Incorrect Answer Types:

> Could Be True answers are attractive because they can possibly occur, but they are incorrect because they do not have to be true.

> Exaggerated answers take information from the stimulus and then stretch that information to make a broader statement that is not supported by the stimulus.

> New Information answers include information not explicitly mentioned in the stimulus. Be careful with these answers: first examine the scope of the stimulus to make sure the "new" information does not fall under the umbrella of a term or concept in the stimulus. Second, examine the

answer to make sure it is not the consequence of combining stimulus elements.

The Shell Game occurs when an idea or concept is raised in the stimulus, and then a very similar idea appears in the answer choice, but the idea is changed just enough to be incorrect while remaining attractive.

The Opposite answer is completely opposite of the facts of the stimulus.

The Reverse answer is attractive because it contains familiar elements from the stimulus, but the reversed statement is incorrect because it rearranges those elements to create a new, unsupported statement.

Please complete the problem set and review the answer key and explanations. *Answers on Page 88*

1. Some argue that laws are instituted at least in part to help establish a particular moral fabric in society. But the primary function of law is surely to help order society so that its institutions, organizations, and citizenry can work together harmoniously, regardless of any further moral aims of the law. Indeed, the highest courts have on occasion treated moral beliefs based on conscience or religious faith as grounds for making exceptions in the application of laws.

   The statements above, if true, most strongly support which one of the following?

   (A) The manner in which laws are applied sometimes takes into account the beliefs of the people governed by those laws.
   (B) The law has as one of its functions the ordering of society but is devoid of moral aims.
   (C) Actions based on religious belief or on moral conviction tend to receive the protection of the highest courts.
   (D) The way a society is ordered by law should not reflect any moral convictions about the way society ought to be ordered.
   (E) The best way to promote cooperation among a society's institutions, organizations, and citizenry is to institute order in that society by means of law.

2. Newtonian physics dominated science for over two centuries. It found consistently successful application, becoming one of the most highly substantiated and accepted theories in the history of science. Nevertheless, Einstein's theories came to show the fundamental limits of Newtonian physics and to surpass the Newtonian view in the early 1900s, giving rise once again to a physics that has so far enjoyed wide success.

   Which one of the following logically follows from the statements above?

   (A) The history of physics is characterized by a pattern of one successful theory subsequently surpassed by another.
   (B) Long-standing success or substantiation of a theory of physics is no guarantee that the theory will continue to be dominant indefinitely.
   (C) Every theory of physics, no matter how successful, is eventually surpassed by one that is more successful.
   (D) Once a theory of physics is accepted, it will remain dominant for centuries.
   (E) If a long-accepted theory of physics is surpassed, it must be surpassed by a theory that is equally successful.

3. The solidity of bridge piers built on pilings depends largely on how deep the pilings are driven. Prior to 1700, pilings were driven to "refusal," that is, to the point at which they refused to go any deeper. In a 1588 inquiry into the solidity of piers for Venice's Rialto Bridge, it was determined that the bridge's builder, Antonio Da Ponte, had met the contemporary standard for refusal: he had caused the pilings to be driven until additional penetration into the ground was no greater than two inches after twenty-four hammer blows.

    Which one of the following can properly be inferred from the passage?

    (A) The Rialto Bridge was built on unsafe pilings.
    (B) The standard of refusal was not sufficient to ensure the safety of a bridge.
    (C) Da Ponte's standard of refusal was less strict than that of other bridge builders of his day.
    (D) After 1588, no bridges were built on pilings that were driven to the point of refusal.
    (E) It is possible that the pilings of the Rialto Bridge could have been driven deeper even after the standard of refusal had been met.

4. Every moral theory developed in the Western tradition purports to tell us what a good life is. However, most people would judge someone who perfectly embodied the ideals of any one of these theories not to be living a good life—the kind of life they would want for themselves and their children.

    The statements above, if true, most strongly support which one of the following?

    (A) Most people desire a life for themselves and their children that is better than a merely good life.
    (B) A person who fits the ideals of one moral theory in the Western tradition would not necessarily fit the ideals of another.
    (C) Most people have a conception of a good life that does not match that of any moral theory in the Western tradition.
    (D) A good life as described by moral theories in the Western tradition cannot be realized.
    (E) It is impossible to develop a theory that accurately describes what a good life is.

5. Mystery stories often feature a brilliant detective and the detective's dull companion. Clues are presented in the story, and the companion wrongly infers an inaccurate solution to the mystery using the same clues that the detective uses to deduce the correct solution. Thus, the author's strategy of including the dull companion gives readers a chance to solve the mystery while also diverting them from the correct solution.

    Which one of the following is most strongly supported by the information above?

    (A) Most mystery stories feature a brilliant detective who solves the mystery presented in the story.
    (B) Mystery readers often solve the mystery in a story simply by spotting the mistakes in the reasoning of the detective's dull companion in that story.
    (C) Some mystery stories give readers enough clues to infer the correct solution to the mystery.
    (D) The actions of the brilliant detective in a mystery story rarely divert readers from the actions of the detective's dull companion.
    (E) The detective's dull companion in a mystery story generally uncovers the misleading clues that divert readers from the mystery's correct solution.

6. Cézanne's art inspired the next generation of artists, twentieth-century modernist creators of abstract art. While most experts rank Cézanne as an early modernist, a small few reject this idea. Françoise Cachin, for example, bluntly states that such an ascription is "overplayed," and says that Cézanne's work is "too often observed from a modern point of view."

    Which one of the following statements is most strongly supported by the information above?

    (A) Cézanne's work is highly controversial.
    (B) Cézanne was an early creator of abstract art.
    (C) Cézanne's work helped to develop modernism.
    (D) Modern art owes less to Cézanne than many experts believe.
    (E) Cézanne's work tends to be misinterpreted as modernist.

Must Be True Problem Set Answer Key

All answer keys in this book indicate the question number, the question type classification, and the correct answer.

Question #1. Must. The correct answer choice is (A)

Unlike many Must Be True question stimuli, this stimulus contains an argument. The conclusion is in the second sentence: "the primary function of law is surely to help order society so that its institutions, organizations, and citizenry can work together harmoniously, regardless of any further moral aims of the law." The stimulus also begins with the "Some argue that..." construction, and as usual, is followed by a conclusion that argues against the position established in the first sentence (see "A Commonly Used Construction" in Chapter Two if this sounds unfamiliar). The last sentence is a premise that proves to be key for choosing the correct answer.

Answer choice (A): This correct answer is largely a paraphrase of the last sentence.

Answer choice (B): While the author certainly agrees with the first part of the sentence, in the second part the phrase "devoid of moral aims" is too strong to be supported by the information in the stimulus. The last sentence indicates that morality has some effect on the law and invalidates the "devoid" claim.

Answer choice (C): This is an Exaggerated answer. Although the last sentence indicates that religious faith has been grounds for making exceptions in the application of law, the stimulus does not indicate that actions based on religious or moral belief *tend* to receive the protection of the highest courts.

Answer choice (D): The author indicates that the "primary function" of law is to help order society; the author does not indicate that this is the one and only function of law. The answer choice overstates the case by saying that a society ordered by law should *not reflect any* moral convictions about the ordering.

Answer choice (E): No mention is made of the "best way" to promote cooperation, only that the primary function of law is to promote such cooperation.

Question #2. Must. The correct answer choice is (B)

The stimulus tells the story of recent physics theories: Newtonian physics was preeminent for over two centuries, and despite widespread acknowledgment and confirmation it was surpassed by Einsteinian physics in the early 1900s.

Answer choice (A): The two theories cited in the stimulus are not sufficient to form a *pattern*, which is the basis of answer choice (A).

Must Be True Problem Set Answer Key

Answer choice (B): This is the correct answer choice. As shown by the case of Newtonian physics, success and substantiation is no guarantee of dominance.

Answer choice (C): This is an Exaggerated answer that takes one instance and exaggerates it into a pattern. Although Newtonian physics was surpassed, this does not prove that *every* theory of physics will eventually be surpassed. The answer goes farther than the facts of the stimulus and fails the Fact Test.

Answer choice (D): Like answer choice (C), this answer goes too far. Although some theories of physics have been dominant for centuries, there is no guarantee that every theory will be dominant for that long.

Answer choice (E): Even though Einsteinian physics has enjoyed wide success in surpassing Newtonian physics, nowhere in the stimulus is there evidence to prove that each theory *must be* surpassed by an equally successful theory.

Question #3. Must. The correct answer choice is (E)

This interesting stimulus contains two definitions of "refusal:" an initial definition that implies refusal is a point at which pilings will go no further, and then a second, contemporary standards definition of refusal that reveals that refusal is a point at which additional penetration into the ground is no greater than two inches after twenty-four hammer blows. The stimulus is a fact set, and thus there is no conclusion present.

Answer choice (A): Although there was an inquiry into the solidity of the piers of the Rialto Bridge, the results of that inquiry are not disclosed. The only other information we are given is that the pilings of the Rialto Bridge met the contemporary standard of refusal, but this is not sufficient to indicate whether the pilings of this particular bridge were safe. Hence, this answer fails the Fact Test and is incorrect.

Answer choice (B): Similar to answer choice (A), we have insufficient information to make this judgment.

Answer choice (C): This answer is somewhat opposite of the information in the stimulus, which states that Da Ponte had met the contemporary standard of refusal.

Answer choice (D): This is another Opposite answer. The stimulus indicates that bridges built prior to 1700 were driven to the point of refusal.

Answer choice (E): This is the correct answer choice. As stated in the stimulus, "he had caused the pilings to be driven until additional penetration into the ground was no greater than two inches after twenty-four hammer blows." The statement indicates that additional penetration was possible with a sufficient number of hammer blows.

Must Be True Problem Set Answer Key

Question #4. Must. The correct answer choice is (C)

This is a fact set. Note the strength of the modifiers in this stimulus—"every," "most," and "any." We should be able to use this narrow scope to support a fairly strong statement, but be careful: the test makers know this too and they will supply several answer choices that are worded strongly. Make sure you select an answer that conforms to the facts.

Answer choice (A): The phrase "better than a merely good life" goes beyond the statements in the stimulus.

Answer choice (B): This answer is incorrect because we are not given information about how the moral theories are different, or if they are differ at all. The only detail we are told is that the theories all have one thing in common—they tell us what a good life is. Since the answer choice makes a claim based on differences between theories, it cannot be correct.

Answer choice (C): This is the correct answer choice. At first glance, this answer choice may seem a bit strong in saying the conception would not match that of *any* moral theory. But, as discussed above, we can support this because the stimulus uses very strong language, specifically stating "*most* people would judge someone who perfectly embodied the ideals of *any* one of these theories *not* to be living a good life." (italics added).

Answer choice (D): This answer is worded strongly but it quickly fails the Fact Test. Nothing is said to indicate that the life described by one of the moral theories cannot be realized.

Answer choice (E): This answer also has strong language, but it goes too far in saying that it is *impossible* to develop a theory that accurately describes a good life.

Question #5. Must. The correct answer choice is (C)

The last sentence contains a conclusion, and this conclusion is the primary evidence that supports answer choice (C).

Answer choice (A): The word "often" in the first sentence is the key to this answer choice. "Often" means frequently, but frequently is not the same as "most." Had the stimulus said "more often than not," that would mean "most" and this answer choice would be correct.

Answer choice (B): We cannot determine if readers of mystery stories solve the mystery simply by spotting the errors of the dull companion.

Answer choice (C): This is the correct answer choice. The second sentence indicates that "clues are presented in the story...the detective uses to deduce the correct solution." Combined with the last sentence, which states "the author's strategy...gives readers a chance to solve the mystery," this answer choice is proven by facts.

Answer choice (D): Look for the facts in the stimulus—do they support this answer? Although the dull companion diverts readers from the correct solution, we do not know if actions of the brilliant detective rarely divert readers from the actions of the dull companion.

Answer choice (E): This is a tricky answer choice if you do not read closely. The stimulus states that the dull companion infers a wrong solution from clues that the brilliant detective ultimately uses to solve the mystery. Answer choice (E) states that the dull companion uncovers misleading clues. This is incorrect; the interpretation of the clues is misleading, not the clues themselves.

Question #6. Must. The correct answer choice is (C)

The final three problems in this section are harder than the previous five. This problem is answered correctly by about 45% of test takers and is classified as difficult (the hardest GMAT questions have success rates under 20%. Fortunately, questions this difficult appear infrequently). Students can miss questions for a variety of reasons:

1. The stimulus is difficult to understand.
2. The question stem is difficult to classify (very rare) or confusing.
3. The correct answer is deceptive, causing students to avoid it.
4. One (or more) of the incorrect answers is attractive, drawing students to it.

Given that the stimulus is a simple fact set and that none of the incorrect answers attracted more than 15% of test takers, the difficulty in this problem apparently lies in the correct answer.

Answer choice (A): The controversy in the stimulus is about the categorization of Cézanne as an artist, not about Cézanne's work. Further, even if the answer did correctly reference the categorization controversy, the answer would still be suspect because of the word "highly." The stimulus indicates that only a small few reject the categorization of Cézanne as an early modernist and most experts accept it.

Answer choice (B): The stimulus asserts that Cézanne *inspired* the creators of abstract art, not that Cézanne himself created abstract art.

Answer choice (C): This correct answer is a paraphrase of the first sentence. The deceptiveness of this answer lies in two areas:

1. The substitution of "develop" for "inspire." Some students feel the word "develop" is too strong, but if Cézanne inspired the creators of the next generation of art then he helped develop it.

2. The use of the word "modernism." Some students are thrown off by "modernism" because they expect to see "abstract" instead. The stimulus is careful about saying "twentieth-century modernist creators of abstract art." Notice how the test makers use answer choice (B)—which mentions "abstract"—to subtly prepare you to make this error.

Must Be True Problem Set Answer Key

Answer choice (D): The first sentence indicates that Cézanne inspired the modernist creators. The rest of the stimulus discusses a disagreement about the categorization of Cézanne that is not resolved in favor of either group. Hence, there is no way for us to determine if modern art owes less to Cézanne than many experts believe.

Answer choice (E): The word "tends" is the problem in this answer choice. Logically, "tends" means "most." So, according to answer choice (E), Cézanne's work is usually misinterpreted as modernist. The stimulus disagrees with this view: only a "small few" reject the categorization of Cézanne as a modernist whereas the majority accepts it. Further, the disagreement in the stimulus involves art experts, and from their view we would dispute answer choice (E). Answer choice (E) can also be understood as involving all interpretation of Cézanne's work—whether by art expert or not—and from this perspective the answer is still unsupported since the views of others are not discussed in the stimulus.

CHAPTER FIVE: WEAKEN QUESTIONS

Weaken Questions

Weaken questions require you to select the answer choice that undermines the author's argument as decisively as possible. Overall, Weaken questions are the most frequently appearing Critical Reasoning question type on the GMAT.

Because Weaken questions are in the Third Family, these questions require a different approach than the Must Be True and Main Point questions we have covered so far. In addition to the Primary Objectives, keep the following rules in mind when approaching Weaken questions:

Third Family Information Model:

1. The stimulus will contain an argument. Because you are asked to weaken the author's reasoning, and reasoning requires a conclusion, an argument will always be present. In order to maximize your chances of success you must identify, isolate, and assess the premises and the conclusion of the argument. Only by understanding the structure of the argument can you gain the perspective necessary to attack the author's position.

2. Focus on the conclusion. Almost all correct Weaken answer choices impact the conclusion. The more you know about the specifics of the conclusion, the better armed you will be to differentiate between correct and incorrect answers.

3. The information in the stimulus is suspect. There are often reasoning errors present, and you must read the argument very carefully.

4. Weaken questions often yield strong prephrases. Be sure to actively consider the range of possible answers before proceeding to the answer choices.

5. The answer choices are accepted as given, even if they include "new" information. Unlike Must Be True questions, Weaken answer choices can bring into consideration information outside of or tangential to the stimulus. Just because a fact or idea is not mentioned in the stimulus is *not* grounds for dismissing an answer choice. Your task is to determine which answer choice best attacks the argument in the stimulus.

Remember, most Weaken question stems tell you to accept the answer choices as true.

By following the Primary Objectives and focusing on the points above, you will maximize your chances of success on Weaken questions.

Weaken question stems typically contain the following two features:

1. The stem uses the word "weaken" or a synonym. Following are some examples of words or phrases used to indicate that your task is to weaken the argument:

> weaken
> attack
> undermine
> refute
> argue against
> call into question
> cast doubt
> challenge
> damage
> counter

2. The stem indicates that you should accept the answer choices as true, usually with the following phrase:

> "Which of the following, if true, ..."

Here are several Weaken question stem examples:

"Which of the following, if true, most seriously weakens the argument above?"

"Which of the following, if true, casts the most doubt on the conclusion drawn above?"

"Which of the following, if true, most calls into question the claim above?"

"Which of the following, if true, is most damaging to the conclusion above?"

"Which of the following, if known, is evidence that contradicts the hypothesis above?"

"Which of the following, if discovered, would be evidence against the speculation above?"

How to Weaken an Argument

The key to weakening a GMAT argument is to attack the conclusion. But, keep in mind that to attack is not the same as to destroy. Although an answer that destroys the conclusion would be correct, this rarely occurs because of the minimal space allotted to answer choices. Instead, you are more likely to encounter an answer that hurts the argument but does not ultimately destroy the author's position. When evaluating an answer, ask yourself, "Would this answer choice make the author reconsider his or her position or force the author to respond?" If so, you have the correct answer.

You do not need to find an answer that destroys the author's position. Instead, simply find an answer that hurts the argument.

Because arguments are made up of premises and conclusions, you can safely assume that these are the parts you must attack in order to weaken an argument. Let us discuss each part, and the likelihood that each would be attacked by an answer choice.

1. The Premises

   One of the classic ways to attack an argument is to attack the premises on which the conclusion rests. Regrettably, this form of attack is rarely used on the GMAT because when a premise is attacked, the answer choice is easy to spot. Literally, the answer will contradict one of the premises, and most students are capable of reading an argument and then identifying an answer that simply negates a premise.

The one time you might see an answer choice attack a premise is when that "premise" is a sub-conclusion. That is, when a conclusion of one premise is used as a premise to support another conclusion.

   In practice, almost all correct GMAT Weaken question answers leave the premises untouched.

2. The Conclusion

   The conclusion is the part of the argument that is most likely to be attacked, but the correct answer choice will not simply contradict the conclusion. Instead, the correct answer will undermine the conclusion by showing that the conclusion fails to account for some element or possibility. In this sense, the correct answer often shows that the conclusion does not necessarily follow from the premises even if the premises are true. Consider the following example:

   All my neighbors own blue cars. Therefore I own a blue car.

   Even though the statement that the neighbors have blue cars is entirely reasonable, the weakness in the argument is that this fact has no impact on the color of the car I own. In this overly simplified problem, the correct weakening answer would be something along the lines of, "The cars of one's neighbors have no determinative effect on the car any individual owns." Would that conclusively

Assumptions will be discussed in more detail in Chapter Seven.

CR

disprove that I own a blue car? No. Does it show that perhaps I do not own a blue car? Yes. Does it disprove that my neighbors own blue cars? No.

Answers that weaken the argument's conclusion will attack assumptions made by the author. In the example above, the author assumes that the neighbors' ownership of blue cars has an impact on the color of the car that he owns. If this assumption were shown to be questionable, the argument would be undermined.

The stimuli for weaken questions contain errors of assumption. This makes sense, because the easiest argument to weaken is one that already has a flaw. Typically, the author will fail to consider other possibilities or leave out a key piece of information. In this sense the author assumes that these elements do not exist when he or she makes the conclusion, and if you see a gap or hole in the argument immediately consider that the correct answer might attack this hole.

As you consider possible answers, always look for the one that attacks the way the author arrived at the conclusion. Do not worry about the premises and instead focus on the effect the answer has on the conclusion.

Personalizing helps you see the argument from a very involved perspective, and that helps you assess the strength of each answer.

So, we know that we must first focus on the conclusion and how the author arrived at the conclusion. The second key to weakening arguments is to personalize the argument. Most students perform considerably better when they see the argument from their perspective as opposed to trying to understand the issues abstractly. When analyzing the author's argument, imagine how you would respond if you were talking directly to the author. Would you use answer choice (A) or would you prefer answer choice (B)? Students who personalize the argument often properly dismiss answer choices that they would have otherwise wasted time considering.

Common Weakening Scenarios

Although there are many classical logical fallacies, the most common of which we will discuss in the Flaw in the Reasoning section, several scenarios that occur in GMAT Weaken question stimuli are easy to recognize and attack:

1. Incomplete Information. The author fails to consider all of the possibilities, or relies upon evidence that is incomplete. This flaw can be attacked by bringing up new possibilities or information.

2. Improper Comparison. The author attempts to compare two or more items that are essentially different.

3. Qualified Conclusion. The author qualifies or limits the conclusion in such a way as to leave the argument open to attack.

While these three scenarios are not the only ways an argument can be weak, they encompass a large proportion of the errors that appear in GMAT stimuli.

Three Incorrect Answer Traps

There are certain incorrect answer choices that appear frequently in Weaken questions:

1. Opposite Answers. As discussed in the Must Be True question chapter, these answers do the exact opposite of what is needed. In this case, they strengthen the argument as opposed to weakening it. Although you might think answers of this type are easy to avoid, they can be very tricky. To analogize, have you ever gotten on a freeway thinking you were going south when in fact you later discovered you were going north? It is easy to make a mistake when you head in the exact opposite direction. In the same way, Opposite answers lure the test taker by presenting information that relates perfectly to the argument, but just in the wrong manner.

2. Shell Game Answers. Like Opposite answers, the Shell Game is the same as in the Must Be True discussion. Remember, a Shell Game occurs when an idea or concept is raised in the stimulus and then a very similar idea appears in the answer choice, but the idea is changed just enough to be incorrect but still attractive. In Weaken questions, the Shell Game is usually used to attack a conclusion that is similar to, but slightly different from, the one presented in the stimulus. Later in this chapter you will see some excellent examples of this answer type.

3. Out of Scope Answers. These answers simply miss the point of the argument and raise issues that are either not related to the argument or tangential to the argument.

While these three answer types are not the only ways an answer choice can be attractively incorrect, they appear frequently enough that you should be familiar with each form.

Some of the wrong answer types from the Must Be True chapter do not apply to Weaken questions. For example, the New Information answer is usually wrong in a Must Be True question, but not in a Weaken question, because new information is acceptable in the answer choices.

Weaken Questions Analyzed

In the following questions we will discuss the form of the stimulus and answer choices against the background of our discussion so far. Please take a moment to complete the following problem:

1. Carl is clearly an incompetent detective. He has solved a smaller percentage of the cases assigned to him in the last 3 years—only 1 out of 25—than any other detective on the police force.

    Which one of the following, if true, most seriously weakens the argument above?

    (A) Because the police chief regards Carl as the most capable detective, she assigns him only the most difficult cases, ones that others have failed to solve.
    (B) Before he became a detective, Carl was a neighborhood police officer and was highly respected by the residents of the neighborhood he patrolled.
    (C) Detectives on the police force on which Carl serves are provided with extensive resources, including the use of a large computer database, to help them solve crimes.
    (D) Carl was previously a detective in a police department in another city, and in the 4 years he spent there, he solved only 1 out of 30 crimes.
    (E) Many of the officers in the police department in which Carl serves were hired or promoted within the last 5 years.

This would be classified as an easy question, but as a starting point for our discussion that is helpful. The structure of the argument is simple, and it is easy to see why the premise does not undeniably prove the conclusion. The answers contain several predictable forms, and this is the type of question you should quickly destroy. You do not need to spend a great deal of time trying to find a specific prephrased answer because there are so many possibilities, and the answers can be eliminated without a great deal of time spent considering which are Losers and which are Contenders.

The stimulus uses a premise about success rate to form a conclusion about Carl's competency as a detective. Ask yourself—does the premise prove the conclusion? No, because there are many factors that could have affected Carl's performance. In this sense, the stimulus has incomplete information, and we should try to discover a relevant piece of information in one of the answer choices that will shed more light on why Carl's success rate is so low. Use this knowledge to make a general prephrase that indicates you are looking for a piece of information that shows Carl's success rate is not as low as it seems or that other factors limited Carl's performance.

Answer choice (A): This is the correct answer choice. We discover that Carl receives the hardest cases, and one would expect that the hardest cases would yield a lower success rate. Notice that this answer does not attack the premises. Even though they are still true, the conclusion is undermined by the new evidence. This is typical of most Weaken question answers—the premises are not addressed and the focus is on the conclusion.

Answer choice (B): This answer is irrelevant. It tries to use the opinion of others about Carl's performance in one capacity to refute facts about his performance in another capacity. Personalize the answer—is this the answer you would offer to weaken the argument against Carl if he were your friend?

Answer choice (C): This is an Opposite answer that strengthens the claim that Carl is incompetent by showing that Carl was not deprived of certain resources for solving cases.

Answer choice (D): This is another Opposite answer that strengthens the claim that Carl is incompetent. This time, the answer shows that Carl has a previous record of poor performance.

Answer choice (E): This answer goes beyond the scope of the argument by discussing the promotions of other officers. These promotions do not impact Carl's job and no information is given about Carl's promotions. If you are thinking that perhaps Carl's poor performance is a result of dissatisfaction over the promotions of others, then you are assuming too much.

Prephrasing is often easier with Weaken questions than with some other question types. Simply put, many people are good at attacking a position and prephrasing puts that skill to use.

CR

Now we will move to a somewhat harder question. Please take a moment to complete the following problem:

2. Beverage company representative: The plastic rings that hold six-packs of beverage cans together pose a threat to wild animals, which often become entangled in the discarded rings and suffocate as a result. Following our lead, all beverage companies will soon use only those rings consisting of a new plastic that disintegrates after only three days' exposure to sunlight. Once we all complete the switchover from the old to the new plastic rings, therefore, the threat of suffocation that plastic rings pose to wild animals will be eliminated.

Which one of the following, if true, most seriously weakens the representative's argument?

(A) The switchover to the new plastic rings will take at least two more years to complete.

(B) After the beverage companies have switched over to the new plastic rings, a substantial number of the old plastic rings will persist in most aquatic and woodland environments.

(C) The new plastic rings are slightly less expensive than the old rings.

(D) The new plastic rings rarely disintegrate during shipping of beverage six-packs because most trucks that transport canned beverages protect their cargo from sunlight.

(E) The new plastic rings disintegrate into substances that are harmful to aquatic animals when ingested in substantial quantities by them.

In two-speaker stimuli where you are asked to weaken the argument of one of the speakers, the test makers often use misdirection and place an answer choice that weakens the argument of the other speaker.

The conclusion of this argument is the final sentence, which contains the conclusion indicator "therefore," and the conclusion contains a qualification that the threat of suffocation will be eliminated *after* the switchover is complete. The premises supporting this conclusion are that the new plastic rings will be used by all companies and that the rings disintegrate after three days' exposure to sunlight. Personalize this argument and ask yourself—are there any holes in this argument? Yes, there are several. The most obvious is, "What if an animal becomes entangled in the new rings before they can disintegrate?" In this question, however, that avenue of attack is not used (this was a two-question stimulus and that idea was used in the other question) but there is no way to know this prior to attempting the question.

Answer choice (A): This answer does not hurt the argument because the author qualified the conclusion to account for the date of the switchover, thereby inoculating against this avenue of attack. From a personalizing standpoint, imagine what would happen if you raised this issue to the beverage company representative—he or she would simply say, "Yes, that may be the case, but I noted in my conclusion that the program would be effective *once the switchover is complete*." This is an attractive answer because it raises a point that would be a difficult public relations issue to address. Regardless, this does not hurt the argument given by the beverage company representative, and that is the task at hand.

Answer choice (B): This is the correct answer choice. Most people select answer choice (E), but as you will see, (E) is incorrect. This answer undermines the representative's conclusion by showing that even after the switchover is complete, the threat to animals from plastic rings will persist. Note the carefully worded nature of the conclusion—the representative does not say the threat from *new* plastic rings will be eliminated, but rather the threat from plastic rings, which includes both old and new rings.

Answer choice (C): This out-of-scope answer addresses an issue that is irrelevant to the representative's argument.

Answer choice (D): While this is nice information from a customer service standpoint (you do not want your six-pack of beer falling apart as you walk out of the store), this answer does not affect the conclusion because it does not address the threat of suffocation to animals.

Answer choice (E): This is the most commonly chosen answer, and it is a perfect example of a Shell Game. In this case, the answer preys upon test takers who fail to heed Primary Objective #4: "Read closely and know precisely what the author said. Do not generalize!" Many test takers read the conclusion and think, "So when they start using these new rings, it will make things better for the animals." When these test takers get to answer choice (E), the answer looks extremely attractive because it indicates that the implementation of the new rings will also have a harmful effect. With this thinking in mind, many test takers select answer choice (E) thinking it undermines the conclusion and they are certain they have nailed the question. However, the conclusion is specifically about suffocation, and answer choice (E) does not address suffocation. Instead, answer choice (E) is a shell game that attacks a conclusion that is similar to but different from the actual conclusion. Remember, one of the rules for weakening arguments is to focus on the conclusion, and knowing the details of the conclusion is part of that focus.

Finally, the placement of answer choice (E) is no accident. Most students do not immediately identify answer choice (B) as the correct answer, and even those that keep it as a Contender often feel it could be stronger. Then, just when things are starting to look bleak, answer choice (E) pops up sounding fairly reasonable. Most people breathe a sigh of relief and select the answer without carefully examining the contents. Never choose answer choice (E) just because the first four answers are not overly attractive! Always make a thorough

Answer choice (E) is a great place for the test makers to place an attractive wrong answer because (E) is the last answer that a student will read, and the contents of (E) "reverberate" in the test taker's mind and begin to sound reasonable.

In that same vein, answer choice (A) is a great place to put the correct answer if the stimulus is exceedingly difficult to understand or if the question stem is extremely unusual. Why? Because most test takers use the first answer choice in a difficult problem to get a handle on what they are reading and the type of answers they will see. If a problem is tough, it can be difficult to immediately identify answer choice (A) as correct. Then, by the time they have read all five answers, they are prone to have forgotten the details of the first answer choice.

analysis of every answer choice and remember that the test makers know that people get nervous if none of the first four answer choices jump out at them. Do not let the test makers draw you into a trap!

Final Note

We will continue our discussion of Weaken questions in the next chapter, which addresses Cause and Effect Reasoning. We will also continue to discuss argumentation in more detail as we progress through the Second Family of questions and into Method of Reasoning and Parallel Reasoning.

The following page is a review of key points from this chapter. After the review, there is a short problem set to help test your knowledge of these ideas. The problem set is followed by an answer key with explanations. Good luck!

Weaken Question Type Review

Weaken questions require you to select an answer choice that undermines the author's argument as decisively as possible. Keep these fundamental rules in mind when you approach Weaken questions:

1. The stimulus will contain an argument.

2. Focus on the conclusion.

3. The information in the stimulus is suspect. There are often reasoning errors present, and you must read the argument very carefully.

4. Weaken questions often yield strong prephrases.

5. The answer choices are accepted as given, even if they include "new" information.

The conclusion is the part of the argument that is most likely to be attacked, but the correct answer choice will not simply contradict the conclusion. Instead, the correct answer will undermine the conclusion by showing that the conclusion fails to account for some element or possibility. In this sense, the correct answer often shows that the conclusion does not necessarily follow from the premises even if the premises are true.

Several scenarios that can occur in GMAT Weaken question stimuli are easy to recognize and attack:

1. Incomplete Information.

2. Improper Comparison.

3. Qualified Conclusion.

There are certain incorrect answer choices that appear frequently in Weaken questions:

1. Opposite Answers.

2. Shell Game Answers.

3. Out of Scope Answers.

Weaken Question Problem Set

Please complete the problem set and review the answer key and explanations. *Answers on Page 107*

1. Human beings have cognitive faculties that are superior to those of other animals, and once humans become aware of these, they cannot be made happy by anything that does not involve gratification of these faculties.

   Which one of the following statements, if true, most calls into question the view above?

   (A) Certain animals—dolphins and chimpanzees, for example—appear to be capable of rational communication.
   (B) Many people familiar both with intellectual stimulation and with physical pleasures enjoy the latter more.
   (C) Someone who never experienced classical music as a child will usually prefer popular music as an adult.
   (D) Many people who are serious athletes consider themselves to be happy.
   (E) Many people who are serious athletes love gourmet food.

2. Loggerhead turtles live and breed in distinct groups, of which some are in the Pacific Ocean and some are in the Atlantic. New evidence suggests that juvenile Pacific loggerheads that feed near the Baja peninsula hatch in Japanese waters 10,000 kilometers away. Ninety-five percent of the DNA samples taken from the Baja turtles match those taken from turtles at the Japanese nesting sites.

   Which one of the following, if true, most seriously weakens the reasoning above?

   (A) Nesting sites of loggerhead turtles have been found off the Pacific coast of North America several thousand kilometers north of the Baja peninsula.
   (B) The distance between nesting sites and feeding sites of Atlantic loggerhead turtles is less than 5,000 kilometers.
   (C) Loggerhead hatchlings in Japanese waters have been declining in number for the last decade while the number of nesting sites near the Baja peninsula has remained constant.
   (D) Ninety-five percent of the DNA samples taken from the Baja turtles match those taken from Atlantic loggerhead turtles.
   (E) Commercial aquariums have been successfully breeding Atlantic loggerheads with Pacific loggerheads for the last five years.

Weaken Question Problem Set

3. People who have specialized knowledge about a scientific or technical issue are systematically excluded from juries for trials where the issue is relevant. Thus, trial by jury is not a fair means of settling disputes involving such issues.

Which one of the following, if true, most seriously weakens the argument?

(A) The more complicated the issue being litigated, the less likely it is that a juror without specialized knowledge of the field involved will be able to comprehend the testimony being given.

(B) The more a juror knows about a particular scientific or technical issue involved in a trial, the more likely it is that the juror will be prejudiced in favor of one of the litigating parties before the trial begins.

(C) Appointing an impartial arbitrator is not a fair means of settling disputes involving scientific or technical issues, because arbitrators tend to favor settlements in which both parties compromise on the issues.

(D) Experts who give testimony on scientific or technical issues tend to hedge their conclusions by discussing the possibility of error.

(E) Expert witnesses in specialized fields often command fees that are so high that many people involved in litigation cannot afford their services.

4. The five senses have traditionally been viewed as distinct yet complementary. Each sense is thought to have its own range of stimuli that are incapable of stimulating the other senses. However, recent research has discovered that some people taste a banana and claim that they are tasting blue, or see a color and say that it has a specific smell. This shows that such people, called synesthesiacs, have senses that do not respect the usual boundaries between the five recognized senses.

Which one of the following statements, if true, most seriously weakens the argument?

(A) Synesthesiacs demonstrate a general, systematic impairment in their ability to use and understand words.

(B) Recent evidence strongly suggests that there are other senses besides sight, touch, smell, hearing, and taste.

(C) The particular ways in which sensory experiences overlap in synesthesiacs follow a definite pattern.

(D) The synesthetic phenomenon has been described in the legends of various cultures.

(E) Synesthesiacs can be temporarily rid of their synesthetic experiences by the use of drugs.

5. Archaeologist: A skeleton of a North American mastodon that became extinct at the peak of the Ice Age was recently discovered. It contains a human-made projectile dissimilar to any found in that part of Eurasia closest to North America. Thus, since Eurasians did not settle in North America until shortly before the peak of the Ice Age, the first Eurasian settlers in North America probably came from a more distant part of Eurasia.

Which one of the following, if true, most seriously weakens the archaeologist's argument?

(A) The projectile found in the mastodon does not resemble any that were used in Eurasia before or during the Ice Age.

(B) The people who occupied the Eurasian area closest to North America remained nomadic throughout the Ice Age.

(C) The skeleton of a bear from the same place and time as the mastodon skeleton contains a similar projectile.

(D) Other North American artifacts from the peak of the Ice Age are similar to ones from the same time found in more distant parts of Eurasia.

(E) Climatic conditions in North America just before the Ice Age were more conducive to human habitation than were those in the part of Eurasia closest to North America at that time.

6. Lobsters and other crustaceans eaten by humans are more likely to contract gill diseases when sewage contaminates their water. Under a recent proposal, millions of gallons of local sewage each day would be rerouted many kilometers offshore. Although this would substantially reduce the amount of sewage in the harbor where lobsters are caught, the proposal is pointless, because hardly any lobsters live long enough to be harmed by those diseases.

Which one of the following, if true, most seriously weakens the argument?

(A) Contaminants in the harbor other than sewage are equally harmful to lobsters.

(B) Lobsters, like other crustaceans, live longer in the open ocean than in industrial harbors.

(C) Lobsters breed as readily in sewage-contaminated water as in unpolluted water.

(D) Gill diseases cannot be detected by examining the surface of the lobster.

(E) Humans often become ill as a result of eating lobsters with gill diseases.

Question #1. Weaken. The correct answer choice is (B)

This is a nice straightforward question to start the problem set. The conclusion of the argument appears at the end of the stimulus: human beings "cannot be made happy by anything that does not involve gratification of these [cognitive] faculties." To weaken the argument we must show that individuals can be made happy without gratification of the cognitive faculties. If you do not know the meaning of "cognitive," the problem can be challenging. Cognitive means "relating to the mental process of knowing, including reasoning and judgment." In other words, cognitive faculties are thinking and analyzing, etc.

Answer choice (A): This answer attempts to attack the first premise, but fails. Although it is fantastic news that dolphins and chimps can rationally communicate, this fact has no impact on the argument at hand. Even though they have this communication ability, human cognitive faculties can still be superior.

Answer choice (B): This is the correct answer choice, and a somewhat risqué one at that. By showing that many people enjoy the physical more than the cognitive, the answer shows that people can be made happy by gratification of something other than cognitive faculties. Cognitive faculties, being mental in nature, are of course distinct from physical pleasures.

Additionally, this answer has the benefit of addressing the phrase in the stimulus regarding awareness of cognitive faculties: "once humans become aware of these..." In this answer, unlike others, the individuals are known to be familiar with cognitive faculties. While we believe that recognition of cognitive faculties is inherent in adults (or some of the named types in other answers, such as *serious athletes*, who by definition would have to be teens or adults), this answer is stronger because it explicitly addresses the issue.

Answer choice (C): A preference for a certain type of music is likely a cognition-driven preference, and this preference is expressed by an adult who would certainly be aware of cognitive faculties. And, since no suggestion is made that individuals can be made happy without gratification of the cognitive faculties, this answer is incorrect.

Answer choice (D): This can be an attractive answer at first, but it depends on the assumption that the serious athletes are happy due to their athletic endeavors. However, that connection is not explicitly stated, and it could be that the serious athletes are happy because of some gratification of their cognitive faculties, in their respective sport or otherwise.

Answer choice (E): This answer is similar to answer choice (D). A gourmet is a connoisseur of food and drink, and a connoisseur is a person with deep or special knowledge of a subject. In this sense, there would be a cognitive element to the enjoyment of gourmet food. As such, this answer may serve to slightly strengthen the argument because it shows that an individual with experience with the non-cognitive still retains a love of the cognitive.

Weaken Problem Set Answer Key

Question #2. Weaken. The correct answer choice is (D)

The argument uses the premise that 95 percent of the DNA samples of Baja turtles and Japanese turtles match to conclude that Baja turtles hatch in Japanese waters 10,000 kilometers away. Although this sounds like convincing statistical evidence (especially because most people are conditioned to accept DNA-related evidence as irrefutable), the presence of statistics alone does not prove the argument. For example, consider the following statistic using DNA evidence: humans and chimpanzees share about 98% of their DNA (we share about 75% of our DNA with dogs, for that matter). The point is that mere percentages do not prove a definite connection. Regardless of whether or not you understood the weakness of the statistic, you should have been skeptical of the reference to *juvenile* turtles travelling *10,000* kilometers. Such a lengthy trip by a juvenile animal is unlikely, and calls into question the soundness of the argument.

Answer choice (A): This answer does not impact the argument because no details—DNA or otherwise—are given about the turtles at these nesting sites off the Pacific coast of North America.

Answer choice (B): The fact that Atlantic turtles have nesting and feeding sites no more than 5,000 kilometers apart does not attack the argument because the argument is about *Baja* turtles.

Answer choice (C): This answer attempts to weaken the argument by inducing you to conclude that if the Japanese hatchlings are declining but Baja sites are constant, then the Baja sites cannot be supplied by the Japanese hatchlings. But, the answer choice moves from the number of *hatchlings* to the number of *sites*. Even with a declining number of hatchlings, the number of sites could remain constant, albeit with fewer turtles at each. Because of this possibility, the answer does not undermine the argument.

Answer choice (D): This is the correct answer choice. If 95 percent of the Baja samples match *Atlantic* samples, this shows that the 95 percent result in the stimulus is not indicative of origin, and thus the Baja turtles did not have to take the 10,000 kilometer trip.

Answer choice (E): The breeding between species was not an issue in the stimulus.

Question #3. Weaken. The correct answer choice is (B)

The first sentence is a premise, and the second sentence is the conclusion of this argument. To attack this conclusion, look for an answer choice that shows that the exclusion of knowledgeable individuals from scientific or technical issue trials is a fair way of proceeding in these trials.

Answer choice (A): This is an Opposite answer that strengthens the conclusion. If specialized knowledge of these issues makes it more likely that the juror can comprehend the testimony being given, then these individuals should not be excluded from juries, and their exclusion makes trial by jury an unfair means of resolving a dispute.

Answer choice (B): This is the correct answer choice. If the specialized knowledge is likely to produce a prejudice in a juror, then by all means they should be excluded from the jury. Thus, instead of trial by jury being an unfair means, it is made more fair by the exclusion of these individuals. The answer is a tricky one because most people initially think the answer agrees with the argument. It agrees with the principle of the premise, but not with the conclusion drawn from that premise.

108

Weaken Problem Set Answer Key

Answer choice (C): This answer simply notes that arbitrators are not a fair means of settling scientific or technical issue debates. This has no impact on the fairness of jury trials involving these same issues.

Answer choice (D): This answer is about the *experts* testifying at scientific or technical issue trials. This information does not attack the claim that jury trials are unfair because of the exclusion of *jurors* with knowledge of these issues.

Answer choice (E): This answer can be eliminated by reasoning similar to that used to eliminate answer choice (D).

Question #4. Weaken. The correct answer choice is (A)

The conclusion is in the last sentence, that some people "have senses that do not respect the usual boundaries between the five recognized senses." Instead of keeping their senses distinct, these individuals have an overlap.

Incidentally, the condition discussed in the stimulus is not made up: synesthesiacs (or synesthetes) have a real condition known as synesthesia. Regardless of that fact, you must find an answer choice that undermines the conclusion of the argument, something that would suggest their senses do respect the usual boundaries.

Answer choice (A): This is the correct answer choice. If the synesthesiacs have a systematic impairment in their use of language it may not be that their senses overlap but rather that they lack the ability to properly express themselves. Thus, their claim to taste a banana and see blue might not be a reflection of that actually occurring but rather a reflection of the words they use to describe taste. If so, this would undermine the conclusion that the senses of synesthesiacs do overlap. This is a difficult answer to identify as correct, and less than 50% of test takers are able to do so.

Answer choice (B): The appeal of this answer—and many students keep this as a Contender—is that it suggests that perhaps other senses are operating, and some test takers make the judgment that these additional senses account for the sensory overlap in synesthesiacs. Unfortunately, that judgment is not supported by the answer choice. Not enough information is provided by the answer choice to say what role, if any, is played by these other senses.

Answer choice (C): This is the most popular wrong answer choice. Do not forget to personalize the argument and consider how the author would react if faced with this answer. Would he or she surrender and admit the answer overpowers the argument? Doubtful. The author would probably react to this answer by saying something along these lines, "Exactly. Since all the individuals are synesthesiacs and suffer from the same condition, it is not surprising that there would be patterns in the way the senses overlap. Just as everyone afflicted with emphysema has difficulty breathing, the sensory patterns exhibited by synesthesiacs are just a product of the condition. The fact that their senses do not follow the usual boundaries and do so in certain ways is to be expected." So, instead of surrendering to the answer, the author would indicate that the answer agrees with the conclusion.

Weaken Problem Set Answer Key

Answer choice (D): This answer is out of the scope of the argument. The "legendary" status of synesthesiacs does not shed any light on the operation of their five senses.

Answer choice (E): If anything, this may strengthen the argument by indicating that the synesthesiacs are experiencing some type of phenomenon. Beyond that point, however, no information is given to suggest that their senses respect the usual boundaries.

Question #5. Weaken. The correct answer choice is (A)

The stimulus sets up an interesting argument that appears fairly reasonable. A mastodon skeleton has been found containing a human-made projectile dissimilar to those of the part of Eurasia *closest* to North America and because Eurasians did not settle in North America until shortly before the peak of the Ice Age, the first Eurasian settlers of North America probably came from a *more distant* part of Eurasia than the area nearest North America. To make a very rough analogy using dialects, it is like a resident of Washington, D.C. saying, "The visitors we just met did not sound like they were from Virginia, so they must be from a much more distant part of the U.S." Reading that rough analogy, you can see that the speaker has assumed that the visitors are from the U.S. Of course, that does not have to be the case—they could be from England or France or elsewhere. The same form of assumption has occurred in the argument, and the author has assumed that the *projectile* is of Eurasian origin.

Answer choice (A): This is the correct answer choice. This answer hurts the argument by indicating that the projectile is apparently not Eurasian, suggesting that the first Eurasian settlers could have come from any part of Eurasia, including the area closest to North America.

Answer choice (B): This is the most attractive wrong answer, but regardless, this answer does not hurt the argument. Some students attempt to conclude that since the people were nomadic, they could have moved to areas farther away and found projectiles like the one in the mastodon. However, even though these individuals remained nomadic, they were apparently nomadic within the area of Eurasia closest to North America because the answer clearly states, "The people who *occupied* the Eurasia area closest to North America..." Hence, they did not necessarily occupy other areas and this answer does not hurt the argument.

Answer choice (C): This Opposite answer supports the argument by showing that the projectile in the mastodon was not a one-time, anomalous occurrence. If other, similar projectiles come to light, then the author's position would be strengthened.

Answer choice (D): This Opposite answer supports the argument by connecting other artifacts of the same age as the projectile to parts of Eurasia more distant than the area of Eurasia closest to North America. This adds further evidence to the idea that the first Eurasian settlers of North America probably came from a more distant part of Eurasia than the area nearest North America.

Answer choice (E): This Opposite answer supports the argument by indicating that the part of Eurasia closest to North America may not have been inhabited just before the Ice Age. If this area was uninhabitable, then it is more likely that settlers coming to North America came from more distant regions.

110

Question #6. Weaken. The correct answer choice is (E)

This is a great separator question, and approximately one student in three answers this question correctly. However, some students are able to annihilate this question because they see a reference in the first line that raises an important issue that goes unanswered. That reference is to lobsters "eaten by humans." The argument asserts that diverting the sewage in the harbor is a moot point because hardly any lobsters live long enough to be harmed by the diseases caused by the sewage. This may be, but what about the humans who eat the lobsters that live in the sewage-contaminated environment? The author fails to address this point.

The conclusion of the argument is near the end: "the proposal is pointless," and this is based on the premise that "hardly any lobsters live long enough to be harmed by those diseases."

Answer choice (A): The argument is based on the sewage contamination of the harbor. Although other contaminants may be present, they are not addressed by the argument, and thus this answer does not undermine the author's position.

Answer choice (B): This answer has no impact because the argument is about lobsters that are caught *in the harbor*. So, while lobsters in the open ocean may live longer, the author's point about lobsters in the harbor not living long enough to contract a gill disease is untouched.

Answer choice (C): The issue is not breeding frequency but longevity. So, while we are pleased to hear that lobsters in sewage-contaminated waters breed frequently, this fact does not impact an argument based on the age and disease contraction.

Answer choice (D): Although whether the lobsters contract a gill disease is a critical issue in the argument, the method of determining whether a lobster has a disease is not a critical issue. Again, keep in mind the heart of the argument:

> Premise: "hardly any lobsters live long enough to be harmed by those diseases."
> Conclusion: "the proposal [to reroute harbor sewage] is pointless."

Nothing in that argument concerns the detection of the gill diseases.

Answer choice (E): This is the correct answer choice. As discussed above, the author fails to address the effect of the contaminated lobsters on humans who consume them, and this answer attacks that hole. If humans become ill as a result of eating lobsters with gill diseases, and gill diseases are more likely to arise when the lobsters live in the sewage-contaminated waters, then the conclusion that the proposal is pointless is incorrect.

CHAPTER SIX: CAUSE AND EFFECT REASONING

CR

What is Causality?

When examining events, people naturally seek to explain why things happened. This search often results in cause and effect reasoning, which asserts or denies that one thing causes another, or that one thing is caused by another. On the GMAT, cause and effect reasoning appears in many Critical Reasoning problems, often in the conclusion where the author mistakenly claims that one event causes another. For example:

> Last week IBM announced a quarterly deficit and the stock market dropped 10 points. Thus, IBM's announcement must have caused the drop.

Like the above conclusion, most causal conclusions are flawed because there can be alternate explanations for the stated relationship: another cause could account for the effect; a third event could have caused both the stated cause and effect; the situation may in fact be reversed; the events may be related but not causally; or the entire occurrence could be the result of chance.

In short, causality occurs when one event is said to make another occur. The *cause* is the event that makes the other occur; the *effect* is the event that follows from the cause. By definition, the cause must occur before the effect, and the cause is the "activator" or "ignitor" in the relationship. The effect always happens at some point in time after the cause.

How to Recognize Causality

A cause and effect relationship has a signature characteristic—the cause *makes* the effect happen. Thus, there is an identifiable type of expression used to indicate that a causal relationship is present. The list on the following page contains a number of the phrases used by the makers of the GMAT to introduce causality, and you should be on the lookout for those when reading Critical Reasoning stimuli.

Causality is the most-tested logical concept in GMAT Critical Reasoning stimuli. The second most tested concept is Numbers and Percentages, which will be addressed in Chapter Nine.

As mentioned before, this section of the book is about GMAT logic, not general philosophy. Therefore, we will not go into an analysis of David Hume's *Inquiry* or Mill's Methods (both of which address causality) because although those discussions are interesting, they do not apply to the GMAT.

The following terms often introduce a cause and effect relationship:

caused by
because of
responsible for
reason for
leads to
induced by
promoted by
determined by
produced by
product of
played a role in
was a factor in
is an effect of

Be sure to memorize this list!

Because of the variety of the English language, there are many alternate phrases that can introduce causality. However, those phrases would all have the similar characteristic of suggesting that one event *made* another occur.

Causality in the Conclusion versus Causality in the Premises

Causal statements can be found in the premise or conclusion of an argument. If the causal statement is the conclusion, then the reasoning is flawed. If the causal statement is the premise, then the argument may be flawed, but not because of the causal statement. Because of this difference, one of the critical issues in determining whether flawed causal reasoning is present is identifying where in the argument the causal assertion is made. The classic mistaken cause and effect reasoning we will refer to throughout this book occurs when a causal assertion is made in the *conclusion*, or the conclusion presumes a causal relationship. Let us examine the difference between an argument with a causal premise and one with a causal conclusion.

In the GMAT world, when a cause and effect statement appears as the conclusion, the conclusion is flawed. In the real world that may not be the case because a preponderance of evidence can be gathered or visual evidence can be used to prove a relationship.

This is an argument with a causal conclusion:

Premise: In North America, people drink a lot of milk.

Premise: There is a high frequency of cancer in North America.

Conclusion: Therefore, drinking milk causes cancer.

In this case, the author takes two events that occur together and concludes that one causes the other. This conclusion is in error for the reasons discussed on the first page of this chapter.

If a causal claim is made in the premises, however, then no *causal* reasoning error exists in the argument (of course, the argument may be flawed in other ways). As mentioned previously, the makers of the GMAT tend to allow premises to go unchallenged (they are more concerned with the reasoning that follows from a premise) and it is considered acceptable for an author to begin his argument by stating a causal relationship and then continuing from there:

Premise: Drinking milk causes cancer.

Premise: The residents of North America drink a lot of milk.

Conclusion: Therefore, in North America there is a high frequency of cancer among the residents.

The second example is considered valid reasoning because the author takes a causal principle and follows it to its logical conclusion. Generally, causal reasoning occurs in a format similar to the first example, but there are GMAT problems similar to the second example.

Situations That Can Lead to Errors of Causality

There are two scenarios that tend to lead to causal conclusions in Critical Reasoning questions:

1. One event occurs before another

    When one event occurs before another event, many people fall into the trap of assuming that the first event caused the second event. This does not have to be the case, as shown by the following famous example:

    > Every morning the rooster crows before the sun rises. Hence, the rooster must cause the sun to rise.

    The example contains a ludicrous conclusion, and shows why it is dangerous to simply assume that the first event must have caused the second event.

2. Two (or more) events occur at the same time

    When two events occur simultaneously, many people assume that one event caused the other. While one event could have caused the other, the two events could be the result of a third event, or the two events could simply be correlated without one causing the other.

    The following example shows how a third event can cause both events:

    > The consumption of ice cream has been found to correlate with the murder rate. Therefore, consuming ice cream must cause one to be more likely to commit murder.

If you have taken a logic course, you will recognize the first scenario produces the *Post Hoc, Ergo Propter Hoc* fallacy.

In the second example, the two events could simply be correlated. A positive correlation is a relationship where the two values move together. A negative correlation is one where the two values move in opposite directions, such as with age and eyesight (the older you get, the worse your eyesight gets).

As you might imagine, the conclusion of the example does not have to be true (yes, go ahead and eat that Ben and Jerry's!), and the two events can be explained as the effects of a single cause: hot weather. When the weather is warmer, ice cream consumption and the murder rate tend to rise (this example is actually true, especially for large cities).

The Central Assumption of Causal Conclusions

Understanding the assumption that is at the heart of a causal conclusion is essential to knowing why certain answers will be correct or incorrect. Most students assume that the GMAT makes basic assumptions that are similar to the real world; this is untrue and is a dangerous mistake to make.

When we discuss causality in the real world, there is an inherent understanding that a given cause is just one possible cause of the effect, and that there are other causes that could also produce the same effect. This is reasonable because we have the ability to observe a variety of cause and effect scenarios, and experience shows us that different actions can have the same result. The makers of the GMAT do *not* think this way. When a GMAT speaker concludes that one occurrence caused another, that speaker also assumes that the stated cause is the *only* possible cause of the effect and that consequently the stated cause will *always* produce the effect. This assumption is incredibly extreme and far-reaching, and often leads to surprising answer choices that would appear incorrect unless you understand this assumption. Consider the following example:

Premise:	Average temperatures are higher at the equator than in any other area.
Premise:	Individuals living at or near the equator tend to have lower per-capita incomes than individuals living elsewhere.
Conclusion:	Therefore, higher average temperatures cause lower per-capita incomes.

This argument is a classic flawed causal argument wherein two premises with a basic connection (living at the equator) are used as the basis of a conclusion that states that the connection is such that one of the elements actually makes the other occur. The conclusion is flawed because it is not necessary that one of the elements caused the other to occur: the two could simply be correlated in some way or the connection could be random.

In the real world, we would tend to look at an argument like the one above and think that while the conclusion is possible, there are also other things that could cause the lower per-capita income of individuals residing at or near the equator, such as a lack of natural resources. *This is not how speakers on the GMAT view the relationship.* When a GMAT speaker makes an argument like the one above, he or she believes that the *only* cause is the one stated in the conclusion and that there are *no other* causes that can create that particular effect. Why is this the case? Because for a GMAT speaker to come to that conclusion, he or she must have weighed and considered every possible alternative and then rejected each one. Otherwise, why would the speaker draw the given conclusion? In the final analysis, to say that higher average temperatures cause lower per-capita incomes the speaker must also believe that nothing else could be the cause of lower per-capita incomes.

Thus, in every argument with a causal conclusion that appears on the GMAT, the speaker believes that the stated cause is in fact the only cause and all other theoretically possible causes are not, in fact, actual causes. This is an incredibly powerful assumption, and the results of this assumption are most evident in Weaken, Strengthen, and Assumption questions. We will discuss this effect on Strengthen and Assumption questions in a later chapter. Following is a brief analysis of the effect of this assumption on Weaken questions.

Answer choices that otherwise appear irrelevant will suddenly be obviously correct when you understand the central causal assumption.

How to Attack a Causal Conclusion

Whenever you identify a causal relationship in the conclusion of a GMAT problem, immediately prepare to either weaken or strengthen the argument. Attacking a cause and effect relationship in Weaken questions almost always consists of performing one of the following tasks:

Stimuli containing causal arguments are often followed by Weaken, Strengthen, Assumption, or Flaw questions.

A. Find an alternate cause for the stated effect

Because the author believes there is only one cause, identifying another cause weakens the conclusion.

B. Show that even when the cause occurs, the effect does not occur

This type of answer often appears in the form of a counterexample. Because the author believes that the cause always produces the effect, any scenario where the cause occurs and the effect does not weaken the conclusion.

C. Show that although the effect occurs, the cause did not occur

This type of answer often appears in the form of a counterexample. Because the author believes that the effect is always produced by the same cause, any scenario where the effect occurs and the cause does not weaken the conclusion.

D. Show that the stated relationship is reversed

Because the author believes that the cause and effect relationship is correctly stated, showing that the relationship is backwards (the claimed effect is actually the cause of the claimed cause) undermines the conclusion.

E. Show that a statistical problem exists with the data used to make the causal statement

If the data used to make a causal statement are in error, then the validity of the causal claim is in question.

Diagramming Causality

Causal statements can be quickly and easily represented by an arrow diagram, and in this book we use designators ("C" for cause and "E" for effect) above the terms when diagramming. We use these designators to make the meaning of the diagram clear. During the GMAT, however, students should not write out the designators on the scratch paper (they should just use the arrow diagram) because they want to go as fast as possible.

Here is an example of a causal diagram:

Statement: "Smoking causes cancer."

S = smoking
C = cancer

$$\underline{C} \qquad \underline{E}$$
$$S \longrightarrow C$$

During the GMAT, the choice to create an arrow diagram for a causal statement is yours.

As you diagram a causal statement, you will face a decision about how to represent each element of the relationship. Because writing out the entire condition would be onerous, the best approach is to use a symbol to represent each condition. For example, we have already used "S" to represent the idea of "smoking." The choice of symbol is yours, and different students will choose different representations. For example, to represent a phrase such as "they must have studied for the test," you could choose "Study" or the more efficient "S." Whatever you decide to choose, the symbolization must make sense to you and it must be clear. Regardless of how you choose to diagram an element, once you use a certain representation within a problem, stick with that representation throughout the duration of the question.

A Cause and Effect Problems Analyzed

Please take a moment to complete the following problem:

1. People with high blood pressure are generally more nervous and anxious than people who do not have high blood pressure. This fact shows that this particular combination of personality traits—the so-called hypertensive personality—is likely to cause a person with these traits to develop high blood pressure.

    The reasoning in the argument is most vulnerable to criticism on the grounds that the argument

    (A) fails to define the term "hypertensive personality"
    (B) presupposes that people have permanent personality traits
    (C) simply restates the claim that there is a "hypertensive personality" without providing evidence to support that claim
    (D) takes a correlation between personality traits and high blood pressure as proof that the traits cause high blood pressure
    (E) focuses on nervousness and anxiety only, ignoring other personality traits that people with high blood pressure might have

This is a Flaw in the Reasoning question and although we have not discussed this question type, based on your knowledge of causal reasoning we can proceed without a detailed understanding of the question form. You should have identified the following argument structure in the question above:

Premise: People with high blood pressure are generally more nervous and anxious than people who do not have high blood pressure.

Premise: This particular combination of personality traits is called the hypertensive personality.

Conclusion: The hypertensive personality is likely to cause a person to develop high blood pressure.

The premises indicate that certain individuals have both high blood pressure and the hypertensive personality. From this information we cannot draw any conclusions, but the author makes the classic GMAT error of concluding that one of the conditions causes the other. Your job is to find the answer that describes this error of reasoning.

From the "Situations That Can Lead to Errors of Causality" discussion, the scenario in this stimulus falls under item 2—"Two (or more) events occur at the same time." As described in that section, "While one event could have caused the other, the two events could be the result of a third event, or the two events could simply be correlated without one causing the other." Thus, you should search either for an answer that states that the author forgot that a third event could have caused the two events or that the author mistook correlation for causation. Answer choice (D) describes the latter.

Answer choice (A): This is an Opposite answer because the stimulus defines the hypertensive personality as one with the traits of nervousness and anxiety.

Answer choice (B): The permanence of the traits is not an issue in the stimulus.

Answer choice (C): Although the argument does act as described in this answer choice, this is not an error. On the GMAT, authors have the right to make premises that contain certain claims. Remember, the focus is not on the premises but where the author goes with the argument once a premise is created.

Answer choice (D): This is the correct answer choice. The conclusion can be diagrammed as:

HP = hypertensive personality
HBP = high blood pressure

$$\underline{C} \qquad\qquad \underline{E}$$
$$HP \longrightarrow HBP$$

This answer choice describes a classic error of causality: two events occurring simultaneously are mistakenly interpreted to be in a causal relationship. There are many other possibilities for the arrangement: the two events could be caused by a third event (for example, genetics could cause both a hypertensive personality and high blood pressure), the events could be reversed (the high blood pressure could actually cause the hypertensive personality), or there may be situations where the two do not occur together.

Answer choice (E): Although the argument does act as described in this answer choice, this is not an error. The author is allowed to focus on nervousness and anxiety to the exclusion of other traits. To analogize, imagine a speaker says, "The Kansas City Royals have bad pitching and this makes them a bad team." The Kansas City Royals might also wear blue, but the speaker is not obligated to mention that trait when discussing why the Royals are a bad baseball team. In much the same way, the author of this stimulus is not obligated to mention other traits people with high blood pressure may have.

Causal Reasoning Review

Causality occurs when one event is said to make another occur. The *cause* is the event that makes the other occur; the *effect* is the event that follows from the cause.

Most causal conclusions are flawed because there can be alternate explanations for the stated relationship: some other cause could account for the effect; some third event could have caused both the stated cause and effect; the situation may in fact be reversed; the events may be related but not causally; or the entire occurrence could be the result of chance.

Causal statements can be used in the premise or conclusion of an argument. If the causal statement is the conclusion, then the reasoning is flawed. If the causal statement is a premise, then the argument may be flawed, but not because of the causal statement.

There are two scenarios that tend to lead to causal conclusions in Critical Reasoning questions:

1. One event occurs before another
2. Two (or more) events occur at the same time

When a GMAT speaker concludes that one occurrence caused another, that speaker also assumes that the stated cause is the *only* possible cause of the effect and that the stated cause will *always* produce the effect.

In Weaken questions, attacking a cause and effect relationship almost always consists of performing one of the following tasks:

A. Find an alternate cause for the stated effect
B. Show that even when the cause occurs, the effect does not occur
C. Show that although the effect occurs, the cause did not occur
D. Show that the stated relationship is in fact reversed
E. Show a statistical problem exists with the data used to make the causal statement

Final Note

Causal reasoning occurs in many different question types, and the discussion in this chapter is designed to acquaint you with situations that produce causal statements, how to identify a causal statement, and some of the ways that causality appears in GMAT problems. We will revisit these concepts as we discuss other question types.

As you examine GMAT questions, remember that causal reasoning may or may not be present in the stimulus. Your job is to recognize causality when it appears and react accordingly. If causality is not present, you do not need to worry about it.

On the following page is a short problem set to help you work with some of the ideas. The problem set is followed by an answer key with explanations. Good luck!

Please complete the problem set and review the answer key and explanations. *Answers on Page 125*

1. The number of airplanes equipped with a new anticollision device has increased steadily during the past two years. During the same period, it has become increasingly common for key information about an airplane's altitude and speed to disappear suddenly from air traffic controllers' screens. The new anticollision device, which operates at the same frequency as air traffic radar, is therefore responsible for the sudden disappearance of key information.

    Which one of the following, if true, most seriously weakens the argument?

    (A) The new anticollision device has already prevented a considerable number of mid-air collisions.
    (B) It was not until the new anticollision device was introduced that key information first began disappearing suddenly from controllers' screens.
    (C) The new anticollision device is scheduled to be moved to a different frequency within the next two to three months.
    (D) Key information began disappearing from controllers' screens three months before the new anticollision device was first tested.
    (E) The sudden disappearance of key information from controllers' screens has occurred only at relatively large airports.

2. Most antidepressant drugs cause weight gain. While dieting can help reduce the amount of weight gained while taking such antidepressants, some weight gain is unlikely to be preventable.

    The information above most strongly supports which one of the following?

    (A) A physician should not prescribe any antidepressant drug for a patient if that patient is overweight.
    (B) People who are trying to lose weight should not ask their doctors for an antidepressant drug.
    (C) At least some patients taking antidepressant drugs gain weight as a result of taking them.
    (D) The weight gain experienced by patients taking antidepressant drugs should be attributed to lack of dieting.
    (E) All patients taking antidepressant drugs should diet to maintain their weight.

3. Violent crime in this town is becoming a serious problem. Compared to last year, local law enforcement agencies have responded to 17 percent more calls involving violent crimes, showing that the average citizen of this town is more likely than ever to become a victim of a violent crime.

Which one of the following, if true, most seriously weakens the argument?

(A) The town's overall crime rate appears to have risen slightly this year compared to the same period last year.

(B) In general, persons under the age of 65 are less likely to be victims of violent crimes than persons over the age of 65.

(C) As a result of the town's community outreach programs, more people than ever are willing to report violent crimes to the proper authorities.

(D) In response to worries about violent crime, the town has recently opened a community center providing supervised activities for teenagers.

(E) Community officials have shown that a relatively small number of repeat offenders commit the majority of violent crimes in the town.

4. Medical researcher: As expected, records covering the last four years of ten major hospitals indicate that babies born prematurely were more likely to have low birth weights and to suffer from health problems than were babies not born prematurely. These records also indicate that mothers who had received adequate prenatal care were less likely to have low birth weight babies than were mothers who had received inadequate prenatal care. Adequate prenatal care, therefore, significantly decreases the risk of low birth weight babies.

Which one of the following, if true, most weakens the medical researcher's argument?

(A) The hospital records indicate that many babies that are born with normal birth weights are born to mothers who had inadequate prenatal care.

(B) Mothers giving birth prematurely are routinely classified by hospitals as having received inadequate prenatal care when the record of that care is not available.

(C) The hospital records indicate that low birth weight babies were routinely classified as having been born prematurely.

(D) Some babies not born prematurely, whose mothers received adequate prenatal care, have low birth weights.

(E) Women who receive adequate prenatal care are less likely to give birth prematurely than are women who do not receive adequate prenatal care.

Causal Reasoning Problem Set Answer Key

Question #1. The correct answer choice is (D)

The stimulus commits the classic error of assuming that because two events occur simultaneously that one must cause the other. The phrase used to indicate causality is "responsible for."

> D = anticollision device
> SD = sudden disappearance of key information

$$\underline{C} \qquad\qquad \underline{E}$$

$$D \longrightarrow SD$$

The question stem asks you to weaken the argument, and according to the "How to Attack a Causal Conclusion" section you should be on the lookout for one of several primary methods of attacking the argument.

Answer choice (A): This answer presents *another effect* of the cause, but this additional effect does not weaken the argument. To analogize this answer to a different argument, imagine a scenario where a speaker concludes that playing football makes a person more prone to sustaining a leg injury. Would suggesting that playing football makes a person more prone to a head injury (another effect) undermine the first statement? No.

Answer choice (B): This is an Opposite answer that supports the conclusion. By showing that the key information did not disappear prior to the appearance of the anticollision device, the argument is strengthened because the likelihood that the device is at fault is increased.

Answer choice (C): This information has no effect on determining if the device causes the information to disappear from the screen because it references an event that has yet to occur.

Answer choice (D): This is the correct answer choice, and this answer falls into the third category for weakening a causal argument: "Show that although the effect exists, the cause did not occur." In this instance, the effect of information disappearing from the screen occurred prior to the creation of the supposed causal agent, the anticollision device.

Answer choice (E): This answer choice has no impact on the argument. We cannot make a judgment based on the size of the airport because the argument did not mention airport size or anything directly related to airport size.

Question #2. Must-CE. The correct answer choice is (C)

The causal relationship in this problem appears in the premise, and the argument is structured as follows:

Premise: Most antidepressant drugs cause weight gain.

Premise: Dieting can help reduce the amount of weight gained while taking such antidepressants

Conclusion: Some weight gain is unlikely to be preventable.

Note that the causal premise specifically states that "most" antidepressants cause weight gain, not necessarily all antidepressants. Also, the second premise specifically refers to antidepressants causing weight gain (the use of "such" indicates this). The second premise also indicates that the *amount gained* can be reduced, not that dieting can stop weight gain. Perhaps the antidepressants cause a twenty pound weight gain, but dieting can reduce that to a ten pound total gain.

The question stem is a Must Be True, and thus you must accept the stimulus information and find an answer that is proven by that information.

Answer choice (A): This is an Exaggerated answer. The stimulus indicates that *most* antidepressants cause weight gain, leaving open the possibility that some do not. This answer choice references *any* antidepressant drug. Further, the stimulus does not address the role of a physician or the advisability of prescribing certain drugs under certain conditions. The benefits of prescribing an antidepressant that causes weight gain to an overweight patient may well outweigh the negatives (pun intended).

Answer choice (B): This is also an Exaggerated answer. The stimulus allows for antidepressants that do not cause weight gain.

Answer choice (C): This is the correct answer choice. Some individuals taking antidepressants that cause weight gain will gain weight even though dieting can reduce the amount of the gain.

Answer choice (D): This is an Opposite answer. The stimulus and correct answer both indicate that people taking the weight gain-causing antidepressants will gain weight regardless of whether they diet. Thus, the weight gain cannot be attributed to a lack of dieting.

Answer choice (E): This answer is too strong. Not all patients necessarily take antidepressants that cause weight gain, so those that do not might not need to diet to maintain their weight. Also, some patients who do take weight gain-causing antidepressants might be too thin for their own good and could benefit from a weight gain-causing antidepressant.

Question #3. Weaken-CE. The correct answer choice is (C)

The premise contains information concerning a rise in the number of calls involving violent crimes compared to last year. This is where smart GMAT reading comes into play: does the argument say there is more crime, or does it say there are more *calls* reporting crime? Recognizing the difference is critical for successfully solving this problem. The conclusion about citizens being more likely to be victimized by a violent crime indicates the author believes the following causal relationship:

GNC = greater number of violent crimes
MC = more calls involving violent crimes

$$\underline{C} \qquad\qquad \underline{E}$$

$$\text{GNC} \longrightarrow \text{MC}$$

Literally, the author believes that there are more violent crimes and therefore the police are responding to more violent crime calls.

The question stem asks you to weaken the argument, and the correct answer falls into one of the five basic methods for weakening a causal argument.

Answer choice (A): This is an Opposite answer that strengthens the argument.

Answer choice (B): Because the argument is about "the average citizen of this town," information about victims of a certain age is not relevant.

Answer choice (C): This is the correct answer choice. By showing that people are more willing to report crimes (and thus call them in for response), an alternate cause for the rise in the number of calls is given.

Answer choice (D): This answer only addresses an effect of the concern over crime, and does not address the causal relationship that underlies the argument.

Answer choice (E): This answer does not address a possible rise in crime or the reasons for the rise in responses to calls involving violent crime.

Question #4. Weaken-CE. The correct answer choice is (B)

The premises contain correlations, and the conclusion makes a causal claim:

PC = adequate prenatal care
DR = decrease risk of low birth weight babies

$$\underline{C} \qquad\qquad \underline{E}$$

$$PC \longrightarrow DR$$

The question stem asks you to weaken the argument, and the correct answer falls into one of the five basic methods for weakening a causal argument.

Answer choice (A): The conclusion specifically states that mothers who had received adequate prenatal care were *less likely* to have low birth weight babies than mothers who had received inadequate prenatal care. Thus, although mothers who received inadequate prenatal care have a higher likelihood of having low birth weight babies, this likelihood still allows for many babies to be born of normal weight. In a later chapter we will explore the ways the GMAT uses numbers and statistics to confuse test takers, but for now, consider this analogy: The Detroit Tigers are more likely to lose a baseball game than any other team, but even so, they can still win a number of games. In the same way, the aforementioned mothers may be more likely to have low birth weight babies, but they can still give birth to babies of normal weight. Hence, answer choice (A) does not attack the argument.

Answer choice (B): This is the correct answer choice. The answer choice falls into the category of "Showing a statistical problem exists with the data used to make the causal statement." By indicating that mothers without prenatal care records are automatically classified as mothers receiving inadequate prenatal care, the answer undermines the relationship in the argument because the data used to make the conclusion is unreliable.

Answer choice (C): The conclusion is about low birth weight babies, not premature babies. Even if low birth weight babies were routinely classified as premature, that would not affect the conclusion.

Answer choice (D): Similar to answer choice (A), the likelihoods discussed in the stimulus allow for this possibility. Hence, this answer cannot hurt the argument.

Answer choice (E): If anything, this answer strengthens the argument since it shows that adequate prenatal care has a powerful positive effect.

Chapter Seven: Strengthen and Assumption Questions

The Second Family

With this chapter, we begin our exposition of the Second Family of questions. Two of the question types within this family—Strengthen and Assumption—are considered to be among the hardest Critical Reasoning question types. These two question types are closely related and will be examined consecutively in this chapter. The remaining Second Family question type—Resolve the Paradox—will be examined in the next chapter.

Although all Second Family question types are related by their shared information model, there are distinct differences between each question type that ultimately determine the exact nature of the correct answer. Your performance on these questions will depend on your ability to distinguish each question type and understand the task you must fulfill.

Some students compare the Second Family information model diagram to the Third Family (Weaken) model and assume the two groups are exact opposites. While Strengthen and Weaken questions require you to perform opposite tasks, there are many similarities between the two types in terms of how information is used in each question. Assumption questions are variations on the Strengthen theme.

In addition to the Primary Objectives, keep these fundamental rules in mind when approaching Strengthen and Assumption questions:

1. The stimulus will contain an argument. Because you are being asked about the author's reasoning, and reasoning requires a conclusion, an argument will almost always be present. In order to maximize your chances of success you must identify, isolate, and assess the premises and the conclusion of the argument. Only by understanding the structure of the argument can you gain the perspective necessary to understand the author's position.

2. Focus on the conclusion. Almost all correct answer choices impact the conclusion. The more you know about the specifics of the conclusion, the better armed you will be to differentiate between correct and incorrect answers.

3. The information in the stimulus is suspect. There are often reasoning errors present, and you must read the argument very carefully in

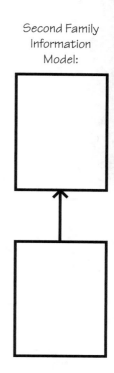

Second Family Information Model:

CR

order to know how to shore up the argument.

4. These questions often yield strong prephrases. Make sure you actively consider the range of possible answers before proceeding to the answer choices.

5. The answer choices are accepted as given, even if they include "new" information. Like Weaken questions, the answer choices to the problems in this chapter can bring into consideration information outside of or tangential to the stimulus. Just because a fact or idea is not mentioned in the stimulus is *not* grounds for dismissing an answer choice.

By following the Primary Objectives and focusing on the points above, you will maximize your chances for success on these questions.

The Difference Between Strengthen and Assumption Questions

Chapter Three contained a basic definition of each question type. Now we will expand those definitions and compare and contrast each type:

Strengthen questions ask you to support the argument in any way possible. This type of answer has great range, as the additional support provided by the answer choice could be relatively minor or major. Speaking in numerical terms, any answer choice that strengthens the argument, whether by 1% or by 100%, is correct.

An assumption is simply an unstated premise of the argument.

Assumption questions ask you to identify a statement that the argument assumes or supposes. An assumption is simply an unstated premise—what must be true in order for the argument to be true. An assumption can therefore be defined as something that is *necessary* for the argument to be true.

Because the two question types are confusingly similar, let's use a simple example to clarify the difference among the correct answer choices that appear with each question type:

An argument concludes that a teenager is an outstanding golfer.

In an Assumption question, the correct answer could be: "The teenager almost always hits the ball" or "The teenager almost never swings and misses the ball." Either statement is an assumption of the argument; otherwise how could the teenager be an outstanding golfer?

In a Strengthen question, the correct answer could be: "The teenager won a local club tournament." This answer choice supports the idea that the teenager is an outstanding golfer, but does not undeniably prove the teenager to be outstanding (what if the tournament was composed primarily of pre-teen players?) nor is the answer an assumption of the conclusion.

Admittedly, this is a simple example, but take a moment to examine the different types of answers to each question.

Strengthen Questions

Strengthen questions ask you to identify the answer choice that best supports the argument. The correct answer choice does not necessarily justify the argument, nor is the correct answer choice necessarily an assumption of the argument. The correct answer choice simply helps the argument in some way.

Most Strengthen question stems typically contain the following two features:

1. The stem uses the word "strengthen" or a synonym. Following are some examples of words or phrases used to indicate that your task is to strengthen the argument:

> strengthen
> support
> helps
> most justifies

2. The stem indicates that you should accept the answer choices as true, usually with the following phrase:

> "Which of the following, if true, ..."

Following are several Strengthen question stem examples:

"Which of the following, if true, most strengthens the argument?"

"Which of the following, if true, most strongly supports the statement above?"

"Which of the following, if true, does most to justify the conclusion above?"

"Each of the following, if true, supports the claim above EXCEPT:"

Whether you are finding an assumption of the argument or strengthening the conclusion, you are doing something positive for the stimulus.

How to Strengthen an Argument

Use the following points to effectively strengthen arguments:

1. Identify the conclusion—this is what you are trying to strengthen!

    Because Strengthen questions are the polar opposite of Weaken questions, the correct approach to supporting a GMAT argument is to help the author's conclusion. When evaluating an answer, ask yourself, "Would this answer choice assist the author in some way?" If so, you have the correct answer.

2. Personalize the argument.

    Personalizing allows you to see the argument from a very involved perspective and helps you assess the strength of each answer.

3. Look for weaknesses in the argument.

    This may seem like a strange recommendation since your task is to strengthen the argument, but a weak spot in an argument is tailor-made for an answer that eliminates that weakness. If you see a weakness or flaw in the argument, look for an answer that eliminates the weakness. In other words, close any gap or hole in the argument.

    Many Strengthen questions require students to find the missing link between a premise and the conclusion. These missing links are assumptions made by the author, and bringing an assumption to light strengthens the argument because it validates part of the author's thinking. This idea will be discussed further in the Assumption section of this chapter.

4. Arguments that contain analogies or use surveys rely upon the validity of those analogies and surveys. Answer choices that strengthen the analogy or survey, or establish their soundness, are usually correct.

5. Remember that the correct answer can strengthen the argument just a little or a lot. This variation is what makes these questions difficult.

Three Incorrect Answer Traps

The same type of wrong answer traps appear in Strengthen as in Weaken questions:

The stimuli for Strengthen and Weaken questions tend to be similar: both often contain faulty reasoning.

1. Opposite Answers. These answers do the exact opposite of what is needed—they weaken the argument. Because of their direct relation to the conclusion they are tempting, despite the fact that they result in consequences opposite of those intended.

2. Shell Game Answers. Remember, a Shell Game occurs when an idea or concept is raised in the stimulus and then a very similar idea appears in the answer choice, but the idea is changed just enough to be incorrect but still attractive. In Strengthen questions, the Shell Game is usually used to support a conclusion that is similar to, but slightly different from, the one presented in the stimulus.

3. Out of Scope Answers. These answers simply miss the point of the argument and support issues that are either unrelated to the argument or tangential to the argument.

These three answer types are not the only ways an answer choice can be attractively incorrect, but they appear frequently enough that you should be familiar with each form.

Strengthen Questions Analyzed

Please take a moment to complete the following problem:

1. Advertisement: At most jewelry stores, the person assessing the diamond is the person selling it so you can see why an assessor might say that a diamond is of higher quality than it really is. But because all diamonds sold at Gem World are certified in writing, you're assured of a fair price when purchasing a diamond from Gem World.

The reasoning in the advertisement would be most strengthened if which one of the following were true?

(A) Many jewelry stores other than Gem World also provide written certification of the quality of their diamonds.

(B) The certifications of diamonds at Gem World are written by people with years of experience in appraising gems.

(C) The diamonds sold at Gem World are generally of higher quality than those sold at other jewelry stores.

(D) The diamond market is so volatile that prices of the most expensive diamonds can change by hundreds of dollars from one day to the next.

(E) The written certifications of diamonds at Gem World are provided by an independent company of gem specialists.

The stimulus is prefaced by the word "advertisement." One quirk of the GMAT is that most GMAT stimuli preceded by this word contain faulty or deceptive logic. Thus, whenever you see this word prefacing a stimulus, be on the lookout for misleading or flawed reasoning.

The argument is constructed as follows:

> Premise: At most jewelry stores, the person assessing the diamond is the person selling it.

> Premise/Sub-conclusion:
> So you can see why an assessor might say that a diamond is of higher quality than it really is.

> Premise: All diamonds sold at Gem World are certified in writing,

> Conclusion: You're assured of a fair price when purchasing a diamond from Gem World.

Remember, a conclusion that is then used as a premise to support another conclusion is called a Sub-conclusion.

The first sentence contains a premise and conclusion that relies on the assumption that financial motivation might cause a person to lie about the quality of the item. According to the advertisement, at Gem World there is no such worry because the diamonds are certified in writing. Think for a moment—does that reasoning sound bulletproof? If you were standing there in the store and you were told that Gem World has written certification, wouldn't you ask *who* does the certification? This is the essence of personalizing the argument—place yourself inside the situation and think how you would react. As soon as you do that in this question, the weakness in the argument becomes apparent. Then, since this is a Strengthen question, you can look for an answer choice that eliminates this weakness. Answer choice (E) addresses the hole in the argument by indicating that the individuals who provide the written certification are not the same people who are selling the diamonds at Gem World.

There are other errors in the stimulus, such as assuming that a written certification equals a fair price. The certification may have no impact on the actual price of the diamond, or perhaps it could even be used to raise the price unjustly. These problems are ignored by the answer choices, and the test makers have that right.

Answer choice (A): The conclusion addresses the fair price of diamonds *at Gem World*, not other stores. Hence, the fact that other stores have written certification does not help the Gem World advertisement.

Answer choice (B): This is an answer many people keep as a Contender. The answer is incorrect because it fails to address the point raised in the first sentence, namely that the person assessing the diamond has a personal stake in the outcome. This "accountability" issue is the central point of the argument, and without knowing the source of the certifications, this answer does not strengthen the argument.

Answer choice (C): The argument asserts that a fair price is assured when purchasing *a* diamond at Gem World. No claim to comparative quality is made in the advertisement, and thus this answer does not strengthen the argument.

Answer choice (D): If anything, this answer may hurt the argument since it indicates that a fair price may not be obtainable at Gem World due to price volatility. If prices change daily, then Gem World may be selling diamonds at a price that does not reflect current market value. However, the answer choice specifically mentions "the most expensive diamonds" and there is no guarantee that Gem World carries diamonds in this price range. So, at best, the answer choice has no effect on the argument and is therefore incorrect.

Answer choice (E): This is the correct answer choice. As mentioned above, this answer addresses the separation of the certification writer from the seller and thereby strengthens the reasoning.

One thing that makes the GMAT difficult is that the test makers have so many options for testing you. In this question they could have chosen to strengthen a different part of the argument.

Please take a moment to complete the following problem:

2. Statistician: A financial magazine claimed that its survey of its subscribers showed that North Americans are more concerned about their personal finances than about politics. One question was: "Which do you think about more: politics or the joy of earning money?" This question is clearly biased. Also, the readers of the magazine are a self-selecting sample. Thus, there is reason to be skeptical about the conclusion drawn in the magazine's survey.

Each of the following, if true, would strengthen the statistician's argument EXCEPT:

(A) The credibility of the magazine has been called into question on a number of occasions.
(B) The conclusions drawn in most magazine surveys have eventually been disproved.
(C) Other surveys suggest that North Americans are just as concerned about politics as they are about finances.
(D) There is reason to be skeptical about the results of surveys that are biased and unrepresentative.
(E) Other surveys suggest that North Americans are concerned not only with politics and finances, but also with social issues.

This problem is more difficult than the previous problem, in part because this is an Except question. As you recall, in a Strengthen Except question the four incorrect answers strengthen the argument and the correct answer either has no effect on the argument or weakens the argument.

The statistician's statement begins with a variation of the classic GMAT construction "Some people claim..." As discussed in Chapter Two, when this construction is used, the author almost always argues against the claim made by the people. Here, a financial magazine has claimed that a survey proves that North Americans are more concerned about personal finances than politics. The statistician attacks two elements of the survey—there was a biased question and the sampling was faulty—and concludes the magazine's claim is questionable. Let us take a closer look at the statistician's two premises:

1. One question was biased.

    The key to understanding this claim is the phrasing of the question in the magazine: "the *joy* of earning money." By describing politics neutrally but describing earning money as a fun activity, the question inappropriately suggests to the magazine reader that one activity is more interesting than the other. This bias undermines the integrity of the survey.

2. The sample was self-selecting.

> A self-selecting sample is one in which individuals decide whether to participate. As you might expect, only those interested in the topic tend to participate and this creates a bias in the results. Because the survey was of subscribers to a financial magazine and not of the general North American population, those participating in the sample are not necessarily representative of North Americans and thus the magazine cannot reliably draw a conclusion about North Americans.

As mentioned previously, surveys that are conducted properly are considered reliable by the makers of the GMAT.

Hence, the statistician's position appears reasonably strong. Nonetheless, you are asked to eliminate four answers that will strengthen it further.

Earlier in this chapter we mentioned that the test makers believe in the validity of surveys, polls, etc. This question does not affect that position; in this situation the survey itself is the topic of discussion. Normally, that is not the case, and unless a survey or poll is shown to be questionable, you can typically accept the results knowing that the test makers believe survey results are valid.

Answer choice (A): This answer asserts that the magazine has credibility issues and thereby supports the conclusion that there should be skepticism regarding the magazine's activities.

Answer choice (B): This answer attacks the integrity of magazine surveys, and therefore supports the idea that there is reason to be skeptical of this magazine survey. Frankly, this is a weak answer because the validity of surveys in other magazines do not necessarily reflect on the validity of this magazine's survey. Nonetheless, only about five percent of test takers select this answer, as most people are able to recognize the intent of the test makers.

Answer choice (C): This answer supports the argument because other surveys suggest that North Americans are not more concerned about finances than politics. Because this counters the claim of the magazine, the answer supports the statistician's conclusion that there is reason to be skeptical of the magazine's survey.

Answer choice (D): Because the statistician has shown the survey to be biased and unrepresentative, this answer choice supports the statistician's conclusion.

Answer choice (E): This is the correct answer choice. The answer has no impact on the statistician's argument because a third topic—social issues—was not part of the magazine's survey, nor does this answer suggest anything about the preference of North Americans for finance or politics. Because the answer has no impact, it is correct in a StrengthenX question.

Causality and Strengthen Questions

Because Strengthen and Weaken questions require you to perform opposite tasks, to strengthen a causal conclusion you take the exact opposite approach that you would in a Weaken question.

In Strengthen questions, supporting a cause and effect relationship almost always consists of performing one of the following tasks:

A. Eliminate any alternate causes for the stated effect

Because the author believes there is only one cause (the stated cause in the argument), eliminating other possible causes strengthens the conclusion.

B. Show that when the cause occurs, the effect occurs

Because the author believes that the cause always produces the effect, any scenario where the cause occurs and the effect follows lends credibility to the conclusion. This type of answer can appear in the form of an example.

C. Show that when the cause does not occur, the effect does not occur

Using the reasoning in the previous point, any scenario where the cause does not occur and the effect does not occur supports the conclusion. This type of answer also can appear in the form of a example.

D. Eliminate the possibility that the stated relationship is reversed

Because the author believes that the cause and effect relationship is correctly stated, eliminating the possibility that the relationship is backwards (the claimed effect is actually the cause of the claimed cause) strengthens the conclusion.

E. Show that the data used to make the causal statement are accurate, or eliminate possible problems with the data

If the data used to make a causal statement are in error, then the validity of the causal claim is in question. Any information that eliminates error or reduces the possibility of error will support the argument.

Take a moment to consider each of these items, as they will reappear in the discussion of causality and Assumption questions—the approach will be identical for that combination.

Remember, to strengthen a causal argument you must perform tasks that are opposite of those that weaken a causal argument.

Please take a moment to complete the following problem:

3. Modern navigation systems, which are found in most of today's commercial aircraft, are made with low-power circuitry, which is more susceptible to interference than the vacuum-tube circuitry found in older planes. During landing, navigation systems receive radio signals from the airport to guide the plane to the runway. Recently, one plane with low-power circuitry veered off course during landing, its dials dimming, when a passenger turned on a laptop computer. Clearly, modern aircraft navigation systems are being put at risk by the electronic devices that passengers carry on board, such as cassette players and laptop computers.

Which one of the following, if true, LEAST strengthens the argument above?

(A) After the laptop computer was turned off, the plane regained course and its navigation instruments and dials returned to normal.

(B) When in use all electronic devices emit electromagnetic radiation, which is known to interfere with circuitry.

(C) No problems with navigational equipment or instrument dials have been reported on flights with no passenger-owned electronic devices on board.

(D) Significant electromagnetic radiation from portable electronic devices can travel up to eight meters, and some passenger seats on modern aircraft are located within four meters of the navigation systems.

(E) Planes were first equipped with low-power circuitry at about the same time portable electronic devices became popular.

The conclusion of the argument is based on the causal assumption that electronic devices cause a disturbance in low-power circuitry, creating an obvious danger:

ED = electronic devices
I = interference with low-power circuitry

$$\underline{C} \qquad\qquad \underline{E}$$

$$ED \longrightarrow I$$

The "Least equals Except" principle applies only when the terms appear in the question stem.

The question stem is a StrengthenX (remember, *Least* works like *Except* in question stems) and thus the four incorrect answers will each strengthen the argument. As you attack the answer choices, look for the five causal strengthening answer types discussed earlier.

Answer choice (A): This answer choice strengthens the argument by showing that when the cause is absent, the effect does not occur (Type C). Once the laptop was turned off, the cause disappeared, and according to the author's beliefs, the effect should then disappear as well.

Answer choice (B): This answer strengthens the argument by showing that the data used to make the conclusion are accurate (Type E). By stating that *all* electronic devices emit radiation, the answer choice closes a hole in the argument.

Answer choice (C): This answer choice strengthens the argument by showing that when the cause is absent, the effect does not occur (Type C).

Answer choice (D): This answer strengthens the argument by showing that the data used to make the conclusion are accurate (Type E). By showing that radiation can travel far enough to reach the cockpit, the cause is confirmed as possible.

Answer choice (E): This is the correct answer choice. The fact that the circuitry and electronic devices became popular at the same time does not offer any supporting evidence to the contention that the electronic devices cause the interference with the low power circuitry. This answer has no effect on the argument and is therefore correct.

This is the third Strengthen question in a row with (E) as the correct answer choice. This is not a pattern, just an incidental and meaningless result of the questions selected for this section.

Strengthen Question Type Review

Strengthen questions ask you to identify the answer choice that best supports the argument.

Use the following points to effectively strengthen arguments:

1. Identify the conclusion—this is what you are trying to strengthen!

2. Personalize the argument.

3. Look for weaknesses or holes in the argument.

The same type of wrong answer traps appear in Strengthen as in Weaken questions:

1. Opposite Answers.

2. Shell Game Answers.

3. Out of Scope Answers.

In Strengthen questions, supporting a cause and effect relationship almost always consists of performing one of the following tasks:

A. Eliminate any alternate causes for the stated effect

B. Show that when the cause occurs, the effect occurs

C. Show that when the cause does not occur, the effect does not occur

D. Eliminate the possibility that the stated relationship is reversed

E. Show that the data used to make the causal statement is accurate, or eliminate possible problems with the data

Although you do not need to memorize the types of wrong answer choices that appear in Strengthen questions, you must memorize the ways to strengthen a causal argument.

Strengthen Question Problem Set

Please complete the problem set and review the answer key and explanations. *Answers on Page 144*

1. According to the theory of continental drift, in prehistoric times, many of today's separate continents were part of a single huge landmass. As the plates on which this landmass rested began to move, the mass broke apart, and ocean water filled the newly created chasms. It is hypothesized, for example, that South America was once joined on its east coast with what is now the west coast of Africa.

    Which one of the following discoveries, if it were made, would most support the above hypothesis about South America and Africa?

    (A) A large band of ancient rock of a rare type along the east coast of South America is of the same type as a band on the west coast of Africa.
    (B) Many people today living in Brazil are genetically quite similar to many western Africans.
    (C) The climates of western Africa and of the east coast of South America resemble each other.
    (D) Some of the oldest tribes of people living in eastern South America speak languages linguistically similar to various languages spoken by certain western African peoples.
    (E) Several species of plants found in western Africa closely resemble plants growing in South America.

2. Medical doctor: Sleep deprivation is the cause of many social ills, ranging from irritability to potentially dangerous instances of impaired decision making. Most people today suffer from sleep deprivation to some degree. Therefore we should restructure the workday to allow people flexibility in scheduling their work hours.

    Which one of the following, if true, would most strengthen the medical doctor's argument?

    (A) The primary cause of sleep deprivation is overwork.
    (B) Employees would get more sleep if they had greater latitude in scheduling their work hours.
    (C) Individuals vary widely in the amount of sleep they require.
    (D) More people would suffer from sleep deprivation today than did in the past if the average number of hours worked per week had not decreased.
    (E) The extent of one's sleep deprivation is proportional to the length of one's workday.

3. Toxicologist: A survey of oil-refinery workers who work with MBTE, an ingredient currently used in some smog-reducing gasolines, found an alarming incidence of complaints about headaches, fatigue, and shortness of breath. Since gasoline containing MBTE will soon be widely used, we can expect an increased incidence of headaches, fatigue, and shortness of breath.

Each of the following, if true, strengthens the toxicologist's argument EXCEPT:

(A) Most oil-refinery workers who do not work with MBTE do not have serious health problems involving headaches, fatigue, and shortness of breath.

(B) Headaches, fatigue, and shortness of breath are among the symptoms of several medical conditions that are potentially serious threats to public health.

(C) Since the time when gasoline containing MBTE was first introduced in a few metropolitan areas, those areas reported an increase in the number of complaints about headaches, fatigue, and shortness of breath.

(D) Regions in which only gasoline containing MBTE is used have a much greater incidence of headaches, fatigue, and shortness of breath than do similar regions in which only MBTE-free gasoline is used.

(E) The oil-refinery workers surveyed were carefully selected to be representative of the broader population in their medical histories prior to exposure to MBTE, as well as in other relevant respects.

4. Galanin is a protein found in the brain. In an experiment, rats that consistently chose to eat fatty foods when offered a choice between lean and fatty foods were found to have significantly higher concentrations of galanin in their brains than did rats that consistently chose lean over fatty foods. These facts strongly support the conclusion that galanin causes rats to crave fatty foods.

Which one of the following, if true, most supports the argument?

(A) The craving for fatty foods does not invariably result in a rat's choosing those foods over lean foods.

(B) The brains of the rats that consistently chose to eat fatty foods did not contain significantly more fat than did the brains of rats that consistently chose lean foods.

(C) The chemical components of galanin are present in both fatty foods and lean foods.

(D) The rats that preferred fatty foods had the higher concentrations of galanin in their brains before they were offered fatty foods.

(E) Rats that metabolize fat less efficiently than do other rats develop high concentrations of galanin in their brains.

Question #1. Strengthen. The correct answer choice is (A)

The theory discussed in the stimulus is a real scientific hypothesis, often called the "Pangaea Theory." Alfred Wegener, who has been the subject of other GMAT questions, theorized in 1915 that Pangaea was a "supercontinent" composed of all landmasses. The theory is attractive because when the shape of today's continents is examined, the continents roughly fit together.

The question stem specifically asks you to strengthen the hypothesis that South America and Africa were once joined. To do so, you must identify evidence about the landmasses, as this is the evidence that the hypothesis in the stimulus relies upon.

Answer choice (A): This is the correct answer choice, and this is the only answer that addresses the land. By tying the rock strata of each continent together, the answer supports the idea that there was once a physical connection between the two continents. A high percentage of test takers correctly identify this answer.

Answer choice (B): This answer addresses people, not land. As with the earlier turtle question, the genetic similarity could be the result of humans from different areas sharing a large amount of DNA.

Answer choice (C): The similarity of climates does not help establish that the landmasses were once connected. For example, the similarity could be the result of both continents largely straddling the equator.

Answer choice (D): The language of the people does not mean the continents were connected. Australians and Americans share the same language, but this is because both areas were populated in modern times by English-speaking people from Britain.

Answer choice (E): The resemblance of plants in both areas does not suggest or strengthen the idea that the continents were joined. Plant similarities could be the result of climate, or perhaps of man-made propagation efforts.

CR

Question #2. Strengthen. The correct answer choice is (B)

Following is the structure of the medical doctor's argument:

Premise: Sleep deprivation is the cause of many social ills, ranging from irritability to potentially dangerous instances of impaired decision making.

Premise: Most people today suffer from sleep deprivation to some degree.

Conclusion: Therefore we should restructure the workday to allow people flexibility in scheduling their work hours.

The first premise contains a causal assertion (not a causal conclusion), and the second premise indicates that most people suffer from the stated cause. This combination would lead to the conclusion that most people have a social ill (which could be irritability or impaired decision making, or something in between). However, the conclusion in the argument leaps over this idea to conclude that the workday should be restructured. The missing link—or assumption—in the argument is that restructuring the workday would alleviate the sleep deprivation. As always, whenever you see a gap in the argument, you can strengthen the argument by eliminating that gap. By relating sleep to work, answer choice (B) closes the gap in the argument.

Answer choice (A): This is a tricky answer, and the key word is "overwork." While the author clearly believes that work schedules affect sleep, this does not mean that employees are being overworked. For example, a person may be sleep deprived because they have to come into work at 8 A.M. Perhaps they have children so they must get up very early to take care of their family. The person might then work a normal eight hour day and be sleep deprived not because of overwork but because of rising early.

Answer choice (B): This is the correct answer choice. By indicating that employees would avoid sleep deprivation with a revised workday, this answer affirms that the leap made in the argument is not an unreasonable one.

Answer choice (C): This answer may hurt the argument by suggesting that some individuals cannot be helped by the restructuring of the workday. At best, this answer has no impact on the argument because we already know that most people suffer from sleep deprivation to some degree.

Answer choice (D): This answer addresses the fact that the hours worked per week has decreased. But the argument is not about the average number of hours worked, but rather the way that those hours affect sleep. Thus, this answer does not help the conclusion that people should be allowed flexibility in scheduling.

Answer choice (E): The argument does not suggest that the workday will be shortened, only that the day will be structured so that people have more flexibility in scheduling their hours. Thus, knowing that the extent of sleep deprivation is proportional to the length of one's workday does not strengthen the argument.

Strengthen Problem Set Answer Key

Question #3. StrengthenX-CE. The correct answer choice is (B)

The conclusion of the argument reflects a causal relationship:

> MBTE = MBTE used
> II = increased incidence of headaches, fatigue, and shortness of breath

$$\underline{C} \qquad\qquad \underline{E}$$

$$\text{MBTE} \longrightarrow \text{II}$$

The question stem is a StrengthenX, and therefore the four wrong answers will support the argument. With a stimulus containing causal reasoning and a StrengthenX question, expect to see wrong answers that come from the five different "Causality and Strengthen Questions" categories to help the argument.

Answer choice (A): This answer shows that when the cause is not present, then the effect is not present. Thus, the answer strengthens the argument and is incorrect.

Answer choice (B): This is the correct answer choice. By indicating that the symptoms discussed in the stimulus can be the effects of several potentially serious public health threats, the author offers up possible alternate causes for the symptoms. These alternate causes would weaken the argument, and therefore this is the correct answer.

Answer choice (C): This answer affirms that when the cause occurs, then the effect occurs. The answer therefore strengthens the argument.

Answer choice (D): Like answer choice (C), this answer shows that when the cause is present, then the effect is present, and makes the case stronger by comparing that scenario to regions where the cause is absent, and the effect is not as pronounced as when the cause is present."

Answer choice (E): This answer choice strengthens the argument by showing that the data used to make the argument are accurate.

Question #4. Strengthen-CE. The correct answer choice is (D)

This stimulus also contains causal reasoning—the conclusion takes a correlation and turns it into a causal relationship:

G = higher concentration of galanin in the brain
CFF = crave fatty foods

$$\underset{G}{\underline{C}} \longrightarrow \underset{CFF}{\underline{E}}$$

As with all causal arguments, once you identify the causality, you must immediately look to the question stem and then attack. In this instance, the author simply assumes that galanin is the cause. Why can't the fatty foods lead to higher concentrations of galanin?

Answer choice (A): If anything, this answer choice may hurt the argument by showing that the cravings do not always lead to choosing fatty foods. But, since the author uses the phrase "consistently chose" to describe the choices of the rats, an answer stating that rats did not "invariably" choose fatty foods has no effect on the argument.

Answer choice (B): This is a Shell Game answer because the test makers try to get you to fall for an answer that addresses the wrong issue. The argument discusses the concentration of galanin in the brains of rats; no mention is made of the fat content of the brains of rats. This answer, which focuses on the fat content in the brains of rats, therefore offers no support to the argument. Even though the brain might not contain more fat, a rat could still consistently choose and eat foods with a higher fat content.

Answer choice (C): The argument is that galanin *in the brain* causes rats to crave fatty foods. The fact that galanin is in the food does not help that assertion and may actually hurt the argument.

Answer choice (D): This is the correct answer choice. The answer strengthens the argument by eliminating the possibility that the stated causal relationship is reversed: if the rats had higher concentrations of galanin prior to eating the fatty foods, then the fatty foods cannot be the cause of the higher concentration of galanin. As discussed earlier in the chapter, this approach strengthens the argument by making it more likely that the author had the original relationship correct.

Answer choice (E): This answer choice hurts the argument by suggesting that the causal relationship in the conclusion is reversed. Remember that in Strengthen questions you can expect to see Opposite answers, and this is one.

Assumption Questions

An argument can be analogized to a house: the premises are like walls, the conclusion is like the roof, and the assumptions are like the foundation.

As with a house foundation, an assumption is a hidden part of the structure, but critical to the integrity of the structure—all the other elements rest upon it.

For many students, Assumption questions are the most difficult type of Critical Reasoning problem. An assumption is simply an unstated premise of the argument; that is, an integral component of the argument that the author takes for granted and leaves unsaid. In our daily lives we make thousands of assumptions, but they make sense because they have context and we have experience with the way the world works. Think for a moment about the many assumptions required during the simple act of ordering a meal at a restaurant. You assume that: the prices on the menu are correct; the items on the menu are available; the description of the food is reasonably accurate; the waiter will understand what you say when you order; the food will not sicken or kill you; the restaurant will accept your payment, et cetera. In a GMAT question, you are faced with the difficult task of figuring out the author's mindset and determining what assumption he or she made when formulating the argument. This task is unlike any other on the GMAT.

Because an assumption is an integral component of the author's argument, a piece that must be true in order for the conclusion to be true, assumptions are *necessary* for the conclusion. Hence, the answer you select as correct must contain a statement that the author relies upon and is fully committed to in the argument. Think of an assumption as the foundation of the argument, a statement that the premises and conclusion rest upon. If an answer choice contains a statement that the author might only think *could* be true, or if the statement contains additional information that the author is not committed to, then the answer is incorrect. In many respects, an assumption can be considered a minimalist answer. Because the statement must be something the author believed when forming the argument, assumption answer choices cannot contain extraneous information. For example, let us say that an argument requires the assumption "all dogs are intelligent." The correct answer could be that statement, or even a subset statement such as "all black dogs are intelligent" or "all large dogs are intelligent" (black dogs and large dogs being subsets of the overall group of dogs, of course). But, additional information would rule out the answer, as in the following case: "All dogs and cats are intelligent." The additional information about cats is not part of the author's assumption, and would make the answer choice incorrect.

The correct answer to an Assumption question is a statement the author must believe in order for the conclusion to make sense.

Because assumptions are described as what must be true in order for the conclusion to be true, some students ask about the difference between Must Be True question answers and Assumption question answers. The difference is one that can be described as *before* versus *after*: Assumption answers contain statements that were *used to make* the conclusion; Must Be True answers contain statements that *follow from* the argument made in the stimulus. In both cases, however, there is a stringent requirement that must be met: Must Be True answers must be proven by the information in the stimulus; Assumption answers contain statements the author must believe in order for the conclusion to be valid.

Question stem examples:

"The argument in the passage depends on which of the following assumptions?"

"The argument above assumes that"

"The conclusion above is based on which of the following assumptions?"

"Which of the following is an assumption made in drawing the conclusion above?"

"The conclusion of the argument above cannot be true unless which of the following is true"

The Supporter/Defender Assumption Model™

Most GMAT publications and courses present a limited description of assumptions. An assumption is described solely as a linking statement, one that links two premises or links a premise to the conclusion. If no other description of assumptions is given, this limited presentation cheats students of the possibility of fully understanding the way assumptions work within arguments and the way they are tested by the makers of the exam.

On the GMAT, assumptions play one of two roles—the Supporter or the Defender. The Supporter role is the traditional linking role, where an assumption connects the pieces of the argument. Consider the following example:

> All male citizens of Athens had the right to vote. Therefore, Socrates had the right to vote in Athens.

The linking assumption is that Socrates was a male citizen of Athens. This connects the premise element of male citizens having the right to vote and the conclusion element that Socrates had the right to vote (affiliated assumptions are "Socrates was male" and "Socrates was a citizen of Athens").

Supporters often connect "new" or "rogue" pieces of information in the argument, and we typically use the term "new" or "rogue" to refer to an element that appears only in the conclusion or only in a premise. Thus, the conclusion in a Supporter argument often contains a piece of information not previously seen in the argument. In the example above, for instance, "Socrates" is a new element in the conclusion. These "new" elements create gaps in the argument, and Supporter assumptions on the GMAT are often relatively easy for students to identify because they can see the gap in the argument. The Supporter assumption, by definition, closes the hole by linking the elements together. Should you ever see a gap or a new element in the conclusion, a Supporter assumption answer will almost certainly close the gap or link the new element back to the premises.

If you see a weakness in the argument, look for an answer that eliminates the weakness or assumes that it does not exist. In other words, close the gaps in the argument.

The Defender role is entirely different, and Defender assumptions protect the argument by eliminating ideas that could weaken the argument. Consider our discussion from Chapter Two:

> "When you read a GMAT argument from the perspective of the author, keep in mind that he or she believes that their argument is sound. In other words, they do not knowingly make errors of reasoning. This is a fascinating point because it means that GMAT authors, as part of the GMAT world, function as if the points they raise and the conclusions they make have been well-considered and are airtight."

This fundamental truth of the GMAT has a dramatic impact when you consider the range of assumptions that must be made by a GMAT author. In order to believe the argument is "well-considered and airtight," an author must assume that every possible objection has been considered and rejected. Consider the following causal argument:

> People who read a lot are more intelligent than other people. Thus, reading must cause a person to be intelligent.

Although the conclusion is questionable (for example, the situation may be reversed: intelligence might be the cause of reading a lot), in the author's mind *all* other alternative explanations are assumed not to exist. Literally, the author assumes that any idea that would weaken the argument is impossible and cannot occur. Consider some of the statements that would attack the conclusion above:

> Sleeping more than eight hours causes a person to be intelligent.

> Regular exercise causes a person to be intelligent.

> A high-protein diet causes a person to be intelligent.

> Genetics cause a person to be intelligent.

Each of these ideas would undermine the conclusion, but they are assumed by the author *not* to be possible, and the author therefore makes the following assumptions in the original argument:

> Sleeping more than eight hours does not cause a person to be intelligent.

> Regular exercise does not cause a person to be intelligent.

> A high-protein diet does not cause a person to be intelligent.

> Genetics do not cause a person to be intelligent.

These assumptions protect the argument against statements that would undermine the conclusion. In this sense, they "defend" the argument by showing that a possible avenue of attack has been eliminated (assumed not to exist). As you can see, this list could go on and on because the author assumes *every* alternate cause does not exist. This means that although the argument only discussed reading and intelligence, we suddenly find ourselves with assumptions addressing a wide variety of topics that were never discussed in the stimulus. In a typical argument, there are an infinite number of assumptions possible, with most of those coming on the Defender side. Books and courses that focus solely on the Supporter role miss these assumptions, and students who do not understand how Defenders work will often summarily dismiss answer choices that later prove to be correct.

Supporter answer choices lend themselves well to prephrasing. Defender answers do not because there are too many possibilities to choose from.

By assuming that any threat to the argument does not exist, the author can present the argument and claim it is valid. If the author knew of imperfections and still presented the argument without a caveat, then the author would be hard-pressed to claim that this conclusion—especially an absolute one—was reasonable.

If there is no obvious weakness in the argument and you are faced with an Assumption question, expect to see a Defender answer choice.

Let's review the two roles played by assumptions:

Supporter Assumption: These assumptions link together new or rogue elements in the stimulus or fill logical gaps in the argument.

Defender Assumption: These assumptions contain statements that eliminate ideas or assertions that would undermine the conclusion. In this sense, they "defend" the argument by showing that a possible source of attack has been eliminated.

Let us examine examples of each type. Please take a moment to complete the following question:

1. Art historian: Great works of art have often elicited outrage when first presented; in Europe, Stravinsky's *Rite of Spring* prompted a riot, and Manet's *Déjeuner sur l'herbe* elicited outrage and derision. So, since it is clear that art is often shocking, we should not hesitate to use public funds to support works of art that many people find shocking.

    Which one of the following is an assumption that the art historian's argument requires in order for its conclusion to be properly drawn?

    (A) Most art is shocking.
    (B) Stravinsky and Manet received public funding for their art.
    (C) Art used to be more shocking than it currently is.
    (D) Public funds should support art.
    (E) Anything that shocks is art.

Once you understand the way Supporters work, they can often be predicted after you read an argument.

This is a very challenging Supporter assumption, and only about half of the test takers identify the correct answer. Take a close look at the conclusion: "we should not hesitate to use public funds to support works of art that many people find shocking." Did "public funds" appear anywhere else in the argument? No. Given our discussion about linking new elements that appear in the conclusion, you should have recognized that a new element was present and responded accordingly. Given that Supporters connect new elements, one would suspect that the correct answer would include this element and that either answer choice (B) or (D) was correct. Take a look at the argument structure:

Premise:	Great works of art have often elicited outrage when first presented; in Europe, Stravinsky's *Rite of Spring* prompted a riot, and Manet's *Déjeuner sur l'herbe* elicited outrage and derision.
Premise:	Art is often shocking.
Conclusion:	We should not hesitate to use public funds to support works of art that many people find shocking.

As is often the case with GMAT stimuli, the argument is based on real events. During the notorious 1913 premiere of the ballet *Rite of Spring*, the rioting crowd inside and outside the theater was so loud the pit orchestra director had difficulty conducting.

However, because the structure of the last sentence in the stimulus ("So, since...") suggests that the author uses the second premise to prove the conclusion, you should focus on the relationship between those two pieces. For the author to say that art is shocking and therefore art should be publicly funded, the author must assume that art is worthy of public support. This assumption is reflected in answer choice (D), the correct answer.

Answer choice (A): The author states that "art is often shocking" but does not assume that *most* art is shocking.

Answer choice (B): This is the most popular wrong answer choice. In the argument, is the author committed to believing that Stravinsky and Manet received public funding? Does the author need this statement in order for the rest of the argument to work? No. The author uses Stravinsky and Manet as examples of artists whose work caused shock, but the author never assumes that those individuals received public funding. Think for a moment—does the conclusion rest on the fact that Stravinsky and Manet received public funding?

Answer choice (C): The author makes no statement regarding the "shock level" of today's art, and thus there is no way to determine if an assumption has been made comparing the shock level of past and present art.

Answer choice (D): This is the correct answer choice. The answer acts as a Supporter and connects the elements in the final sentence.

Answer choice (E): The author states that "art is often shocking," but there is no indication that a conditional assumption has been made stating that anything that shocks is art.

Now let us look at a Defender assumption. Please take a moment to complete the following question:

2. In Western economies, more energy is used to operate buildings than to operate transportation. Much of the decline in energy consumption since the oil crisis of 1973 is due to more efficient use of energy in homes and offices. New building technologies, which make lighting, heating, and ventilation systems more efficient, have cut billions of dollars from energy bills in the West. Since energy savings from these efficiencies save several billion dollars per year today, we can conclude that 50 to 100 years from now they will save more than $200 billion per year (calculated in current dollars).

On which one of the following assumptions does the argument rely?

(A) Technology used to make buildings energy efficient will not become prohibitively expensive over the next century.

(B) Another oil crisis will occur in the next 50 to 100 years.

(C) Buildings will gradually become a less important consumer of energy than transportation.

(D) Energy bills in the West will be $200 billion lower in the next 50 to 100 years.

(E) Energy-efficient technologies based on new scientific principles will be introduced in the next 50 to 100 years.

Unlike Supporter assumptions, Defender assumptions are extremely hard to prephrase because there are so many possibilities for the test makers to choose from. The correct answer in this problem is a Defender, but it is unlikely that anyone could have predicted the answer. Compare this to the previous problem, where many students were able to prephrase the correct Supporter answer.

Now, focus on the final sentence of the argument, which contains a premise and conclusion:

Premise: Energy savings from these efficiencies [new building technologies] save several billion dollars per year today.

Conclusion: 50 to 100 years from now they will save more than $200 billion per year (calculated in current dollars).

So, according to the author, the new building technologies—which are already saving billions—will continue to do the same in the future and the savings will be even greater, relatively.

Answer choice (A): This is the correct answer choice, and a classic Defender. If the money-saving and energy-saving technology becomes too expensive to use in the next 100 years, the savings expected will not materialize. Because this idea would clearly weaken the argument, the author assumes that it does not exist, and answer choice (A) denies that the technology will become prohibitively expensive over the next century.

Answer choice (B): Although there has been an energy usage decline since the 1973 oil crisis, the author does not assume that there will be another crisis in the next 50 to 100 years. Look at the conclusion—does there seem to be a reliance on the idea in this answer? No.

Answer choice (C): Although this answer plays with the idea mentioned in the first sentence of the stimulus—that more energy is used to operate buildings than to operate transportation—no assumption is made that buildings will become a less important consumer of energy. True, buildings have saved billions in operating in costs, but the conclusion is about future savings and not about comparing buildings to transportation.

Answer choice (D): The argument is specific about technologies *saving* more than $200 billion per year; the author does not assume that the *total* bill in the next 50 to 100 years will be lower by $200 billion.

Answer choice (E): The argument is about current technologies saving money in the future. The author does not make an assumption regarding new technologies being introduced in the future.

The Assumption Negation Technique™

Do not use the Assumption Negation Technique on all five answer choices. The process is too time-consuming and you can usually knock out a few answer choices without working too hard. Only apply the technique once you have narrowed the field.

Only a few types of GMAT questions allow you to double-check your answer. Assumption questions are one of those types, and you should use the Assumption Negation Technique to decide between Contenders or to confirm that the answer you have chosen is correct.

The purpose of this technique is to take an Assumption question, which is generally difficult for most students, and turn it into a Weaken question, which is easier for most students. *This technique can only be used on Assumption questions.* To apply the technique take the following steps:

1. Logically negate the answer choices under consideration.

   We will discuss negation later in this section, but negating a statement means to alter the sentence so the meaning is logically opposite of what was originally stated. Negation largely consists of taking a "not" out of a sentence when one is present, or putting a "not" in a sentence if one is not present. For example, "The congressman always votes for gun control" becomes "The congressman does not always vote for gun control" when properly negated.

2. The negated answer choice that attacks the argument will be the correct answer.

   When the correct answer choice is negated, the answer *must* weaken the argument. This will occur because of the *necessary* nature of an assumption.

   The consequence of negating an assumption is that the validity of the conclusion is called into question. In other words, when you take away (negate) an assumption—a building block of the argument—it calls into question the integrity of the entire reasoning structure. Accordingly, negating the answer choices turns an Assumption question into a Weaken question.

Negating Statements

Negating a statement consists of creating the *logical* opposite of the statement. The logical opposite is the statement that denies the truth of the original statement, and a logical opposite is different than the *polar* opposite. For example, consider the following statement:

> I went to the beach every day last week.

The logical opposite is the statement requiring the least amount of "work" to negate the original statement:

> I did not go to the beach every day last week.

The polar opposite typically goes much further:

> I did not go to the beach *any* day last week.

For GMAT purposes, the logical opposite is the statement you should seek when negating, and in order to do this you must understand logical opposition.

Logical Opposition

The concept of logical opposition appears frequently on the GMAT in a variety of forms. A complete knowledge of the logical opposites that most often appear will provide you with a framework that eliminates uncertainties and ultimately leads to skilled GMAT performance. Consider the following question:

> What is the logical opposite of sweet?

Most people reply "sour" to the above question. While "sour" is an opposite of "sweet," it is considered the polar opposite of "sweet," not the logical opposite. A logical opposite will always completely divide the subject under consideration into two parts. Sweet and sour fail as logical opposites since tastes such as bland or bitter remain unclassified. The correct logical opposite of "sweet" is in fact "not sweet." "Sweet" and "not sweet" divide the taste spectrum into two complete parts, and tastes such as bland and bitter now clearly fall into the "not sweet" category. This same type of oppositional reasoning also applies to other everyday subjects such as color (what is the logical opposite of white?) and temperature (what is the logical opposite of hot?).

To help visualize pairs of opposites within a subject, we use an Opposition Construct. An Opposition Construct efficiently summarizes subjects within a limited spectrum of possibilities, such as quantity:

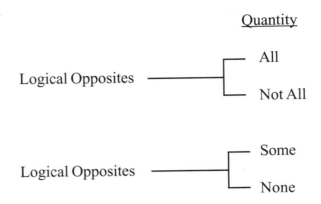

In this quantity construct, the range of possibilities extends from All to None. Thus, these two "ends" are polar opposites. There are also two pairs of logical opposites: All versus Not All and Some versus None. These logical opposites hold in both directions: for example, Some is the precise logical opposite of None, and None is the precise logical opposite of Some. The relationship between the four logical possibilities of quantity becomes more complex when we examine pairs such as Some and All. Imagine for a moment that we have between 0 and 100 marbles. According to the above construct, each logical possibility represents the following:

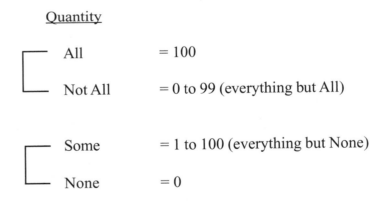

By looking closely at the quantities each possibility represents, we can see that Some (1 to 100) actually includes All (100). This makes sense because Some, if it is to be the exact logical opposite of None, should include every other possibility besides None. The same relationship also holds true for Not All (0 to 99) and None (0).

The relationship between Some and Not All is also interesting. Some (1 to 100) and Not All (0 to 99) are largely the same, but they differ significantly at the extremes. Some actually includes All, the opposite of Not All, and Not All includes None, the opposite of Some. As a point of definition Not All is the same as Some Are Not.

The same line of reasoning applies to other subjects that often appear on the GMAT:

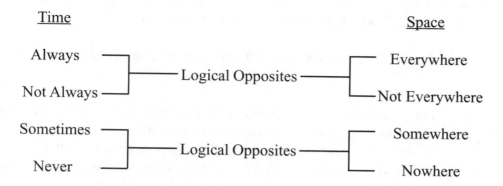

The Time and Space constructs are very similar to the Quantity construct. For example, Always is somewhat equivalent to "All of the time." Everywhere could be said to be "All of the space." Thus, learning one of these constructs makes it easy to learn the other two.

Three Quirks of Assumption Question Answer Choices

Over the years, certain recurring traits have appeared in Assumption answer choices. Recognizing these quirks may help you eliminate wrong answers or more quickly identify the correct answer at crunch time.

1. Watch for answers starting with the phrase "at least one" or "at least some."

    For some reason, when an Assumption answer choice starts with either of the above constructions the chances are unusually high that the answer will be correct. However, if you spot an answer with that construction, do not simply assume the answer is correct; instead, use the proper negation ("None") and check the answer with the Assumption Negation Technique.

2. Avoid answers that claim an idea was the most important consideration for the author.

    These answers typically use constructions such as "the primary purpose," "the top priority," or "the main factor." In every Assumption question these answers have been wrong. And, unless, the author specifically discusses the prioritization of ideas in the stimulus, these answers will continue to be wrong because an author can always claim that the idea under discussion was very important but not necessarily the most important idea.

3. Watch for the use of "not" or negatives in assumption answer choices.

    Because most students are conditioned to think of assumptions as positive connecting elements, the appearance of a negative in an Assumption answer choice often causes the answer to be classified a Loser. Do not rule out a negative answer choice just because you are used to seeing assumptions as a positive part of the argument. As we have seen with Defender answer choices, one role an assumption can play is to eliminate ideas that could attack the argument. To do so, Defender answer choices frequently contain negative terms such as "no," "not," and "never." One benefit of this negative language is that Defender answer choices can usually be negated quite easily.

In an Assumption question, there can be only one answer that will hurt the argument when negated. If you negate the answers and think that two or more hurt the argument, you have made a mistake.

Assumptions and Causality

The central assumption of causality was stated in the last chapter:

> "When a GMAT speaker concludes that one occurrence caused another, that speaker also assumes that the stated cause is the *only* possible cause of the effect and that the stated cause will *always* produce the effect."

Thus, because the author always assumes that the stated cause is the only cause, Assumption answer choices tend to work exactly like Strengthen answer choices in arguments with causal reasoning. The correct answer to an Assumption question will normally fit one of the following categories:

A. Eliminates an alternate cause for the stated effect

Because the author believes there is only one cause (the stated cause in the argument), the author assumes no other cause exists.

B. Shows that when the cause occurs, the effect occurs

Because the author believes that the cause always produces the effect, assumption answers will affirm this relationship.

C. Shows that when the cause does not occur, the effect does not occur

Using the reasoning in the previous point, the author will always assume that when the cause does not occur, the effect will not occur.

D. Eliminates the possibility that the stated relationship is reversed

Because the author believes that the cause-and-effect relationship is correctly stated, the author assumes that the relationship cannot be backwards (the claimed effect is actually the cause of the claimed cause).

E. Shows that the data used to make the causal statement are accurate, or eliminates possible problems with the data

If the data used to make a causal statement are in error, then the validity of the causal claim is in question. The author assumes that this cannot be the case and that the data are accurate.

The above categories should be easy to identify because you should have already memorized them from the Strengthen question section. From now on, when you encounter Assumption questions containing causal reasoning, you will be amazed at how obvious the correct answer will seem. These types of patterns within questions are what make improvement on the GMAT possible, and when you become comfortable with the ideas, your speed will also increase.

Please take a moment to complete the following problem:

3. Doctors in Britain have long suspected that patients who wear tinted eyeglasses are abnormally prone to depression and hypochondria. Psychological tests given there to hospital patients admitted for physical complaints like heart pain and digestive distress confirmed such a relationship. Perhaps people whose relationship to the world is psychologically painful choose such glasses to reduce visual stimulation, which is perceived as irritating. At any rate, it can be concluded that when such glasses are worn, it is because the wearer has a tendency to be depressed or hypochondriacal.

The argument assumes which one of the following?

(A) Depression is not caused in some cases by an organic condition of the body.
(B) Wearers do not think of the tinted glasses as a means of distancing themselves from other people.
(C) Depression can have many causes, including actual conditions about which it is reasonable for anyone to be depressed.
(D) For hypochondriacs wearing tinted glasses, the glasses serve as a visual signal to others that the wearer's health is delicate.
(E) The tinting does not dim light to the eye enough to depress the wearer's mood substantially.

The conclusion of this argument is causal in nature ("because" is the indicator):

Depression = tendency to be depressed or hypochondriacal
Glasses = glasses are worn

$$\underline{C} \qquad\qquad \underline{E}$$

$$\text{Depression} \longrightarrow \text{Glasses}$$

The answer choices are very interesting as they all relate to either the cause or effect, or both. Answer choices (A) and (C) are similar in that they both discuss what causes depression (the cause of the cause). But the author has made no assumption about what *causes* depression, only that depression causes a person to wear glasses. Therefore, both of these answers are incorrect. Similarly, answer choices (B) and (D) both discuss the effects of wearing glasses (the effects of the effect). Again, this is not a part of the author's argument. Because answer choices (A), (B), (C), and (D) discuss issues that occur either "before" or "after" the causal relationship in the conclusion, they are incorrect.

Answer choice (E): This is the correct answer choice. Answer choice (E) is a Defender that eliminates the possibility that the stated relationship is reversed (Type D in the Assumptions and Causality discussion). Remember, if the glasses actually cause the wearer to be depressed, this scenario would hurt the argument, so the author assumes the possibility cannot exist. Note how tricky this answer could be, especially if you had not been exposed to the way the test makers think about causality and assumptions. With the right information, the answer can be identified as part of a larger pattern on the GMAT, and this allows you to solve the problem quickly and confidently. While it may take a bit of work to memorize the different assumptions inherent in causal arguments, the payoff is more than worth the effort.

Assumption—Fill in the Blank Questions

A number of GMAT questions contain a stimulus that ends with a blank space. The question stem then asks you to fill in the blank with an appropriate answer. While not one of the most common question types, a Fill in the Blank question can throw off test takers who are surprised by the unusual stimulus formation. No need to worry; on the GMAT these are almost always Assumption questions in disguise (and when they are not Assumption questions they are Must Be True/Main Point questions—more on this in a moment).

The placement of the blank in the stimulus is not random—the blank is always at the very end of the stimulus. There is a premise indicator at the start of the sentence to help you recognize that you are being asked to fill in a missing premise, which is of course the same as an assumption. In order to achieve this goal, you must read the stimulus for clues revealing the direction of the argument and the author's beliefs.

First, here are some sample sentences to give you an example of how the sentence with the blank appears:

> "...because _____."

> "...is the fact that _____."

> "...is that _____."

> "...since _____."

As you can see, just prior to the blank is a premise indicator; this is the signal that you must supply an assumption of the argument.

Assumption Question Type Review

An assumption is simply an unstated premise of the argument; that is, an integral component of the argument that the author takes for granted and leaves unsaid.

The answer you select as correct must contain a statement that the author relies upon and is fully committed to in the argument.

On the GMAT, assumptions play one of two roles: the Supporter or the Defender:

Supporter Assumption: These assumptions link together new or rogue elements in the stimulus or fill logical gaps in the argument.

Defender Assumption: These assumptions contain statements that eliminate ideas or assertions that would undermine the conclusion. In this sense, they "defend" the argument by showing that a possible avenue of attack has been eliminated (assumed not to exist).

Use the Assumption Negation Technique to decide between Contenders or to confirm that the answer you have chosen is correct. The purpose of this technique is to take an Assumption question, which is generally more difficult, and turn it into a Weaken question. *This technique can only be used on Assumption questions.* Take the following steps to apply this technique:

1. Logically negate the answer choices under consideration.

2. The negated answer choice that attacks the argument will be the correct answer.

Negating a statement consists of creating the *logical* opposite of the statement. The logical opposite is the statement that denies the truth of the original statement, and the logical opposite is different than the polar opposite.

Assumption answer choices tend to work exactly like Strengthen answer choices in arguments with causal reasoning. Because the author always assumes the stated cause is the only cause, the correct answer to an Assumption question will normally fit one of the following categories:

A. Eliminates an alternate cause for the stated effect

B. Shows that when the cause occurs, the effect occurs

C. Shows that when the cause does not occur, the effect does not occur

D. Eliminates the possibility that the stated relationship is reversed

E. Shows that the data used to make the causal statement are accurate, or eliminates possible problems with the data

Fill in the Blank questions are almost always Assumption questions in disguise (and when they are not Assumption questions they are Must Be True/Main Point questions). The placement of the blank is always at the very end of the stimulus. There is a premise indicator at the start of the sentence to help you recognize that you are being asked to fill in a missing premise, which is of course the same as an assumption. In order to achieve this goal, you must read the stimulus for clues revealing the direction of the argument and the author's beliefs.

Please complete the problem set and review the answer key and explanations. *Answers on Page 169*

1. Barnes: The two newest employees at this company have salaries that are too high for the simple tasks normally assigned to new employees and duties that are too complex for inexperienced workers. Hence, the salaries and the complexity of the duties of these two newest employees should be reduced.

    Which one of the following is an assumption on which Barnes's argument depends?

    (A) The duties of the two newest employees are not less complex than any others in the company.
    (B) It is because of the complex duties assigned that the two newest employees are being paid more than is usually paid to newly hired employees.
    (C) The two newest employees are not experienced at their occupations.
    (D) Barnes was not hired at a higher-than-average starting salary.
    (E) The salaries of the two newest employees are no higher than the salaries that other companies pay for workers with a similar level of experience.

2. The current pattern of human consumption of resources, in which we rely on nonrenewable resources, for example metal ore, must eventually change. Since there is only so much metal ore available, ultimately we must either do without or turn to renewable resources to take its place.

    Which one of the following is an assumption required by the argument?

    (A) There are renewable resource replacements for all of the nonrenewable resources currently being consumed.
    (B) We cannot indefinitely replace exhausted nonrenewable resources with other nonrenewable resources.
    (C) A renewable resource cannot be exhausted by human consumption.
    (D) Consumption of nonrenewable resources will not continue to increase in the near future.
    (E) Ultimately we cannot do without nonrenewable resources.

Assumption Question Problem Set

3. In humans, ingested protein is broken down into amino acids, all of which must compete to enter the brain. Subsequent ingestion of sugars leads to the production of insulin, a hormone that breaks down the sugars and also rids the bloodstream of residual amino acids, except for tryptophan. Tryptophan then slips into the brain uncontested and is transformed into the chemical serotonin, increasing the brain's serotonin level. Thus, sugars can play a major role in mood elevation, helping one to feel relaxed and anxiety-free.

    Which one of the following is an assumption on which the argument depends?

    (A) Elevation of mood and freedom from anxiety require increasing the level of serotonin in the brain.
    (B) Failure to consume foods rich in sugars results in anxiety and a lowering of mood.
    (C) Serotonin can be produced naturally only if tryptophan is present in the bloodstream.
    (D) Increasing the level of serotonin in the brain promotes relaxation and freedom from anxiety.
    (E) The consumption of protein-rich foods results in anxiety and a lowering of mood.

4. Publicity campaigns for endangered species are unlikely to have much impact on the most important environmental problems, for while the ease of attributing feelings to large mammals facilitates evoking sympathy for them, it is more difficult to elicit sympathy for other kinds of organisms, such as the soil microorganisms on which large ecosystems and agriculture depend.

    Which one of the following is an assumption on which the argument depends?

    (A) The most important environmental problems involve endangered species other than large mammals.
    (B) Microorganisms cannot experience pain or have other feelings.
    (C) Publicity campaigns for the environment are the most effective when they elicit sympathy for some organism.
    (D) People ignore environmental problems unless they believe the problems will affect creatures with which they sympathize.
    (E) An organism can be environmentally significant only if it affects large ecosystems or agriculture.

Question #1. Assumption. The correct answer choice is (C)

The stimulus to this problem contains a Shell Game, and you must read closely in order to identify it: in the first sentence the author equates "new employees" with "inexperienced workers." Of course, a new employee is not necessarily inexperienced (the employee could have transferred from another company, etc.). The assumption that new employees are inexperienced is reflected in the correct answer, (C).

Answer choice (A): The author notes that the duties of the two new employees are too complex for them, but the author does not compare or imply a comparison to the tasks of other workers.

Answer choice (B): The author makes no assumption as to why the two new employees are being paid the salary they receive, only that their salary should be reduced. For example, the reason the employees are paid more could be that they are related to the owner of the company.

Answer choice (C): This is the correct answer choice, a Supporter.

Answer choice (D): This answer is an immediate Loser. No discussion or assumption is made about Barnes' salary.

Answer choice (E): This answer would hurt the argument, and therefore it can never be an assumption of the argument.

Question #2. Assumption. The correct answer choice is (B)

The structure of the argument is as follows:

Premise:	There is only so much metal ore available.
Subconclusion/ Premise:	Ultimately we must either do without or turn to renewable resources to take its place.
Conclusion:	The current pattern of human consumption of resources, in which we rely on nonrenewable resources, for example metal ore, must eventually change.

At first glance the argument does not seem to have any holes. This would suggest a Defender answer is coming, and indeed that is the case.

Answer choice (A): The author does not need to assume this statement because the stimulus specifically indicates that "we must either *do without* or turn to renewable resources." Since doing without is an option, the author is not assuming there are renewable replacements for all nonrenewable resources currently being consumed.

Assumption Problem Set Answer Key

Answer choice (B): This is the correct answer choice. This answer defends the conclusion that the consumption pattern must change by indicating that it would *not* be possible to simply replace one nonrenewable resource with another nonrenewable resource. If this answer did not make sense at first glance, you should have noted the negative language and then negated the answer. Using the Assumption Negation Technique, the following would clearly attack the conclusion: "We *can* indefinitely replace exhausted nonrenewable resources with other nonrenewable resources." If the nonrenewable resources can be indefinitely replaced, why do we need to change our consumption habits?

Answer choice (C): The author's argument concerns changing current consumption habits. Although the author does suggest turning to renewable resources, this alone would represent a change. The author does not make a long-term assumption that renewable resources can never be depleted. When faced with the negation of the answer choice, the author would likely reply: "If that eventuality does occur, then perhaps we will have to do without. In the meantime, we still need to change our consumption habits." As you can see, the negation has not undermined the author's position, and so this answer is incorrect.

Answer choice (D): The author does not make statements or assumptions about actual consumption patterns in the *near future*, only statements regarding what must *eventually* occur.

Answer choice (E): This answer, when rephrased to eliminate the double negative, reads as "Ultimately we must have nonrenewable resources." Because this answer hurts the argument, the answer is incorrect.

Question #3. Assumption. The correct answer choice is (D)

The importance of this problem is not just in answering it correctly, but also in answering it quickly. A major portion of GMAT success is speed related, and a question like this is an opportunity to gain time. The first step is to recognize the argument structure:

Premise:	In humans, ingested protein is broken down into amino acids, all of which must compete to enter the brain.
Premise:	Subsequent ingestion of sugars leads to the production of insulin, a hormone that breaks down the sugars and also rids the bloodstream of residual amino acids, except for tryptophan.
Premise:	Tryptophan then slips into the brain uncontested and is transformed into the chemical serotonin, increasing the brain's serotonin level.
Conclusion:	Sugars can play a major role in mood elevation, helping one to feel relaxed and anxiety-free.

At this point in your preparation, you should constantly be on the lookout for new elements that appear in the conclusion. This problem contains the new conclusion element of "a major role in mood elevation, helping one to feel relaxed and anxiety-free." Because this element immediately follows the assertion that the brain's serotonin level has been increased, you should attack the answer choices by looking for an answer that fits the Supporter relationship that an increase serotonin leads to an elevated mood. Only answer choices (A) and (D) contain these two elements, and you should examine them first as you seek to accelerate through this problem:

Answer choice (A): Although the author assumes that raising the level of serotonin is sufficient to elevate mood, this answer claims that it is necessary. Hence, this answer is incorrect.

Answer choice (D): This is the correct answer choice. The author states that after the action of the sugars, more serotonin enters the brain. The author then concludes that this leads to a mood elevation. Thus, the author assumes that serotonin has an effect on the mood level.

Answer choice (B): The argument refers to what happens when sugars are ingested. No assumption is made about what occurs when foods rich in sugars are not ingested.

Answer choice (C): Although the argument states that tryptophan is transformed into serotonin, no assumption is made that this is the only way serotonin is produced.

Answer choice (E): The author does not assume the statement in this answer. We know from the first sentence of the stimulus that ingested protein is broken down into amino acids which compete to enter the brain. This competition could result in mood elevation even without the ingestion of sugars since some amino acids will enter the brain (some could be tryptophan, for example). Thus, since the author's argument contains a scenario that would allow for the opposite of this answer choice to occur, this answer is not an assumption of the argument.

Question #4. Assumption. The correct answer choice is (A)

This is a challenging problem because two of the wrong answer choices are attractive. The argument itself is not overly complex, but you must pay attention to the language. Consider the conclusion of the argument:

> "Publicity campaigns for endangered species are unlikely to have much impact on the most important environmental problems."

Answer choice (A): This is the correct answer choice. Ask yourself, why is it that these campaigns are unlikely to have much impact on the *most important* problems? According to the premises, the reason is that "it is more difficult to elicit sympathy for other kinds of organisms [than large mammals]." The reasoning shows that the author believes there is a connection between the important problems and organisms that are not large mammals. This Supporter connection is perfectly reflected in answer choice (A), the correct answer. Again, when faced with an Assumption question, remember to look for connections between rogue elements in the argument, and then seek that connection in the answer choices.

Answer choice (B): The argument is about eliciting sympathy, and no assumption is made about microorganisms *experiencing* pain.

Assumption Problem Set Answer Key

Answer choice (C): This is a Shell Game answer. The conclusion is specific about "publicity campaigns for endangered species" as they relate to environmental problems. This answer refers to "publicity campaigns" in general—a different concept. It may be that the most effective publicity campaign for the environment has nothing to do with organisms. Consequently, this answer is not an assumption of the argument.

Answer choice (D): This answer choice is worded too strongly and is an Exaggerated answer. "Ignore" goes further than what the author implies. The author indicates that it is "*more difficult* to elicit sympathy for other kinds of organisms," but the author does not say it is impossible to get sympathy from individuals if a non-large mammal is involved. Further, the argument is specific about the impact on the "most important" problems, and this answer goes well beyond that domain.

Answer choice (E): The microorganisms discussed at the end of the argument are an example ("such as"); therefore, the author does not assume this type of relationship must be true in order for the conclusion to be true.

CHAPTER EIGHT: RESOLVE THE PARADOX QUESTIONS

Resolve the Paradox Questions

Resolve the Paradox questions are generally easy to spot because of their distinctive stimuli: each stimulus presents a situation where two ideas or occurrences contradict each other. Because most people are very good at recognizing these paradox scenarios, they usually know after reading the stimulus that a Resolve the Paradox question is coming up.

Stimulus Peculiarities

Besides the discrepant or contradictory facts, most Resolve the Paradox stimuli contain the following features:

1. No conclusion

   One of the hallmarks of a Resolve the Paradox question is that the stimulus does not contain a conclusion. The author is not attempting to persuade you, he or she just presents two sets of contradictory facts. Thus, when you read a stimulus without a conclusion that contains a paradox, expect to see a Resolve question. If you read a fact set that does not contain a paradox, expect to see a Must Be True question or a Cannot Be True question (less likely).

2. Language of contradiction

   In order to present a paradox, the test makers use language that signals a contradiction is present, such as:

   > But
   > However
   > Yet
   > Although
   > Paradoxically
   > Surprisingly

If you can recognize the paradox present in the stimulus, you will have a head start on prephrasing the answer and completing the problem more quickly.

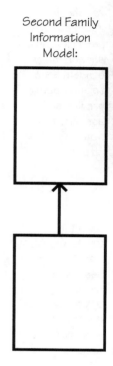

Second Family Information Model:

CR

Question Stem Features

Resolve the Paradox question stems are easy to identify, and typically contain the following features:

1. An indication that the answer choices should be accepted as true

    Because Resolve the Paradox questions fall into the Second Question Family, you must accept the answer choices as true and then see if they resolve the paradox. Typically, the question stem will contain a phrase such as, "which of the *following*, if true, ..."

2. Key words that indicate your task is to resolve a problem

    To convey the nature of your task, Resolve the Paradox question stems usually use words from both of the lists below. The first list contains words used to describe the action you must take, the second list contains words used to describe the paradox present in the stimulus:

Action	Problem
Resolve	Paradox
Explain	Discrepancy
Reconcile	Contradiction
	Conflict
	Puzzle

Here are several Resolve the Paradox question stem examples:

"Which of the following, if true, most helps to resolve the apparent paradox?"

"Which of the following, if true, most helps to explain the discrepancy described above?"

"Which of the following, if true, best reconciles the seeming discrepancy described above?"

"Which of the following hypotheses best explains the contrast described above?"

Active Resolution

When first presented with a Resolve question, most students seek an answer choice that destroys or disproves one side of the situation. They follow the reasoning that if one side can be proven false, then the paradox will be eliminated. While this is true, the test makers know that such an answer would be obvious (it would simply contradict part of the facts given in the stimulus) and thus this type of answer does not appear in these questions. Instead, the correct answer will actively resolve the paradox, that is, it will allow both sides to be factually correct and it will either explain how the situation came into being or add a piece of information that shows how the two ideas or occurrences can coexist.

Because you are not seeking to disprove one side of the situation, you must select the answer choice that contains a *possible cause* of the situation. So, when examining answers, ask yourself if the answer choice could lead to the situation in the stimulus. If so, the answer is correct.

Please take a moment to complete the following problem:

1. Provinces and states with stringent car safety requirements, including required use of seat belts and annual safety inspections, have on average higher rates of accidents per kilometer driven than do provinces and states with less stringent requirements. Nevertheless, most highway safety experts agree that more stringent requirements do reduce accident rates.

   Which one of the following, if true, most helps to reconcile the safety experts' belief with the apparently contrary evidence described above?

   (A) Annual safety inspections ensure that car tires are replaced before they grow old.
   (B) Drivers often become overconfident after their cars have passed a thorough safety inspection.
   (C) The roads in provinces and states with stringent car safety programs are far more congested and therefore dangerous than in other provinces and states.
   (D) Psychological studies show that drivers who regularly wear seat belts often come to think of themselves as serious drivers, which for a few people discourages reckless driving.
   (E) Provinces and states with stringent car safety requirements have, on average, many more kilometers of roads then do other provinces and states.

The correct answer will positively resolve the paradox so that both sides are true and the conditions in the stimulus have been met.

If an answer supports or proves only one side of the paradox, that answer will be incorrect. The correct answer must show how both sides coexist.

The paradox in the argument is that the provinces and states that have more stringent safety requirements also have higher average rates of accidents. Even so, experts agree that the more stringent requirements actually are effective. This type of "surprisingly low/high rate of success" scenario has appeared in a number of Resolve the Paradox questions, including the following:

An anti-theft device is known to reduce theft, but cars using the anti-theft device are stolen at a higher rate than cars without the device.

Explanation: The device is placed on highly desirable cars that are prone to being stolen, and the device actually lessens the rate at which they are stolen.

A surgeon has a low success rate while operating, but the director of the hospital claims the surgeon is the best on the staff.

Explanation: The surgeon operates on the most complex and challenging cases.

A bill collector has the lowest rate of success in collecting bills, but his manager claims he is the best in the field.

Explanation: The bill collector is assigned the toughest cases to handle.

These scenarios underscore the issue present in the question: other factors in the situation make it more difficult to be successful. With the car safety requirements, you should look for an answer that shows that there is a situation with the roads that affects the accident rates. A second possible explanation is that the seat belts are not actually used by a majority of drivers and the safety inspections are not made or are rubber-stamp certifications. This answer is less likely to appear because it is fairly obvious.

Answer choice (A): The stimulus specifies that annual safety inspections—regardless of what is examined—are already in place. Therefore, this answer does not explain why the average rate of accidents is higher in those states.

Answer choice (B): Assuming that overconfidence leads to accidents, the answer could support the assertion that states with more stringent requirements have higher accident rates. But, this answer would also suggest that the experts are wrong in saying that more stringent standards reduce accident rates, so this answer cannot be correct.

Answer choice (C): This is the correct answer choice, and the answer conforms to the discussion above. If the roads are generally more dangerous, then the stringent requirements could reduce the accident rate while at the same time the accident rate could remain relatively high. Since this scenario allows all sides of the situation to be correct and it explains how the situation could occur, this is the correct answer.

Answer choice (D): This answer supports only one side of the paradox. The answer confirms that the experts are correct, but it does not explain why these provinces have higher accident rates. Thus, as explained in the second sidebar on page 175, it does not resolve the paradox.

Answer choice (E): This answer appears attractive at first, but the number of miles of roadway in the provinces is irrelevant because the stimulus specifically references "accidents per kilometer driven." Since the accident rate is calculated as per-miles-driven, the actual number of miles of roadway is irrelevant.

Address the Facts

When attempting to resolve the paradox in the stimulus, you must address the facts of the situation. Many incorrect answers will try to lure you with reasonable solutions that do not quite meet the stated facts. These answers are incorrect. The correct answer *must* conform to the specifics of the stimulus otherwise how could it resolve or explain the situation?

Please take a moment to complete the following problem:

2. Calories consumed in excess of those with which the body needs to be provided to maintain its weight are normally stored as fat and the body gains weight. Alcoholic beverages are laden with calories. However, those people who regularly drink two or three alcoholic beverages a day and thereby exceed the caloric intake necessary to maintain their weight do not in general gain weight.

    Which one of the following, if true, most helps to resolve the apparent discrepancy?

    (A) Some people who regularly drink two or three alcoholic beverages a day avoid exceeding the caloric intake necessary to maintain their weight by decreasing caloric intake from other sources.
    (B) Excess calories consumed by people who regularly drink two or three alcoholic beverages a day tend to be dissipated as heat.
    (C) Some people who do not drink alcoholic beverages but who eat high-calorie foods do not gain weight.
    (D) Many people who regularly drink more than three alcoholic beverages a day do not gain weight.
    (E) Some people who take in fewer calories than are normally necessary to maintain their weight do not lose weight.

The paradox in this problem is that alcohol drinkers who surpass the threshold for calorie intake should gain weight, but they do not. Most people, upon reading the stimulus, prephrase an answer involving exercise or some other way to work off the expected weight gain. Unfortunately, a perfect match to this prephrase does not appear, and instead students are faced with a tricky answer that preys upon this general idea while at the same time it fails to meet the circumstances in the stimulus.

Answer choice (A): Read closely! The stimulus specifies that people who regularly drink two or three alcoholic beverages a day thereby *exceed* the necessary caloric intake. This answer, which discusses individuals who *avoid exceeding* the caloric intake necessary, therefore addresses a different group of people from that in the stimulus. Since information about a different group of people does not explain the situation, this answer is incorrect.

This answer is attractive because it uses the idea of getting rid of or avoiding calories, but it violates one of the precepts of the stimulus. Remember, you must look very closely at the circumstances in the stimulus and make sure that the answer you select matches those circumstances.

Answer choice (B): This is the correct answer choice. If the excess calories are dissipated as heat, then there would be no weight gain. Hence, alcohol drinkers can consume excess calories and still not gain weight.

Some students object to this answer because the situation seems unrealistic. Can heat dissipation actually work off dozens if not hundreds of calories? According to the question stem, yes. Remember, the question stem tells you that each answer choice should be taken as true. Since this answer choice clearly states that the excess calories tend to be dissipated, you must accept that as true and then analyze what effect that would have.

Answer choice (C): The stimulus discusses "people who regularly drink two or three alcoholic beverages a day and thereby exceed the caloric intake necessary." This answer choice addresses a different group of people than those discussed in the stimulus.

Answer choice (D): The first flaw in this answer is that it simply states that individuals consuming alcohol do not gain weight but it offers no *explanation* for why these people have no weight gain. The second flaw in the problem is that it addresses the wrong group of people. The stimulus discusses people who drink two or three alcoholic beverages a day; this answer addresses people who drink *more than* three alcoholic beverages a day.

Answer choice (E): Again, this answer discusses a different group of people than those in the stimulus. The stimulus discusses people who exceed the necessary caloric intake; this answer addresses people who do not meet the necessary caloric intake.

Resolve the Paradox Question Review

Each Resolve the Paradox stimulus presents a situation where two ideas or occurrences contradict each other.

Besides the discrepant or contradictory facts, most Resolve the Paradox stimuli contain the following features:

1. No conclusion
2. Language of contradiction

The correct answer will actively resolve the paradox—it will allow both sides to be factually correct and it will either explain how the situation came into being or add a piece of information that shows how the two ideas or occurrences can coexist.

Because you are not seeking to disprove one side of the situation, you must select the answer choice that contains a *possible cause* of the situation. So, when examining answers, ask yourself if the answer choice could lead to the situation in the stimulus. If so, the answer is correct. The following types of answers are incorrect:

1. Explains only one side of the paradox

   If an answer supports or proves only one side of the paradox, that answer will be incorrect. The correct answer must show how both sides coexist.

2. Similarities and differences

   If the stimulus contains a paradox where two items are similar, then an answer choice that explains a difference between the two cannot be correct.

   Conversely, if the stimulus contains a paradox where two items are different, then an answer choice that explains why the two are similar cannot be correct.

   In short, a similarity cannot explain a difference, and a difference cannot explain a similarity.

When attempting to resolve the problem in the stimulus, you must address the facts of the situation. Many answers will try to lure you with reasonable solutions that do not quite meet the stated facts. These answers are incorrect.

All Resolve the Paradox questions require you to seek a cause of the scenario in the stimulus. However, we do not classify these questions as "CE" questions because the causality does not appear in the stimulus. The CE designator is reserved solely for indicating when causality is featured as the form of reasoning in an argument.

Resolve the Paradox Question Problem Set

Please complete the problem set and review the answer key and explanations. *Answers on Page 182*

1. Industry experts expect improvements in job safety training to lead to safer work environments. A recent survey indicated, however, that for manufacturers who improved job safety training during the 1980s, the number of on-the-job accidents tended to increase in the months immediately following the changes in the training programs.

   Which one of the following, if true, most helps to resolve the apparent discrepancy in the passage above?

   (A) A similar survey found that the number of on-the-job accidents remained constant after job safety training in the transportation sector was improved.

   (B) Manufacturers tend to improve their job safety training only when they are increasing the size of their workforce.

   (C) Manufacturers tend to improve job safety training only after they have noticed that the number of on-the-job accidents has increased.

   (D) It is likely that the increase in the number of on-the-job accidents experienced by many companies was not merely a random fluctuation.

   (E) Significant safety measures, such as protective equipment and government safety inspections, were in place well before the improvements in job safety training.

2. Cigarette companies claim that manufacturing both low- and high-nicotine cigarettes allows smokers to choose how much nicotine they want. However, a recent study has shown that the levels of nicotine found in the blood of smokers who smoke one pack of cigarettes per day are identical at the end of a day's worth of smoking, whatever the level of nicotine in the cigarettes they smoke.

   Which one of the following, if true, most helps to explain the finding of the nicotine study?

   (A) Blood cannot absorb more nicotine per day than that found in the smoke from a package of the lowest-nicotine cigarettes available.

   (B) Smokers of the lowest-nicotine cigarettes available generally smoke more cigarettes per day than smokers of high-nicotine cigarettes.

   (C) Most nicotine is absorbed into the blood of a smoker even if it is delivered in smaller quantities.

   (D) The level of tar in cigarettes is higher in low-nicotine cigarettes than it is in some high-nicotine cigarettes.

   (E) When taking in nicotine by smoking cigarettes is discontinued, the level of nicotine in the blood decreases steadily.

3. Raisins are made by drying grapes in the sun. Although some of the sugar in the grapes is caramelized in the process, nothing is added. Moreover, the only thing removed from the grapes is the water that evaporates during the drying, and water contains no calories or nutrients. The fact that raisins contain more iron per calorie than grapes do is thus puzzling.

    Which one of the following, if true, most helps to explain why raisins contain more iron per calorie than do grapes?

    (A) Since grapes are bigger than raisins, it takes several bunches of grapes to provide the same amount of iron as a handful of raisins does.
    (B) Caramelized sugar cannot be digested, so its calories do not count toward the calorie content of raisins.
    (C) The body can absorb iron and other nutrients more quickly from grapes than from raisins because of the relatively high water content of grapes.
    (D) Raisins, but not grapes, are available year-round, so many people get a greater share of their yearly iron intake from raisins than from grapes.
    (E) Raisins are often eaten in combination with other iron-containing foods, while grapes are usually eaten by themselves.

4. Vervet monkeys use different alarm calls to warn each other of nearby predators, depending on whether the danger comes from land or from the air.

    Which one of the following, if true, contributes most to an explanation of the behavior of vervet monkeys described above?

    (A) By varying the pitch of its alarm call, a vervet monkey can indicate the number of predators approaching.
    (B) Different land-based predators are responsible for different numbers of vervet monkey deaths.
    (C) No predators that pose a danger to vervet monkeys can attack both from land and from the air.
    (D) Vervet monkeys avoid land-based predators by climbing trees but avoid predation from the air by diving into foliage.
    (E) Certain land-based predators feed only on vervet monkeys, whereas every predator that attacks vervet monkeys from the air feeds on many different animals.

Resolve the Paradox Problem Set Answer Key

Question #1. Resolve. The correct answer choice is (B)

The paradox in the stimulus is: for manufacturers who improved job safety training during the 1980s there was an increase in the number of on-the-job accidents.

Answer choice (A): This answer does not provide an explanation for the paradox in the stimulus. Some students eliminate this answer because it addresses the transportation industry, but information about the transportation industry could be used to analogically explain the issue in the manufacturing industry (but, to be correct the answer would have to offer some further relevant parallel between the two industries).

Answer choice (B): This is the correct answer choice. If the workforce is increasing, more accidents would be expected. Thus, safety training could improve the safety of the work environment (as measured by average number of accidents per worker, for example) while at the same time the number of total accidents could increase. Because this answer allows both sides to be true and it explains the circumstance in the stimulus, this answer is correct. In Chapter Nine we will discuss average versus total numbers, and that will further explain the construction of this question.

Answer choice (C): This would explain an increase in accidents *before* the improvements in job safety training, but the issue in the stimulus is an increase *after* the improvements in safety training.

Answer choice (D): This answer further confuses the issue. If the fluctuation *was* random, that could explain how an increase in accidents could follow safety training. By stating that the increase was *not* random, a possible cause of the scenario is eliminated.

Answer choice (E): This answer shows that the level of safety was at least minimal prior to the safety training, but this does not help explain why an increase in accidents followed the training.

Question #2. Resolve. The correct answer choice is (A)

In rough terms, the paradox in the stimulus is that smokers of one pack of low-nicotine cigarettes have an identical nicotine level at the end of the day as smokers of one pack of high-nicotine cigarettes. This similarity must be explained by a similarity, not a difference.

Answer choice (A): This is the correct answer choice. The answer choice indicates that there is a similarity in the blood such that the maximum amount of nicotine absorbed is identical for everyone. Because the maximum amount of nicotine absorbed per day is equal to the amount of nicotine in a pack of low-nicotine cigarettes, each person absorbs the amount of nicotine equal to that in the low-nicotine pack regardless of the type of cigarette smoked. Additional nicotine is not absorbed into the blood of smokers of the high-nicotine brand. Since this answer explains the paradox, this is the correct answer.

Answer choice (B): Read closely! The stimulus is specifically about smokers who "smoke one pack of cigarettes per day." This answer discusses smoking different numbers of cigarettes and thus it fails to meet the circumstances in the stimulus.

Answer choice (C): This answer confuses the issue because it indicates that most nicotine is absorbed into

Resolve the Paradox Problem Set Answer Key

the system. From this fact one would expect that those smoking high-nicotine cigarettes would have higher nicotine levels than low-nicotine cigarette smokers.

Answer choice (D): The stimulus does not address the level of tar in cigarettes, nor can we make any judgment about how tar affects nicotine levels.

Answer choice (E): This would apply to any smoker, and as this addresses an effect that occurs after smoking is stopped, it does not help us understand why the nicotine rose to identical levels regardless of the kind of cigarette smoked.

Question #3. Resolve. The correct answer choice is (B)

The paradox in the stimulus is that raisins contain more iron per calorie than grapes even though the two are almost identical in composition. But there is a difference: "some of the sugar in grapes is caramelized" as the grapes are dried in the sun. Since this is the only stated difference between the two that could affect the calorie count (water has no calories), you should focus on an answer that discusses this difference.

Answer choice (A): This answer essentially states that grapes are bigger than raisins, and you need several bunches to equal a handful of raisins. The issue is not the size of the grapes or raisins!

Answer choice (B): This is the correct answer choice. If the iron content in the raisins and grapes is identical, but raisins have fewer calories for counting purposes, then the iron per calorie will be higher for raisins, as highlighted by the following example:

	Raisins	Grapes
Units of Iron	100	100
Countable Calories	10	20
Iron per Calorie	10	5

Note that the paradox could have addressed any common element between raisins and grapes (such as fiber or fat), and raisins would always have the higher per calorie content since they contain fewer countable calories.

Answer choice (C): The paradox in the stimulus does not involve the rate at which the body can absorb iron or any other nutrient. This answer misses the point and is incorrect.

Answer choice (D): The availability of raisins and grapes is not an issue in the stimulus. The answer then discusses iron, but the point made about yearly intake is irrelevant.

Answer choice (E): The comparison in the stimulus is between grapes and raisins. This answer, which brings in other food items, is irrelevant.

Question #4. Resolve. The correct answer choice is (D)

The situation in the stimulus is that vervet monkeys use different calls depending on where predators come from. The correct answer must explain why the calls are different (again, difference versus similarity is an issue). Note that the stimulus does not contain a true paradox, just an odd situation that is presented without explanation.

Answer choice (A): This answer states that vervet monkeys vary the calls in order to indicate the number of predators, but the answer does not explain why different calls are used for land versus air predators. This answer is attractive because it shows that different calls can be used to indicate different things, but it is wrong because it does not explain the behavior of the monkeys as described in the stimulus.

Answer choice (B): This answer addresses only land-based predators and does not explain the difference described in the stimulus.

Answer choice (C): This answer states that the predators using land attacks are different from the predators using air attacks, but this information does not explain why vervet monkeys use different calls to indicate that fact.

Answer choice (D): This is the correct answer choice. Because vervet monkeys react to predators in different ways, they would need to know if the predator was coming by land or air. Hence, the different calls are used to tell the monkeys whether they should climb trees or dive into the foliage. Since this answer explains the behavior of vervet monkeys, this answer is correct.

Answer choice (E): The diet of selected predators of vervet monkeys is irrelevant and does not help explain why vervet monkeys use different calls depending on the direction of the attack.

CHAPTER NINE: NUMBERS AND PERCENTAGES

Numbers and Percentages

Like Cause and Effect Reasoning, the concept of Numbers and Percentages is featured in many GMAT stimuli. Although most people are comfortable working with numbers or percentages because they come up so frequently in daily life (for example in balancing a checking account, dividing a bar tab, or adding up a grocery bill), the makers of the GMAT often prey upon several widely-held misconceptions:

Misconception #1:   Increasing percentages automatically lead to increasing numbers.

Most people assume that if a percentage becomes larger, the number that corresponds to that percentage must also get larger. This is not necessarily true because the overall size of the group under discussion could get smaller. For example, consider the following argument: "Auto manufacturer X increased their United States market share from 10% last year to 25% this year. Therefore, Company X sold more cars in the United States this year than last." This is true if the size of the U.S. car market stayed the same or became larger. But if the size of the U.S. car market decreased by enough, the argument would not be valid, as in the following example:

	Last Year	This Year
Total number of cars sold in the United States	1000	200
X's market share	10%	25%
X's total car sales in the United States	100	50

Thus, even though auto manufacturer X's market share increased to 25%, because the size of the entire market decreased significantly, X actually sold fewer cars in the United States.

CR

When identifying problems that contain numbers or percentages as part of the reasoning, we use a "#%" notation, as in "Must-#%."

Of course, if the overall total remains constant, an increasing percentage does translate into a larger number. But on the GMAT the size of the total is usually not given.

If the percentage increases but the corresponding number decreases, then the overall total must have decreased.

If the percentage decreases but the corresponding number increases, then the overall total must have increased.

If the number increases but the corresponding percentage decreases, then the overall total must have increased.

In each of the first four misconceptions the makers of the test attempt to lure you into making an assumption about the size of the overall total.

If the number decreases but the corresponding percentage increases, then the overall total must have decreased.

Misconception #2: Decreasing percentages automatically lead to decreasing numbers.

This misconception is the opposite of Misconception #1. Just because a percentage decreases does not necessarily mean that the corresponding number must become smaller. Reversing the years in the previous example proves this point.

Misconception #3: Increasing numbers automatically lead to increasing percentages.

Just as increasing percentages do not automatically translate into increasing numbers, the reverse is also true. Consider the following example: "The number of bicycle-related accidents rose dramatically from last month to this month. Therefore, bicycle-related accidents must make up a greater percentage of all road accidents this month." This conclusion can be true, but it does not have to be true, as shown by the following example:

	Last Month	This Month
Number of bicycle-related accidents	10	30
Total number of road accidents	100	600
Percentage of total accidents that are bicycle-related	10%	5%

Thus, even though the number of bicycle-related accidents tripled, the percentage of total road accidents that were bicycle-related dropped because the *total number* of road accidents rose so dramatically.

Misconception #4: Decreasing numbers automatically lead to decreasing percentages.

This misconception is the opposite of Misconception #3. Just because a number decreases does not necessarily mean that the corresponding percentage must become smaller. Reversing the months in the previous example proves this point.

Misconception #5:   Large numbers automatically mean large percentages, and small numbers automatically mean small percentages.

In 2008, Porsche sold just over 26,000 cars in the United States. While 26,000 is certainly a large number, it represented only about 1/5 of 1% of total U.S. car sales in 2008. Remember, the size of a number does not reveal anything about the percentage that number represents unless you know something about the size of the overall total that number is drawn from.

Misconception #6:   Large percentages automatically mean large numbers, and small percentages automatically mean small numbers.

This misconception is the reverse of Misconception #5. A figure such as 90% sounds impressively large, but if you have 90% of $5, that really isn't too impressive, is it?

Numerical situations normally hinge on three elements: an overall total, a number within that total, and a percentage within the total. GMAT problems will often give you one of the elements, but without at least two elements present, you cannot make a definitive judgment about what is occurring with another element. When you are given just percentage information, you cannot make a judgment about numbers. Likewise, when you are given just numerical information you cannot make a judgment about percentages.

In a moment, we will explore this idea by examining several GMAT questions. But first, you must be able to recognize number and percentage ideas when they appear on the GMAT:

Words used to introduce numerical ideas:

    Amount
    Quantity
    Sum
    Total
    Count
    Tally

Words used to introduce percentage ideas:

Percent
Proportion
Fraction
Ratio
Incidence
Likelihood
Probability
Segment
Share

Three words on the percentage list—"incidence," "likelihood," and "probability"—bear further discussion. Each of these words relates to the chances that an event will occur, and when the GMAT makers uses phrases such as "more likely" or "less likely" they are telling you that the percentage chances are greater than 50% or less than 50%, respectively. In fact, a wide variety of phrases can be used to introduce percentage ideas, including such disparate phrases as "more prone to" or "occurs with a high frequency."

With these indicators in mind, please take a moment to complete the following question:

1. From 1973 to 1989 total energy use in this country increased less than 10 percent. However, the use of electrical energy in this country during this same period grew by more than 50 percent, as did the gross national product—the total value of all goods and services produced in the nation.

    If the statements above are true, then which one of the following must also be true?

    (A) Most of the energy used in this country in 1989 was electrical energy.
    (B) From 1973 to 1989 there was a decline in the use of energy other than electrical energy in this country.
    (C) From 1973 to 1989 there was an increase in the proportion of energy use in this country that consisted of electrical energy use.
    (D) In 1989 electrical energy constituted a larger proportion of the energy used to produce the gross national product than did any other form of energy.
    (E) In 1973 the electrical energy that was produced constituted a smaller proportion of the gross national product than did all other forms of energy combined.

Like the vast majority of Must Be True problems, the stimulus does not contain a conclusion. We are given the following facts, however:

From 1973 to 1989 total energy use increased less than 10%.

During this same period, the use of electrical energy grew by more than 50%.

During this same period, the gross national product (GNP) grew by more than 50%.

A careful examination of the second sentence reveals that there is no stated connection between the growth of the GNP and the increase in the use of electrical energy. If you assume that the use of electrical energy somehow caused the growth of the GNP, you are guilty of making an unwarranted causal assumption. Because there is no stated connection between the two other than they both grew by more than 50%, any answer that attempts to connect the two is incorrect. Answer choices (D) and (E) can both be eliminated by this reasoning.

Now that we recognize that the GNP issue is only a red herring, let us examine the percentages that are given in the stimulus. The 50% increase in electrical energy gives the impression that the jump must have been substantial. But we know from Misconception #6 that a large percentage does not automatically mean a large number. For example, in this problem it is possible that the 50% increase in electrical energy use was a jump from 2 units to 3 units. The possibility that electrical energy use in 1973 was a relatively small percentage of overall energy use directly undermines answer choice (A), as shown by the following example:

	1973	1989
Total energy use (in units)	100	109
Electrical energy use (in units)	10	15
Percentage of total energy use that was electrical	10%	13+%

A close analysis of the chart also reveals that answer choice (B) can be eliminated. In the example, the use of energy other than electrical energy rose from 90 units to 94 units.

Although the example disproves answer choices (A) and (B), obviously you do not have time to make a chart during the test to examine each possibility, so is there a faster way to eliminate the first two answers? Yes—consider the previous discussion point that information about percentages does not tell us about the numbers. With that idea in mind, because the stimulus contains only percentage information (even though there are two percentages), you should be very suspicious of answer choice (A) (which states that the number of electrical units used was greater) and answer choice (B) (which states that the use of non-electrical energy declined) since they both contain numerical information. At the same time, you should be attracted to an answer such as (C) because it contains only percentage information, and as it turns out, **answer choice (C) is correct.**

Because the misconceptions discussed earlier have a predictable effect when you try to make inferences, you can use the following general rules for Must Be True questions:

The rules to the right address the classic combination of a stimulus with numbers and percentages information and a Must Be True question.

1. If the stimulus contains percentage or proportion information only, avoid answers that contain hard numbers.

    Example Stimulus Sentence:

    The car market share of Company X declined this year.

    Avoid answers which say:

    Company X sold a smaller number of cars this year.

    Company X sold a greater amount of cars this year.

2. If the stimulus contains only numerical information, avoid answers that contain percentage or proportion information.

    Example Stimulus Sentence:

    Company Y sold fewer computers this year.

    Avoid answers which say:

    Company Y now has a lower share of the computer market.

    Company Y now possesses a greater proportion of the computer market.

3. If the stimulus contains both percentage and numerical information, any answer choice that contains numbers, percentages, or both *may* be true.

Please keep in mind that these rules are very general. You must read the stimulus closely and carefully to determine exactly what information is present because the makers of the GMAT are experts at camouflaging or obscuring important information in order to test your ability to understand complex argumentation.

Please take a moment to complete the following question:

2. The number of North American children who are obese—that is, who have more body fat than do 85 percent of North American children their age—is steadily increasing, according to four major studies conducted over the past 15 years.

    If the finding reported above is correct, it can be properly concluded that

    (A)   when four major studies all produce similar results, those studies must be accurate
    (B)   North American children have been progressively less physically active over the past 15 years
    (C)   the number of North American children who are not obese increased over the past 15 years
    (D)   over the past 15 years, the number of North American children who are underweight has declined
    (E)   the incidence of obesity in North American children tends to increase as the children grow older

Like the previous question, this is a Must Be True question with a stimulus that does not contain a conclusion. But, this stimulus does provide information about both the numbers and percentages of obese children, and so you can end up with an answer that has either a number or a percentage (though a numerical answer is more likely since the percentage is fixed at a constant 15% in the stimulus).

The numerical information comes from the phrase, "The number of North American children who are obese...is steadily increasing." The percentage information comes from the phrase, "children who are obese—that is, who have more body fat than do 85 percent of North American children their age." The percentage information defines obese children as those who fall into the top 15% among all children their age in terms of body fat, and therefore the percentage is known to be constant. The numerical information tells us that the actual number of obese children is increasing (and since this is a Must Be True question we can accept that information as accurate).

Answer choice (A): This answer is incorrect because there is no evidence in the stimulus to support it. Although the stimulus mentioned four major studies that apparently agreed about the increase in the number of obese children, it would be an exaggeration to say that any time four major studies produce similar results they *must* be accurate.

Answer choice (B): This answer proposes a causal reason for why the number of obese children is growing. From the information in the stimulus we cannot determine the cause of the rise in obesity, so answer choice (B) is also wrong.

Answer choice (C): This is the correct answer choice. Consider the following example:

> 15 years ago—100 total children of similar age

> | | | |
> |---|---|---|
> | Number of obese children | 15 | = 15% |
> | Number of non-obese children | 85 | |

Now, let us say that the number of obese children has risen to 150 children today:

> Today

> | | |
> |---|---|
> | Number of obese children | 150 |

So far we have conformed to the information given in the stimulus: the actual number of obese children is rising. However, although the number of obese children has now risen to 150, the definition of obesity ("more body fat than 85 percent of North American children") remains unchanged. Since this is the case, the 150 obese children today must still comprise the top 15% of the total child population. Consequently, the remaining 85% of non-obese children must now be 850:

> Today

> | | |
> |---|---|
> | Number of non-obese children | 850 |

(150 is 15% of 1000, and thus 85% of 1000 is 850)

Answer choice (C) is fully supported because the stimulus provides information about both the number and percentage of obese children. As stated earlier, if the stimulus provides information about both the numbers and percentages in a situation, then you can select any supported answer choice that contains either numbers or percentages. Note the emphasis on the word "supported." In the obesity problem, GMAC could easily have written an *incorrect* answer choice that says, "The number of North American children who are not obese *decreased* over the past 15 years."

Answer choice (D): This answer addresses "underweight" children, who are neither defined nor discussed in the stimulus.

Answer choice (E): This answer is directly contradicted by the information in the stimulus, which states that the incidence of obesity is definitionally set at a constant 15%.

Markets and Market Share

Entire books have been written about market operations, so a lengthy discussion of this topic is beyond the scope of this book.

The makers of the GMAT expect you to understand the operation of markets and the concept of market share. Market operation includes supply and demand, production, pricing, and profit. None of these concepts should be unfamiliar to you as they are a routine part of business.

Market share is simply the portion of a market that a company controls. The market share can be measured either in terms of revenues (sales) or units sold. For example:

Heinz has a 60% market share of the $500 million ketchup market.

Jif brand peanut butter sold 80 million units last year, a 30% market share.

Like all numbers and percentages problems, market share is a comparative term, as opposed to an absolute term. Thus, many market share questions hinge on one of the Misconceptions discussed in this chapter.

Because market share is a numbers and percentages concept, market share can change when factors in the market change. For example, a company can gain market share (percentage) if the market shrinks and they maintain a constant size, or if they grow in an unchanging market. However, a company losing market share does not mean that their sales decreased, only that they became a smaller entity in the market relative to the whole (for example, the market grew and they stayed the same size). Similarly, a company could lose sales and still gain market share if the overall market became smaller.

Regardless of the size of a market and even though the total amount of the market can shift, the total market share must always add up to 100%.

Please take a moment to complete the following question:

3. Rumored declines in automobile-industry revenues are exaggerated. It is true that automobile manufacturers' share of the industry's revenues fell from 65 percent two years ago to 50 percent today, but over the same period suppliers of automobile parts had their share increase from 15 percent to 20 percent and service companies (for example, distributors, dealers, and repairers) had their share increase from 20 percent to 30 percent.

Which one of the following best indicates why the statistics given above provide by themselves no evidence for the conclusion they are intended to support?

(A) The possibility is left open that the statistics for manufacturers' share of revenues come from a different source than the other statistics.

(B) No matter what changes the automobile industry's overall revenues undergo, the total of all shares of these revenues must be 100 percent.

(C) No explanation is given for why the revenue shares of different sectors of the industry changed.

(D) Manufacturers and parts companies depend for their revenue on dealers' success in selling cars.

(E) Revenues are an important factor but are not the only factor in determining profits.

The conclusion of the argument states that the rumored declines in automobile-industry revenues are exaggerated (a numerical statement), but the premises provided in support of this argument only address the market share percentages of the three groups that have automobile-industry revenues (percentage statements). The percentage statements used by the author only indicates that the percentages have changed, not whether overall revenue has changed:

	2 Years Ago	Today
Manufacturers' share	65%	50%
Suppliers' share	15%	20%
Service companies' share	20%	30%
Total market size in %	100%	100%

Although the composition of the market has changed in terms of the market share of each group, this fact tells us nothing about industry revenues because market shares will always add up to 100% regardless of the actual dollars involved. Thus, automobile-industry revenues could have fallen dramatically and the percentages above could still be accurate.

Answer choice (A): Although it is true that the possibility is left open that the statistics for the manufacturers' share may come from a different source, this does not address the fundamental percentage-to-number error in the argument.

Answer choice (B): This is the correct answer choice. The answer reveals the error of the author: the changing market shares of different groups have no impact on the actual amount of revenues. In all instances, the market shares will add up to 100%, so a discussion of shifts within this 100% is meaningless as far as making a determination of whether revenues declined.

Answer choice (C): This is not a flaw of the argument. The author is allowed to simply note that the shares changed and use those facts to draw a conclusion. In the argument the conclusion is faulty, but not for the reason cited in this answer.

Answer choice (D): The interrelationship of the groups named in the stimulus is not an issue in determining whether the conclusion is in error.

Answer choice (E): The argument is about revenues, and information about profits will not describe the error in the reasoning.

CR

Numbers and Percentages Review

The makers of the GMAT often prey upon several widely-held misconceptions:

Misconception #1:   Increasing percentages automatically lead to increasing numbers.

Misconception #2:   Decreasing percentages automatically lead to decreasing numbers.

Misconception #3:   Increasing numbers automatically lead to increasing percentages.

Misconception #4:   Decreasing numbers automatically lead to decreasing percentages.

Misconception #5:   Large numbers automatically mean large percentages, and small numbers automatically mean small percentages.

Misconception #6:   Large percentages automatically mean large numbers, and small percentages automatically mean small numbers.

Words that introduce numerical ideas:

    Amount
    Quantity
    Sum
    Total
    Count
    Tally

Words that introduce percentage ideas:

    Percent
    Proportion
    Fraction
    Ratio
    Incidence
    Likelihood
    Probability
    Segment
    Share

Use the following general rules for Must Be True questions:

1. If the stimulus contains percentage or proportion information only, avoid answers that contain hard numbers.

2. If the stimulus contains only numerical information, avoid answers that contain percentage or proportion information.

3. If the stimulus contains both percentage and numerical information, any answer choice that contains numbers, percentages, or both *may* be true.

Use the following general rules for Weaken and Strengthen questions:

> To weaken or strengthen an argument containing numbers and percentages, look carefully for information about the total amount(s)— does the argument make an assumption based on one of the misconceptions discussed earlier?

Market share is simply the portion of a market that a company controls. Market share can be measured either in terms of revenues (sales) or units sold. Regardless of the size of a market, total market share must always add up to 100%.

Numbers and Percentages Problem Set

Please complete the problem set and review the answer key and explanations. *Answers on Page 201*

CR

1. Politician: Those economists who claim that consumer price increases have averaged less than 3 percent over the last year are mistaken. They clearly have not shopped anywhere recently. Gasoline is up 10 percent over the last year; my auto insurance, 12 percent; newspapers, 15 percent; propane, 13 percent; bread, 50 percent.

   The reasoning in the politician's argument is most vulnerable to criticism on the grounds that the argument

   (A) impugns the character of the economists rather than addressing their arguments
   (B) fails to show that the economists mentioned are not experts in the area of consumer prices
   (C) mistakenly infers that something is not true from the claim that it has not been shown to be so
   (D) uses evidence drawn from a small sample that may well be unrepresentative
   (E) attempts to persuade by making an emotional appeal

2. Ditrama is a federation made up of three autonomous regions: Korva, Mitro, and Guadar. Under the federal revenue-sharing plan, each region receives a share of federal revenues equal to the share of the total population of Ditrama residing in that region, as shown by a yearly population survey. Last year, the percentage of federal revenues Korva received for its share decreased somewhat even though the population survey on which the revenue-sharing was based showed that Korva's population had increased.

   If the statements above are true, which one of the following must also have been shown by the population survey on which last year's revenue-sharing in Ditrama was based?

   (A) Of the three regions, Korva had the smallest number of residents.
   (B) The population of Korva grew by a smaller percentage than it did in previous years.
   (C) The populations of Mitro and Guadar each increased by a percentage that exceeded the percentage by which the population of Korva increased.
   (D) Of the three regions, Korva's numerical increase in population was the smallest.
   (E) Korva's population grew by a smaller percentage than did the population of at least one of the other two autonomous regions.

CR

3. In 1980, Country A had a per capita gross domestic product (GDP) that was $5,000 higher than that of the European Economic Community. By 1990, the difference, when adjusted for inflation, had increased to $6,000. Since a rising per capita GDP indicates a rising average standard of living, the average standard of living in Country A must have risen between 1980 and 1990.

    Which one of the following is an assumption on which the argument depends?

    (A) Between 1980 and 1990, Country A and the European Economic Community experienced the same percentage increase in population.

    (B) Between 1980 and 1990, the average standard of living in the European Economic Community fell.

    (C) Some member countries of the European Economic Community had, during the 1980s, a higher average standard of living than Country A.

    (D) The per capita GDP of the European Economic Community was not lower by more than $1,000 in 1990 than it had been in 1980.

    (E) In 1990, no member country of the European Economic Community had a per capita GDP higher than that of Country A.

Numbers and Percentages Problem Set Answer Key

Question #1. Flaw-#%. The correct answer choice is (D)

The politician's argument is that the claims that price increases have averaged less than 3 percent are wrong, and in support of that position the politician cites several examples of price increases, each of which is greater than 3 percent. As mentioned in one of the chapter sidebars, "an average is a composite number, and within the average there can be a significant degree of variation and no single entity need embody the exact characteristic of the average (for example, the average weight of a 1 pound rock and a 99 pound rock is 50 pounds)." In making the argument, the politician has focused on several individual examples while ignoring the fact that an average is a compilation of many different numbers. Answer choice (D) perfectly captures the essence of this sampling error.

Answer choice (A): The argument does not contain a source or *ad hominem* attack. Simply stating that a position is wrong is different from criticizing the character of that person.

Answer choice (B): To properly claim that the economists are wrong does not require showing that they are not pricing experts, and hence this answer is incorrect.

Answer choice (C): The politician attempts to refute the position by providing evidence about large price increases for certain products. This process, which involves facts, is different from inferring that a claim is false because it has not been shown to be true. This answer choice would better describe an argument such as the following: "you have not proven that God exists, so there must be no God."

Answer choice (D): This is the correct answer choice. Citing several examples to refute an average is a doomed strategy.

Answer choice (E): There is no appeal to emotion present; percentages are used to make the argument.

Question #2. Must-#%. The correct answer choice is (E)

The situation in Ditrama is as follows:

> Under the federal revenue-sharing plan, each region receives a share of federal revenues equal to the *share of the total population* of Ditrama residing in that region, as shown by a yearly population survey.

> Last year, the *percentage* of federal revenues Korva received for its share *decreased* somewhat even though the population survey on which the revenue-sharing was based showed that Korva's *population had increased*.

If the total population of Korva increased but at the same time they experienced a decrease in revenue allocation, the only possible solution is that the total population of Ditrama increased by more than the Korva increase. Thus, you must seek an answer that indicates that the total population increased more than Korva's population increased. But be careful: this question is one of high difficulty because the test makers do not make it easy to spot the correct answer.

Answer choice (A): Either Mitro or Guadar could have a smaller number of residents than Korva.

Answer choice (B): This answer is impossible to prove because we do not have information about the population growth of Korva in the years prior to the last one.

Answer choice (C): This is the most popular wrong answer choice. The key error is the claim that "Mitro and Guadar *each* increased by a percentage that exceeded" Korva's increase. Although it must be true that at least one exceeded Korva's increase, it does not have to be true that both exceeded Korva, as shown by the following example:

	Before	After (Last Year)
Total Population of Ditrama	30 (100%)	100 (100%)
Population of Korva (people/percent of total)	10 (33%)	15 (15%)
Population of Mitro (people/percent of total)	10 (33%)	10 (10%)
Population of Guadar (people/percent of total)	10 (33%)	75 (75%)

In the example above, only one of the other regions had a population increase that exceeded Korva; the other did not. Hence this answer choice is incorrect. Note also that this example disproves answer choice (A) as well.

Numbers and Percentages Problem Set Answer Key

Answer choice (D): As shown by the previous example, this answer is incorrect.

Answer choice (E): This is the correct answer choice. From the stimulus we know that Korva had a population increase, but a revenue drop. So, the total population of Ditrama must have increased by more than Korva's increase, and for this to happen, at least one other region must have had an increase in population that exceeded Korva's.

Note that the scenario in answer choice (C) would force answer choice (E) to be correct, and based on the Uniqueness Rule of Answer Choices, answer (C) is incorrect for that reason alone.

Question #3. Assumption-#%. The correct answer choice is (D)

This is a challenging question. The author makes the following argument:

Premise:	In 1980, Country A had a per capita gross domestic product (GDP) that was $5,000 higher than that of the European Economic Community.
Premise:	By 1990, the difference, when adjusted for inflation, had increased to $6,000.
Premise:	A rising per capita GDP indicates a rising average standard of living.
Conclusion:	The average standard of living in Country A must have risen between 1980 and 1990.

The author has fallen into the trap of believing that an increase in the difference between GDP's means that the *actual* GDP of Country A has increased. Since that is not necessarily the case based on the difference, you should look for the answer that assumes the total GDP of country A has not decreased.

Answer choice (A): The stimulus is clear that the GDP is a "per capita" (per person) figure. Hence, the author does not need to make an assumption regarding actual population increases.

Answer choice (B): The author does need to assume this is true because a bigger GDP gap does not prove that either must have fallen; the actual GDP of both Country A and the European Economic Community (EEC) could rise and the author's argument would still be valid.

Answer choice (C): In the argument the author uses the GDP of the entire EEC. Since the figure for the EEC would necessarily be an average drawn from the numbers of multiple countries, the author does not need to make any assumptions about figures for individual countries within the EEC.

Continued on next page.

Answer choice (D): This is the correct answer choice. In order to conclude that an increasing difference in GDP translates to an actual increase in GDP, the author must assume that the GDP of the point of comparison, the EEC, did not fall dramatically. Consider the following example, which assigns actual numbers to the GDP of each group in 1980, and then shows a variety of possibilities for the numbers in 1990:

	1980	#1: 1990	#2: 1990	#3: 1990	#4: 1990
GDP of Country A	105	107	156	96	105
GDP of the EEC	100	101	150	90	99
Difference	+5	+6	+6	+6	+6

Each of the four examples for 1990 is consistent with the claim that there is a $6000 difference between the GDP of Country A and the GDP of the EEC. The first two examples for 1990, #1 and #2, show that the total GDP of Country A, and therefore the standard of living as defined in the stimulus, has risen. Example #3 shows that even though the gap has increased between the two groups, the actual GDP of Country A has *decreased*, and therefore the standard of living in Country A has decreased. This is inconsistent with the author's conclusion, so the author must be assuming that this type of scenario cannot occur. In example #4, we see a second example that is incompatible with the author's conclusion, one where the gap remains at $6000, but the GDP of Country A remains the same. The author must assume that the fourth scenario also cannot occur, and that the GDP of the EEC cannot drop by the $1000 that is the amount of the increase in the gap. Hence, the author must assume that if the GDP of the EEC drops, it drops by less than $1000, and therefore answer choice (D) is correct.

This is clearly a confusing answer, but do not forget that you can always apply the Assumption Negation Technique to any answer choice in an Assumption question. Answer choice (D), when negated, reads: "The per capita GDP of the European Economic Community was lower by more than $1,000 in 1990 than it had been in 1980." This negation would definitely weaken the argument because it would create a scenario like #3 or one even worse than #4. Because the answer choice weakens the argument when negated, it must be the correct answer.

Answer choice (E): This answer is incorrect for the same reason cited in answer choice (C): since the figure for the EEC would necessarily be an average drawn from the numbers of multiple countries, the author does not need to make any assumptions about the figures for individual countries within the EEC, regardless of year.

Section Two:

Reading Comprehension

RC

RC

CHAPTER TEN: THE BASICS OF READING COMPREHENSION

The Reading Comprehension Passages

The focus of this section is on the Reading Comprehension portion of the GMAT. The Reading Comprehension passages are each up to 350 words long, and can be based on a variety of topics from the social sciences, the physical or biological sciences, humanities, or business related fields such as economics or marketing. Each passage is accompanied by questions that require you to interpret the passage, apply information from the passage, or draw inferences from your reading of the passage. These questions are presented on a split computer screen, allowing the reading passage to remain visible on the left side of the screen, while the associated question and answer choices appear on the right. Of course, the amount of time you spend on each passage set will vary with the reading difficulty of the passage, the difficulty of the questions, and the total number of questions per passage.

Why Reading Comprehension?

Each portion of the GMAT verbal section is designed to test abilities required of students earning an M.B.A. The Critical Reasoning section measures your skills in argumentation and logic. The Sentence Correction section tests your ability to understand and apply the complex rules of English grammar. Reading Comprehension, a section included in many standardized tests, provides a test of skills particularly important to students and professionals. MBA students are required to read significant portions of dense text throughout their studies, and business professionals must often be ready to do the same in their normal course of business.

The Section Directions

Each Reading Comprehension passage is prefaced by the following directions:

> "The questions in this group are based on the contents of a passage. After reading the passage, choose the best answer to each question. Answer all questions following the passage on the basis of what is <u>stated</u> or <u>implied in the passage.</u>"

Because these directions precede each Reading Comprehension passage, you should familiarize yourself with them now. Once the GMAT begins, *never* waste time reading the directions for any section.

Let us examine these directions more closely. Consider the following sentence: "Answer all questions following the passage on the basis of what is <u>stated</u> or <u>implied in the passage.</u>" Thus, the test makers indicate that you

RC

are to use the statements of the author of the passage to prove and disprove answer choices. You do not need to bring in additional information aside from the typical ideas that the average American would be expected to believe on the basis of generally known and accepted facts. For example, you would be expected to understand the *basics* of how the weather works, or how supply and demand works, but not the specifics of either. Please note this does not mean that the GMAT cannot set up scenarios where they discuss ideas that are extreme or outside the bounds of common knowledge, such as a passage about a difficult scientific or legal concept. The test makers can and do discuss complex or extreme ideas; in these cases, they give you context for the situation by providing additional information.

Always be sure to read every answer choice before making a selection. If you read only one or two answer choices and then decide you have the correct one, you could end up choosing an answer that has some merit but is not as good as a later answer. One of the test makers' favorite tricks is to place a highly attractive wrong answer choice immediately before the correct answer choice in the hopes that you will pick the wrong answer choice and then move to the next question without reading any of the other answers.

You should read all five answer choices in each question.

Passage Topics

Reading Comprehension passages are drawn from a wide variety of disciplines, including science, business, and humanities. Thus, you will typically encounter passage sets with widely varying topical matter.

Please note that the topic of the passage is not necessarily indicative of the level of difficulty. That is, some Science passages are easy, some are difficult. The same goes for Business related passages, Humanities passages, etc. In the next chapter we will discuss how to attack any type of passage, and we will discuss how the underlying structure of passages can be analyzed regardless of the passage topic. Topic is examined here so that you understand the nature of what you will be reading. In some cases, knowing the topic can help you make informed decisions about the viewpoints that will be presented therein, and in many cases, students perform better on passages that contain a subject matter that is familiar to them.

RC

Approaching the Passages

Every Reading Comprehension passage set contains two separate parts: the passage and the questions. When examining the two parts for the first time, students sometimes wonder about the best strategy for attacking the passages: Should I skim the passage? Should I read just the first and last sentence of each paragraph of the passage? The answer is *Read the passage in its entirety and then attack the questions*. That is, first read the entire passage with an eye towards capturing the main ideas, viewpoints, tone, and structure of the passage, and then proceed to the questions. Although this may seem like a reasonable, even obvious approach, we mention it here because some GMAT texts advocate skimming the passage. Let us take a moment to discuss some of the various reading approaches that you *might* consider using, but should avoid:

We will discuss how to systematically break down each passage shortly.

1. **DO NOT** skim the passage, then do each question, returning to the passage as needed.

   In theory, it might seem that skimming could add some degree of efficiency, but in practice this is not the case. In fact, this approach actually reflects a fundamental misunderstanding of the nature of the Reading Comprehension passages.

   Skimming might be sufficient to absorb lighter materials, such as newspapers or magazines, but that is because those types of materials are written with simplicity in mind. A newspaper editor wants readers to know half the story by the time they have read the headline, and magazines put the most attention-grabbing pictures on their covers; these publications are trying to draw you in, to entice you to make a purchase. The makers of the GMAT, on the other hand, are well aware that they are dealing with a captive audience; they do not feel any pressure to entertain (as you may have noticed), and passages are chosen based on completely different criteria.

   For many, skimming is a natural reaction to a time-constrained test, but unfortunately the test-makers are well aware of this tendency— the passages they use are chosen in part because they evade quick and simple analysis. In practice, the time "saved" on the front end skimming a passage is more than lost on the back end. In the question section, the skimmer invariably finds the need to go back and re-read, and is often not sufficiently familiar with the passage structure to locate relevant reference points quickly.

2. **DO NOT** read just the first and last sentence of each paragraph of the passage, and then do each question, returning to the passage as needed.

RC

This type of "super-skimming" may also sound good in theory; the idea of breezing through the passages, trying to pick up the big picture ideas, may sound appealing, but again, these passages unfortunately do not work that way. This shorthand and ineffective approach is based in part on the common misconception that the main idea of every paragraph appears in the first or last sentence. While this may often hold true, we will see that this is not always the case. After all, the makers of the GMAT are extremely sharp, and they are familiar with these common approaches as well. That may be why many passages will not follow this general rule— the test makers do not like for passages to follow such a simple prescribed formula.

This approach is basically an even more simplistic and ineffective variation of skimming that provides neither substantive knowledge of the information in the passage nor familiarity with the structure sufficient to locate important reference points.

The bottom line is that your reading approach must be maximally effective for all passages. The flawed strategies above, although perhaps effective in some limited contexts, do not consistently produce solid results.
Having discussed some common practices to avoid, let us now consider the proper way to attack a GMAT passage:

1. Read the passage for an understanding of structure and detail, for viewpoints and for themes, and for the author's tone. Make notations as needed.

2. After reading the passage, consider each question, only returning to the passage when necessary to confirm your answers.

These are the basic steps to a proper approach to the Reading Comprehension passages; each step will be discussed in greater detail.

Your Focus While Reading

Have you ever reached the second, or even third, paragraph of an article or reading passage and suddenly realized that you had no idea what you had just been reading? Many students have had this uncomfortable experience at some point. How are we able to read with our eyes while our minds are elsewhere? Ironically, it is our familiarity with the act of reading that has allowed many to develop the "skill" to do so without 100% focus. This approach might be fine for the morning newspaper or a favorite magazine, but these publications tend to be more simply written, and they are unaccompanied by difficult questions. GMAT passages, on the other hand, are chosen for their tendency to elude this type of unfocused approach. Faced with this type of reading, many people "zone out" and lose concentration. Thus, your state of mind when approaching these passages is extremely important.

Giving yourself the simple instruction, "read the passage," allows your mind too much free reign to wander as your eyes gloss over the words. Instead, you should take a more active approach, breaking down the passage as you go, creating something of a running translation, and effectively outlining and notating, as we will discuss further. Yes, it can be difficult to focus for long stretches of time, but you must train yourself through practice to keep your concentration at as high a level as possible.

When starting a section, keep the following tips to keep in mind:

- Channel any nervous energy into intensity.

- Enjoy reading the passages—make them into a game or learning exercise.

- If you lose focus, take a deep breath, refocus, and then return to the task at hand.

- Read aggressively, not passively. Actively engage the material and think about the consequences of what you are reading.

Note: Strong readers have many advantages on this test, but becoming an effective reader obviously has significant value in many contexts. As you practice applying the approaches discussed in this book, keep in mind that they are applicable to reading in general, and not meant solely to help you achieve a high GMAT score (although this is obviously one of the benefits of having an effective approach to reading).

Your Attitude While Reading

Many students approach the Reading Comprehension passages with anxiety, concerned about the prospect of reading dense passages with difficult structures and unfamiliar terminology. As is the case with every section of the GMAT, maintaining the proper mind set is vital; in this section, expectations of boredom or anxiety can become self-fulfilling prophecies. If you wish to perform well, you must approach the passages with a positive, energetic, and enthusiastic attitude.

It is vital that you avoid a negative attitude as you practice and improve your approach to reading. Some passages might cover topics that you do not find inherently interesting, but you should not resent the authors for it! These passages are presented not to delight and amuse, but rather to test your reading

GMAT reading is unlike the reading most people engage in on a day to day basis. For example, newspapers and magazines, and even most novels, are written with an eye towards presenting the material in the clearest and most interesting fashion possible. GMAT Reading Comprehension passages, on the other hand, are not written in this manner. They are often written in an academic style that is, at times, dense and complex.

RC

A positive attitude is perhaps the most underrated factor in GMAT success. Virtually all high-scoring students expect to do well on the GMAT, and this mind set helps them avoid distractions during the exam, and it helps them overcome any adversity they might face.

comprehension skills. Some students approach the passages as puzzles to solve, while others read the passages and try to learn new things from them. Either way, the truth of the matter is that if you do not try to enjoy reading the passages or get some value from them, you will be hard-pressed to perform well.

Some students get annoyed by the academic style of writing of the exam, but this is just part of the test. The passages in this section are not meant to be easy, and the test makers know that the way the passages are written and constructed can be off-putting to many students. You must simply ignore this situation, and take on the passages as a challenge.

Understand the *Type* of Difficulty in the Reading Comprehension Passages

There is a widespread misconception among test takers that because one's reading level is difficult to improve (having been developed over many years), one's performance on the Reading Comprehension passages is also unlikely to change. This belief reflects a common misunderstanding about the specific type of difficulty associated with reading GMAT passages. Keeping in mind that the test makers only have about a half of a page to get their points across, GMAT authors are limited as to the degree of depth that can be reached. This is not to say that these passages are simple, but that the challenge often comes from sources other than conceptual difficulty.

The GMAT is designed not only as a test of conceptual abilities—it is also a test of intimidation. So, how do the test makers ensure that the passages are challenging? Often by choosing subjects that seem daunting; many passages are based on esoteric topics, filled with sophisticated-sounding scientific or technical terms. It is vital that you avoid intimidation as a response to words or phrases which you have never seen. Since the makers of the GMAT do not expect or require outside knowledge with regard to Reading Comprehension passage topics, unfamiliar terms or phrases will almost always be surrounded by context clues. These issues will be covered further in our discussion of reading and notating strategy; for now it is important to understand that unfamiliar words or phrases do not necessarily make a passage any more conceptually difficult, as long as you do not react with discomfort at the prospect of seeing novel terms or phrases.

Many Reading Comprehension passages discuss conflicts between different viewpoints, and this can make the reading inherently more interesting. Getting involved in the argument will make the passage more enjoyable for you and will also allow you to focus more clearly on the material.

Reading Speed and Returning to the Passage

The amount of time that you spend reading the passage has a direct effect on your ability to comfortably complete all of the questions. At the same time, the makers of the GMAT have extraordinarily high expectations about the level of knowledge you should retain when you read a passage. Many questions will test your knowledge of small, seemingly nitpicky variations in phrasing, and reading carelessly is GMAT suicide. Thus, every test taker is placed at the nexus of two competing elements: the need for speed (caused by the timed element) and the need for patience (caused by the detailed reading requirement). How well you manage these two elements strongly determines how well you perform.

Although it may sound rather ordinary, the best approach is to read each passage at the high end of your normal reading speed. If possible, you should try to step it up a notch or two, but reading too quickly will cause you to miss much of the detailed information presented in the passage and will force you to reread most of the passage. On the other hand, reading too slowly will prevent you from having adequate time to answer all of the questions, and that will also prevent you from answering all the questions.

One thing to be aware of as you read is that you do not need to remember every single detail of the passage. Instead, you simply need to remember the basic structure of the passage so you will know where to return when answering the questions. We will discuss this in more detail when we discuss passage structure.

Everyone's reading speed is different, and over the next several chapters we will focus on improving your GMAT reading ability. Improving your reading ability will, in part, consist of teaching you what to look for when reading the passages. Once your ability improves, you will be able to move through the passages and questions more quickly.

Please note that the primary aim of this book is not to just make you a *faster* reader (your natural reading speed has been developed over many years and is hard to increase by itself in a short period of time). Instead, as you become more adept with effective approaches to the passages, you will likely be able to attack the passage sets far more proficiently. The goal here is to make you a *better* reader with a greater knowledge of what to look for, and this will result in your becoming a faster reader.

In seeking to increase reading speed, some students ask us about speed reading courses. In our extensive experience, speed reading techniques do not work on GMAT passages because of the way the passages are written and constructed. GMAT passages are written in a detailed style filled with built-in traps and formations, and speed reading techniques are not designed to detect these elements.

RC

Active Reading and Anticipation

The best readers read actively. That is, they engage the material and consider the implications of each statement as they read. They also use their involvement in the material to constantly anticipate what will occur next in the passage. This type of reading takes focus and a positive attitude, as discussed earlier, but it also takes practice.

The first part of this section is devoted to examining the theory of approaching the passages and questions, whereas the second part of the section is focused on applying those ideas and discussing passage elements.

Let us take a moment to examine several short sections of text, and use those sections to highlight the idea of how active reading leads to anticipating what comes next:

> Governmental reforms, loosening of regulations, and the opening of markets each played a role in fueling China's economic growth over the last quarter-century.

After reading this section, one could deduce that there are a number of directions this passage could go. For example, a detailed analysis of each of the three listed factors in the economic growth could be presented, or further implications of the growth could be discussed. Let's add the next two sentences—which complete this paragraph— and see where the author goes:

> Governmental reforms, loosening of regulations, and the opening of markets each played a role in fueling China's economic growth over the last quarter-century. Within the economy, the two most important segments
> (5)   are industry and agriculture. However, industry has grown at a significantly faster pace than agriculture.

If you were reading this passage, when you reached this juncture, you should have a fairly good idea of the possible directions the author can take with the *next* paragraph. Consider for a moment the information that has been presented thus far:

- Three factors were named as playing a role in China's economic growth over the last quarter-century.

- The economy is stated to have two key segments.

- One of those two segments is said to have grown at a much faster rate than the other segment.

Clearly, the logical direction to take at this point would be to either explain why industry has grown at a faster rate or why agriculture has grown at a slower rate, or both. There does seem to be a slightly higher likelihood that the author will focus on industry because the exact phrase used was, "industry has grown at a significantly faster pace than agriculture," and this phrasing puts the emphasis on "industry."

214

Let's see which direction the author chose:

> Governmental reforms, loosening of regulations, and the opening of markets each played a role in fueling China's economic growth over the last quarter-century. Within the economy, the two most important segments
> (5) are industry and agriculture. However, industry has grown at a significantly faster pace than agriculture.
>
> The growth in industry has occurred largely in the urban areas of China, and has been primarily spurred by a focus on technology and heavy manufacturing. This
> (10) emphasis, however, has not come without costs.

Not surprisingly, the author chose to address the industrial side of the economic growth, in this case by focusing on the segments within industry that have been the most important. Of course, as you continue to read, being correct in your anticipation should not cause you to stop reading actively. As the passage moves forward you should continue to "look ahead" mentally. For example, the last sentence in the text above suggests that the next topic of discussion will be the costs associated with the industrial economic growth.

As a reader, anticipating what will come next in the passage is a habit you should seek to cultivate. By constantly thinking about the possible directions the author can take, you will gain a richer perspective on the story being told by the author. Of course, at times, you might be incorrect in your prediction of what will come next. This is not a problem—you will still be able to absorb what is presented and there is no associated time loss. Simply put, there are tremendous benefits to be gained from actively reading, with no downside.

RC

Active Reading Drill

The following drill is presented to reinforce the valuable habit of reacting to important verbal cues. Most students are likely to be familiar with the meanings of important transitional words such as "furthermore" and "however," but again, the most effective readers react when they see these sorts of transitions, which can often allow the reader to predict the next turn of the passage. After each of the following examples, take a moment to consider what is likely to come next in the passage, and write down your predictions. *Answers on the next page*

1. After developing her initial hypothesis, early studies yielded consistently positive results; in fact,...

_____

_____

_____

2. As a result of his childhood accomplishments, Rhee found many opportunities that would have been inaccessible to lesser known talents. Notwithstanding his early successes,...

_____

_____

_____

3. Martindale was generally scorned by his contemporaries, who characterized him as an artist who lacked the imagination to create anything truly original, as well as the self-awareness to perceive his own shortcomings. Modern critics, however...

_____

_____

_____

4. Many American constitutional scholars argue that in making legal determinations, the Supreme Court should comply whenever possible with the original intent of drafters of the Constitution. At the same time,...

_____

_____

_____

5. Most experts in the field who were first told of Dr. Jane's hypothesis were initially skeptical, but...

_____

_____

_____

Active Reading Drill Answer Key

1. In this case, the words "in fact" tell us that the next information provided will likely continue to support the positive results yielded by early studies.

2. "Notwithstanding," which basically means "in spite of," tells us that the passage is about to take a turn; although Rhee did apparently enjoy early success, we are soon likely to be told of some challenge(s) that appeared in spite of Rhee's early achievements and opportunities.

3. The word "however" in this example is a clear indication that there is contrast between contemporaries' characterizations and those of modern critics, so it is likely that modern critics are going to have nicer things to say about Martindale.

4. If taken out of context, "at the same time" might appear to continue a thought, but the phrase is often more akin to "on the other hand." Here, the author begins by telling us that, according to many, Supreme Court decisions should be based on the Constitution's original intent. "At the same time" is likely in this case to be followed by some limitation on the advisability of this notion (e.g., "At the same time, many facets of modern life were not envisioned by the founders.")

5. "But" is a fairly obvious clue that the passage is about to take a new turn. If we are told of skepticism at first, followed by "but," then it is likely that the author is about to discuss how the hypothesis was confirmed, or possibly how Dr. Jane was able to overcome the initial skepticism of the experts.

RC

Analyzing the Passage Using VIEWSTAMP

Having dispensed with the generalities, we now turn to the specifics of analyzing Reading Comprehension passages. In this section, we will focus on the five main elements you must identify when reading each passage.

As you begin reading the passage, initially focus on making a quick analysis of the topic under discussion. What area has the author chosen to write about? You will be more familiar with some topics than with others, but do not assume that everything you know "outside" of the passage regarding the topic is true and applies to the passage. Instead, use the statements from the passage to answer the questions.

After you have ascertained the topic, as you progress into the passage you must carefully track the following five key elements:

1. The various groups and viewpoints discussed within the passage.
2. The tone or attitude of each group or individual.
3. The argument made by each group or individual.
4. The main point of the passage.
5. The structure of the passage and the organization of ideas.

To remember these five critical elements, we use the acronym VIEWSTAMP:

VIEW	= the different **VIEW**points in the passage
S	= the **S**tructure of the passage
T	= the **T**one of the passage
A	= the **A**rguments in the passage
MP	= the **M**ain **P**oint

Let us examine each of these five elements in detail.

1. Viewpoint Identification and Analysis

A viewpoint is the position or approach taken by a person or group. On the GMAT, Reading Comprehension passages may contain one viewpoint, or might reflect several different viewpoints. These viewpoints can be the author's or those of groups discussed by the author.

As you read, you must identify each viewpoint that is presented in the passage. This is a fairly easy process—whenever a new group or individual viewpoint is discussed, simply note the presence of that group. Consider the opening paragraph from the following passage:

A single passage usually contains anywhere from 25 to 65 lines, generally spread across two to five paragraphs.

This is the order that we will discuss the five elements in, not the order they appear in the acronym. This is the most logical order for discussion purposes.

This section discusses the "VIEW" in VIEWSTAMP. The "VIEW" stands for Viewpoints.

The World Wide Web, a network of electronically
produced and interconnected (or "linked") sites, called
pages, that are accessible via personal computer, raises
legal issues about the rights of owners of intellectual
(5)   property, notably those who create documents for
inclusion on Web pages. Some of these owners of
intellectual property claim that unless copyright law is
strengthened, intellectual property on the Web will not
be protected from copyright infringement. Web users,
(10)   however, claim that if their ability to access
information on Web pages is reduced, the Web cannot
live up to its potential as an open, interactive medium
of communication.

Let us take a moment to analyze this paragraph, section by section.

Lines 1-6

Not all of the text on the GMAT is presented with a definable
viewpoint. Many Reading Comprehension passages begin with a
statement of facts or a description of the situation. In these sections,
no viewpoint is presented. Throughout this book, we will refer to these
sections as "viewpoint neutral." The first five and a half lines of this
passage are viewpoint neutral, simply providing a description of the
Web and the fact that this system raises legal issues. Yes, "owners of
intellectual property" are mentioned, but since no viewpoint is ascribed
to them (as yet), there is no need to note them as a group.

Many Reading Comprehension passages begin with a Viewpoint Neutral discussion that provides context for the passage.

Lines 6-9

The sixth line of the paragraph presents the first identifiable viewpoint
of the passage, held by "Some of these owners of intellectual
property." These owners have an identifiable viewpoint, namely that
"unless copyright law is strengthened, intellectual property on the
Web will not be protected from copyright infringement." You can
note the presence of this viewpoint element in a variety of ways,
from underlining or circling the name of the group to placing a visual
marker off to the side (we will discuss passage notation in more detail
in a later section).

Lines 9-14

Not unusually, a second viewpoint is also presented in the first
paragraph. This viewpoint, of "Web users," is somewhat contrary to
the previous viewpoint presented.

Test takers might ask, "What is the importance of tracking all of the viewpoints in a given Reading Comprehension passage?" There are several excellent reasons:

1. Tracking the viewpoints will help you disentangle the mass of information contained in every Reading Comprehension passage.

2. Within the questions, you will be asked to identify the viewpoints presented in the passages and to differentiate between those viewpoints. Answer choices will often present different viewpoints in order to test your ability to distinguish between groups.

In the paragraph under examination, the two viewpoints are presented "back-to-back." This is done intentionally so that the test makers can test your ability to compare and contrast different views. Of course, some test takers fail to distinguish these views, and they are much more prone to fall prey to questions that test the difference between these viewpoints.

In the above paragraph, the views are presented very clearly, and each group is easy to identify. Unfortunately, viewpoints will not always be presented with such clarity. Consider the following opening paragraph from a different sample passage:

> Many critics agree that the primary characteristic of Senegalese filmmaker Ousmane Sembène's work is its sociopolitical commitment. Sembène was trained in Moscow in the cinematic methods of socialist
> (5) realism, and he asserts that his films are not meant to entertain his compatriots, but rather to raise their awareness of the past and present realities of their society. But his originality as a filmmaker lies most strikingly in his having successfully adapted film,
> (10) originally a Western cultural medium, to the needs, pace, and structures of West African culture. In particular, Sembène has found within African oral culture techniques and strategies that enable him to express his views and to reach both literate and
> (15) nonliterate Senegalese viewers.

The first sentence introduces the view of "Many critics" and how they view the work of Ousmane Sembène. The second sentence (line 3) begins with a viewpoint neutral statement, but the second half of that sentence (line 5) begins with "he asserts," a reference to Sembène and how he views his films. So, the first two sentences each contain a different group and viewpoint. The third and fourth sentences may at first appear to be viewpoint neutral, but in fact this section is an opinion, and as this opinion is not ascribed to any particular group, it must be the opinion and viewpoint of the author. Thus, this paragraph contains three separate viewpoints:

RC

An opinion presented without reference to any group is typically the author's opinion.

Many critics agree that the primary characteristic
of Senegalese filmmaker Ousmane Sembène's work is
its sociopolitical commitment. Sembène was trained
in Moscow in the cinematic methods of socialist
(5)   realism, and he asserts that his films are not meant to
entertain his compatriots, but rather to raise their
awareness of the past and present realities of their
society. But his originality as a filmmaker lies most
strikingly in his having successfully adapted film,
(10)   originally a Western cultural medium, to the needs,
pace, and structures of West African culture. In
particular, Sembène has found within African oral
culture techniques and strategies that enable him to
express his views and to reach both literate and
(15)   nonliterate Senegalese viewers.

Many Critics' View

Sembène's View

Author's View

Of course, not all viewpoints are presented in separate sentences. In an effort
to confuse test takers, the test makers sometimes introduce two viewpoints in
a single sentence, as in the following example:

While the proponents of the Futurism art movement
believed that the past was an era to be ignored, some
critics assert that, ironically, for the Futurists to break
from the past would have required a more thorough
(5)   understanding of history on their part.

In the sentence above, two views are introduced: that of the proponents of
Futurism, and that of the critics of Futurism. However, although the sentence
contains two opposing views, tracking those elements is no more difficult than
when the views are presented in separate sentences. Again, we will discuss
notating the views in a later section.

When we begin our discussion of the questions that typically accompany
GMAT passages, we will revisit the importance of a viewpoint-based analysis.
In the meantime, always remember to identify the various viewpoints that you
encounter in a Reading Comprehension passage.

2. Tone/Attitude

This section discusses the "T" in the VIEWSTAMP acronym. The "T" stands for Tone.

Identifying the group or individual behind each viewpoint is usually easy. Identifying the tone or attitude of each group can sometimes be more challenging. Attitude is the state of mind or feeling that each group takes to the subject matter at hand, and for our purposes, "attitude" and "tone" will be used interchangeably.

The author's attitude is revealed through the author's choice of words. For example, is the author indifferent? Critical? Convinced? Skeptical? Hopeful? To make a determination of attitude, you must carefully examine the words used by the author. Is the opinion of the author positive or negative? By how much?

In most passages, GMAT authors tend not to be extreme in their opinions. As mentioned earlier in this chapter, most passages are drawn from academic or professional publications, and the authors in these publications attempt to offer reasoned arguments in support of their position, arguments that will sway the average reader. In doing so, they often present counterarguments and acknowledge the position of the other side. This fact does not mean that they cannot have strong opinions; it just means that they will not use extremely passionate or fiery language. Thus, one does not often see an author whose tone would be described as "jubilant," "tempestuous," or "depressed."

Most GMAT authors do not display an extreme attitude or tone.

Note also that tone is representative of the passage as a whole, and not just of a single section. An author who exhibited strong support for a position throughout the passage but then at the very end of the passage acknowledged that critics existed would not be said to be "concerned" or "negative." In other words, the tone exhibited in the last few lines would not override or outweigh the positive support that author displayed earlier. Instead, such a section would simply modify the overall tone of the author, to something along the lines of "reasoned optimism" or "positive but realistic."

Of course, the author is not the only one with a distinct tone. Each viewpoint group has tone as well, but determining that tone can sometimes be far more difficult because their position is filtered through the author's words. That is, the author chooses all of the words in the passage, so the viewpoint of each group is harder to discern at times because their views are given to you secondhand. This typically results in a limited range of tones. So, although an author's tone can be quite complex, usually the tone of other viewpoint groups is less complex, and can often be reduced to a simple agree/disagree position. Thus, although you must know the viewpoint of each group in the passage, as far as attitude, you are primarily concerned with the attitude of the author.

RC

Let us analyze a few excerpts and examine the idea of tone further. Consider the following section of text:

> There are signs that the animosity between the two companies is diminishing.

In the section above, the author's attitude towards the occurrence appears to be neutral. The information is presented factually, and no valuation of the diminishing animosity is provided. Consider, however, how this passage would read if one additional word were inserted:

> Fortunately, there are signs that the animosity between the two companies is diminishing.

With the addition of "fortunately," the author's attitude towards the occurrence is now clear—the diminishment of the animosity is a positive occurrence. Other word choices would obviously have a different effect. For example, choosing "unfortunately" instead of "fortunately" would reverse the author's position on the diminishing disagreement .

Of course, GMAT passages are comprised of more than a single sentence, and sometimes no indicator words are present. The following text segment from the prior section typifies how a passage can begin:

> The World Wide Web, a network of electronically produced and interconnected (or "linked") sites, called pages, that are accessible via personal computer, raises legal issues about the rights of owners of intellectual
> (5) property, notably those who create documents for inclusion on Web pages. Some of these owners of intellectual property claim that unless copyright law is strengthened, intellectual property on the Web will not be protected from copyright infringement. Web users,
> (10) however, claim that if their ability to access information on Web pages is reduced, the Web cannot live up to its potential as an open, interactive medium of communication.

Lines 1-6 are viewpoint neutral, and thus the tone is neutral as well. The author simply presents the topic at hand, and he or she does so in a matter-of-fact manner. One would not say that the author is "happy," or "serious," or "sad."

Lines 6-9 present the first definable group in the passage, "Some of these owners of intellectual property." We know from prior analysis that their viewpoint is that copyright law should be strengthened, but their tone is harder to discern. Are they furious? Belligerent? Reasonable? There is really no way to know because no indication of their attitude is made other than the obvious fact that they believe copyright law should be strengthened and thus they disagree with other groups who believe it should be weakened. How they approach that disagreement, however, is not stated in the passage.

Lines 9-14 present a new viewpoint, that of "Web users." However, other than understanding that this group's viewpoint is somewhat contrary to the owners of intellectual property, we cannot make a determination of the tone of their argument. There is no indication that they are focused, or intense, or happy. Like the previous group, there is simply not enough information to determine their exact attitude toward the subject matter.

Now, let's take a moment to examine a section of text from the end of this same passage:

> Changing copyright law to benefit owners of
> intellectual property is thus ill-advised because it
> would impede the development of the Web as a public
> (55)   forum dedicated to the free exchange of ideas.

Consider the author's position in this section of text. The choice of the words "ill-advised" reveals the author's attitude to be strongly negative toward changing the copyright law to benefit owners. The "negative" part is easy to spot, but how do you know it is "strongly negative?" Think for a moment of some of the other words the author could have chosen instead of "ill-advised" that would also convey negativity. Here are just a few examples, each of which conveys negativity, but not to the degree conveyed by "ill-advised":

> "Changing copyright law to benefit owners of intellectual property is thus a *concern* because it...

> "Changing copyright law to benefit owners of intellectual property is thus *troubling* because it..."

> "Changing copyright law to benefit owners of intellectual property is thus an *issue* because it..."

In each example, the word chosen to convey negativity is not as strong or as harsh as "ill-advised." In the annals of GMAT passages, "ill-advised" is a relatively strong negative term. Of course, the author could have chosen to go even more negative, but that would begin to sound unreasonable:

RC

"Changing copyright law to benefit owners of intellectual property would thus be *ridiculous* because..."

"Changing copyright law to benefit owners of intellectual property would thus be *preposterous* because..."

"Changing copyright law to benefit owners of intellectual property would thus be *disastrous* because..."

These word choices, while possible, tend not to occur on the GMAT because they convey such extreme emotion. Regardless, the point is that in examining attitude, you must carefully consider the word choices used by the author of the passage. The rule is that small changes in word choice can have a large effect on the overall tone of the passage.

Because tracking viewpoints and tone is such a critical ability, the next several pages contain a drill that will help test and strengthen your ability to identify various viewpoints and their accompanying tones.

RC

Viewpoint and Attitude Identification Drill

Each of the following items presents a paragraph. Read each item and identify the viewpoints present. Then, in the spaces that follow each paragraph, fill in the proper line references, respective viewpoints, and any associated tone or attitude. *Answers on Page 229*

Passage 1:

Federal rules of evidence have long prohibited the presentation in court of many types of "hearsay" (evidence recounted second-hand, rather than reported directly by a witness), based on the notion
(5)   that only the most readily verifiable evidence should be allowed consideration by any court in making its determinations. Dr. Kinsley has argued, however, that the rules of evidence as currently written are unacceptably overreaching, precluding
(10)   the use of too many types of evidence whose value would far outweigh any associated detriment if allowed court admissibility. But modern hearsay rules have been written with good reason.

Lines: _____
Viewpoint: _____

Lines: _____
Viewpoint: _____

Lines: _____
Viewpoint: _____

Passage 2:

In the years which preceded Roger Bannister's record breaking performance, it was widely believed that the human body was not equipped to complete a mile-long run in under four minutes;
(5)   human lungs, many leading experts asserted, could never deliver sufficient oxygen, and the heart could not undergo such physical stress. Bannister, undeterred, believed that he could reach the goal that he had set in 1952.

Lines: _____
Viewpoint: _____

Lines: _____
Viewpoint: _____

RC

Viewpoint and Attitude Identification Drill

<u>Passage 3:</u>

Friedman suggested monetary manipulation to
bring the supply and demand for money to an
artificial equilibrium, but, as Margaret Thatcher and
many others have since learned, the application of
(5)   these principles in the real world often brings about
results contrary to those predicted from the ivory
towers of abstract economic theory.

Lines: _____
Viewpoint: _____

Lines: _____
Viewpoint: _____

<u>Passage 4:</u>

The first cardiac pacemaker was the brainchild of
John Hopps, a Canadian electrical engineer who, in
1941, while researching hypothermia and the use
of heat from radio frequencies to restore
(5)   body temperature, found that mechanical or
electrical stimulation can restart a heart that has
stopped under conditions of extreme cold. The
earliest versions of the pacemaker were heavy
pieces of equipment which were far too large for
(10)   implantation, and instead had to be rolled on
wheels and kept attached to the patient at all times.
Modern science has seen a striking decrease in the
size of these devices, which are now small enough
to be surgically placed under the skin, allowing
(15)   them to remain virtually undetectable externally.

Lines: _____
Viewpoint: _____

Viewpoint and Attitude Identification Drill

On the other side of the interpretation debate
are those who believe that the Constitution was
meant to be a "living document," whose proper
construction would readily adapt to an evolving

(5) nation. Judges who subscribe to this perspective
are often referred to by strict constructionists as
judicial activists who are trying to take law-making
power away from the legislative branch of
the government. These judges, however, consider

(10) themselves interpreters, not activists. The framers
specifically allowed for constitutional amendment,
and afforded significant power to the judicial
branch; they felt that the Constitution was to
provide a framework but would have to adapt to a

(15) changing nation.

Lines: _____
Viewpoint: _____

Lines: _____
Viewpoint: _____

Lines: _____
Viewpoint: _____

Lines: _____
Viewpoint: _____

Viewpoint and Attitude Identification Drill Answers

1. Lines 1-7: This section is not attributed to any particular party, so it must come from the author. As this portion is purely informational, there is no tone at this point.

    Lines 7-12: This is the perspective of Dr. Kinsley. By using the term "unacceptably," Kinsley appears to have a fairly strong negative opinion about the breadth of hearsay prohibitions as currently written.

    Lines 12-13: This excerpt is also not attributed to anyone, so it is the author at this point who takes issue with Kinsley's argument, asserting that the hearsay rules have a reasonable foundation.

2. Lines 1-7: In the beginning of this paragraph, the author apprises us of a widely held belief about the body's limitations, followed by a more specific attribution of related assertions to many leading experts.

    Lines 7-9: Here the author makes the switch to the perspective of Bannister. There is not too much attitude reflected here, although Bannister is characterized as fairly confident.

3. Lines 1-3: The first two lines provide Friedman's suggestion as a simple presentation of information.

    Lines 3-7: This portion, which is not specifically attributed to anyone else, provides the perspective of the author, who takes a very negative attitude, clearly reflected in the reference to "ivory tower theory;" the author is not a fan of Friedman's suggestion of monetary manipulation.

4. Lines 1-15: This excerpt does not provide multiple viewpoints; it is simply the author's presentation of information about the history of the cardiac pacemaker and its inventor. As is sometimes the case with science passages, this selection reflects a relatively neutral tone.

5. Lines 1-5: This is the viewpoint of the "living document" proponents, and the tone is fairly matter-of-fact.

    Lines 5-9: Here the author presents the perspective of the strict constructionists, who take a negative tone with regard to the "living document" judges.

    Lines 9-10: At this point we are presented with the perspective of the so-called "judicial activists," who believe that they are simply offering interpretations rather than newly made laws.

    Lines 10-12: Here we are provided with information about the beliefs of the framers, with an attitude that lends more support to the idea of the Constitution as a living document.

3. Passage Argumentation

This section discusses the "A" in VIEWSTAMP. The "A" stands for Arguments.

Identifying viewpoints and tone is critical to getting a generalized feel for how a passage unfolds. Understanding the arguments will help you understand the details of the passage. GMAT Reading Comprehension passages consist of premises and conclusions just as in the Critical Reasoning section. Thus revisiting those concepts, which are covered in the first section of this book, will be very helpful in approaching Reading Comprehension passages as well.

4. The Main Point

In the Critical Reasoning section of this book, our discussion of argumentation was at the detail level, discussing the words that authors use to introduce certain types of argumentative elements. Identifying ideas at the elemental level is an important ability, and one that will serve you well throughout the GMAT, as well as in business school. However, a large number of Reading Comprehension questions will ask you broad questions such as the Main Point of the author's argument. Consequently, you must also see the "big picture" as you read, and develop an ability to track the author's major themes and intents.

This section discusses the "MP" in the VIEWSTAMP acronym. The "MP" stands for Main Point.

The main point of a passage is the central idea, or ultimate conclusion, that the author is attempting to prove. Although in the majority of passages the main point is stated in the first paragraph, it is not always the case that the main point appears in the first or second sentence. The main point of many passages has appeared in the final sentence of the first paragraph or in the first sentence of the second paragraph, or, at times, in the last paragraph. So, although the main point is often in the first paragraph, the test makers have the ability to place the main point anywhere in the passage.

The main point of a passage is the central idea that the author is attempting to prove or relay.

As you read, you must identify the author's conclusions and track how they link together. What is the ultimate aim of the author's statements? What is he or she attempting to prove? Are some conclusions used to support others? If so, which is the primary conclusion? The key to identifying a main point is to remember that, although the main point may be stated succinctly in a sentence or two, all paragraphs of the passage must support the main point. Thus, the main point will not just reflect the argument contained in a single paragraph.

RC

5. Passage Structure

Many students, when first beginning to work with Reading Comprehension passages, attempt to remember every single detail of the passage. Given the limits of human short-term memory, this is an impossible task. Fortunately, it is also an unnecessary one. Built into your test taking strategy should be the expectation that you will frequently return to the passage during the questions to confirm and disconfirm answer choices.

In order to successfully return to the passage, however, you must attempt to identify the underlying logical structure of the passage as you read. This will help you quickly find information once you begin to answer the questions. For example, some passages open by stating the background of a thesis that will be challenged later in the passage. In the following paragraphs the author will present an alternative viewpoint to the thesis and perhaps specific counterexamples which provide support for the alternative view. Awareness of this general structure will allow you to reduce the time you spend searching for information when you need to refer back to the passage.

Fortunately, identifying the logical structure of a passage does not require any training in logic or in logical terminology. You simply need to be able to describe in general terms the order in which things are presented in the passage. This is most often connected to specific paragraphs of a passage, as in, "The first paragraph introduces the jury unanimity requirement, and then presents the viewpoints of the critics of unanimity. At the start of the second paragraph, the author takes a strong position that jury unanimity is essential. The second and third paragraphs support that position—paragraph two states that the costs of hung juries are minimal, and paragraph three states that unanimous verdicts lead to fairer verdicts." With a brief synopsis such as this one, you could confidently return to the passage as needed. Question about the critic's position? Most likely the answer will be found in the first paragraph. Question about verdict fairness? Most likely the answer will be found in the last paragraph.

Note that your structural analysis is *not* written down during the exam; instead, you simply hold the idea mentally. Thus, in a nutshell, your structural analysis must be compact enough to be mentally retained, and it must also provide enough basic detail to serve as a guide when you return to the passage. Also keep in mind that if you need to refresh your memory, you can glance at your notes for clues.

Of course, the Viewpoint Analysis approach we discussed briefly before will also help you identify and control the structure of the passage. Understanding the views of the various players in the passage will greatly assist in your ability to understand the passage as a whole. Identifying the main point and author's tone will also make this task easier.

This section discusses the "S" in the VIEWSTAMP acronym. The "S" stands for Structure.

RC

Do not worry about the fact that you will not be able to remember every detail. Remember, the answers to every problem are already on the page, and thus your task is simply to be able to identify the correct answer, not to remember every single thing about the passage.

Passage Analysis and Structure Identification Drill

Using the principles described in this section, provide a distilled version of the information presented, as well as a basic structural analysis, of the following passage excerpts.
Answers on Page 235

Example:

> The okapi, a forest mammal of central Africa, has presented zoologists with a number of difficult questions since they first learned of its existence in 1900. The first was how to classify it, because it was horselike in dimension, and bore patches of striped hide similar to a zebra's (a relative of the horse), zoologists first classified it as a member of the horse family but further studies showed that, despite okapis' coloration and short necks, their closest relatives were giraffes. The okapi's rightful place within the giraffe family is confirmed by its skin-covered horns (in males), two-lobed canine teeth, and long prehensile tongue.

Distilled Version: The okapi, a central African mammal discovered in 1900, was first classified with the horse family based on its size and hide. Zoologists later decided the okapi was related to the giraffe, based on its canine teeth, long tongue, and horns in males.

Structural Analysis: Introduce the okapi, and the difficulties of classification, first thought to be related to the horse, then the giraffe. Provide specific evidence which supports the animal's relation to the giraffe.

Passage 1:

> Most scientists who study the psychological effects of alcoholic beverages have assumed that wine, like beer or distilled spirits, is a drink whose only active ingredient is alcohol. Because of this assumption, these scientists have rarely investigated the effects of wine as distinct from other forms of alcoholic beverages. Nevertheless, unlike other alcoholic beverages, wine has for centuries been thought to have healthful effects that these scientists—who not only make no distinction among wine, beer, and distilled spirits but also study only the excessive or abusive intake of these beverages—have obscured.

Distilled Version: _____
_____
_____
_____

Structural Analysis: _____
_____
_____

Passage 2:

Many political economists believe that the soundest indicator of the economic health of a nation is the nation's gross national product (GNP) per capita—a figure reached by dividing the total value of the goods produced yearly in a nation by its population and taken to be a measure of the welfare of the nation's residents. But there are many factors affecting residents' welfare that are not captured by per capita GNP; human indicators, while sometimes more difficult to calculate or document, provide sounder measures of a nations' progress than does the indicator championed by these economists. These human indicators include nutrition and life expectancy; birth weight and level of infant mortality; ratio of population level to availability of resources; employment opportunities; and the ability of governments to provide services such as education, clean water, medicine, public transportation, and mass communication for their residents.

Distilled Version:_____

_____

_____

_____

Structural Analysis:_____

_____

_____

Passage 3:

Traditionally, members of a community such as a town or neighborhood share a common location and sense of necessary interdependence that includes, for example, mutual respect and emotional support. But as modern societies grow more technological and sometimes more alienating, people tend to spend less time in the kinds of interactions that their communities require in order to thrive. Meanwhile, technology has made it possible for individuals to interact via personal computer with others who are geographically distant. Advocates claim that these computer conferences, in which large numbers of participants communicate by typing comments that are immediately read by other participants and responding immediately to those comments they read, function as communities that can substitute for traditional interactions with neighbors.

Distilled Version:_____

_____

_____

Structural Analysis:_____

_____

_____

RC

Passage 4:

Experts anticipate that global atmospheric concentrations of carbon dioxide (CO_2) will have doubled by the end of the twenty-first century. It is known that CO_2 can contribute to global warming by trapping solar energy that is being reradiated as heat from the Earth's surface. However, some research has suggested that elevated CO_2 levels could enhance the photosynthetic rates of plants, resulting in a lush world of agricultural abundance, and that this CO_2 fertilization effect might eventually decrease the rate of global warming. The increased vegetation in such an environment could be counted on to draw more CO_2 from the atmosphere. The level of CO_2 would thus increase at a lower rate than many experts have predicted.

Distilled Version: _____
_____
_____
_____

Structural Analysis: _____
_____
_____

Passage 5:

One of the greatest challenges facing medical students today, apart from absorbing volumes of technical information and learning habits of scientific thought, is that of remaining empathetic to the needs of patients in the face of such rigorous training. Requiring students to immerse themselves completely in medical coursework risks disconnecting them from the personal and ethical aspects of doctoring, and such strictly scientific thinking is insufficient for grappling with modern ethical dilemmas. For these reasons, aspiring physicians need to develop new ways of thinking about and interacting with patients. Training in ethics that takes narrative literature as its primary subject is one method of accomplishing this.

Distilled Version: _____
_____
_____
_____

Structural Analysis: _____
_____
_____

Passage Analysis and Structure Identification Drill Answer Key

Note: It is unlikely that your answers will exactly match the answers below; these are merely suggested analyses of the passage excerpts. However, you should focus on whether your analysis of each excerpt provides similar sufficient basic detail and can be easily understood and retained.

Passage 1:
Distilled Version: Scientists usually group wine along with other alcoholic beverages, presuming its only active ingredient to be alcohol. Science seldom considers wine on its own, instead focusing on the excessive intake or abuse of alcohol, obscuring wine's distinct beneficial properties.
Structural Analysis: Introduce common assumption about wine, point out how the assumption caused a course of action. Assert that wine has healthful effects, and that science's focus on abuse obscures the perceived healthful effects of wine.

Passage 2:
Distilled Version: Many mistakenly believe a nation's health is best reflected by its per capita GNP. A more accurate measure deals with human indicators, which reflect a population's general health, basic resources provided, and access to opportunities such as education and employment.
Structural Analysis: Introduce concept of GNP as indicator of economic health. List factors that do not show up in GNP indicator (with clear intent of calling into question its accuracy as an indicator).

Passage 3:
Distilled Version: Communities have historically been based on neighbor relationships which can provide respect and support. Technology has reduced traditional interactions in favor of more computer-based communications; advocates claim this provides a reasonable substitute for traditional communities.
Structural Analysis: Describe attributes of a traditional community, and fact that modern technology leads many to have computer based interactions over great distances. Introduce advocates' viewpoint, which is that such computer interaction can substitute for the traditional community.

Passage 4:
Distilled Version: Global CO_2 could double by the end of the century. CO_2 can trap the Earth's heat, and contribute to global warming. But research indicates that CO_2 might enhance photosynthesis, catalyzing growth of plants, which would in turn absorb more CO_2. This could eventually decrease the rate of global warming.
Structural Analysis: Introduce expert prediction that CO_2 will double by the end of the century. State that CO_2 can contribute to global warming but may also eventually decrease the rate of global warming by working with vegetation to promote absorption.

Passage 5:
Distilled Version: In addition to standard medical study, medical students need empathy for their patients. Immersive training can desensitize these students to personal and ethical issues. To develop abilities with empathetic patient interaction, one approach is ethics training with narrative literature.
Structural Analysis: Introduce medical students' challenge of remaining empathetic in spite of complete immersion in scientific thought. Introduce option of ethics training as one way to promote their staying connected to ethical aspects.

A Sample Passage Analyzed

Take several minutes to read the following practice GMAT passage (time is not critical for this exercise). Look for the five crucial elements of VIEWSTAMP that we discussed within this chapter:

1. The various groups and viewpoints discussed within the passage. (VIEW)
2. The tone or attitude of each group or individual. (T)
3. The argument made by each group or individual. (A)
4. The main point of the passage. (MP)
5. The structure of the passage and the organization of ideas. (S)

Please note that we will not examine any questions just yet, but the passage and the five VIEWSTAMP elements are discussed on the following pages.

James Joyce, the Irish poet considered by many to be among the most influential writers of the modern era, is probably known best as the author of Ulysses, the modernist novel first published in
(5) 1922. To say that Joyce's writings are subject to complex and varied interpretation would be an understatement; the author continues to provide fodder for modern scholarly journals, and countless books and articles by subsequent
(10) authors have been dedicated solely to the assessment of his often enigmatic works. One such work is an obscure collection of short stories known as "Finn's Hotel."

For many years, the tales which comprise
(15) "Finn's Hotel" were believed by most scholars to be nothing more than a series of preliminary sketches the amalgamation of which was eventually to serve as the basis for the author's more famous "Finnegan's Wake." Recently,
(20) however, a Joyce scholar in Ireland has offered a new perspective on the collection. Danis Rose, an independent writer who has been developing his own critical edition of "Finnegan's Wake" for over fifteen years, will soon release a previously
(25) unpublished collection by Joyce (the works involved have been published before, but never as a collection). Rather than early drafts of a later work, says Rose, the collection represents its own anthology of distinct works—one which provides
(30) important insights about the writer's path from Ulysses to Finnegan's Wake.

Rose arrived at his conclusions about the anthology after examining correspondence between Joyce and the poet's patron, Harriet
(35) Shaw Weaver. These letters only recently became available, which explains why the "Finn's Hotel" stories had been mischaracterized for so many years.

Sample Passage—Analysis

Paragraph One:

This passage begins with an introduction to James Joyce, a writer best known as the author of the modernist novel *Ulysses*. Joyce's writings, we are told, are not easily understood; despite the fact that Joyce was published in the early 20th century, the writer's works are still the subject of varied and complex interpretations among modern scholars. Like many GMAT authors, the writer of this passage begins with a paragraph that is viewpoint neutral—an opinion-free presentation of facts, intended to provide context for the subsequent discussion of the anthology of obscure stories known as *Finn's Hotel*.

Paragraph Two:

The author begins this second paragraph with the perspective of "most scholars," who perceived the stories from *Finn's Hotel* as nothing more than early sketches which were to provide the foundation for Joyce's later, better-known work, *Finnegan's Wake*. At line 19 of the passage, the author begins the presentation of the alternate viewpoint of Danis Rose, a writer who argues that the stories of *Finn's Hotel* are not early drafts of *Finnegan's Wake*. Rose instead asserts that these stories are important in their own right, reflecting the evolution which took place between Joyce's writing of *Ulysses* and that of *Finnegan's Wake*. Structurally, the author opens this paragraph with the perspective of "most scholars," and closes with Rose's rebuttal of that position.

Paragraph Three:

The author begins the final paragraph with the fact that Rose's perspective is based on correspondence between Joyce and his patron, Harriet Shaw Weaver. Until this point in the passage, different viewpoints have been discussed, but the author's opinion has not been presented. Beginning at line 35, the author's perspective finally becomes clear: Because the patron correspondences were previously unavailable, the author asserts, the stories from the Joyce anthology were "mischaracterized" for years. The claim that the *Finn's Hotel* stories had been mischaracterized (presumably by the scholars referenced in the second paragraph) reflects the author's opinion, not empirical fact. This final sentence of the passage clarifies the position of the author, who shares Rose's perspective.

Let us review each of the five critical VIEWSTAMP elements in the passage:

1. The various groups and viewpoints discussed within the passage.

   There are three main viewpoints presented in the passage: that of "most scholars," that of Danis Rose, and that of the author. Rose and the author are in agreement, and both oppose the referenced scholars.

2. The tone or attitude of each group or individual.

> Rose and the scholars are at odds, but the tone of the disagreement does not appear to be acrimonious. For example, critics "believed" and Rose "has offered a new perspective." Those are fairly mild words that simply indicate general disagreement, not particularly strong opposition.

> The author appears to disagree with the scholars to a greater degree. In lines 37-38, the author asserts that "the *Finn's Hotel* stories had been mischaracterized for so many years," to indicate that he or she does not share the position of "most scholars."

3. The argument made by each group or individual.

> The "scholars" referenced by the author in line 15 argue that *Finn's Hotel* represents nothing more than early drafts for Joyce's later work, *Finnegan's Wake*.

> Rose and the author disagree with the scholars: the author calls the scholar's perspective a "mischaracterization," and Danis asserts that the anthology should be considered a group of distinct works, providing "important insights" about Joyce's progression as a writer.

4. The main point of the passage.

> The main point of the passage is presented at the end of the second paragraph, where the author discusses Rose's assertion that the stories of *Finn's Hotel* make up an important anthology rather than just sketches for the production of the later, more famous *Finnegan's Wake*.

5. The structure of the passage and the organization of ideas.

> The structure of the passage is as follows: The first paragraph discusses Joyce and some of the poet's works, including *Finn's Hotel*. The second paragraph presents the scholars' perspective on the anthology, and introduces Rose and his alternate viewpoint on the matter. The third paragraph reflects the perspective of the author, who agrees with Rose.

Overall, this is a solid passage—several viewpoints exist, clear authorial position and attitude are presented, and reasonably clear structure and argumentation exist. Granted, the topic may not be the most exciting, but you can engage yourself by focusing on the disagreement between the parties.

Sample Passage—Analysis

One final note: If you can consistently apply the five VIEWSTAMP ideas we have discussed throughout this chapter, you will be in an excellent position to attack the questions. Once we have examined the various question types which will accompany the passages, you will have a powerful arsenal of tools to dissect each problem, and, in many cases, you will discover that you know what the correct answer will say before you even begin reading the five answer choices.

CHAPTER ELEVEN: PASSAGE ELEMENTS AND FORMATIONS

Chapter Preview

This chapter will cover sources of passage difficulty and examine the elements and formations that appear in passages which tend to generate questions. That is, we will look at why passages are hard and what passage elements the test makers tend to ask about. The preceding chapter introduced the "big picture" elements that you must always track, whereas this chapter will present the more detailed elements that you should note. In the next chapter we will discuss individual question types.

Sources of Difficulty: The Test Makers' Arsenal

There are several general ways the makers of the test can increase the level of difficulty of any given passage. Before examining the specific elements that the test makers like to test, reviewing the general methods that can be used to increase difficulty is helpful.

The following five methods are the primary ways used by the test makers to alter the perception of difficulty that students have about individual passages:

Challenging Topic or Terminology

In some passages, the choice of topic makes the passage seem more difficult to some students. For example, many students fear the appearance of a science-related passage on the GMAT. As we will discuss later, you should not be afraid or unduly worried by science passages (or any passage, for that matter). That said, an unfamiliar or complex topic can make a passage harder, but only incrementally so because the test makers are forced to explain the main concepts of the passage, regardless of the topic. Thus, there may be a few moments of anxiety while you are forced to adjust to an unknown topic, but the test makers will always give you the information needed to answer the questions. As outlined below, other methods are far more effective at making a passage difficult.

The use of complicated terminology usually concerns students as well. Reading a passage that contains words or ideas that you do not recognize is intimidating and usually confusing. As mentioned in the previous chapter, you should not be intimidated by unknown concepts, mainly because the test makers must *always* define any term or concept not in common public usage.

When you encounter unknown words, they will generally fall into one of two categories: new terms related to the concept under discussion or unknown vocabulary words. In the case of terms related to the concept under discussion (such as *Monetarism* or *Meteor Streams*), the test makers will define the term or concept for you in the text, sometimes briefly using synonyms, sometimes in greater detail. Unknown vocabulary words can be more challenging, but you can use context clues from the surrounding text to help determine the meaning of words you do not recognize. We will briefly discuss this point again later in this chapter.

Challenging Writing Style

The test makers carefully choose whether a passage will have a clear, easy-to-read writing style or a dense, convoluted writing style. Obviously, writing style has a tremendous effect on passage difficulty because even the easiest of concepts can become difficult to understand if the writing style is intentionally complex.

In the first few lines of a passage, it is difficult to tell whether the writing style will be challenging. If you do encounter a passage that has a very difficult-to-read style, use some of the tips in the next section to focus on the elements most likely to be tested.

Multiple Viewpoints

In the preceding chapter we discussed the importance of tracking viewpoints while reading. We will discuss this again in a few pages, but be aware that one easy way for the test makers to increase difficulty is to add more viewpoints. Tracking viewpoints in a passage with only two viewpoints is easy; tracking viewpoints in a passage with several can be far more challenging. The more viewpoints present, the easier it is to confuse them, or forget who said what. This is especially true because when more viewpoints are present, the test makers typically insert extensive compare-and-contrast sections, which make separating and mastering each view more difficult.

Difficult Questions/Answers

The difficulty of a passage can also be altered by the nature of the questions. For example, if the questions are unusual in nature, or, more frequently, if the answer choices are difficult to separate, then the passage set itself will be difficult or time-consuming. Thus, even an easily understandable passage can turn challenging once you start attacking the questions. Later we will discuss question type in detail, and provide you with an effective approach for attacking any question you face.

As you develop the ability to see through the topic and focus on the writing style, you will notice that many passages are not as complex as their topics might suggest.

RC

Passage Elements That Generate Questions

As you read, there are certain specific passage elements that should jump out at you, primarily because history has reflected the test makers' tendency to use these elements as the basis of questions.

For purposes of clarity, we will divide these elements into two groups: viewpoint-specific elements and text-based elements.

Viewpoint-Specific Elements

Analysis of viewpoints is one of the major approaches we use in attacking the passages, and in the previous chapter we discussed this approach in depth. Because separating viewpoints allows you to divide the passage into logical, trackable units, the process helps you to more easily understand the passage and to disentangle the many disparate ideas in each passage. Viewpoints also play a large role in the main themes of the passage, so they also are the source of many of the questions asked by the test makers. For example, questions about the main point, authorities cited by the author, or the perspective of any of the players in the passage are all related to viewpoints, and thus tracking viewpoints not only makes understanding the passage itself easier, it automatically assists you in answering a *significant* portion of the questions. Thus, while reading you must always focus on identifying each viewpoint in the passage.

When considering viewpoints, be aware that one of the favorite tricks of the test makers is to use competing perspectives, a trick that involves presenting two or more viewpoints on the same subject, with each viewpoint containing slightly different elements (but often sharing some similar elements). Here is an example:

Topic: Nuclear power

Viewpoint 1: Nuclear power plants are efficient generators of energy, but they present serious long-term environmental concerns because of the problems associated with storing radioactive waste in the form of spent fuel.

Viewpoint 2: Nuclear power is the most efficient way to produce energy, and the waste problems associated with them, while significant, are lesser than those associated with more traditional energy production methods, such as those involving coal.

In the form above, the difference and similarity in viewpoints is easy to identify, but subtleties exist ("efficient generators" vs. "most efficient way," and "serious long-term environmental concerns" vs. "significant, are lesser," to name two). But imagine for a moment that the two views are woven together in a passage, and some extraneous information is also interspersed. When you finally attack the questions a few minutes later, it would be very easy to have forgotten the exact similarities and differences, especially if other viewpoints were present.

Thus, competing perspectives can be quite tricky because it is easy to confuse different views, and, of course, questions about these elements make certain to closely test whether you understand the exact differences between the different viewpoints.

Because viewpoint analysis was a main feature in the last chapter, we will move on for the moment, but in the passages we analyze in later chapters we will prominently feature this element (and all the elements in VIEWSTAMP) in our analysis.

Text-based Questions

In one sense, all questions are based on the text. In using the name "text-based," we refer to elements that appear directly in the text as an identifiable part—definitions, lists, compare/contrast sections, or dates, for example—and not the broader and somewhat more abstract elements such as main points, author's purposes, or passage structure. Under this definition, text-based questions will often be smaller pieces, sometimes just a single word, but sometimes short sections of the text. In this sense, these are the "nuts and bolts" elements that you should be aware of when reading.

These are the elements we will discuss (not in order of importance):

1. Initial Information/Closing Information
2. Dates and Numbers
3. Definitions
4. Examples
5. Difficult words or phrases
6. Enumerations/Lists
7. Text Questions

RC

1. Initial Information/Closing Information

The information presented in the first five lines of a passage—especially the details—is often forgotten by students. This occurs because at the very beginning of a passage you are focused on figuring out the topic and the author's general position, and thus seemingly minor details are hard to retain.

Similarly, the information presented in the last five lines is often forgotten because the average student is eager to jump to the questions and thus skims over the material at the very end of the passage. Thus, the test makers occasionally question you on your knowledge of information contained at the very beginning or end of the passage, so you must always make sure to check these areas if you are having difficulty answering a question, especially when you seem to have no idea where the answer might be (again, this would most likely occur with detail or fact-based questions).

2. Dates and Numbers

When a GMAT author references more than one date or era, creating a simple timeline can be an effective way to maintain relative perspective, whether the comparison spans days or centuries.

Dates often provide useful markers within a passage, allowing you "before" and "after" points to return to when searching for answers. While in some passages the use of dates is incidental, in other passages, a chronology is created, and then some of the questions will test your ability to understand the timeline. The general rule is that the more dates you see in a passage, the more important it is that you make note of them.

Numbers are usually less important than dates, but when numbers are used in a comparative sense, or as part of an explanation, the test makers will sometimes check your comprehension of their meaning.

3. Definitions

Identifying definitions serves two purposes: in those cases where you do not understand the term or concept it helps you to clarify the idea, and even when you do understand the concept the test makers will sometimes test you on your understanding of the definition.

The typical definition is presented in the immediate vicinity of the word or concept, like so:

> In England the burden of history weighs heavily on common law, the unwritten code of time-honored laws derived largely from English judicial custom and precedent.

In the section above, the clause after the comma provides the definition for the term *common law*. Of course, some definitions are much shorter, such as this sentence which includes the one-word definition of *maize*:

> Every culture that has adopted the cultivation of maize—also known as corn—has been radically changed by it.

Regardless of the length of a definition, you should make sure that you are comfortable with the term being defined. If you encounter an idea or term that you think should be defined but do not see a definition in the immediate vicinity, then the definition will probably be presented relatively soon (explicitly or through context clues), and the test makers are simply trying to trick you with a "trap of separation," which we will discuss later in this chapter.

Whenever you see an unfamiliar term or concept defined, be sure to take note; if the test makers have provided a clear definition or description, they generally expect you to be able to locate the reference.

4. Examples

GMAT authors often use examples to explain or underscore the points they are making. Logically, these examples serve as broad premises that support the conclusion of the author. Functionally, they help you to understand the typically more abstract point that the author is making, and so they can be quite helpful especially when you are having difficulty understanding the argument.

Examples can be short and specific to a single point, or they can be substantial and involved and appear throughout the passage. Always remember, though, that the example is not the main conclusion or point of the author; generally, examples are provided to support or explain the main conclusion.

The words "for example" are the most common way that examples are introduced, but the following terms all have been used:

> For example
> For instance
> A case in point is
> As shown by
> As demonstrated by

Examples are not the main conclusion or point of the author; the point being proven or explained by the example is the main conclusion or point.

Whenever you see these terms, immediately note what point is being shown. Here is an example:

> In science, serendipity often plays a crucial role in discoveries. For instance, Teflon was discovered by a scientist attempting to find a new gas for use in refrigeration.

Above, the author has introduces a concept (that good luck often plays a part in new discoveries), and immediately exemplifies the concept with the introductory phrase, "for instance."

RC

5. Difficult Words or Phrases

As mentioned earlier, challenging words or phrases are items that you should note while reading, but you should not become overly distressed if you do not immediately know what the terms mean. Terms outside the common public domain of knowledge (such as *circumpolar vortex*) are always explained, and unknown vocabulary words (such as *vituperate*) can often be defined by the context of usage. Acronyms are always explained.

The key thing to remember is that even if you do not understand a word, you will still understand virtually all other words in the passage, and so the possible downside of not knowing one word is very small. Simply bypass the word and then see if it is explained in some way later in the text or by context.

6. Lists and Enumerations

A number of passages feature sections where the author explains an idea by providing a list of points that support or explain the position. When these lists occur, you are almost always tested on your understanding of some or all of the items on the list.

The listed items do not appear as bullet points. Rather, they usually appear using a construction similar to one of the following:

> "First...Second...Third..."
> "First...Second...In addition..."
> "First...Second...Third...Last..."
> "(1)...(2)..."
> "Initially...And...Further..."
> "One possibility is...another possibility is...A final possibility..."

The lists usually contain one of two types of items: a list of reasons (premises) that explain why an action was taken or why a circumstance came into being, or a list of examples that relate to the point at hand.

A list of premises may appear as follows:

> The move towards political systems less dependent on monarchical structures came about for several reasons. First, the monetary and military abuses of the royalty placed several governments in severe financial hardship and created a strong undercurrent of discontent and resentment among the populace. Second, the uncertainty over personal human and property rights caused select elements within the upper class to become convinced that a more concrete and accountable political system was necessary, one insulated from the vagaries of royalty. And finally, problems with succession created a political environment fraught with uncertainty and turmoil.

"Circumpolar vortex" describes the high-altitude westerly winds that circle the Northern hemisphere at the middle latitudes.

To "vituperate" is to berate or address harshly.

RC

A list of examples might appear as follows:

> Developing nations have used a number of ingenious methods to increase energy production—and therefore gross economic capacity—while at the same time maintaining a commitment to sustaining the environment. Microfinanced solar projects in India, Brazil, and Vietnam have all yielded power systems able to sustain towns and villages in remote areas, all without a material impact on local resources. A wind farm in Morocco is a successful collaboration between three commercial firms and the government, and now outputs 50 megawatts. In Tibet, where there are no significant or obtainable fossil fuel resources, the Nagqu geothermal energy field provides 300 kilowatts of power in more cost-effective fashion than could any fossil fuel generators.

In the example above, the listed items are not numbered or introduced as list items, but a list of examples connected to specific countries is presented nonetheless. When reading, you must be prepared to encounter lists of items that are not clearly marked in the text. Any time an author presents a series of examples, you should recognize it and expect to capitalize on that list when you begin answering the questions.

7. Text Questions

When an author poses a question in the passage, in most instances the author goes on to immediately answer that question. Thus, tracking the presence of text questions is critical because it provides you with an outline for where the passage will go next. And, because these questions are often central to the theme of the passage, there is usually a question that revolves around the answer to the question.

Most often, text questions are posed in the traditional manner, with a question mark, as follows:

> So, what was the ultimate impact of the court's ruling on property rights for the Aleutian Islanders?

However, questions can be posed without the traditional question mark, as in this example:

> And thus, researchers concluded that some other explanation was needed to account for the difference in temperatures.

In the example, the sentence implies that there is a question regarding the temperature difference, and this implicit question is likely to then be answered in the text.

Text questions can be explicitly or implicitly presented in the passage.

RC

Causal reasoning and conditional reasoning appear frequently in the Critical Reasoning questions of the GMAT, but less so with the Reading Comprehension passages. Still, recognizing each reasoning type when it appears is extremely helpful because this can provide a framework that helps you understand the arguments being made.

Let's briefly review causal and conditional reasoning:

Causal Reasoning

Cause and effect reasoning asserts or denies that one thing causes another, or that one thing is caused by another. The cause is the event that makes the other occur; the effect is the event that follows from the cause. By definition, the cause must occur before the effect, and the cause is the "activator" or "ignitor" in the relationship. The effect always happens at some point in time after the cause.

Causality in Reading Comprehension usually is discussed in the context of why certain events occurred. The terms that typically introduce causality—such as *caused by*, *reason for*, or *product of*—are still used, but then the author often goes on to discuss the reasons behind the occurrence in depth.

Causality, when it appears in Reading Comprehension, is not normally viewed as flawed reasoning, and GMAT authors usually make an effort to explain the reasoning behind their causal assertions.

Conditional Reasoning

Conditional reasoning is the broad name given to logical relationships composed of sufficient and necessary conditions. Any conditional relationship consists of at least one sufficient condition and at least one necessary condition. A sufficient condition is an event or circumstance whose occurrence indicates that a necessary condition must also occur. A necessary condition is an event or circumstance whose occurrence is required in order for a sufficient condition to occur. In other words, if a sufficient condition occurs, you automatically know that the necessary condition also occurs. If a necessary condition occurs, then it is possible but not certain that the sufficient condition will occur.

Conditional relationships in Reading Comprehension passages tend to be unobtrusive, usually occurring as a sideline point to a larger argument. For example, a passage might discuss monetary policy, and in the course of doing so make a conditional assertion such as, "The only way to decrease monetary volatility is to tightly control the supply of money." In this sense, conditionality is usually not the focus or Main Point of a passage, but instead it is a type of reasoning that occurs while discussing or supporting other points.

Of the two types of reasoning, causal reasoning appears more frequently than conditional reasoning in the Reading Comprehension passages. This difference is due to the fact that many passages attempt to address why certain events occurred, and in doing so they naturally fall into causal explanations.

When either of the two reasoning types appears, it is usually discussed in more expansive terms, and the casual or conditional argument is broad and seldom based on single words or sentences. For example, consider the following paragraph:

> While prescriptions for medications are at an all time high, hyperactivity in children appears to be attributable in many cases to diet. Excessive ingestion of processed sugars, for example, has been linked to various disorders. In a recent study of children diagnosed with hyperactivity, many subjects displayed a more positive response to sugar restriction than to traditionally prescribed medication.

In the first sentence, a cause-and-effect relationship is asserted, and then the remainder of the paragraph builds the case for the assertion. Of course, causal or conditional reasoning assertions need not be limited to a single paragraph; entire passages can be built around a single causal or conditional idea.

Pitfalls to Avoid

While there are many concrete elements to track when reading a passage, there are also a number of text formations and configurations you should recognize. These formations are often used to generate questions, and in this sense they function as possible "traps" for the unwary test taker. The following section reviews the most frequently appearing traps, and examines each in detail.

Traps of Similarities and Distinctions™

These sections of text discuss in detail items that have both similarities and differences. By comparing and contrasting the items in a continuous section of text, the test makers create the possibility of confusion (by comparison, if the discussion of the concepts was separated into discrete sections, the information would be easier to control).

You should not become bogged down in trying to memorize every detail. Instead, take down a simple notation about a given section or paragraph, so that if you are asked about the details you can quickly return to the passage and sort out the specifics.

Compare-and-contrast sections appear very frequently in Reading Comprehension passages, and you should expect to see one or more on your exam.

Trap of Separation™

One of the favorite tricks of the test makers is to take related pieces of information and then physically separate those pieces by a number of lines of text that discuss a different concept. Then, in the questions, the test makers ask you a question about the concept in order to examine your ability to track related concepts in the face of unrelated (and likely confusing) information.

In some especially insidious instances, in the question stem the test makers will specifically refer you to just one of the places where the concept is discussed (for example, "In lines 12-14, the author..."), but this will not be the place in the passage that contains the information needed to answer the question. This trap, known as the Trap of Question Misdirection, can be very difficult to handle because most questions that specifically refer you to a place in the passage are indeed referring you to the area where the information needed to answer the question resides. Later we will discuss specific reference questions in more detail.

One reason this trick works is that there is a natural tendency on the part of readers to assume that pieces of information that are related should be in close proximity. The logical and linear writing style used in newspapers and

If a list of comparisons and contrasts starts to get complicated, a simple note ("paragraph two: mills compared") allows you to keep that section in perspective and move on to the rest of the passage.

The Trap of Question Misdirection occurs when the test makers use a specific line reference in the question stem to direct you to a place in the passage where the correct answer will not be found.

textbooks tends to support this belief, and many students bring those beliefs to the GMAT. However, as we have already discussed, the test makers want to present passages that test your ability to comprehend difficult material, and so they use certain methods to create greater complexity in the passages.

Of course, just as information that is separated can be related, information that is in close proximity does not have to be connected, as discussed next.

Trap of Proximity™

Just because two ideas are presented in close physical proximity to one another within a passage does not mean that they are related. As mentioned in the prior section, the expectation of most readers is that information that is physically close together will be related. This does not have to be the case, and the makers of the GMAT will set up situations to test your ability to make that distinction.

Trap of Inserted Alternate Viewpoint ™

Another trick of the test makers is to discuss a particular viewpoint, and in the middle of that discussion insert a new viewpoint. This technique is used to test your ability to track different perspectives and to know who said what.

Traps of Chronology™

Traps of chronology relate to the placement and order of items within the passage, and the tendency of many readers to believe that when one item is presented before another, then the first item occurred first or caused the second item. These two traps are called the Trap of Order and the Trap of Cause:

Trap of Order

Some students make the mistake of believing that because an item is discussed before another item, the first item likely predated the second item. Unless explicitly stated or inherently obvious, this does not have to be the case.

Trap of Cause

Other students make the mistake of assuming that when one item is discussed before another item, then the first item must have caused the second item. This assumption is unwarranted. The easiest way to discern the author's intentions is to carefully examine the language used by the writer because causal relationships almost always feature one or more of the words that indicate causality (such as *caused by, produced by, determined*, etc).

The simple truth is that the order of presentation of the items in the passage does not indicate any temporal or causal relationship between those items.

Passage Topic Traps™

Previously we discussed how passages on any topic could be easy or difficult. Difficulty is more a function of writing style, the number of viewpoints, and the exact concepts under discussion than of the general topic of the passage. That said, the test makers will occasionally use the topic to catch test takers off-guard. This can occur because when the typical student begins reading a passage, the topic often frames their expectation. For example, science passages are thought to be challenging whereas passages about humanities are less feared. The test makers are well aware of these ingrained expectations, and they at times play a sort of "bait and switch" game with students, especially by making a passage initially look hard or easy and then radically changing the level of difficulty after the first few lines or first paragraph.

The point to draw from this discussion is that you should not assume that a topic or passage will be easy or hard just from the first line or paragraph. The test makers love to play with the expectations of students, and one of their favorite tricks is to turn those expectations on their head.

Final Chapter Note

In review, the approach we advocate is a multi-level one. While reading, you should constantly track the five major VIEWSTAMP elements discussed in the previous chapter: the various groups and viewpoints discussed within the passage, the tone or attitude of each group or individual, the argument made by each group or individual, the main point of the passage, and the structure of the passage and the organization of ideas. At the same time, you must also keep an eye on the smaller elements that appear throughout the text, items such as examples and definitions, or forms of reasoning, to name a few. While this approach may sound complicated, with practice it becomes second nature, and soon you will find that you are able to answer many questions very quickly and with more confidence. Later we will present a review of all of the ideas from the previous chapters in the Reading Comprehension section of the book, in order to give you a concise guide to approaching any passage.

In addition, on the following pages is a drill that will test your ability to recognize the elements discussed in this chapter.

Passage Elements and Formations Recognition Drill

Analyze the following passage excerpts, noting the components discussed in this chapter. In the space provided, list any of the notable passage formations, elements, or reasoning structures, and then provide a brief summary of the material in each excerpt. *Answers on Page 257*

Passage 1:

Intellectual authority is defined as the authority of arguments that prevail by virtue of good reasoning and do not depend on coercion or convention. A contrasting notion, institutional authority, refers to the power of social institutions to enforce acceptance of arguments that may or may not possess intellectual authority. The authority wielded by legal systems is especially interesting because such systems are institutions that nonetheless aspire to a purely intellectual authority.

Analysis: _____

_____

_____

_____

_____

_____

Passage 2:

The morass of evidentiary technicalities often made it unlikely that the truth would emerge in a judicial contest, no matter how expensive and protracted. Reform was frustrated both by the vested interests of lawyers and by the profession's reverence for tradition and precedent. Bentham's prescription was revolutionary: virtually all evidence tending to prove or disprove the issue in dispute should be admissible. Narrow exceptions were envisioned: instances in which the trouble or expense of presenting or considering proof outweighed its value, confessions to a Catholic priest, and a few other instances.

Analysis: _____

_____

_____

_____

_____

_____

Passage 3:

In *The Dynamic of Apocalypse*, John Lowe attempts to solve the mystery of the collapse of the Classic Mayan civilization. Lowe bases his study on a detailed examination of the known archeological record. Like previous investigators, Lowe relies on dated monuments to construct a step-by-step account of the actual collapse. Using the erection of new monuments as a means to determine a site's occupation span, Lowe assumes that once new monuments ceased to be built, a site had been abandoned. Lowe's analysis of the evidence suggests that construction of new monuments continued to increase between A.D. 672 and 751, but that the civilization stopped expanding geographically; new construction took place almost exclusively in established settlements. The first signs of trouble followed. Monument inscriptions indicated that between 751 and 790, long standing alliances started to break down. Evidence also indicates that between 790 and 830, the death rate in Classic Mayan cities outstripped the birthrate. After approximately 830, construction stopped throughout the area, and within 100 years, the Classic Mayan civilization all but vanished.

Analysis: _____

_____

_____

_____

_____

_____

_____

_____

_____

_____

_____

_____

_____

_____

_____

_____

Passage 4:

Sifting though the tangled details of court cases, Staves demonstrates that, despite surface changes, a rhetoric of equality, and occasional decisions supporting women's financial power, definitions of men's and women's property remained inconsistent—generally to women's detriment. For example, dower lands (properly inherited by wives after their husbands' deaths) could not be sold, but "curtesy" property (inherited by husbands from their wives) could be sold. Furthermore, comparatively new concepts that developed in conjunction with the marriage contract, such as jointure, pin money and separate maintenance, were compromised by peculiar rules. For instance, if a woman spent her pin money (money paid by the husband according to the marriage contract for the wife's personal items) on possessions other than clothes she could not sell them; in effect they belonged to her husband. In addition, a wife could sue for pin money only up to a year in arrears—which rendered a suit impractical. Similarly, separate maintenance allowances (stated sums of money for the wife's support if husband and wife agreed to part) were complicated by the fact that if a couple tried to agree in a marriage contract on an amount, they were admitting that a supposedly indissoluble bond could be dissolved, an assumption courts could not recognize. Eighteenth-century historians underplayed these inconsistencies, calling them "little contrarieties" that would soon vanish. Staves shows, however, that as judges gained power over decisions on marriage contracts, they tended to fall back on pre-1660 assumptions about property.

Analysis: _____

_____

_____

_____

_____

_____

_____

_____

_____

_____

_____

_____

_____

_____

RC

Passage 5:

People's opinions about the degree of privacy that electronic mail should have vary depending on whose electronic mail system is being used and who is reading the messages. Does a government office, for example, have the right to destroy electronic messages created in the course of running the government, thereby denying public access to such documents? Some hold that government offices should issue guidelines that allow their staff to delete such electronic records, and defend this practice by claiming that the messages thus deleted already exist in paper versions whose destruction is forbidden. Opponents of such practices argue that the paper versions often omit such information as who received the messages and when they received them, information commonly carried on electronic mail systems. Government officials, opponents maintain, are civil servants; the public should thus have the right to review any documents created during the conducting of government business.

Analysis: _____

_____

_____

_____

_____

_____

_____

_____

_____

_____

_____

_____

_____

Passage 1: In this passage we are presented with two contrasting <u>definitions</u>. Whenever a word, phrase or concept is defined, it is probably worth noting, by learning the definition or being able to reference its location in the passage when needed. This selection can be distilled as follows:

> Intellectual authority is based on good reasoning. Institutional authority is based on enforcement and coercion. Legal systems base their power on institutional authority, but would generally like to think of their authority as having basis in good reason.

Passage 2: If there is a trap reflected here, it is the author's <u>challenging writing style</u>; this selection is not written in a particularly accessible way, and the information in the passage can be broken down into far simpler terms:

> Technical evidence rules made it tough to bring out the truth, no matter how much time one spent in court. But these rules were supported by tradition and by self-interested lawyers, so change did not come easily. Bentham's approach was completely different: admit anything that provides proof, with few narrow exceptions.

Passage 3: In this passage, the author provides several relevant dates, so the creation of a simple <u>timeline</u> can be helpful in tracking information and developing a clear perspective:

> In *The Dynamics of the Apocalypse*, Lowe investigates the mystery of the Classic Mayans using archeological records, assuming that a given site was occupied as long as new monument construction was taking place. Lowe's timeline of eventual decline:

672-751	751-790	790-830	930 ("w/in 100 yrs")
New monuments (in established settlements)	Alliances breaking down	Death rate higher than birthrate	Classic Mayans "all but vanished"

Passage 4: This excerpt discusses the unfair treatment of women (despite lip service to equality). The author provides a <u>list</u> of <u>examples</u> of this inequity, which we should note:

> A. Following the death of a spouse, men could sell inherited property; women could not.
> B. A wife's possessions (other than clothes) purchased with "pin money" were basically considered the belongings of the husband—court treatment supported this.
> C. No prenuptial agreements, because marriage was meant to be seen as a lifelong bond.

This sort of treatment continued despite downplay and predictions that it would dissipate.

Passage 5: Here the author presents a <u>text question</u>, in the second sentence of the passage above. When we see such a question, we should always take note; it often provides an inquiry central to the discussion (as is the case here). This passage also provides an example of <u>multiple viewpoints</u> presented side by side:

> Should the government be allowed to destroy electronic government documents?
> Some say yes—they are just e-copies of protected paper documents.
> Others say no—they provide sender/receiver information, which should also be public.

CHAPTER TWELVE: THE QUESTIONS AND ANSWER CHOICES

The Questions

Each Reading Comprehension passage on the GMAT is accompanied by a group of four to eight questions. The question stems cover a wide range of tasks, and will variously ask you to:

- describe the main point or primary purpose of the passage

- describe the structure and organization of the passage

- identify the viewpoint of the author or the viewpoint of subjects discussed within the passage

- identify details of the passage or statements proven by the passage

- describe the meaning, function, or purpose of words or phrases in the passage

- strengthen, weaken, or parallel elements of the passage

- augment or expand the passage

Analyzing the Question Stem

At first glance, Reading Comprehension passages appear to have a multitude of different types of question stems. The test makers create this impression by varying the words used in each question stem. As we will see shortly, even though they use different words, many of these question stems are identical in terms of what you are asked to do.

In order to easily handle the different questions, we categorize the question stems that appear on the GMAT. Fortunately, every question stem can be defined as a certain type, and the more familiar you are with the question types, the faster you can respond when faced with individual questions. Thus, one of your tasks is to learn each question type and become familiar with the characteristics that define each type. We will help you accomplish this goal by including a variety of question type identification drills and by examining each type of question in detail.

The makers of the GMAT warn: "If you have some familiarity with the material presented in a passage, do not let this knowledge influence your choice of answers to the questions. Answer all questions on the basis of what is stated or implied in the passage itself."

RC

The Location Element™

All Reading Comprehension question stems reveal where in the passage you should begin your search for the correct answer. This element is called "location," and you should always establish location as you read each question stem.

Location can be divided into three categories—Specific Reference, Concept Reference, and Global Reference:

Specific Reference (SR). These question stems refer you to a specific numbered line, paragraph, or sentence. For example:

"The author of the passage uses the phrase 'the flux within society' (line 42) primarily in order to"

"Which one of the following best defines the word 'political' as it is used in the third paragraph of the passage?"

"Which one of the following would best exemplify the kind of interpretive theory referred to in the first sentence of the third paragraph of the passage?"

In some Specific Reference questions, the answer choices refer you to specific lines within the passage:

Which one of the following, in its context in the passage, most clearly reveals the attitude of the author toward the proponents of the Post-Modern Movement?

(A)   "spirit" (lines 8-9)
(B)   "tended to" (line 43)
(C)   "innovation" (line 26)
(D)   "conveniently" (line 30)
(E)   "inaccuracy" (line 47)

Although the correct information in a Specific Reference question is not always found in the exact lines referenced, those line references are always an excellent starting point for your analysis.

To attack Specific Reference questions that refer to an exact line number or sentence, always return to the passage and start reading three to five lines above the reference, or from the most logical nearby starting point such as the start of a paragraph. To attack Specific Reference questions that refer to a paragraph, return to the passage and consider the paragraph in question. We will discuss this approach in more detail when we begin dissecting individual passages.

Make sure to read each question stem very carefully. Some stems direct you to focus on certain areas of the passage and if you miss these clues, the problem becomes much more difficult.

RC

To attack Specific Reference questions, return to the passage and start reading three to five lines above the reference, or from the most logical nearby starting point such as the start of a paragraph.

A thorough understanding of the organization of the passage allows for quick access to the information necessary to attack Concept Reference questions.

Concept Reference (CR). Some questions refer you to ideas or themes within the passage that are not identified by a specific line or paragraph reference, but that are identifiable because the ideas are clearly enunciated or expressed within one or two areas of the passage. When reading questions that contain concept references, you should typically know where to search in the passage for the relevant information even though no line reference is given. Examples include:

"The passage suggests which one of the following about the behavior of *A. aperta* in conflict situations?"

"The author's discussion of telephone answering machines serves primarily to"

"The passage indicates that prior to the use of pollen analysis in the study of the history of Irish landscape, at least some historians believed which one of the following?"

In each of the above instances, although no specific location reference is given, an engaged student would know where in the passage to begin searching for the correct answer, and he or she would then return to the passage and take a moment to review the relevant information.

Global Reference (GR). Global Reference questions ask about the passage as a whole, or they fail to identify a defined area or isolated concept within the question stem. For example:

"Which one of the following most accurately expresses the main point of the passage?"

"The primary purpose of the passage is to"

"Information in the passage most strongly supports which one of the following statements?"

Understanding the "big picture" is vital, since many of the questions on any given passage are likely to be Global Reference questions.

Although they might at first seem intimidating, many Global questions can be answered from your initial reading of the passage. For example, you know that you are always seeking to identify the main point of the passage as you read, so the presence of a Main Point question should not alarm you or cause you any undue work. On the other hand, Global questions that ask you to prove statements drawn from the passage can be time consuming because they typically require you to return to the passage and cross-check each answer choice.

Note that not every question stem that refers to a concept is a Concept Reference question. For example, if an entire passage is about Hemingway, and the question stem asks about the views of Hemingway, that question would be classified as Global. We will discuss this classification in more detail when we examine individual questions.

As we classify Reading Comprehension questions, location will always appear as the first element of the classification. Thus, every question classification in this book will begin with the shorthand reference of SR, CR, or GR.

The concept of location should not be an unexpected one. Since you are tested on the depth of your understanding of each passage, you should expect that the test makers will want to ask about different parts of the passage.

Throughout this book, all questions are first classified as one of these three types. There are also additional indicators designating question type, etc.

RC

Location Designation Drill

Each of the following items contains a sample question stem. In the space provided, categorize each stem into one of the three Location designations: Specific Reference (SR), Concept Reference (CR), and Global Reference (GR). While we realize that you have not yet worked directly with each question type, by considering the designations now you will have an advantage as you attack future questions. Later in this chapter we will present more comprehensive Identify the Question Stem drills to further strengthen your abilities. *Answers on the next page*

1. Question Stem: "Which one of the following most accurately describes the organization of the material presented in the passage?"

   Location Designation: _____

2. Question Stem: "The third paragraph of the passage provides the most support for which one of the following inferences?"

   Location Designation: _____

3. Question Stem: "The discussion of the chaos of physical systems is intended to perform which one of the following functions in the passage?"

   Location Designation: _____

4. Question Stem: "The author mentions the egg-laying ability of each kind of mite (lines 20 - 23) primarily in order to support which one of the following claims?"

   Location Designation: _____

5. Question Stem: "Which one of the following is mentioned in the passage as an important characteristic of many statutes that frustrates the application of computerized legal reasoning systems?"

   Location Designation: _____

6. Question Stem: "Which one of the following titles most completely and accurately describes the contents of the passage?"

   Location Designation: _____

Location Designation Drill Answer Key

The typical student misses a few questions in this drill. Do not worry about how many you miss; the point of this drill is to acquaint you with the idea of Location as it is presented in different question stems. As you see more examples of each type of question, your ability to correctly identify the Location element will improve.

1. Location Type: Global Reference

Because this stem asks about the "organization of the material presented in the passage," it references the passage as a whole and is thus best described as a Global Reference question.

2. Location Type: Specific Reference

This stem specifically references the "third paragraph of the passage," and so this is a Specific Reference question.

3. Location Type: Concept Reference

This question stem does not refer to a specific line or paragraph, so it cannot be a Specific Reference question. The reference to "discussion of the chaos of physical systems" is enough to suggest that this is more specific than a Global Reference question, and hence this question is classified as a Concept Reference question.

4. Location Type: Specific Reference

This stem specifically references the "lines 20-23," and therefore this is a Specific Reference question.

5. Location Type: Concept Reference

This question stem does not refer to a specific line or paragraph, so it cannot be a Specific Reference question. However, the question also does not refer to the passage in general, and the idea mentioned in the stem is specific enough to suggest that this is a Concept Reference question.

6. Location Type: Global Reference

This stem discusses the "contents of the passage," and is thus best described as a Global Reference question.

RC

After establishing Location, the next element you must identify when reading question stems is the type of question that you face. The questions which accompany the Reading Comprehension passages are similar to the Critical Reasoning questions, and virtually all question stems that appear in the Reading Comprehension passages of the GMAT can be classified into one of six different types:

Many of the question types discussed in the Critical Reasoning section are also covered here.

1. Must Be True/Most Supported
2. Main Point
3. Strengthen
4. Weaken
5. Parallel Reasoning
6. Cannot Be True

Note that some of the other Critical Reasoning question types, such as Justify the Conclusion or Resolve the Paradox, *could* appear with a Reading Comprehension passage, but they appear so infrequently that a discussion of those types is not useful.

You must correctly analyze and classify every question stem because the question stem ultimately determines the nature of the correct answer choice. A mistake in analyzing the question stem almost invariably leads to a missed question. Properly identifying the question stem type will allow you to proceed quickly and with confidence, and in some cases it will help you determine the correct answer before you read any of the five answer choices.

Occasionally, students ask if we refer to the question types by number or by name. We always refer to the questions by name, as that is an easier and more efficient approach. Numerical question type classification systems force you to add two unnecessary levels of abstraction to your thinking process. For example, consider a question that asks you to "weaken" the argument. In a numerical question classification system, you must first recognize that the question asks you to weaken the argument, then you must classify that question into a numerical category (say, Type 4), and then you must translate Type 4 to mean "Weaken." Literally, numerical classification systems force you to perform an abstract, circular translation of the meaning of the question, and the translation process is both time-consuming and valueless.

In the following pages we will briefly discuss each of the primary Reading Comprehension question types.

1. Must Be True/Most Supported

This category is simply known as "Must Be True." Must Be True questions ask you to identify the answer choice that is best proven by the information in the stimulus. Question stem examples:

"If the statements above are true, which one of the following must also be true?"

"Which one of the following can be properly inferred from the passage?"

Must Be True questions are the dominant category with the Reading Comprehension passages. This should not be surprising, considering that Reading Comprehension is about trying to understand a lengthy passage of text. The best way to test your comprehension of this information is to ask a series of questions aimed at determining whether you understood the facts of what you read.

Many of the Must Be True questions which accompany the Reading Comprehension passages ask you to perform a more specific action, such as to identify the author's viewpoint or the function of a word or phrase. In the next section we will examine these attributes in more detail and discuss each type of Must Be True question.

2. Main Point

Main Point questions are a variant of Must Be True questions. As you might expect, a Main Point question asks you to find the primary focus of the passage. Question stem example:

"The main point of the argument is that"

Main Point questions often appear as the very first question in a given passage set. This placement is beneficial because as you conclude your reading of the passage, you should already know the main point of what you have read.

3. Strengthen

These questions ask you to select the answer choice that provides support for the author's argument or strengthens it in some way. Question stem examples:

"Which one of the following, if true, most strengthens the argument?"

"Which one of the following, if true, most strongly supports the statement above?"

RC

4. <u>Weaken</u>

Weaken questions ask you to attack or undermine the author's argument. Question stem example:

"Which one of the following, if true, most seriously weakens the argument?"

Considered together, Strengthen and Weaken questions appear far less frequently than Must Be True questions.

5. <u>Parallel Reasoning</u>

Parallel Reasoning questions ask you to identify the answer choice that contains reasoning most similar in structure to the reasoning presented in the stimulus. Question stem example:

"Which one of the following arguments is most similar in its pattern of reasoning to the argument above?"

Like Strengthen and Weaken Questions, Parallel Reasoning questions appear less frequently than Must Be True questions.

6. <u>Cannot Be True</u>

Cannot Be True questions ask you to identify the answer choice that cannot be true or is most weakened based on the information in the stimulus. Question stem example:

"If the statements above are true, which one of the following CANNOT be true?"

These questions often appear with the modifier "Least," which will be discussed in more detail in a later section of this chapter.

Other question type elements will also be discussed, most notably question variants (such as Author's Perspective questions) and overlays (such as Principle questions). Those will be discussed later in this chapter.

Question Classification (Up to this point)

From a classification standpoint, at this point we have established that every question which accompanies a Reading Comprehension passage has two elements: Location and Question Type. When questions are classified in this book, those two elements are always listed in order, as follows:

Location, Question Type

Here are several sample question classifications featuring both elements:

SR, Must
   (Location: Specific Reference, Type: Must Be True)

CR, Strengthen
   (Location: Concept Reference, Type: Strengthen)

GR, MP
   (Location: Global Reference, Type: Main Point)

SR, Parallel
   (Location: Specific Reference, Type: Parallel Reasoning)

The next page contains a drill designed to strengthen your ability to correctly classify questions.

RC

Identify the Question Type Drill

Each of the following items contains a sample question stem. In the space provided, categorize each stem into one of the three Location designations: Specific Reference (SR), Concept Reference (CR), and Global Reference (GR), and then categorize each stem into one of the six main Reading Comprehension Question Types: Must Be True, Main Point, Strengthen, Weaken, Parallel Reasoning, or Cannot be True. While we realize that you have not yet worked directly with each question type, by considering the designations now you will have an advantage as you attack future questions. *Answers on Page 270*

1. Question Stem: "Which one of the following, if true, would lend the most support to the view of most 20th century critics?"

    Classification: _____

2. Question Stem: "The author would most likely disagree with which one of the following statements?"

    Classification: _____

3. Question Stem: "Which one of the following most accurately describes the author's purpose in referring to literature of the past as being "unfairly burdened" (line 51) in some cases?"

    Classification: _____

4. Question Stem: "Which one of the following most accurately expresses the main point of the passage?"

    Classification: _____

5. Question Stem: "Which one of the following, if true, would most call into question the author's assertion in the last sentence of the passage?"

    Classification: _____

6. Question Stem: "In discussing the tangential details of events, the passage contrasts their original significance in the courtroom (lines 52-59). This contrast is most closely analogous to which one of the following?"

    Classification: _____

7. Question Stem: "Which one of the following most accurately describes the organization of the passage?"

    Classification: _____

8. Question Stem: "Which one of the following, if true, most weakens the author's criticism of the assumption that parasitic interactions generally evolve toward symbiosis?"

    Classification: _____

9. Question Stem: "The author of the passage would be most likely to agree with which one of the following statements?"

    Classification: _____

10. Question Stem: "Which one of the following would, if true, most strengthen the claim made by the author in the last sentence of the passage (lines 49-52)?"

    Classification: _____

11. Question Stem: "Which one of the following, if true, offers the most support for Rose's hypothesis?"

    Classification: _____

12. Question Stem: "According to the passage, the elimination of which one of the following obstacles enabled scientists to identify the evolutionary origins of the platypus?

    Classification: _____

13. Question Stem: "Which one of the following is most similar to the relationship described in the passage between the new methods of the industry and pre-twentieth-century methods?"

    Classification: _____

14. Question Stem: "The third paragraph of the passage most strongly supports which one of the following inferences?"

    Classification: _____

Identify the Question Stem Drill Answer Key

The typical student misses about half of the questions in this drill. Do not worry about how many you miss; the point of this drill is to acquaint you with the different question stems. As you see more examples of each type of question, your ability to correctly identify each stem will improve.

1. CR, Strengthen
Location: Here we are asked to find the answer choice that would support a particular view referenced from the passage, so this is a <u>Concept Reference</u> question.
Type: The presence of the phrase "Which of the following, if true," generally introduces either a Strengthen or a Weaken question. In this case, since the correct answer will support the referenced view, this is clearly a <u>Strengthen</u> question.

2. GR, Cannot
Location: This example provides no direction, conceptual or otherwise, as to location in the passage. It is therefore a <u>Global Reference</u> question.
Type: This question requires you to find the answer choice with which the author would disagree. Because the correct answer choice will be inconsistent with the author's attitude, this question stem can be classified as a <u>Cannot Be True</u> question (that is, "according to the author, which of the following cannot be true?").

3. SR, Must
Location: This example provides the exact location of the referenced quote, so this is a <u>Specific Reference</u> question.
Type: The correct answer must pass the Fact Test; in this case it must provide an accurate description of the referenced quote's purpose in the passage. Therefore this question stem falls under the <u>Must Be True</u> category.

4. GR, MP
Location: This common question stem refers to the passage as a whole and is therefore a <u>Global Reference</u> question.
Type: Since this question stem asks for the main point of the passage, this is a clear example of a <u>Main Point</u> question. The correct answer choice will be the one which most accurately and completely reflects the central focus of the passage.

5. SR, Weaken
Location: Although no line reference is provided in this example, the reader is directed specifically to the last sentence of the passage, so this is a <u>Specific Reference</u> question.
Type: A question stem that begins with "Which of the following, if true" is nearly certain to be a Strengthen or Weaken question. In this case, the information in the correct answer will call the referenced assertion into question, so this should be classified as a <u>Weaken</u> question.

6. SR, Parallel
Location: Since an exact line reference is provided, this is a <u>Specific Reference</u> question.
Type: Here the reader is asked to find the answer choice which is most closely analogous to the referenced discussion, which makes this a <u>Parallel</u> question. The correct answer choice will reflect a contrast similar to that discussed in the passage.

7. GR, Must

Location: Since this question stem deals with the entire passage, this is a <u>Global Reference</u> question.
Type: This question requires that the reader understand the overall structure of the given passage, and the correct answer choice must reflect that structure. This is a <u>Must Be True</u> question.

8. CR, Weaken

Location: Although this question does not provide a line reference, it refers to a very specific assumption on the author's part. It is thus a <u>Concept Reference</u> question.
Type: This is one of the more readily recognizable question types, since the word "weaken" is in the question stem; this is a standard <u>Weaken</u> question which in this case requires that the correct answer choice reduce the credibility of the author's referenced criticism.

9. GR, Must

Location: This question deals with the passage as a whole, so this is a <u>Global Reference</u> question.
Type: This common question requires that the reader understand the author's perspective. The correct answer choice must reflect the author's attitude, and pass the Fact Test, so this is a <u>Must Be True</u> question.

10. SR, Strengthen

Location: The line reference at the end of this question stem identifies this example as a <u>Specific Reference</u> question.
Type: The fact that we are asked to strengthen a claim means that this is a <u>Strengthen</u> question, and the correct answer choice must assist the author's argument in some way.

11. GR, Strengthen

Location: Without reading the passage, it might be difficult to assess the scope of this question's reference (although you should immediately recognize that this is <u>not</u> a Specific Reference question). If the passage is largely focused on the referenced hypothesis, this is a <u>Global Reference</u> question.
Type: Since the correct answer choice will somehow support the referenced hypothesis, this is a <u>Strengthen</u> question.

12. CR, Must

Location: This question stem requires the reader to identify a particular obstacle but does not provide its specific location in the passage, so this is a <u>Concept Reference</u> question.
Type: In this case, the correct answer choice will come directly from information provided in the passage, so this is a <u>Must Be True</u> question.

13. CR, Parallel

Location: This question refers to a specific relationship but offers no line references, thus it is a <u>Concept Reference</u> question.
Type: The question stem asks you to find an answer that is "most similar to the relationship" in the passage, and thus this is a <u>Parallel</u> question.

14. SR, Must

Location: Specification of "the third paragraph" makes this a <u>Specific Reference</u> question.
Type: Although this question stem uses the word "supports," the correct answer choice will be the one which, based on the passage, <u>Must Be True</u>.

Reading Comprehension Question Types Examined in Detail

Must Be True/Most Supported Questions

Must Be True questions are, by far, the most important Reading Comprehension question type, since they appear far more frequently than any other question type. Thus, to perform well with Reading Comprehension passages, you must dominate Must Be True questions. In this section we will examine the theory behind Must Be True questions, and then examine a variety of specific Must Be True subtypes. In each instance we will provide helpful tips and strategies to attack each type.

Must Be True questions require you to select an answer choice that is proven by the information presented in the passage. The correct answer choice can be a paraphrase of part of the passage or it can be a logical consequence of one or more parts of the passage. However, when selecting an answer choice, you must find the proof that supports your answer in the passage. We call this the Fact Test™:

> The correct answer to a Must Be True question can always be proven by referring to the facts stated in the passage.

The majority of the questions which accompany the Reading Comprehension passages are Must Be True questions.

The test makers will try to entice you by creating incorrect answer choices that could possibly occur or are likely to occur, but are not certain to occur. You must avoid those answers and select the answer choice that is most clearly supported by what you read. Do not bring in information from outside the passage (aside from commonsense assumptions); all of the information necessary to answer the question resides in the passage.

Must Be True questions require you to read text and understand the facts and details that logically follow. To Weaken or Strengthen an argument, for example, you first need to be able to ascertain the facts and details. The same goes for every other type of question. Because every question type relies on the fact-finding skill used to answer Must Be True questions, your performance on Must Be True questions controls your overall Reading Comprehension score. For this reason, you must lock down the understanding required of this question category: what did you read in the passage and what do you know on the basis of that reading?

Attacking Must Be True Questions

Your approach to Must Be True questions will, in part, be dictated by the Location element specified in each question stem. That is, your approach to an SR, Must question should generally be different than your approach to a GR, Must question. Following, we examine how the difference in Location affects how you attack Must Be True questions.

Specific Reference

As mentioned in the Location section:

> To attack Specific Reference questions that refer to an exact line number or sentence, always return to the passage and start reading three to five lines above the reference, or from the most logical nearby starting point such as the start of a paragraph.

As we will see when discussing specific passages and questions, the "three to five line" recommendation is open-ended because what you are seeking is the most logical starting point for your reading, and that starting point is typically the prior complete sentence or two.

For Specific Reference questions that refer to a paragraph, return to the passage and consider the paragraph in question.

Concept Reference

With Concept Reference questions, you must return to the areas in the passage mentioned in the question stem and quickly review the information. These questions are by nature more vague than Specific Reference questions and so you must rely on your passage notes or memory to return to the correct area.

Global Reference

Global Must Be True questions are usually Main Point, Purpose, or Organization questions, and you will typically not need to refer back to the passage prior to attacking the answer choices because you will already know the answer from your reading. Remember, if you seek to identify the five critical VIEWSTAMP elements of each passage, you will automatically know the answer to every Global Must Be True question. Thus, you would only need to refer back to the passage to eliminate or confirm individual answer choices.

The prevalence of Must Be True questions is incredibly beneficial to you as a test taker because the answer to every Must question resides directly in the text of each passage.

RC

Must Be True Question Subtypes

Although many of the questions which follow the Reading Comprehension passages are straightforward Must Be True questions, many questions are subtypes of the Must Be True category. Fundamentally, these subtypes are approached in exactly the same manner as regular Must Be True questions. That is, the Fact Test applies and you must still be able to justify your answer with evidence from the passage. However, some of these subtypes ask for very specific information, and thus an awareness of the existence of these question types is essential.

Main Point Questions (MP)

Main Point questions may be the question type most familiar to test takers. Many of the standardized tests you have already encountered, such as the SAT, contain questions that ask you to ascertain the Main Point. Even in daily conversation you will hear, "What's your point?" Main Point questions, as you might suspect from the name, ask you to summarize the author's point of view in the passage.

The answer you select must follow from the information in the stimulus. But be careful: even if an answer choice must be true according to the stimulus, if it fails to capture the main point it cannot be correct. This is the central truth of Main Point questions: Like all Must Be True question variants, the correct answer must pass the Fact Test, but with the additional criterion that the correct answer choice must capture the author's point.

A complete understanding of any passaage requires that you identify the main point, even when a passage does not include a Main Point question.

As discussed previously, one key to identifying a main point is to remember that, although the main point may be stated succinctly in a sentence or two, all paragraphs of the passage must support the main point. Thus, the main point will not just reflect the argument contained in a single paragraph. To assess the situation, apply the viewpoint identification approach and argument identification methods discussed previously. These two VIEWSTAMP items will direct you toward the Main Point during your reading of the passage. Thereafter, you will be in excellent position to answer any Main Point question.

The Main Point question stem format is remarkably consistent, with the primary feature being a request for you to identify the conclusion or point of the argument, as in the following examples:

> "Which one of the following most accurately expresses the main point of the passage?"

> "Which one of the following statements best expresses the main idea of the passage?"

Two types of *incorrect* answers frequently appear in Main Point questions:

1. Answers that are true but do not encapsulate the author's point.

2. Answers that repeat portions of the passage but not the Main Point.

Each answer type is attractive because they are true based on what you have read. However, neither summarizes the author's main point and therefore both are incorrect.

Purpose/Function Questions (P)

At the Specific Reference and Concept Reference level, Purpose questions ask why the author referred to a particular word, phrase, or idea. To determine the reasons behind the author's use of words or ideas, refer to the context around the reference, using context clues and your knowledge of the viewpoints and structure of the passage. Here are several example question stems:

"The author of the passage uses the phrase "the flux within Hawaiian society" (line 33) primarily in order to"

"The author's discussion of people's positive moral duty to care for one another (lines 44-49) functions primarily to"

"The author's discussion of telephone answering machines serves primarily to"

"Which one of the following best states the function of the third paragraph of the passage?"

Global Purpose questions are almost always phrased using the words "primary purpose" and ask for the author's main purpose in writing the passage. These questions ask you to describe why the author wrote the passage, and the correct answer is often an abstract version of the main point (and if not, at the very least the answer to a Global Purpose question will agree with the Main Point).

"The primary purpose of the passage is to"

"In the passage, the author seeks primarily to"

Perspective Questions

This categorization contains questions about two of the five VIEWSTAMP elements: viewpoints and tone. These two elements are very closely related, and we combine these two elements in our question classification, using the term "perspective" to capture the idea behind both elements.

Perspective questions can be divided into two categories: questions that ask about the author's views and tone, and questions that ask about the views and tone of one of the other groups discussed in the passage. These two types are discussed on the following page.

Author's Perspective Questions (AP)

Author's Perspective questions ask you to select the answer choice that best reflects the author's views on a subject or the author's attitude toward a subject. Because identifying the position of the author is a critical part of your strategy when reading, normally these questions should be relatively painless:

"The author of the passage would most likely agree with which one of the following statements?"

"It can be inferred that the author of the passage believes which one of the following about the history of modern jurisprudence?"

"It can be reasonably inferred from the passage that the author's attitude is most favorable toward which one of the following?"

Subject Perspective Questions (SP)

In this question type, we use the term "subject" to refer to a person or group who is discussed in the passage. Subject Perspective questions, then, ask you to select the answer choice that best reflects the views or attitude of one of the other groups in the passage. Because identifying all views is a critical part of your strategy when reading, you should be well-prepared for these questions.

Understanding the author's viewpoint is an integral part of mastering any passage.

"Given the information in the passage, which one of the following is Lum most likely to believe?"

"It can be inferred that Peter Goodrich would be most likely to agree with which one of the following statements concerning common law?"

These questions are considered Must Be True questions because the correct answer follows directly from the statements in the passage.

Organization Questions (O)

These questions usually appear in reference to either a specific paragraph or to the passage as a whole, and refer less frequently to specific lines.

At the line level, you are normally asked to identify the way in which pairs of lines relate to each other:

"The logical relationship of lines 8-13 of the passage to lines 23-25 and 49-53 of the passage is most accurately described as"

At a specific paragraph level, you will either be asked to identify the structure of the paragraph, or to identify how one paragraph relates to another paragraph. Question examples include the following:

"Which one of the following most accurately describes the relationship between the second paragraph and the final paragraph?"

"Which one of the following most accurately describes the organization of the material presented in the second and third paragraphs of the passage?"

At the Global level, these questions ask you to describe the overall structure of the passage. For example:

"Which one of the following best describes the organization of the passage?"

"Which one of the following most accurately describes the organization of the material presented in the passage?"

"Which one of the following sequences most accurately and completely corresponds to the presentation of the material in the passage?"

In both the Specific and Global versions, these questions are similar to the Method of Reasoning questions in Critical Reasoning, but they are generally broader. Given that you must track structure as you read, these questions should be fairly straightforward exercises in matching answer choices to what you already know occurred in the passage.

Expansion Questions (E)

Expansion questions require you to extrapolate ideas from the passage to determine one of three elements: where the passage was drawn from or how it could be titled, what sentence or idea could come before the passage, and what sentence or idea could follow the passage. The following examples show the range of phrasing in these questions:

"Which one of the following would be most suitable as a title for this passage if it were to appear as an editorial piece?"

"Which one of the following titles most completely summarizes the contents of the passage?"

"If this passage had been excerpted from a longer text, which one of the following predictions about the near future of U.S. literature would be most likely to appear in that text?"

"Which one of the following sentences would most logically begin a paragraph immediately following the end of the passage?"

"Which one of the following is the most logical continuation of the last paragraph of the passage?"

"Which one of the following sentences could most logically be appended to the end of the last paragraph of the passage?"

Questions about the title or source of the passage typically reflect the Main Point of the passage. Questions asking you to identify pre- or post-passage sentences, however, are usually immediately dependent upon the two or three sentences at the beginning or end of the passage, and then more generally dependent upon the passage as a whole. These questions can be difficult because they ask you to infer the flow and direction of the passage from a somewhat limited set of clues.

Although questions which specifically reference Passage Organization make up only a small percentage of questions in this section, a strong grasp of the structure of a passage will allow you to attack Concept Reference and Specific Reference questions far more efficiently.

RC

Correct Answers in Must Be True Questions

Let us take a moment to discuss two types of answers that will always be correct in a Must Be True question and any Must Be True subtype (except for Main Point questions, as discussed previously).

1. Paraphrased Answers

   Paraphrased Answers are answers that restate a portion of the passage in different terms. Because the language is not exactly the same as in the passage, Paraphrased Answers can be easy to miss. Paraphrased Answers are designed to test your ability to discern the author's exact meaning. Sometimes the answer can appear to be almost too obvious since it is drawn directly from the passage.

2. Answers that are the sum of two or more passage statements (Combination Answers)

   Any answer choice that would result from combining two or more statements in the passage will be correct.

Should you encounter either of the above as an answer choice in a non-Main Point, Must Be True question, select the answer with confidence.

Incorrect Answers in Must Be True Questions

There are several types of answers that appear in Must Be True questions that are incorrect. These answers appear frequently enough that we have provided a review of the major types below. Each answer category below is designed to attract you to an incorrect answer choice. As we begin to look at actual passages and questions in the next chapter, we will examine instances of these types of answers.

1. Could Be True or Likely to Be True Answers

   Because the criteria in the question stem require you to find an answer choice that Must Be True, answers that merely could be true or are even likely to be true are incorrect. These answers are attractive because there is nothing demonstrably wrong with them (for example, they do not contain statements that are counter to the passage). Regardless, like all incorrect answers, these answers fail the Fact Test. Remember, you must select an answer choice that must occur based on what you have read.

   This category of "incorrect answer" is very broad, and some of the types mentioned below will fall under this general idea but place an emphasis on a specific aspect of the answer.

2. Exaggerated Answers

Exaggerated Answers take information from the passage and then stretch that information to make a broader statement that is not supported by the passage. In that sense, this form of answer is a variation of a Could Be True answer since the exaggeration is possible, but not proven based on the information. Here is an example:

> If the passage states, "*Some* software vendors recently implemented more rigorous licensing procedures."

> An incorrect answer would exaggerate one or more of the elements: "*Most* software vendors recently implemented more rigorous licensing procedures." In this example, *some* is exaggerated to *most*. While it could be true that most software vendors made the change, the passage does not prove that it must be true. This type of answer is often paraphrased, creating a deadly combination where the language is similar enough to be attractive but different enough to be incorrect.

Here is another example:

> If the passage states, "Recent advances in the field of molecular biology make it *likely* that many school textbooks will be rewritten."

> The exaggerated and paraphrased version would be: "Many school textbooks about molecular biology will be re-written." In this example, *likely* has been dropped, and this omission exaggerates the certainty of the change. The paraphrase also is problematic because the passage referenced school textbooks whereas the paraphrased answer refers to school textbooks *about molecular biology*.

3. "New" Information Answers

Because correct Must Be True answers must be based on information in the passage or the direct result of combining statements in the passage, be wary of answers that present so-called new information—that is, information not mentioned explicitly in the passage or information that would not fall under the umbrella of a statement made in the passage. For example, if a passage discusses the economic policies of Japan, be careful with an answer that mentions U.S. economic policy. Look closely at the passage—does the information about Japanese economic policy apply to the U.S., or are the test makers trying to get you to fall for an answer that sounds logical but is not directly supported?

4. The Shell Game

The GMAT makers have a variety of psychological tricks they use to entice test takers to select an answer choice. One of their favorites is one we call the Shell Game: an idea or concept is raised in the passage, and then a very similar idea appears in the answer choice, but the idea is changed just enough to be incorrect but still attractive. This trick is called the Shell Game because it abstractly resembles those street corner gambling games where a person hides a small object underneath one of three shells, and then scrambles them on a flat surface while a bettor tries to guess which shell the object is under (similar to three-card Monte). The object of a Shell Game is to trick the bettor into guessing incorrectly by mixing up the shells so quickly and deceptively that the bettor mistakenly selects the wrong shell. The intent of the GMAT makers is the same.

5. The Opposite Answer

As the name suggests, the Opposite Answer provides an answer that is completely opposite of the stated facts of the passage. Opposite Answers are very attractive to students who are reading too quickly or carelessly.

6. The Reverse Answer

Here is a simplified example of how a Reverse Answer works, using italics to indicate the reversed parts:

> The passage might state, "*Many* people have *some* type of security system in their home."

> An incorrect answer then reverses the elements: "*Some* people have *many* types of security systems in their home."

The Reverse Answer is attractive because it contains familiar elements from the passage, but the reversed statement is incorrect because it rearranges those elements to create a new, unsupported statement.

Reverse Answers can occur in any type of question.

7. The Wrong View

Wrong View answers frequently appear in Perspective questions. For example, the question will ask you to identify a statement that agrees with the author's view, but then place one or more answers that would agree with the view of another group in the passage. You can avoid these answers by carefully tracking viewpoints as discussed earlier.

8. Hidden References

Shell Game answers can occur in all GMAT question types, not only in Must Be True questions.

In some Specific Reference questions, you will be sent to a certain location in the passage but the information needed to answer the question will reside elsewhere in the passage, in a section that also touches on the issue in the Specific Reference. This can be difficult to handle if the information is a large number of lines away.

Non-Must Be True Question Types

In this section we examine all other Reading Comprehension question types. As mentioned earlier, these questions appear with far less frequency than Must Be True questions.

Strengthen Questions

Strengthen questions ask you to identify the answer choice that best supports a section of the passage or a particular view from the passage. The correct answer choice does not necessarily prove the argument beyond a shadow of a doubt, nor is the correct answer choice necessarily an assumption of the argument. The correct answer choice simply helps the argument in some way.

Following are examples of Strengthen question stems:

> "Which one of the following would, if true, most strengthen the author's position regarding the practical applicability of the theory presented in the passage?"

> "Which one of the following would, if true, most strengthen the claim made by the author in the last sentence of the passage (lines 47-49)?"

How to Strengthen an Argument

Use the following points to effectively strengthen arguments:

1. Identify what you are trying to strengthen!

   Before you can examine the answer choices, you must know what it is that you must strengthen. When evaluating an answer, ask yourself, "Would this answer choice assist the position in question in some way?" If so, you have the correct answer.

2. Personalize the argument.

   Personalizing allows you to see the argument from a very involved perspective and helps you assess the strength of each answer.

3. Look for weaknesses in the argument.

   This may seem like a strange recommendation since your task is to strengthen the argument, but a weak spot in an argument is tailor-made for an answer that eliminates that weakness. If you see a weakness or flaw in the argument, look for an answer that eliminates the weakness. In other words, close any gap or hole in the argument.

   Many Strengthen questions require students to find the missing link between a premise and the conclusion. These missing links are assumptions made by the author or by the party in question, and bringing an assumption to light strengthens the argument because it validates part of the author's thinking.

4. Remember that the correct answer can strengthen the argument just a little or a lot. This variation is what makes these questions difficult.

Three Incorrect Answer Traps

The following types of wrong answer traps frequently appear in Strengthen questions:

1. Opposite Answers. These answers do the exact opposite of what is needed—they weaken the position in question. Because of their direct relation to the argument they are tempting, despite the fact that they result in consequences opposite of those intended.

2. Shell Game Answers. Remember, a Shell Game occurs when an idea or concept is raised in the passage and then a very similar idea appears in the answer choice, but the idea is changed just enough to be incorrect but still attractive. In Strengthen questions, the Shell Game is usually used to support a conclusion or position that is similar to, but slightly different from, the one presented in the passage.

3. Out of Scope Answers. These answers simply miss the point of the argument and support issues that are either unrelated to the argument or tangential to the argument.

These three answer types are not the only ways an answer choice can be attractively incorrect, but they appear frequently enough that you should be familiar with each form.

Because the same types of wrong answer traps appear in Strengthen as in Weaken questions, the three items above apply to both this section and the following section on Weaken questions.

Weaken Questions

Weaken questions require you to select the answer choice that undermines a position as decisively as possible. In this sense, Weaken questions are the polar opposite of Strengthen questions.

Note that the makers of the GMAT can use a variety of words to indicate that your task is to weaken the argument:

> weaken
> attack
> undermine
> refute
> argue against
> call into question
> cast doubt
> challenge
> damage
> counter

Here are two Weaken question stem examples:

> "Which one of the following, if true, would most weaken the author's argument against harsh punishment for all infractions?"

> "Which one of the following, if true, would most seriously challenge the position of the biologists mentioned in line 19?"

When approaching Weaken questions, always remember to:

1. Isolate and assess the position you are attacking. Only by understanding the structure of the position can you gain the perspective necessary to attack that position.

2. Know the details of what was said in the passage.

3. Accept the answer choices as given, even if they include "new" information. Unlike Must Be True questions, Weaken answer choices can bring into consideration information outside of or tangential to the stimulus. Just because a fact or idea is not mentioned in the passage is not grounds for dismissing an answer choice. Your task is to determine which answer choice best attacks the position.

By focusing on the points above, you will maximize your chances of success on Weaken questions.

Weaken question stems tell you to accept the answer choices as true, so you cannot throw out an answer because it doesn't seem possible.

RC

Some of the wrong answer types from the Must Be True section do not apply to Strengthen and Weaken questions. For example, the New Information answer is usually wrong in a Must Be True question, but not in a Strengthen or Weaken question because new information is acceptable in the answer choices.

Parallel Reasoning Questions

Parallel Reasoning questions ask you to identify the answer choice that contains reasoning most similar in structure to the reasoning in a section of the passage. Because each answer choice is a wholly new argument, these questions force you to evaluate five arguments in one question, and as such they can be quite time consuming (a fact known to and exploited by the test makers).

The typical Reading Comprehension Parallel Reasoning question asks you to parallel the structure of a section or paragraph, and thus you usually need only understand the basic outline of what occurred in the section. Then, select the answer choice that contains the same structure. If you find yourself choosing between two or more answer choices, then simply compare some of the other elements in the passage—intent of the author or group, force and use of premises, the relationship of the premises to a conclusion, and the soundness of the argument.

You do not need to find an answer that destroys the author's position. Instead, simply find an answer that hurts the argument.

Question stem examples:

> "Which one of the following is most analogous to the literary achievements that the author attributes to Maillet?"

> "As described in the passage, re-creating an accident with a computer-generated display is most similar to which one of the following?"

> "Based on the passage, the relationship between strengthening current copyright access to a Web document is most analogous to the relationship between"

Cannot Be True Questions

Cannot Be True questions occur infrequently with Reading Comprehension passages. Nonetheless, a familiarity with the principles behind these questions is helpful.

Question types that appear infrequently, such as Cannot Be True, tend to consume more time because students are not used to seeing those types of questions.

In Cannot Be True questions your task is to identify the answer choice that cannot be true or is most weakened by the information in the passage. Thus, instead of using the information in the passage to prove that one of the answer choices must be true, you must instead prove that one of the answer choices cannot occur, or that it disagrees with the information in the passage.

In the abstract, Cannot Be True questions can be viewed in two ways:

1. Polar Opposite Must Be True Questions

   Cannot Be True questions are the polar opposite of Must Be True questions: rather than prove an answer choice, you disprove an answer choice.

2. Reverse Weaken Questions

Cannot Be True questions are like reverse Weaken questions: use the information in the stimulus to attack one of the answers.

When the word "not" is used in question stems, it is capitalized.

Both question descriptions are similar, and neither sounds very difficult. In practice, however, Cannot Be True questions are tricky because the concept of an answer choice being possibly true and therefore wrong is counter intuitive. This type of question appears very infrequently, but the test makers are savvy and they know Cannot questions can catch test takers off-guard and consume more time than the average question. When you encounter a Cannot Be True question, you must mentally prepare yourself to eliminate answers that could be true or that are possible, and select the one answer choice that cannot be true or that is impossible.

Cannot Be True questions can be worded in a variety of ways, but the gist of the question type is to show that an answer cannot logically follow, as in these examples:

"Which one of the following, if true, is LEAST consistent with Riechart's theory about fighting behavior in spiders?"

"Given the information in the passage, the author is LEAST likely to believe which one of the following?"

Question Modifiers and Overlays

Certain words that sometimes appear in question stems have a powerful impact on the nature of the answer choice you are seeking. The most important of these words are discussed below.

"Most" and "Best" in Question Stems

Many question stems contain the qualifiers "most" or "best." For example, a typical question stem will state, "Which one of the following most accurately expresses the main point of the passage?" or "Which one of the following best expresses the main idea of the passage?" Astute test takers realize that the presence of "most" or "best" opens up a Pandora's box of sorts: by including "most" or "best," there is a possibility that other answer choices will also meet the criteria of the question stem (Main Point, Strengthen, Parallel, etc.), albeit to a lesser extent. In other words, if a question stem says "most weakens," the possibility is that every answer choice weakens the argument and you would be in the unenviable task of having to choose the best of a bunch of good answer choices. *Fortunately, this is not how it works.* Even though "most" or "best" will appear in a number of stems, you can rest assured that only one answer choice will meet the criteria. So, if you see a "most weakens" question stem, only one of the answers will weaken the argument. So, then, why does

Of course, every once in a while two answer choices achieve the desired goal; in those cases you simply choose the better of the two answers. Normally, the difference between the two answers is significant enough for you to make a clear distinction as to which one is superior.

"most" or "best" appear in so many question stems? Because in order to maintain test integrity the test makers need to make sure their credited answer choice is as airtight and defensible as possible. Imagine what would occur if a question stem, let us say a Weaken question, did not include a "most" or "best" qualifier: any answer choice that weakened the argument, even if only very slightly, could then be argued to meet the criteria of the question stem. A situation like this would make constructing the test exceedingly difficult because any given problem might have multiple correct answer choices. To eliminate this predicament, the test makers insert "most" or "best" into the question stem, and then they can always claim there is one and only one correct answer choice.

"Except" and "Least" in Question Stems

The word "except" has a dramatic impact when it appears in a question stem. Because "except" means "other than," when "except" is placed in a question it negates the logical quality of the answer choice you seek. Literally, it turns the intent of the question stem upside down. For example, if a question asks you what must be true, the one correct answer must be true and the other four answers are not necessarily true. If "except" is added to the question stem, as in "Each of the following must be true EXCEPT," the stem is turned around and instead of the correct answer having the characteristic of must be true, the four incorrect answers must be true and the one correct answer is not necessarily true.

Many students, upon encountering "except" in a question stem, make the mistake of assuming that the "except" charges you with seeking the polar opposite. For example, if a question stem asks you to weaken a statement, some students believe that a "Weaken EXCEPT" question stem actually asks you to strengthen the statement. This is incorrect. Although weaken and strengthen are polar opposites, because except means "other than," when a "Weaken EXCEPT" question stem appears, you are asked to find any answer choice other than Weaken. While this could include a strengthening answer choice, it could also include an answer choice that has no effect on the statement. Thus, in a "Weaken EXCEPT" question, the four incorrect answers Weaken the statement and the one correct answer does not weaken the statement (could strengthen or have no effect). Here is another example:

The true effect of "except" is to logically negate the question stem.

"Which one of the following, if true, strengthens the argument above?"

> One correct answer: Strengthen
> Four incorrect answers: Do not Strengthen

"Each of the following, if true, strengthens the argument above EXCEPT:"

> One correct answer: Does not Strengthen
> Four incorrect answers: Strengthen

As you can see from the example, the presence of except has a profound impact upon the meaning of the question stem. Because "except" has this powerful effect, it always appears in all capital letters whenever it is used in a GMAT question stem.

The word "least" has a similar effect to "except" when it appears in a question stem. Although "least" and "except" do not generally have the same meaning, when "least" appears in a question stem you should treat it *exactly the same* as "except." Note: this advice holds true only when this word appears in the question stem! If you see the word "least" elsewhere on the GMAT, consider it to have its usual meaning of "in the lowest or smallest degree."
Because "least," like "except," has such a strong impact on the meaning of a question stem, the test makers kindly place "least" in all capital letters when it appears in a question stem.

In the answer keys to this book, we will designate questions that contain "except" or "least" by placing an "X" at the end of the question stem classification. For example, a "Must Be True EXCEPT" question stem would be classified as "MustX." A "Parallel EXCEPT" question stem would be classified as "ParallelX" and so on. The only exception to this rule will be a question that states, "Each of the following could be true EXCEPT." Those questions will be designated "Cannot Be True."

"Except" is used more frequently in GMAT Reading Comprehension question stems than "least."

RC

Principle Questions

Principle questions (PR) are not a separate question type but are instead an "overlay" that appears in a variety of question types. For example, there are Must Be True Principle questions (Must-PR), Strengthen Principle questions (Strengthen-PR), and Cannot Be True Principle questions (Cannot-PR), among others. In a question stem, the key indicator that the Principle concept is present is the word "principle." Here are two examples:

> "Which one of the following principles can be most clearly said to underlie the author's arguments in the third paragraph?"

> "Given the information in the passage, the author can most reasonably be said to use which one of the following principles to refute the advocates' claim that computer conferences can function as communities (line 15)?"

A principle is a broad rule that specifies what actions or judgments are correct in certain situations. For example, "Some companies are profitable" is not a principle because no rule is involved and no judgment can be drawn from the statement. "All companies should strive to be profitable" is a principle, and one that can be applied to any company.

The degree of generality of principles can vary considerably, and some are much narrower than others. For example, "Children at Smith Elementary School must wear uniforms" is a principle restricted to children attending Smith. The principle does not apply to a child attending a different school. On the other hand, the principle "Any person of voting age has an obligation to vote" applies to a large number of people regardless of background, education, wealth, etc.

The word "proposition" or "precept" can be used in place of "principle."

Because a principle is by definition a broad rule (usually conditional in nature), the presence of the Principle indicator serves to broaden the scope of the question. The question becomes more abstract, and you must analyze the problem to identify the underlying relationships. Functionally, you must take a broad, global proposition and apply it in a specific manner, either to the answer choices (as in a Must or Parallel question) or to the passage (as in a Strengthen or Weaken question).

Question Type Variety

One of the aims of the test makers is to keep you off-balance. An unsettled, frustrated test taker is prone to make mistakes. By mixing up the types of questions you face as well as the location you must search in order to find the proper information, the makers of the test can keep you from getting into a rhythm. For this reason, you will always see a spread of questions within each section, and you will infrequently see the same exact question type twice in a row. Since this situation is a fact of the GMAT, you should be prepared for the quick shifting of mental gears required to move from question to question.

Location, Type, and Sub-type Drill

The following is another collection of sample Reading Comprehension questions. In the space provided, categorize each stem into one of the three Location designations: Specific Reference (SR), Concept Reference (CR), and Global Reference (GR), and then categorize each stem into one of the six main Reading Comprehension Question Types: Must Be True, Main Point, Strengthen, Weaken, Parallel Reasoning, or Cannot be True. In addition, include any relevant sub-type designations as discussed in this chapter: Purpose (P), Organization (O), Author's Perspective (AP), Subject Perspective (SP), Passage Expansion (E), Except (X), or Principle (PR). *Answers on Page 292*

1. Question Stem: "It can be reasonably inferred from the passage that the author's attitude is most favorable toward which one of the following?"

   Question Type: _____

2. Question Stem: "Which one of the following views can most reasonably be attributed to the experts cited in line 39?"

   Question Type: _____

3. Question Stem: "As described in the passage, NASA's approach to solving the dark matter problem is most analogous to which of the following?"

   Question Type: _____

4. Question Stem: "Based on information in the passage, it can be inferred that which one of the following sentences could most logically be added to the passage as a concluding sentence?"

   Question Type: _____

5. Question Stem: "Which one of the following, if true, would most weaken the author's argument against harsh punishment for debtors?"

   Question Type: _____

6. Question Stem: "Which one of the following, if true, would lend the most credence to the author's argument in the second paragraph of the passage?"

   Question Type: _____

7. Question Stem: "Which one of the following best states the main idea of the passage?"

   Question Type: _____

8. Question Stem: "Which one of the following most accurately describes the organization of the passage?"

   Question Type: _____

9. Question Stem: "The passage provides information that answers each of the following questions EXCEPT:"

   Question Type: _____

10. Question Stem: "The author's primary purpose in the passage is"

   Question Type: _____

11. Question Stem: "The logical relationship of lines 7-9 of the passage to lines 23-25 of the passage is most accurately described as"

   Question Type: _____

12. Question Stem: "Which one of the following, if true, would most cast doubt on the author's interpretation of the study involving the family discussed on line 17?"

   Question Type: _____

13. Question Stem: "The passage contains information sufficient to justify inferring which one of the following?"

   Question Type: _____

14. Question Stem: "The author's attitude toward Zeno's development of a new hypothesis about atomic processes can most aptly be described as"

    Question Type: _____

15. Question Stem: "Which one of the following institutions would NOT be covered by the multi-tier classification system proposed by Jacobs?"

    Question Type: _____

16. Question Stem: "Which one of the following most closely expresses the author's intended meaning in using the term "unabashedly" (line 14)?"

    Question Type: _____

17. Question Stem: "The author's attitude toward the studies mentioned in lines 14 - 23 is most likely"

    Question Type: _____

18. Question Stem: "Based on the passage, the author would probably hold that which one of the following principles is fundamental to long-term reduction of recidivism rates?"

    Question Type: _____

19. Question Stem: "Which one of the following most accurately describes the organization of the material presented in the first and second paragraphs of the passage?"

    Question Type: _____

20. Question Stem: "In discussing the tangential details of events, the passage contrasts their original significance to witnesses with their possible significance in the courtroom (lines 52-59). That contrast is most closely analogous to which one of the following?"

    Question Type: _____

Location, Type, and Sub-type Drill Answer Key

The typical student misses at least half of the questions in this drill. Do not worry about how many you miss; the point of this drill is to acquaint you with the different question stems. As you see more examples of each type of question, your ability to correctly identify each stem will improve.

1. GR, Must, AP
Location: This question stem provides no reference points, so this is a Global Reference Question.
Type: The correct answer to this question must reflect the author's attitude as described in the passage, and it must pass the Fact Test. This is a Must Be True question.
Sub-type: Since the question deals with the author's attitude, this is an Author's Perspective question.

2. SR, Must, SP
Location: This question stem provides a line reference, so this is a Specific Reference question.
Type: The correct answer must be consistent with the passage's description of the referenced experts, so this is a Must Be True question.
Sub-Type: Here we are asked about the views of experts cited in the passage, so we must understand their perspective to find the answer to this Subject Perspective question.

3. CR, Parallel
Location: This question stem refers to a particular approach discussed somewhere in the passage, so this is a Concept Reference question.
Type: Here we are asked to parallel the referenced approach, so this is a Parallel Reasoning question (as with most questions that contain the word "analogous").

4. SR, Must, E
Location: This question stem specifies the location by asking for a logical concluding sentence.
Type: The correct answer to this question must provide a logical conclusion, which can be determined based on information from the passage, so this is a Must Be True question.
Sub-type: This question requires that a logical conclusion be added to the end of the passage, which makes this a Passage Expansion question.

5. CR, Weaken
Location: This question deals with a particular argument made by the author, so this is a Concept Reference question (if the entire passage were focused on this one argument, this would then be a Global Reference question).
Type: Since this question asks for the answer choice which will weaken the author's argument, this is of course a Weaken question.

6. SR, Strengthen
Location: The line reference makes this a Specific Reference question.
Type: In this case we are asked to "lend credence" to an argument (otherwise known as "strengthening"). This is a Strengthen question.

7. GR, MP
Location: This question stem regards the passage as a whole, so this is a Global Reference Question.
Type: Since this question asks for the central focus of the passage, this is a Main Point question.

8. GR, Must, O
Location: As this question provides no specific reference points, it is a Global Reference question.
Type: The answer to this question stem will come directly from information in the stimulus, so this is a Must Be True question.
Sub-Type: This is a clear example of an Organization question, which requires that you have an understanding of the overall structure of the passage.

9. GR, MustX
Location: This question references the passage in its entirety, so this is a Global Reference question.
Type: The information needed to answer this question comes directly from the passage, so this is a Must Be True question.
Sub-Type: This is an Except question, so the four incorrect answers in this case will be those choices that can be answered with information provided in the passage. The correct answer choice will be the one that cannot be answered by the passage.

10. GR, Must, P
Location: This common question stem refers to the passage as a whole, and is therefore a Global Reference question.
Type: The answer to this question will be based on information from the passage (and should be prephrased). This is a Must Be True question.
Sup-Type: Since this question asks for the author's main purpose, this is a Purpose question.

11. SR, Must, O
Location: This question refers us specifically to various locations in the passage, so this is a Specific Reference question.
Type: The answer comes from information from the passage, making this a Must Be True question.
Sub-Type: Because this question requires that you understand the structure of the passage, as well as the relationship between various sections of the passage, this is an Organization question.

12. SR, Weaken
Location: The reference to line 17 makes this a Specific Reference question.
Type: When we see a question begin with "Which of the following, if true," we can generally expect either a Strengthen or a Weaken question. In this case, because the correct answer will "cast doubt," this is a Weaken question.

13. GR, Must
Location: This stem gets no more specific than "The passage," so this is a Global Reference question.
Type: Although the wording in this case is somewhat convoluted, if an answer choice must be a "sufficiently justified inference," then it Must Be True.

14. CR, Must, AP
Location: This question stem refers to a particular hypothesis, which makes this a Concept Reference question.
Type: A proper description of the author's attitude will come directly from information in the passage (and therefore should certainly be prephrased), so this is a Must Be True question.
Sub-type: This question requires an understanding of the author's attitude, so it is an Author's Perspective question.

RC

Location, Type, and Sub-type Drill Answer Key

15. CR, Cannot
Location: This question stem deals with a proposed classification system. If this system were the focus of the passage as a whole, this would be a Global Reference question. In the actual passage, however, that is not the case, making this a Concept Reference question.
Type: Since the correct answer choice cannot be covered by the proposed classification, this is a Cannot question.

16. SR, Must, P
Location: This question refers us to line 14, which makes this a Specific Reference question.
Type: The answer to this question should be prephrased, as it will come directly from information offered in the passage. It is a Must Be True question.
Sub-Type: Since this question stem requires that we consider the intended meaning of the given term, it is a Function/Purpose question.

17. SR, Must, AP
Location: This question stem specifies that the study is mentioned in lines 14-23, so this is a Specific Reference question.
Type: This question regards information about the author which comes directly from the stimulus, and the answer must pass the Fact Test. This is a Must Be True question.
Sub-type: This example requires an understanding of the author's attitude, so it is an Author's Perspective question.

18. GR, Must, AP, PR
Location: If this question deals with a passage which focuses on recidivism rates, then this is a Global Reference question. If recidivism only makes up a part of the discussion, this would be a Concept Reference question.
Type: The answer to this question will come from the information offered in the passage, so this is a Must Be True question.
Sub-type: Since this question regards the author's attitude, it is an Author's Perspective question, and because the answer will involve fundamental principles, it is also a Principle question.

19. SR, Must, O
Location: This question refers to a specific portion of the passage, so it is a Specific Reference question.
Type: The answer to this Must Be True question will come from information provided in the passage, and should be prephrased.
Sub-Type: This question stem requires an understanding of the structure of the passage, as it is a Passage Organization question.

20. SR, Parallel
Location: Since this question refers to lines 52-59, it is a Specific Reference question.
Type: This question requires that we find an "analogous contrast," which basically means that we have to find a parallel scenario. This is a Parallel Reasoning question.

Most students tend to simply read the question stem and then move on to the answer choices without further thought. This is disadvantageous because these students run a greater risk of being tempted by the expertly constructed incorrect answer choices. One of the most effective techniques for quickly finding correct answer choices and avoiding incorrect answer choices is prephrasing. Prephrasing an answer involves quickly speculating on what you expect the correct answer will be based on the information in the passage.

Although every answer you prephrase may not be correct, there is great value in considering for a moment what elements could appear in the correct answer choice. Students who regularly prephrase find that they are more readily able to eliminate incorrect answer choices, and of course, many times their prephrased answer is correct. In part, prephrasing puts you in an attacking mindset: if you look ahead and consider a possible answer choice, you are forced to involve yourself in the problem. This process helps keep you alert and in touch with the elements of the problem.

Keep in mind that prephrasing is directly related to attacking the passage; typically, students who closely analyze the five critical elements of the passage can more easily prephrase an answer.

Keep in mind, however, that while the answers to many questions can be prephrased, not all answers can be prephrased. A question that asks, "Which one of the following most accurately states the main point of the passage?" should immediately bring an answer to mind. On the other hand, if a question asks, "To which one of the following questions does the passage most clearly provide an answer?" you cannot prephrase an answer, because you are not given sufficient information to pre-form an opinion. Yes, you will have some general knowledge based on your reading, but because the test makers can choose any angle from the passage, you will probably not come up with a strong prephrase to this question. This should not be a concern—prephrase when you can, and if you cannot, move ahead.

Prephrasing is the GMAT version of the old adage, "An ounce of prevention is worth a pound of cure."

Because of the GMAT's time constraints, some students are afraid to pause between reading the questions and assessing the answers. Always prephrase when possible! Prephrasing is far more efficient, and makes you less susceptible to the test makers' cleverly worded incorrect answer choices.

RC

All GMAT questions have five answer choice options and each question has only one correct, or "credited," response. As with other sections, the correct answer in a Reading Comprehension question must meet the Uniqueness Rule of Answer Choices™, which states that "Every correct answer has a unique logical quality that meets the criteria in the question stem. Every incorrect answer has the opposite logical quality." The correctness of the answer choices themselves conforms to this rule: there is one correct answer choice; the other four answer choices are the opposite of correct, or incorrect. Consider the following specific examples:

1.   Logical Quality of the Correct Answer: Must Be True
      Logical Quality of the Four Incorrect Answers:
            the opposite of Must Be True = Not Necessarily True (could be not necessarily the case or never the case)

2.   Logical Quality of the Correct Answer: Strengthen
      Logical Quality of the Four Incorrect Answers:
            the opposite of Strengthen = Not Strengthen (could be neutral or weaken)

3.   Logical Quality of the Correct Answer: Weaken
      Logical Quality of the Four Incorrect Answers:
            the opposite of Weaken = Not Weaken (could be neutral or strengthen)

Even though there is only one correct answer choice and this answer choice is unique, you still are faced with a difficult task when attempting to determine the correct answer. The test makers have the advantage of time and language on their side. Because identifying the correct answer at first glance can be quite hard, you must always read all five of the answer choices. Students who fail to read all five answer choices open themselves up to missing questions without ever having read the correct answer. There are many classic examples of the test makers' placing highly attractive wrong answer choices just before the correct answer. If you are going to make the time investment of analyzing the stimulus and the question stem, you should also make the wise investment of considering each answer choice.

As you read through each answer choice, sort them into Contenders and Losers. If an answer choice appears somewhat attractive, interesting, or even confusing, keep it as a contender and quickly move on to the next answer choice. You do not want to spend time debating the merits of an answer choice only to find that the next answer choice is superior. However, if an answer choice immediately strikes you as incorrect, classify it as a loser and move on. Once you have evaluated all five answer choices, return to the answer choices that strike you as most likely to be correct and decide which one is correct.

All high-scoring test takers are active and aggressive. Passive test takers tend to be less involved in the exam and therefore more prone to error.

RC

Let us review a concept discussed in the first section of this book: The Contender/Loser separation process, which is exceedingly important, primarily because it saves time. Again consider two students—1 and 2—who each approach the same question, one of whom uses the Contender/Loser approach and the other who does not. Answer choice (D) is correct:

Student 1 (using Contender/Loser)

> Answer choice (A): considers this answer for 10 seconds, keeps it as a Contender.
> Answer choice (B): considers this answer for 5 seconds, eliminates it as a Loser.
> Answer choice (C): considers this answer for 10 seconds, eliminates it as a Loser.
> Answer choice (D): considers this answer for 15 seconds, keeps it as a Contender, and mentally notes that this answer is preferable to answer choice(A).
> Answer choice (E): considers this answer for 10 seconds, would normally keep as a contender, but determines answer choice (D) is superior.

> After a quick review, Student 1 selects answer choice (D) and moves to the next question. Total time spent on the answer choices: 50 seconds (irrespective of the time spent on the stimulus).

Student 2 (considering each answer choice in its entirety)

> Answer choice (A): considers this answer for 10 seconds, is not sure if the answer is correct or incorrect. Returns to stimulus and spends another 15 seconds proving the answer is wrong.
> Answer choice (B): considers this answer for 5 seconds, eliminates it.
> Answer choice (C): considers this answer for 10 seconds, eliminates it.
> Answer choice (D): considers this answer for 15 seconds, notes this is the best answer thus far.
> Answer choice (E): considers this answer for 10 seconds, but determines answer choice (D) is superior.

> After a quick review, Student 2 selects answer choice (D) and moves to the next question. Total time spent on the answer choices: 65 seconds.

Comparison: both students answer the problem correctly, but Student 2 takes 15 more seconds to answer the question than Student 1.
Again, we might note that the time difference in this example is small (15 seconds) we should keep in mind that the extra 15 seconds is for just one problem.

There may be times when you would not read all five answer choices. For example, suppose you only have two minutes left in the section and you determine that answer choice (B) is clearly correct. In that case, you would choose answer choice (B) and then move on to the next question.

Imagine if that same thing occurred on every single Reading Comprehension problem in the section: that extra 15 seconds per question would translate to a loss of 6 minutes and 45 seconds when multiplied across 27 questions in a section! And that lost time would mean that student 2 would get to four or five fewer questions than Student 1, just in this one section. This example underscores an essential GMAT truth: Little things make a big difference, and every single second counts. If you can save even five seconds by employing a certain method, then do so!

Occasionally, students will read and eliminate all five of the answer choices. If this occurs, return to the passage and re-evaluate what you have read. Remember—the information needed to answer the question always resides in the passage, either implicitly or explicitly. If none of the answers are attractive, then you must have missed something key in the passage.

Tricks of the Trade

The individuals who construct standardized tests are called *psychometricians*. Although this job title sounds ominous, breaking this word into its two parts reveals a great deal about the nature of the GMAT. Although we could make a number of jokes about the *psycho* part, this portion of the word refers to psychology; the *metrician* portion relates to metrics or measurement. Thus, the purpose of these individuals is to create a test that measures you in a precise, psychological way. As part of this process, the makers of the GMAT carefully analyze reams of data from every test administration in order to assess the tendencies of test takers. As Arthur Conan Doyle observed through his character Sherlock Holmes, "You can, for example, never foretell what any one man will do, but you can say with precision what an average number will be up to." By studying the actions of all past test takers, the makers of the exam can reliably predict where you will be most likely to make errors. Throughout this book we will reference those pitfalls as they relate to specific questions and passage types. For the moment, we would like to highlight one mental trap you must avoid at all times in any GMAT section: the tendency to dwell on past problems. Many students fall prey to "answering" a problem, and then continuing to think about it as they start the next problem. Obviously, this is distracting and creates an environment where missing the next problem is more likely. When you finish a problem, you must immediately put it out of your mind and move to the next problem with 100% focus. If you let your mind wander back to previous problems, you fall into a deadly trap.

Practicing with Time

Students often ask if they should time themselves while practicing. While every student should take a timed practice GMAT at the very start of their preparation in order to gauge where they stand, not all preparation should be composed of timed exercises. When you learn a new concept or are practicing with a certain technique, you should begin by doing the first several problems untimed in order to get a feel for how the idea operates. Once you feel comfortable with the concept, begin tracking the time it takes you to complete each question. At first, do not worry about completing the passages within a specified time frame, but rather examine how long it takes you to do each passage when you are relaxed. How long does it take you to read the passage? How long to do each question? After doing several passages in this fashion, then begin attempting to read each passage and question set in the general time frame allowed on the test. Thus, you can "ramp up" to the appropriate time per passage.

Final Chapter Note

This concludes our general discussion of Reading Comprehension passages. In the next chapter we will briefly review ideas previously discussed, and then we will use those techniques to work through complete passages and question sets. If, in the future, you find yourself unclear about some of these ideas, please return to the earlier chapters and revisit those concepts.

If you feel as if you are still hazy on some of the ideas discussed so far, do not worry. When discussing the theory that underlies all questions and approaches, the points can sometimes be a bit abstract and dry. In the next chapter we will focus more on the application of these ideas to common Reading Comprehension questions, which often helps to clarify these concepts.

RC

CHAPTER THIRTEEN: PUTTING IT ALL TOGETHER

Chapter Preview

Up until this point we have focused on the methods needed to analyze the passages, and in doing so we have isolated individual sections of text that relate directly to each discussion. Now it is time to combine all of the information you have learned and analyze some complete passage sets. Accordingly, this chapter contains two sections:

1. A review of all elements of the approach we use for Reading Comprehension passages.

2. Two practice Reading Comprehension passages, each with detailed analysis of the passage text and each question.

Reading Approach Review

The following section provides a brief review of the reading approaches discussed in the previous chapters in this section.

Chapter Ten Review

After you have ascertained the topic, as you progress into the passage you must carefully track the following five key VIEWSTAMP elements:

1. The various groups and viewpoints discussed within the passage. (VIEW)
2. The structure of the passage and the organization of ideas. (S)
3. The tone or attitude of each group or individual. (T)
4. The argument made by each group or individual. (A)
5. The main point of the passage. (MP)

Chapter Eleven Review

Sources of Difficulty

There are four general ways the makers of the test can increase the difficulty of any given passage:

1. Challenging Topic or Terminology
2. Challenging Writing Style
3. Multiple Viewpoints
4. Difficult Questions/Answers

Passage Elements That Generate Questions

As you read, there are certain specific passage elements that should jump out at you, primarily because history has shown that the test makers use these elements as the basis of questions. For purposes of clarity, we will divide these elements into two groups:

Viewpoint-Specific Elements

1. Track all viewpoints
2. Be wary of competing perspectives

Text-based Questions

Text-based elements will often be smaller pieces, sometimes just a single word, but sometimes short sections of the text. In this sense, these are the "nuts and bolts" elements that you should be aware of when reading.

These are the seven elements (not in order of importance):
1. Initial Information/Closing Information
2. Dates and Numbers
3. Definitions
4. Examples
5. Difficult Words or Phrases
6. Enumerations/Lists
7. Text Questions

Two Broad Reasoning Structures

Causal reasoning and conditional reasoning appear frequently in the Critical Reasoning questions on the GMAT, but less so with the Reading Comprehension passages.

Causal Reasoning

Cause and effect reasoning asserts or denies that one thing causes another, or that one thing is caused by another. The cause is the event that makes the other occur; the effect is the event that follows from the cause. By definition, the cause must occur before the effect, and the cause is the "activator" or "ignitor" in the relationship. The effect always happens at some point in time after the cause.

Causality in Reading Comprehension usually is discussed in the context of why certain events occurred. The terms that typically introduce causality—such as *caused by*, *reason for*, or *product of*—are still used, but then the author often goes on to discuss the reasons behind the occurrence in depth.

Conditional Reasoning

Conditional reasoning is the broad name given to logical relationships composed of sufficient and necessary conditions. Any conditional relationship consists of at least one sufficient condition and at least one necessary condition.

Conditional relationships in Reading Comprehension passages tend to be unobtrusive, usually occurring as a sideline point to a larger argument.

Of the two types of reasoning, causal reasoning appears more frequently than conditional reasoning with Reading Comprehension passages.

Pitfalls to Avoid

There are a number of text formations and configurations you should recognize. These formations are often used to generate questions, and in this sense they function as possible "traps" for the unwary test taker.

Traps of Similarities and Distinctions

These sections of text discuss in detail items that have both similarities and differences. By comparing and contrasting the items in a continuous section of text, the test makers create the possibility of confusion.

Trap of Separation

One of the favorite tricks of the test makers is to take related pieces of information and then physically separate those pieces by a number of lines of text that discuss a different concept. Then, in the questions, the test makers ask you a question about the concept in order to examine your ability to track related concepts in the face of unrelated (and likely confusing) information.

The Trap of Question Misdirection

This trap occurs when the test makers use a specific line reference in the question stem to direct you to a place in the passage where the correct answer will not be found.

Trap of Proximity

Just because two ideas are placed in physical proximity in a passage does not mean that they are related.

RC

Trap of Inserted Alternate Viewpoint

Another trick of the test makers is to discuss a particular viewpoint, and then in the middle of that discussion insert a new viewpoint.

Traps of Chronology

Traps of chronology relate to the placement and order of items within the passage, and the tendency of many readers to believe that when one item is presented before another, then the first item occurred first or caused the second item. These two traps are called the Trap of Order and the Trap of Cause:

Trap of Order

Some students make the mistake of believing that because an item is discussed before another item then the first item likely predated the second item. Unless explicitly stated or inherently obvious, this does not have to be the case.

Trap of Cause

Other students mistakenly assume that when one item is discussed before another item, then the first item must have caused the second item. This assumption is unwarranted. The easiest way to discern the author's intentions is to carefully examine the language used by the writer because causal relationships almost always feature one or more of the words that indicate causality (such as *caused by*, *produced by*, etc).

The order of presentation of the items in the passage does not indicate any temporal or causal relationship between those items.

Passage Topic Traps

The test makers sometimes use the topic to catch test takers off-guard. Most students have expectations of difficulty based on topic, the test makers at times play a sort of "bait and switch" game with students, by making a passage initially look hard or easy and then radically changing the difficulty after the first few lines or first paragraph.

Two Passages Analyzed

On the following pages two practice GMAT passages are presented, followed by a complete analysis of each passage and all of the corresponding questions. One important note: remember that maintaining a positive attitude is critical! Approach the passages with energy and enthusiasm and you will see your performance improve.

RC

Practice Passage I

For each passage, note the basic information in the text and the VIEWStamp elements, and continue working until you complete the questions. Then, read the corresponding explanation section.

"Dissociative identity disorder," or multiple personality disorder, is a rare psychological disorder in which an individual exhibits entirely different personalities and behaviors. Although the
(5) exact psychological mechanism that creates multiple personalities is not known, psychiatrists have agreed that a severe emotional trauma must occur prior to age seven, the age at which a child's mind matures into a unified identity. In addition to
(10) this trauma, certain familial elements must be present. First, the parents of the child must be in conflict, essentially playing opposing, warring roles in the child's life. Typically, this is manifested by one parent abusing the child and the other parent
(15) denying or ignoring the abuse. Second, if siblings are present, they must be treated differently (and generally better) by the parents than the dissociated child. This difference in treatment is critical since it shows the dissociated child that he or she is
(20) "different" and undeserving of love and other emotional valuation. If all children in a family are treated in a similar fashion, then multiple personality disorder will not tend to occur. The above elements, while necessary for the rise of
(25) multiple personalities, do not guarantee that a child will develop multiple personalities.

1. The passage provides information to answer all of the following questions EXCEPT:

   (A) Are siblings necessary for the creation of multiple personality disorder?
   (B) Will a trauma in a young child's life guarantee the onset of multiple personality disorder?
   (C) How does a child establish multiple personalities?
   (D) What are some of the necessary preconditions for multiple personality disorder?
   (E) How common is the occurance of multiple personality disorder in the population?

2. Which of the following individuals would be the most likely candidate for development of multiple personality disorder?

   (A) A fifteen-year-old female runaway with two abusive parents and two poorly-treated siblings.
   (B) A nine-year-old male with divorced parents and three well-treated sisters.
   (C) A five-year-old female who lost both her parents in a car accident.
   (D) A six-year-old male with one abusive parent and two well-treated brothers.
   (E) A seven-year-old female with two abusive parents and no siblings.

3. In the passage, the author is primarily concerned with doing which of the following?

   (A) Describing a psychiatric problem and proposing a solution.
   (B) Presenting information and drawing conclusions from the information.
   (C) Summarizing the current research into a common psychological disorder.
   (D) Citing evidence to support a view.
   (E) Discussing a phenomenon and several factors required for its development.

4. Which of the following factors is required for the development of dissociative personality disorder?

   I.   Parental conflict
   II. Different parental treatment of siblings, if siblings are present
   III. Early childhood trauma

   (A) I only
   (B) II only
   (C) I and II only
   (D) I and III only
   (E) I, II, and III

Practice Passage II

For business executives, managing the growth of a company at an appropriate rate is a central challenge. For small businesses, the issue is even more critical. An improperly managed small

(5) business usually does not have the necessary cash reserves to overcome mismanagement, and if growth is neither sustained nor managed properly, the existence of the business can be jeopardized.

A number of experts have suggested that a

(10) strong guiding business plan is the key to handling small business growth. A potent and well-formulated plan can lay the foundation for years of rising profitability, and can help a small business prepare for changes in the market. While a strong

(15) business plan can help a business grow, a good plan does not ensure growth. At times, market conditions change so rapidly as to relegate the plan to obsolescence. In other businesses, the plan is not used as intended, or is simply ignored. Evidence

(20) from a number of business case studies suggests that a more important factor in managing growth is the presence of an executive with a clear vision of the business and its market position. If there is also a competent business plan in place, this can assist the

(25) executive, but leaders with a strong market vision can easily overcome the lack of a good business plan.

The truth of this assertion is borne out by the experience of one regional travel agency. Although

(30) the company did not have even a basic business plan in place, they had a forceful, involved leader who understood the dynamics of the marketplace. With the rise of the internet, revenues from the consumer travel market began to wane. Realizing

(35) that the market landscape was changing irrevocably, the executive quickly initiated a retrenchment that dropped most consumer lines of business and instead focused on handling outsourced business travel. By repositioning the company as business

(40) travel specialists and increasing quality of service—24-hour service availability, emergency travel specialists, and business concierges—the company was able increase revenues by over 500% yearly.

1. Which of the following best states the main idea of the passage?

   (A)   Market repositioning by a travel agency can foster growth and increase revenues.
   (B)   A strong business plan, while helpful, is not essential to managing business growth.
   (C)   Ignoring a business plan can be detrimental to the economic well-being of a business.
   (D)   Improperly managed small businesses can run out of cash reserves.
   (E)   A strong executive is necessary for business success.

2. According to the passage, which of the following statements about business growth is likely to be true?

   (A)   The size of the business can affect the importance of growth management.
   (B)   Experts agree on the importance of a strong business plan to business growth.
   (C)   A leader with strong business vision will make a business succeed.
   (D)   Improper management of business growth will kill the business.
   (E)   Regional travel agencies provide a model for general business growth.

3. Which of the following best describes the way the last paragraph functions in the context of the passage?

   (A)   An example is presented to undermine the assertion that a leader with vision can succeed without a business plan.
   (B)   The elements of a company's success are outlined to prove a point about changing market conditions.
   (C)   A chain of reasoning is discussed in order to identify assumptions.
   (D)   A specific example is presented to illustrate a point made in the previous paragraph.
   (E)   The main conclusion of the passage is stated.

4. The author's attitude toward the view that business plans are essential is best described as

   (A)   unequivocal agreement
   (B)   tentative acceptance
   (C)   mild skepticism
   (D)   grudging acceptance
   (E)   studious criticism

RC

Practice Passage I—Answer Key

On the following pages you will find both practice passages replicated, each followed by complete explanations of the questions and answer choices. Your focus should be not only on the accuracy of your responses, but also on the general effectiveness of your note-taking/outlining approach.

"Dissociative identity disorder," or multiple personality disorder, is a rare psychological disorder in which an individual exhibits entirely different personalities and behaviors. Although the
(5) exact psychological mechanism that creates multiple personalities is not known, psychiatrists have agreed that a severe emotional trauma must occur prior to age seven, the age at which a child's mind matures into a unified identity. In addition to
(10) this trauma, certain familial elements must be present. First, the parents of the child must be in conflict, essentially playing opposing, warring roles in the child's life. Typically, this is manifested by one parent abusing the child and the other parent
(15) denying or ignoring the abuse. Second, if siblings are present, they must be treated differently (and generally better) by the parents than the dissociated child. This difference in treatment is critical since it shows the dissociated child that he or she is
(20) "different" and undeserving of love and other emotional valuation. If all children in a family are treated in a similar fashion, then multiple personality disorder will not tend to occur. The above elements, while necessary for the rise of
(25) multiple personalities, do not guarantee that a child will develop multiple personalities.

1. The passage provides information to answer all of the following questions EXCEPT:

(A) Are siblings necessary for the creation of multiple personality disorder?
(B) Will a trauma in a young child's life guarantee the onset of multiple personality disorder?
(C) How does a child establish multiple personalities?
(D) What are some of the necessary preconditions for multiple personality disorder?
(E) How common is the occurance of multiple personality disorder in the population?

2. Which of the following individuals would be the most likely candidate for development of multiple personality disorder?

(A) A fifteen-year-old female runaway with two abusive parents and two poorly-treated siblings.
(B) A nine-year-old male with divorced parents and three well-treated sisters.
(C) A five-year-old female who lost both her parents in a car accident.
(D) A six-year-old male with one abusive parent and two well-treated brothers.
(E) A seven-year-old female with two abusive parents and no siblings.

3. In the passage, the author is primarily concerned with doing which of the following?

(A) Describing a psychiatric problem and proposing a solution.
(B) Presenting information and drawing conclusions from the information.
(C) Summarizing the current research into a common psychological disorder.
(D) Citing evidence to support a view.
(E) Discussing a phenomenon and several factors required for its development.

4. Which of the following factors is required for the development of dissociative personality disorder?

I. Parental conflict
II. Different parental treatment of siblings, if siblings are present
III. Early childhood trauma

(A) I only
(B) II only
(C) I and II only
(D) I and III only
(E) I, II, and III

Practice Passage I—Answer Key

This passage begins with a definition of its topic, "dissociative identity disorder." This term describes the rare case of an individual who displays distinct multiple personalities and behaviors. While the exact cause of the pathology is unknown, the author provides a list of several factors common to those who suffer from this multiple personality disorder:

1) A child must suffer some severe emotional trauma before the age of seven, because this is the age at which a child's mind develops a "unified identity."

2) There must be conflict between the child's parents, typically with one parent who is abusive and the other in denial of, or at least ignoring, this abuse.

3) Finally, if the child has brothers or sisters, the parents' treatment of these siblings must be different from that of the affected child. The author points out that this factor plays an important role, because this different treatment sends the message that the affected child is different, has less value, and is unworthy of love.

One interesting note regarding the factors listed above: Although the author uses the term "first" to introduce the necessity of parental conflict, and uses the term "second" to introduce the requirement of different parental treatment of siblings, these are actually the second and third factors, respectively, required for the development of multiple personality disorder. The first factor, although not presented in list form, is that of severe emotional trauma suffered prior to age seven.

The author closes the paragraph with an important distinction: Although these factors are required for the development of dissociative identity disorder, their presence does not guarantee that the disorder will be developed (in conditional reasoning terms, the presence of these elements is *necessary* to the outcome, but not *sufficient* to guarantee the outcome).

VIEWSTAMP Analysis:

The sole **Viewpoint** presented in this passage is that of the author, who presents facts but neither provides any opinions nor draws any conclusions regarding the topic.

The **Structure** of this passage is quite simple, since the entire passage is composed of only one paragraph, in which the author introduces the concept of dissociative identity disorder, provides a definition of the disorder, and lists factors required for the development of the disorder.

The **Tone** of the passage is unbiased and academic, as the author provides facts about the disorder without drawing any conclusions or presenting any opinions on the matter.

Since this passage is basically a presentation of facts, there is no real **Argument** present, except perhaps for the assertion that the three factors listed are required if the disorder is to be developed.

The **Main Point** of this passage is to introduce and define dissociative identity disorder, and present three factors necessary to its development.

RC

Practice Passage I—Answer Key

Question #1: GR, Must X. The correct answer choice is (C)

Since this is an Except question, the four incorrect answer choices will present questions which are answered by the information provided within the passage, and the correct answer choice will be the one that presents a question which is unanswered by the information in the passage.

Answer choice (A): The question presented in this answer choice is covered in lines 15-16. The author tells us that if siblings are present, they must be treated differently than the affected child. This wording (specifically, the use of the term "if") implies that siblings need not be present.

Answer choice (B): In lines 23-26, the author points out that the factors listed are necessary to the development of the disorder, but do not guarantee its development. Since this question is answered in the passage, this answer choice is incorrect.

Answer choice (C): This is the correct answer choice, because this question is not answered in the passage. Although the elements listed are common to all those who suffer from the disorder, the author points out in lines 5-6 that the exact mechanism which causes the disorder is unknown.

Answer choice (D): This question is answered by the list of factors presented in lines 6-25, so this answer choice cannot be correct.

Answer choice (E): Since dissociative identity disorder is defined as "rare," this question is answered by the information in the passage, making this answer choice incorrect.

Question #2: CR, Must. The correct answer choice is (D)

As discussed earlier in the book, we should prephrase answers whenever possible. In this case, a candidate for multiple personality disorder would likely have suffered early emotional trauma, have parents in conflict, and be treated differently than his or her siblings (if siblings are present).

Answer choice (A): This female would be an unlikely candidate, because there is no clear conflict between the parents (she would be a more likely candidate if one parent ignored or denied the other's abuse), and she also lacks the element of parental treatment which is different from the treatment of her siblings.

Answer choice (B): The information provided in this answer choice is not sufficient to define this male as a likely candidate, because there is no mention of early emotional trauma, abuse, or differential treatment.

Answer choice (C): While this girl seems to have suffered the requisite early emotional trauma, there is no mention of abuse, conflict, or differential treatment, so there is no way to conclude that she is a likely candidate for the disorder.

Answer choice (D): This is the correct answer choice. Although the factors listed do not guarantee that this child will develop dissociative identity disorder, he is clearly the most likely candidate listed, considering the elements present in his case: He is younger than seven, has possibly suffered

RC

severe trauma from abuse, has one abusive parent, and is treated differently than his brothers.

Answer choice (E): This case lacks the opposing parental roles necessary for the development of the disorder, so this answer choice is incorrect.

Question #3: GR, P. The correct answer choice is (E)

The answer to this question should be prephrased as well: The author's primary purpose in this case is to define dissociative identity disorder, and provide a list of elements common to all who suffer from this disorder.

Answer choice (A): Although the author does describe a psychiatric problem, no solution is proposed in the passage.

Answer choice (B): The author is certainly concerned with presenting information about the disorder, but no conclusions are drawn.

Answer choice (C): There is no mention of current research into the disorder, and the author specifically mentions that it is a rare phenomenon.

Answer choice (D): The author does not cite evidence to support any view, choosing instread to merely present facts, so this answer choice is incorrect.

Answer choice (E): This is the correct answer choice, as any solid prephrase would have predicted. The author is primarily concerned with discussing the rare phenomenon of multiple personality disorder, and several factors necessary for development of the disorder.

Question #4: CR, Must. The correct answer choice is (E)

This question is particularly conducive to prephrasing, because all three factors listed below the question are necessary for development of the disorder. Note that factor III (early childhood trauma) is not presented in list form like the others in the passage ("First..." "Second..."), but is nonetheless a requirement for one to become dissociated and develop multiple personalities.

Answer choice (A): This answer choice lists only one of three necessary factors.

Answer choice (B): This answer choice also lists only one element.

Answer choice (C): This answer choice is the most commonly chosen wrong answer, because these are the two factors presented in the passage as "first" and "second." Since early emotional trauma (before age seven) is necessary, however, this answer choice is incorrect.

Answer choice (D): Factor II is also necessary.

Answer choice (E): This is the correct answer choice, because it is the only answer which includes all three elements necessary for the development of dissociative identity disorder.

Practice Passage II—Answer Key

For business executives, managing the growth of a company at an appropriate rate is a central challenge. For small businesses, the issue is even more critical. An improperly managed small
(5) business usually does not have the necessary cash reserves to overcome mismanagement, and if growth is neither sustained nor managed properly, the existence of the business can be jeopardized.

A number of experts have suggested that a
(10) strong guiding business plan is the key to handling small business growth. A potent and well-formulated plan can lay the foundation for years of rising profitability, and can help a small business prepare for changes in the market. While a strong
(15) business plan can help a business grow, a good plan does not ensure growth. At times, market conditions change so rapidly as to relegate the plan to obsolescence. In other businesses, the plan is not used as intended, or is simply ignored. Evidence
(20) from a number of business case studies suggests that a more important factor in managing growth is the presence of an executive with a clear vision of the business and its market position. If there is also a competent business plan in place, this can assist the
(25) executive, but leaders with a strong market vision can easily overcome the lack of a good business plan.

The truth of this assertion is borne out by the experience of one regional travel agency. Although
(30) the company did not have even a basic business plan in place, they had a forceful, involved leader who understood the dynamics of the marketplace. With the rise of the internet, revenues from the consumer travel market began to wane. Realizing
(35) that the market landscape was changing irrevocably, the executive quickly initiated a retrenchment that dropped most consumer lines of business and instead focused on handling outsourced business travel. By repositioning the company as business
(40) travel specialists and increasing quality of service—24-hour service availability, emergency travel specialists, and business concierges—the company was able increase revenues by over 500% yearly.

1. Which of the following best states the main idea of the passage?

   (A) Market repositioning by a travel agency can foster growth and increase revenues.
   (B) A strong business plan, while helpful, is not essential to managing business growth.
   (C) Ignoring a business plan can be detrimental to the economic well-being of a business.
   (D) Improperly managed small businesses can run out of cash reserves.
   (E) A strong executive is necessary for business success.

2. According to the passage, which of the following statements about business growth is likely to be true?

   (A) The size of the business can affect the importance of growth management.
   (B) Experts agree on the importance of a strong business plan to business growth.
   (C) A leader with strong business vision will make a business succeed.
   (D) Improper management of business growth will kill the business.
   (E) Regional travel agencies provide a model for general business growth.

3. Which of the following best describes the way the last paragraph functions in the context of the passage?

   (A) An example is presented to undermine the assertion that a leader with vision can succeed without a business plan.
   (B) The elements of a company's success are outlined to prove a point about changing market conditions.
   (C) A chain of reasoning is discussed in order to identify assumptions.
   (D) A specific example is presented to illustrate a point made in the previous paragraph.
   (E) The main conclusion of the passage is stated.

4. The author's attitude toward the view that business plans are essential is best described as

   (A) unequivocal agreement
   (B) tentative acceptance
   (C) mild skepticism
   (D) grudging acceptance
   (E) studious criticism

Practice Passage II—Answer Key

Paragraph One:

The author begins the first paragraph by presenting one focal point of the passage: the importance of managing the rate of a company's growth. Management of this issue is of particular importance to small businesses, which often lack significant cash reserves and are therefore less resilient to growth mismanagement. Failure to sustain or manage growth can threaten the existence of such companies.

Paragraph Two:

In this paragraph the author presents the perspective of "a number of experts," who assert that a strong business plan is vital to the proper management of a company's growth, creating the basis for long range profit increases and planning for prospective market changes. At this point in the passage (line 14), there is a subtle shift from the opinion of "a number of experts" to the perspective of the author, who points out that a strong business plan can be helpful but does not guarantee business growth, because of rapid market change or failure to stick to the plan. Citing evidence from case studies, the author asserts that an executive with a strong understanding of the market is a more important component of successful growth management, with or without the assistance of a good business plan.

Paragraph Three:

In the final paragraph the author provides practical (though anecdotal) evidence in support of the assertion that a competent executive is more vital to growth management than a solid business plan. The example provided is that of a regional travel agency which had no basic business plan but did have an involved leader with a strong understanding of the market. In response to the advent of the internet and waning consumer travel revenues, the executive repositioned the business to focus primarily on outsourced business travel. In addition, the business improved upon its consumer services in three ways: 1) 24 hour service   2) Emergency travel specialists   3) Business concierge

The author closes the passage by recounting the predictably positive results experienced by the travel agency (over 500% annual growth following the changes), to strenthen the case that a strong leader with vision is more integral to growth management than a compentent business plan.

VIEWSTAMP Analysis:

The **Viewpoints** reflected in this passage are as follows: The first paragraph is entirely factual, and thus viewpoint-neutral. The first sentence of the second paragraph reflects the viewpoint of "a number of experts," who believe that successful growth management depends primarily on a strong business plan. In the the second sentence of this paragraph, however, there is a quick shift to the authors viewpoint (that a strong leader is more important than a strong business plan), with this perspective reflected in the remainder of the passage.

Practice Passage II—Answer Key

The **Structure** of the passage is as follows:

> Paragraph One: Discuss the notion that effective growth management is a major challenge for business executives, and why the issue is of particular concern to small businesses.

> Paragraph Two: Present the "expert" perspective that a competent business plan is the most important factor in small business growth management, and the shortcomings of this viewpoint. Assert that a strong leader who understands the marketplace is more important than a good business plan.

> Paragraph Three: Introduce one real-world example of a small business which thrives with a strong leader despite the fact that there was no business plan in place.

The author's **Tone** is even-handed and well reasoned. When the author takes issue with the perspective of "a number of experts," that disagreement has a reasonable basis (markets can change quickly; business plans can be ignored), and is bolstered by the the practical example provided.

The **Arguments** in the passage are those of the referenced experts who believe that the business plan is the key to effective growth management, and of the author, who provides reason and evidence to back the assertion that a business leader with a clear vision of the market is more vital to success.

The **Main Point** of the passage is that while some say a business plan is the most important component in handling growth management, a very important issue for small businesses, a strong executive who understands the market can help a business to thrive with or without a set plan.

Question #1: GR, MP. The correct answer choice is (B)

The main point, as stated above, is that a business plan can be helpful to managing growth, a strong leader can help a business to thrive in the presence or absence of a business plan.

Answer choice (A): This answer references the specific example provided by the author to speak to the importance of a strong leader, but this point is provided as evidence, not as the main point.

Answer choice (B): This is the correct answer choice. Although the importance of a strong executive is not specifically mentioned in this answer, this is the choice which best reflects the author's main assertion, discussed throughout the passage.

Answer choice (C): This side point is mentioned as one potential vulnerability which exists even in the presence of a competent business plan.

Answer choice (D): This point is not the main focus, but rather speaks to the fact that proper management is of particular importance to a small business.

Answer choice (E): The argument made is that a strong leader can be more vital than a competant business plan—the author never claims that a business <u>can't</u> succeed without such a leader.

Practice Passage II—Answer Key

Question #2: GR, Must. The correct answer choice is (A)

Answer choice (A): This is the correct answer choice. In the first paragraph of the passage, the author discusses why proper growth management is "for small businesses...even more critical."

Answer choice (B): The author references some experts who believe that a solid business plan is vital, but the authors perspective, supported by case studies and the travel agency example, is that the business plan can be helpful but is not absolutely necessary.

Answer choice (C): While a business leader with a strong vision is more *likely* to lead a small business to success, the author never goes so far as to assert that success is guaranteed under strong leadership.

Answer choice (D): Like answer choice (C), the language here is stronger than would be justified by the passage. Improper management may jeopardize a business, but there is no implication that failure is assured by poor management.

Answer choice (E): The regional travel agency happens to be the subject of the example presented in the third paragraph, but the author does not assert that regional travel agencies provide a model for general business growth.

Question #3: SR, O. The correct answer choice is (D)

Like Question #1, this is a question conducive to prephrasing, so we should try to get a good idea of the answer before considering the choices provided. Having already broken down the basic structure of the passage, we know the role played by the third paragraph: the author uses this paragraph to provide the travel agency example, to strengthen the general assertion that a strong leader can bring success to a business, even in the absence of a basic business plan.

Answer choice (A): The case presented exemplifies the point that a strong leader can help to foster success without necessarily requiring a business plan.

Answer choice (B): The elements of the travel agency's success are outlined to prove the point about the importance of a strong leader, not to prove a point about changing market conditions.

Answer choice (C): No assumptions are identified, so this cannot be the correct answer choice.

Answer choice (D): This is the correct answer choice. The example is presented to illustrate the point that while a business plan can be helpful, a plan is not absolutely necessary if the company's leader has a clear understanding of the marketplace.

Answer choice (E): The final paragraph is used to exemplify the main point of the passage, but the main point is stated most clearly in the final sentence of the second paragraph.

Question #4: CR, Must. The correct answer choice is (E)

The author states in line 25 that "leaders with a strong personal vision can easily overcome the lack of a good business plan." The argument has reasonable basis and the author provides an example to support this assertion.

Answer choice (A): The author does not agree that business plans are essential, so this cannot be the correct answer choice.

Answer choice (B): The author does not accept the assertion.

Answer choice (C): This author is skeptical, but the skepticism is far greater than "mild," so this answer choice is incorrect.

Answer choice (D): Again, the author is not accepting of the notion that business plans are the key to effective growth management.

Answer choice (E): This is the correct answer choice. The entire passage is basically a reasoned critique of the assertion that a good business plan is the key to effective growth management.

RC

SECTION THREE:

SENTENCE CORRECTION

CHAPTER FOURTEEN: THE BASICS OF SENTENCE CORRECTION

Grammar Review

Students who do well on Sentence Correction questions possess a sound knowledge of grammar and the use of standard written English. If you feel that you have a firm understanding of grammar, including the parts of speech and parts of a sentence, please proceed with this chapter. However, if you are not completely comfortable with grammar and usage, we strongly urge you to visit the online portion of this book at www.powerscore.com/gvbible. There you will find the Appendix "The Basics of Grammar," which you should read and complete before continuing.

Sentence Correction Question Directions

The directions for Sentence Correction questions are only given once on the test, just before the first Sentence Correction question. The directions will not be repeated. For this reason, as well as for saving time on the GMAT, you should familiarize yourself with the directions now:

> A sentence correction question will introduce a sentence. All or part of the sentence may be underlined. Five ways to phrase the underlined portion will be listed under the sentence. The first answer choice is identical to the underlined portion; the remaining four answer choices are different. If the original underlined portion is best, select the first answer. Otherwise, choose another phrase.

> These questions assess your skill in recognizing the proper use and effectiveness of sentences in standard written English. Your answer must follow the rules of standard written English by using correct grammar, word choice, and sentence construction. Choose the best phrasing that creates the most effective sentence. Your choice should not be awkward, ambiguous, redundant, or grammatically incorrect; rather, the sentence should be clear and concise.

Notice the line "The first answer choice is identical to the underlined portion." Because you have already read the underlined portion of the sentence, you should never read the first answer choice. There is no point in reading the same phrase twice, as it wastes valuable time.

The directions also state that "Your answer must follow the rules of standard written English." Standard English is the variety of English used as the model for proper communication, reflecting correct grammar and usage as dictated by textbooks and style manuals. The GMAT tests the standards of *written* English, which tend to be more formal than the rules of *spoken* English. You should also be aware that the GMAT tests standard written American English, although this is not stated in the directions.

Unlike the ACT or SAT, the GMAT mixes Sentence Correction questions with Reading Comprehension and Critical Reading questions. They are not separated by format or content.

SC

The Parts of a Sentence Correction Question

Each Sentence Correction question contains two parts: the sentence and the five answer choices. All or part of the sentence will be underlined, and the first answer choice is identical to the underlined portion of the sentence:

You must read Answer Choices (B), (C), (D), and (E) before making a selection.

1. At the completion of World War II, Japan agreed to abandon its position as an imperial power, <u>allocated funds for victims in war crimes, and the Treaty of San Francisco was signed.</u>   ← Sentence
    ← Underlined portion

    (A) allocated funds for victims in war crimes, and the Treaty of San Francisco was signed   ← Answer Choice (A) always repeats underlined portion
    (B) to allocate funds for victims in war crimes, and to sign he Treaty of San Francisco
    (C) allocated funds for victims of war crimes, and signed the Treaty of San Francisco
    (D) allocating funds for victims of war crimes, and signing the Treaty of San Francisco   Remaining answer choices
    (E) to allocate funds for victims of war crimes, and the Treaty of San Francisco was signed

The best answer is not always a perfect answer.

As a technical note, an empty answer bubble appears next to each answer choice (rather than the letters A through E) on the real GMAT CAT. However, for the convenience of discussion, we will present problems with the answer choices lettered (A) through (E).

Tested Curriculum

Just as the Verbal portion of the test assesses several different verbal abilities, the Sentence Correction questions test three different areas of language proficiency.

1. *Grammar* (the use of standard written English)
2. *Concise expression* (expression of a complete idea in as few words as possible)
3. *Correct diction* (the choice of appropriate words)

Although the makers of the GMAT purposefully create sentences intended to trick the novice test-taker, they also tend to repeat the same types of errors and test questions. By recognizing a repeated pattern, you can dissect a Sentence Correct question quickly and correctly.

Grammatical offenses are at the root of all GMAT Sentence Correction errors. Problems with wordy phrases or incorrect word choice are usually secondary errors.

SC

CHAPTER FIFTEEN: ERRORS INVOLVING VERBS

Subject and Verb Agreement

The subject of a sentence and its corresponding verb must agree with each other. Similarly, the subject of a clause and its verb must be in agreement. This simply means that singular subjects need singular verbs, and plural subjects need plural verbs:

	CORRECT	INCORRECT
Singular Subject	The *boy* plays cards.	The *boy* play cards.
	The *computer* whirs.	The *computer* whir.
	She needs a haircut.	*She* need a haircut.
Plural Subject	The *boys* play cards.	The *boys* plays cards.
	The *computers* whir.	The *computers* whirs.
	They need a haircut.	*They* needs a haircut.

> Many singular verbs end in *-s* or *-es*, such as *plays*, *catches*, *whirs*, and *needs*. This is especially true for action verbs.

The test will also feature agreement mistakes with the verb *to be* (*am, is, are, was, were, being, been, be*) used both as a linking verb and a helping verb:

	CORRECT	INCORRECT
Singular Subject	*Sam* is tired	*Sam* are tired.
Plural Subject	The *plans* were made.	The *plans* was made.

ETS will make sure that sentences are not so simple on the GMAT, by using four types of sentence constructions to confuse you regarding the agreement of the subject and verb.

1. Phrases between the Subject and the Verb

The most common trick used by GMAC is to insert long phrases between the main subject and verb in an already lengthy sentence. The test makers hope you'll lose track of any agreement issues when other nouns and verbs are present. An example follows:

> The feline leukemia virus, characterized by a loss of appetite, weight loss, poor coat condition, and other debilitating losses, are rampant among cats on the island.   [*Incorrect*]

> Notice that the example sentence is labeled "incorrect." We do not want you to mistake faulty grammar for valid sentence construction.

In this sentence, *virus* is the subject and *are* is the verb. However, there is a long phrase in between listing symptoms of the disease, all of which are in noun format. Note that the last item in the list is plural (*losses*), which makes *are* seem correct: *losses are*. However, the subject is the singular *virus*, and *virus are* creates an agreement problem. In order for the sentence to agree, it must read *virus is*. Remember, a subject is never in a dependent clause, a prepositional phrase, or a phrase separated by commas. Thus, we can mentally eliminate the problem-causing phrase:

> The feline leukemia virus, ~~characterized by a loss of appetite, weight loss, poor coat condition, and other debilitating losses~~, are rampant among cats on the island.   [*Incorrect*]

If needed, you can also eliminate the two prepositional phrases (*among cats* and *on the island*) at the end of the sentence:

> The feline leukemia virus, ~~characterized by a loss of appetite, weight loss, poor coat condition, and other debilitating losses~~, are rampant ~~among cats on the island~~.   [*Incorrect*]

To correct this sentence, change the plural *are* to the singular *is*:

> The feline leukemia virus, characterized by a loss of appetite, weight loss, poor coat condition, and other debilitating losses, is rampant among cats on the island.   [*Correct*]

You should also be aware that phrases are sometimes separated by dashes rather than commas:

> The Tony award-winning plays—*Sunset Boulevard, Rent, The Lion King*, and *The Producers*—was performed by the local theater throughout the summer and autumn seasons. [*Incorrect*]

The titles of the four plays divide the subject *plays* from the verb *was performed*:

> The Tony award-winning plays—~~*Sunset Boulevard, Rent, The Lion King*, and *The Producers*~~—was performed by the local theater throughout the summer and autumn seasons.

> Prepositional phrases: *by the local theater, throughout the summer and autumn seasons*
> Phrase separated by dashes: *Sunset Boulevard, Rent, The Lion King, and The Producers*

The correct agreement is *plays were performed*:

> The Tony award-winning <u>plays</u>—*Sunset Boulevard*, *Rent*, *The Lion King*, and *The Producers*—<u>were performed</u> by the local theater throughout the summer and autumn seasons. [*Correct*]

Even short prepositional phrases can disguise the real subject:

> The scent of apples and cinnamon sticks permeate throughout the cider mill, causing most visitors to purchase snacks while on the tour. [*Incorrect*]

This sentence would be perfect if apples and cinnamon sticks permeate throughout the mill. However, it is the *scent* that is permeating, and since *scent* is singular, the verb must be *permeates*. Remove the phrases and clauses and look again:

> The scent ~~of apples and cinnamon sticks~~ permeate ~~throughout the cider mill, causing most visitors to purchase snacks while on the tour~~. [*Incorrect*]

The sentence should appear as follows:

> The <u>scent</u> of apples and cinnamon sticks <u>permeates</u> throughout the cider mill, causing most visitors to purchase snacks while on the tour. [*Correct*]

Furthermore, beware of GMAC combining short prepositional phrases with long phrases to complicate the sentence even more:

> The number of car accidents involving deer, up seventeen percent from ten years ago and continuing to rise throughout the country, have decreased in Michigan's Upper Peninsula due to the increased use of car-mounted deer whistles by residents. [*Incorrect*]

Can you find the subject and the verb? Are they in agreement? Maybe this will help:

> The number ~~of car accidents~~ involving deer, ~~up seventeen percent from ten years ago and continuing to rise throughout the country~~, have decreased ~~in Michigan's Upper Peninsula due to the increased use of car-mounted deer whistles by residents~~. [*Incorrect*]

Prepositional phrase: *of car accidents, in Michigan's Upper Peninsula, due to the increased use, of car-mounted deer whistles, by residents*

Phrase separated by commas: *up seventeen percent from ten years ago and continuing to rise throughout the country*

The preposition "of" causes a lot of errors on the GMAT. Beware of the use of "of" in expressions such as "the number of...," and "the thought of...."

This one is especially tricky. *Accidents* is not the subject, as most people believe. The subject is *number*, because *accidents* is in the prepositional phrase *of car accidents*. In order for *number* to agree with the verb, it must be *has decreased*, not *have decreased*. GMAC is known to use Sentence Correction questions beginning with *The number of…*, which almost always have Subject Verb agreement problems. The correct sentence is:

The <u>number</u> of car accidents involving deer, up seventeen percent from ten years ago and continuing to rise throughout the country, <u>has decreased</u> in Michigan's Upper Peninsula due to the increased use of car-mounted deer whistles by residents.   [*Correct*]

2. The Subject Follows the Verb

Most sentences in the English language are arranged so that the main subject comes before the verb.

subj.   vb..
<u>She</u> || <u>smiled</u>.

subj.   vb.
The <u>wedding</u> || <u>was held</u> outdoors, despite the threat of rain.

The makers of the GMAT know that this is customary sentence construction, which is why sentences with inverted subjects and verbs make perfect fodder for your test.

An expletive construction on the GMAT is nothing to curse about once you learn how to monitor subject-verb agreement. Expletive constructions occur when a sentence begins with *there*, *here*, or *it*, and they invert the order of the subject and verb:

vb.   subj.
There <u>are</u> many <u>reasons</u> for the tax increase.

vb.   subj.
It <u>has come</u> to my attention <u>that you failed to file the paperwork correctly</u>.

If you are unable to see the true subject in an expletive construction, rearrange the sentence so that the subject comes before the verb:

subj.   vb.
Many <u>reasons</u> for the tax increase <u>are</u> there.

subj.   vb.
<u>That you failed to file the paperwork correctly</u> <u>has come</u> to my attention.

In the last sentence, the subject is a noun clause (*that you have failed to file the paperwork correctly*) acting as a noun.

Of course, expletive constructions on the GMAT will not be this brazenly obvious. They will likely be hidden between clauses and phrases. However, if you follow the subject rule and remove the clauses and phrases, expletive constructions become easier to see:

> According to the latest census, which was released in 2002, there is two television sets per home for every family in America, a statistic that nearly doubled in the last ten years.   [*Incorrect*]

Sentences containing "there is" or "here is" should cause you to immediately confirm subject and verb agreement.

Mentally delete the phrases:

> ~~According to the latest census, which was released in 2002,~~ there is two television sets ~~per home for every family in America, a statistic that nearly doubled in the last ten years~~.   [*Incorrect*]

We are left with *there is two television sets*, but the expletive construction can be rearranged:

> Two television sets is there.

Rearranging sentences is a tactic used by great test takers. Putting the contents into a more-easily recognized form can help you pinpoint errors.

It becomes immediately apparent that the verb, *is*, does not agree with the subject, *sets*. The verb should be plural: *Two television sets are there*. Thus, the corrected sentence looks like:

> According to the latest census, which was released in 2002, there <u>are</u> two television <u>sets</u> per home for every family in America, a statistic that nearly doubled in the last ten years.   [*Correct*]

Expletive constructions can also appear in a dependent clause, which we will examine later in this chapter.

3. Compound Subject

Compound subjects are plural and receive plural verbs:

> <u>Baseball and apple pie</u> <u>are</u> American traditions.
> <u>He and I</u> <u>do not agree</u>.
> <u>A GMAT score, an essay, and a letter of recommendation</u> <u>are required</u> for admission.

On the GMAT, look for longer sentences with a compound subject paired with a singular verb:

> Ernest Hemingway and his contemporaries, all of whom were authors born at the turn of century, was revered for describing the sense of aimlessness felt by their generation.   [*Incorrect*]

SC

The sentence has a compound subject: *Ernest Hemingway and his contemporaries*. Remove the phrases:

> Ernest Hemingway and his contemporaries, ~~all of whom were authors born at the turn of century~~, was revered ~~for describing the sense of aimlessness felt by their generation~~.   [*Incorrect*]

The verb must be plural: *Ernest Hemingway and his contemporaries were revered*:

> <u>Ernest Hemingway and his contemporaries</u>, all of whom were authors born at the turn of century, <u>were revered</u> for describing the sense of aimlessness felt by their generation.   [*Correct*]

An exception to this rule occurs when the compound subject is joined by *or* or *nor*. The noun or pronoun closest to the verb determines the form of the verb; if the nearest noun is singular, the verb is singular. If the closest noun is plural, the verb is plural.

> A napkin or *paper towel* <u>is</u> fine.
> <small>singular</small>

> Either a slice of toast or *eggs* <u>are</u> what I will eat for breakfast.
> <small>plural</small>

With the use of phrases between the subject and verb, recognizing an error in the correct verb form with a compound subject connected by *or* or *nor* can be daunting:

> Once the flight landed, neither the flight attendants nor the captain, who even tried using a hammer, were able to open the emergency exit door. [*Incorrect*]

Once again, remove phrases and dependent clauses:

> ~~Once the flight landed~~, neither the flight attendants nor the captain, ~~who even tried using a hammer~~, were able to open the emergency exit door. [*Incorrect*]

Now you can see that singular *captain* is next to the plural *were*, a violation in subject verb agreement. The sentence may sound correct with a plural verb because it is obvious there is more than one person attempting to open the door. However, *captain*, a singular noun, is closest to the verb, so it must have a singular verb: neither the flight attendants nor the *captain was*:

> Once the flight landed, neither the flight attendants nor the <u>captain</u>, who even tried using a hammer, <u>was</u> able to open the emergency exit door. [*Correct*]

SC

Another exception to the rule occurs when *each* and *every* are attached to the compound subject. In this case, each and every are acting as an adjective, modifying the nouns in the compound subject:

> *Each* child, teenager, and adult
> *Every* nook and cranny

Sentences with *each* and *every* in front of a compound subject must have a singular verb because *each* and *every* are singular. Their use indicates that the subject is referring to a string of individual items, rather than to the items as a group:

> *Each* child, teenager, and adult <u>was</u> wearing a seat belt on the bus.
> *Every* nook and cranny <u>is</u> a possible hiding spot.

Look for *each* and *every* to be used on the GMAT, separated from their verb by a phrase:

> At the Springfield Museum of Art, each painting and sculpture, some purchased for millions of dollars and others found discarded at garage sales, have their history displayed on a board beside the piece. [*Incorrect*]

Mentally remove the phrases and clauses:

> ~~At the Springfield Museum of Art~~, each painting and sculpture, ~~some purchased for millions of dollars and others found discarded at garage sales~~, have their history displayed ~~on a board beside the piece~~. [*Incorrect*]

Because *each* is attached to the compound subject, the verb must be the singular *has* rather than the plural *have*. The plural pronoun *their* must also be changed it *its*: *each painting and sculpture has its history displayed*:

> At the Springfield Museum of Art, <u>each painting and sculpture</u>, some purchased for millions of dollars and others found discarded at garage sales, <u>has</u> its history <u>displayed</u> on a board beside the piece. [*Correct*]

Remember the exception words: the conjunctions *or* and *nor*, and the indefinite adjectives *each* and *every*.

SC

4. Indefinite Pronouns as the Subject

A pronoun that does not refer to any one person or thing in particular, such as *someone*, *many*, or *everybody*, is an **indefinite pronoun**. Most indefinite pronouns have a verb form assigned to their usage, but there are a handful that can be singular or plural:

SINGULAR		PLURAL	BOTH
anybody	neither	both	all
anyone	nobody	few	any
each	no one	many	more
either	somebody	several	most
everybody	someone		none
everyone			some

Most indefinite pronouns have widely-recognized subject verb agreement forms. Take *someone*, for example. You always say "*Someone is home*," rather than "*Someone are home*."

Everybody and *everyone* often give writers a difficult time. The root of each word is singular: *body* and *one*. Therefore *everybody* and *everyone* are always singular:

> Everybody is invited to the party.
> Everyone claps at the end of the movie.

The most troublesome indefinite pronoun, and the one most likely to be tested on the GMAT, is *each*. It is always singular. However, when *each* is coupled with a prepositional phrase ending in a plural noun, it causes trouble:

> At the beginning of the play, each of King Lear's daughters—Goneril, Regan, and Cordelia—appear to be jealous, treacherous, and immoral, but it is soon discovered that Cordelia is virtuous and loyal.   [*Incorrect*]

Remove the phrases and clauses to find the subject and verb:

> ~~At the beginning of the play,~~ each of King Lear's daughters—~~Goneril, Regan, and Cordelia~~—appear to be jealous, treacherous, and immoral, but it is soon discovered ~~that Cordelia is virtuous and loyal~~.   [*Incorrect*]

The subject is *each*, so the verb must be singular:

> Each appears to be jealous, treacherous, and immoral.

Plug the correct verb into the original sentence:

> At the beginning of the play, each of King Lear's daughters—Goneril, Regan, and Cordelia—appears to be jealous, treacherous, and immoral, but it is soon discovered that Cordelia is virtuous and loyal.   [*Correct*]

SC

Subject-Verb Agreement in Dependent Clauses

The errors in the Sentence Correction questions will not be limited to one type of sentence construction. You may experience a Subject Verb agreement problem in a sentence with an expletive construction, a long phrase between the subject and the verb, and an indefinite pronoun as the subject. And all of this may be mixed with another grammatical error, such as wordiness or an illogical comparison!

Similarly, errors in subject and verb agreement are not always limited to the main subject and main verb. You may also find an agreement error in a dependent clause:

> Because a hive of European honeybees produce much more honey than the bees can consume, beekeepers harvest the excess for human consumption.   [*Incorrect*]

If we were to mentally cross out the phrases and clauses, we'd see that the main subject and verb are in agreement:

> ~~Because a hive of European honeybees produce much more honey than the bees can consume~~, beekeepers harvest the excess ~~for human consumption~~.

The subject, *beekeepers*, is in agreement with the verb, *harvest*. If you find that the main subject and verb are in agreement, return to the dependent clause to check its subject and verb agreement:

> Because a hive of European honeybees produce much more honey than the bees can consume

If we remove the prepositional phrase *of European honeybees*, the subject and verb of the dependent clause become clearer, and their non-agreement is apparent:

> *hive produce*

The subject is singular (*hive*), so the verb must be singular (*produces*).

> Because a *hive* of European honeybees *produces* much more honey than the bees can consume, beekeepers harvest the excess for human consumption.   [*Correct*]

The GMAT is more prone to test your knowledge of subject verb agreement among the main parts of the sentence. However, as questions become more difficult, you may see similar errors in dependent clauses. Expect five to ten percent of your questions to test Subject and Verb Agreement.

The subject of a dependent clause will *never* occur in a prepositional phrase.

Subject and Verb Agreement Problem Set

Please complete the problem set and review the answer key and explanations. *Answers on page 330.*

1. According to a study by the American Education Bureau, the average number of calendar days in a school year across the fifty states have increased by nearly twenty five percent since 1950.

   (A) the average number of calendar days in a school year across the fifty states have increased
   (B) across the fifty states, the average number of calendar days in a school year have increased
   (C) the average number of calendar days, across the fifty states, in a school year have increased
   (D) the average number of calendar days in a school year across the fifty states has increased
   (E) the average numbers of calendar days in a school year across the fifty states has increased

2. Information for travelers, such as road maps, hotel directions, or rest area locations, are provided free of charge from the automotive club, long known for its roadside assistance plan.

   (A) are provided free of charge from the automotive club, long known for its
   (B) is provided free of charge from the automotive club, long known for its
   (C) are provided free of charge from the automotive club, long known for their
   (D) is provided free of charge from the automotive club, long known for their
   (E) is to be provided free of charge from the automotive club, long known for their

3. The causes of the American Revolution and the reasons for the colonists' victory—including home field advantage and more strategic generals—is firmly rooted in a citizen's sense of patriotic duty and belonging.

   (A) is firmly rooted in a citizen's sense of
   (B) is rooted firmly in a citizen's sense of
   (C) are a citizen's sense firmly rooted in
   (D) are firmly rooted in a citizen's sense for
   (E) are firmly rooted in a citizen's sense of

4. The reasons for the budget cuts, of which there is dozens, will be revealed at tonight's city council meeting by the mayor and the council members.

   (A) The reasons for the budget cuts, of which there is dozens
   (B) The reason for the budget cuts, of which there is dozens
   (C) The reasons for the budget cut, of which there is dozens
   (D) The reason for the budget cuts, of which there are dozens
   (E) The reasons for the budget cuts, of which there are dozens

5. Tear gas, launched in the form of grenades or aerosol cans, <u>are irritants used by police</u> to calm rioting crowds and unruly mobs.

    (A) are irritants used by police
    (B) used by police, are irritants
    (C) is an irritant used by police
    (D) is an irritants to be used by police
    (E) are irritants for use by police

6. According to the Constitution, neither those senators under 35 years of age <u>nor the representative born outside of the United States are able to run for the position of President</u>.

    (A) nor the representative born outside of the United States are able to run for the position of President
    (B) nor the representative born outside of the United States is running for the position of President
    (C) nor the representative born outside of the United States are running for the position of President
    (D) nor the representative born outside of the United States is not able to run for the position of President
    (E) nor the representative born outside of the United States is able to run for the position of President

Subject Verb and Agreement Problem Set Answer Key

Correct answers are in bold.

1. According to a study by the American Education Bureau, <u>the average number of calendar days in a school year across the fifty states have increased</u> by nearly twenty five percent since 1950.

   (A) the average number of calendar days in a school year across the fifty states have increased
   (B) across the fifty states, the average number of calendar days in a school year have increased
   (C) the average number of calendar days, across the fifty states, in a school year have increased
   (D) the average number of calendar days in a school year across the fifty states has increased
   (E) the average numbers of calendar days in a school year across the fifty states has increased

The sentence has an agreement problem between the subject, *number*, and the verb, *have increased*. Choice (D) puts the singular verb, *has increased*, with the singular subject, *number*. The two prepositional phrases between the subject and the verb—*of calendar days* and *across the fifty states*—are meant to throw off the novice test taker.

2. Information for travelers, such as road maps, hotel directions, or rest area locations, <u>are provided free of charge from the automotive club, long known for its</u> roadside assistance plan.

   (A) are provided free of charge from the automotive club, long known for its
   (B) is provided free of charge from the automotive club, long known for its
   (C) are provided free of charge from the automotive club, long known for their
   (D) is provided free of charge from the automotive club, long known for their
   (E) is to be provided free of charge from the automotive club, long known for their

The sentence has an agreement problem between the subject, *information*, and the verb, *are provided*. Choice (B) puts the singular verb, *is provided*, with the singular subject, *information*. Choice (D) also does this, but it has changed the pronoun *its* to *their*. The word *club* is not plural, thus *their* is an incorrect pronoun. It must stay *its*. Choice (E) changed the entire verb form, consequently changing the timing (tense) of the sentence.

SC

3. The causes of the American Revolution and the reasons for the colonists' victory—including home field advantage and more strategic generals—is firmly rooted in a citizen's sense of patriotic duty and belonging.

    (A)   is firmly rooted in a citizen's sense of
    (B)   is rooted firmly in a citizen's sense of
    (C)   are a citizen's sense firmly rooted in
    (D)   are firmly rooted in a citizen's sense for
    (E)   **are firmly rooted in a citizen's sense of**

The sentence has an agreement problem between the compound subject, *the causes and the reasons*, and the verb, *is firmly rooted*. A compound subject must have a plural verb, *are firmly rooted*. Choice (D) corrects this, but chooses an unidiomatic preposition, *for*. Choice (C) also corrects the subject verb agreement, but rearranges the segment, thus changing the meaning of the sentence.

4. <u>The reasons for the budget cuts, of which there is dozens</u>, will be revealed at tonight's city council meeting by the mayor and the council members.

    (A)   The reasons for the budget cuts, of which there is dozens
    (B)   The reason for the budget cuts, of which there is dozens
    (C)   The reasons for the budget cut, of which there is dozens
    (D)   The reason for the budget cuts, of which there are dozens
    (E)   **The reasons for the budget cuts, of which there are dozens**

The sentence has an agreement problem in the dependent clause, *of which there are dozens*. The dependent clause is an expletive construction, so the subject, *dozens*, does not agree with the verb, *is*. The verb must be *are*. Choice (D) also changes *is* to *are*, but it makes *reason* a singular noun. This changes the meaning of the sentence, and thus Choice (D) is incorrect.

5. Tear gas, launched in the form of grenades or aerosol cans, <u>are irritants used by police</u> to calm rioting crowds and unruly mobs.

    (A)   are irritants used by police
    (B)   used by police, are irritants
    (C)   **is an irritant used by police**
    (D)   is an irritant to be used by police
    (E)   are irritants for use by police

The sentence has an agreement problem between the subject, *tear gas*, and the verb, *are*. *Tear gas* is singular, so the verb must be *is*. This also requires changing *irritants* to the singular form, *an irritant*. Choice (D) also makes this change, but it adds the unnecessary verb *to be*.

6. According to the Constitution, neither those senators under 35 years of age <u>nor the representative born outside of the United States are able to run for the position of President</u>.

(A) nor the representative born outside of the United States are able to run for the position of President
(B) nor the representative born outside of the United States is running for the position of President
(C) nor the representative born outside of the United States are running for the position of President
(D) nor the representative born outside of the United States is not able to run for the position of President
(E) nor the representative born outside of the United States is able to run for the position of President

The sentence has an agreement problem between the compound subject and the verb *are able to run*. When *neither...nor* is used to create a compound subject, the noun closest to the verb determines the verb's form. The nearest noun in this case is in the form of a noun phrase (*the representative born outside of the United States*) which is singular. Therefore, the verb must be singular, *is able to run*. Choice (B) correctly uses *is*, but changes the verb form to *is running*. Choice (D) adds a negative (*not*) to the verb, thus creating a double negative overall.

Another common error involving verbs is the incorrect use of tense. Verb tense expresses the point in time, whether in the past, the present, or in the future, that the action, or lack of action, takes place. It helps a reader visualize when the events in the sentence occur. Consider the following example:

> When Shelly's husband was deployed overseas, she *was married* for two months.

Most students could infer the order of events based on the context of the sentence, but what if it were read literally? It says that at the same time her husband was deployed, Shelly participated in a wedding ceremony that lasted for two months. We use different forms of tense to show the sequence of action:

> When Shelly's husband was deployed overseas, she *had been married* for two months.

The English language has three basic tenses to help us determine the point in time in which an action occurs (*past*, *present*, and *future*), and each of these tenses has four forms they can then take to further convey timing (*simple*, *progressive*, *perfect*, and *perfect progressive*).

Tense	Subj.	Simple
Past	he	walked
Present	he	walks
Future	he	will walk

Tense	Subj.	Progressive
Past	he	was walking
Present	he	is walking
Future	he	will be walking

Tense	Subj.	Perfect
Past	he	had walked
Present	he	has walked
Future	he	will have walked

Tense	Subj.	Perfect Progressive
Past	he	had been walking
Present	he	has been walking
Future	he	will have been walking

The GMAT tests all three tenses and all four forms.

SC

SIMPLE TENSES

Tense	Subj.	Simple
Past	he	walked
Present	he	walks
Future	he	will walk

The Official Guide to GMAT Review refers to simple tenses as indicative tenses.

Simple tenses express an action. A plain and simple action, as their name suggests. The action may or may not have been completed at the time the sentence is uttered or written:

He walked to the store.

The example above uses a simple past tense of the infinitive *to walk*. Did he walk to the store two years ago, or did he leave two minutes ago? Is he back from his walk to the store? This cannot be answered by the simple tense. The purpose of the simple past tense verb is to show that at some point in the past he walked to the store.

Simple Past

As we just saw in the example above, this form simply shows that the action occurred at some point in the past.

I *walked* two miles.
He *walked* over to the woman.
They *walked* away from the fight.

Simple Present

Present tense shows what happens right now, at the moment the sentence is spoken or written. It is also used to state a general fact or truth, or in discussing literature or art.

I *walk* the path every day.
He *walks* the reader through the complexities of the character's mind.
They *walk* around the locker room.

Simple Future

The simple form of future tense shows what will or what may happen at some point in the future. Simple future tenses need *shall* or *will*, which are helping verbs, to convey that the events will occur in the future.

I *will walk* to school tomorrow.
He *shall walk* you home.
They *will not walk* on the grass.

SC

Note that adverbs such as "not" and "never" come between the helping verb and the verb, as in the third sentence.

PROGRESSIVE TENSES

Tense	Subj.	Progressive
Past	he	was walking
Present	he	is walking
Future	he	will be walking

The progressive tenses are aptly named because they are showing progress. With the use of helping verbs, they indicate something happening or being.

Past Progressive

This form shows that the action occurred at a specific time in the past. The ongoing action occurred in the past and has been completed by the time the sentence is spoken or written.

> I *was walking* to the beach when you called.
> She *was not walking* in the crosswalk when the light changed.
> They *were walking* through the parking lot at midnight.

Present Progressive

Present progressive tense shows what is happening now. It is sometimes used interchangeably with the simple present tense, but present progressive indicates a continuation of the action or event.

> I *am walking* to the store to get milk.
> She *is walking* off the plane right now.
> They *are walking* away from the car with their hands above their heads.

Future Progressive

The progressive form of future tense shows what will continue to happen in the future.

> I *will still be walking* to the party when you get there.
> She *will be walking* down the street when he appears out of nowhere.
> They *will not be walking* ten miles a day once winter arrives.

SC

PERFECT TENSES

Tense	Subj.	Perfect
Past	he	had walked
Present	he	has walked
Future	he	will have walked

The perfect tense describes a finished action.

The incorrect use of past perfect test is one of the most common GMAT verb tense errors, which we will cover later in this chapter.

Past Perfect

The past perfect verb tense is used to show action that was started and completed in the past. It is often used in a sentence that discusses two past events that occurred at different times; past perfect is assigned to the first event to distinguish the time of its occurrence from the more recent event. This form shows that the action occurred at some point in the past before another event in the past, so sentences with past perfect tense will have two verbs.

> I *had walked* to the store and back by the time you *got* off the phone.
> He *had walked* to the car before she *sped* out of the parking lot.
> They *had walked* into the backyard when everyone *yelled* "Surprise!"

Present Perfect

Present perfect tense shows something that has happened in the past, that may or may not yet be completed. It often suggests that the past action is influencing events in the present. Present perfect tenses cannot be used in association with words like *yesterday* or *one day*, but can be used with less specific words like *once* or *before*.

> I *have walked* to work for over six years.
> He *has walked* in your shoes.
> They *have walked* around the track ten times.

Future Perfect

The perfect form of future tense shows an action or event that will be completed sometime in the future before another action or event occurs.

> I *will have walked* six miles by the time you get out of bed tomorrow.
> He *will have walked* with a limp for three years this March.
> They *will have walked* for over three hours when the charity relay is over.

PERFECT PROGRESSIVE TENSES

Tense	Subj.	Perfect Progressive
Past	he	had been walking
Present	he	has been walking
Future	he	will have been walking

Past Perfect Progressive

The past perfect progressive tense shows that an action started at some point in the past, continued for a period of time, and was eventually interrupted or stopped by another event in the past.

> I *had been walking* to school for months before I got my new car.
> She *had been walking* in the woods for an hour when she spotted a deer.
> They *hadn't been walking* long when he ran out of breath.

Present Perfect Progressive

Like the present perfect tense, present perfect progressive tense shows an action that started at some point in the past and has continued. However, this tense stresses that the action has continued and is not completed.

> I *have been walking* with you since we moved into the neighborhood.
> She *has been walking* around the mall for hours.
> They *have been walking* past the house every day for ten years.

Future Perfect Progressive

The progressive form of future tense shows an action that began in the past, but will continue until a particular point in the future.

> In ten minutes, I *will have been walking* on the treadmill for an hour.
> She *will have been walking* to the laundry mat for three years by the time
>   she buys a car.
> They *will have been walking* together for six years next May.

SC

Incorrect Verb Tense

On the GMAT, the most common verb tense error is an incorrect use of tense. Look at an example:

> A recent survey has revealed that within the last ten years, many working mothers had chosen to work part time, rather than place their children in daycare full time.   [*Incorrect*]

If you find a Sentence Correction question containing the word "had," immediately check the verb tenses in the sentence.

The verb *had chosen* is in past perfect tense, which indicates that the action was started and ended in the past. However, the sentence describes a situation that is continuing into the present, and possibly the future. Therefore, the present perfect tense, *have chosen*, is required:

> A recent survey has revealed that within the last ten years, many working mothers *have chosen* to work part time, rather than place their children in daycare full time.   [*Correct*]

This example required a switch between past and present, but stayed in the perfect form. Some sentences will stay in the same tense, but require you to change form:

> Never before had the author used as much sarcasm as he had used in his fifth novel.   [*Incorrect*]

In this sentence, we have two events occurring in the past:
1. The use of little sarcasm in books 1, 2, 3, and 4
2. The use of a lot of sarcasm in book 5

However, both verbs are in the past perfect form (*had [the author] used* and *had used*), indicating that the two events are happening at the same time. We know that this is not true, thanks to the phrase *never before* and our knowledge of numbers; the first four books were written prior to the fifth. In a sentence with two separate past events occurring at different times, the past perfect tense is assigned to the first event to distinguish the time of its occurrence from the more recent event. The more recent event receives a simple past tense verb:

> Never before *had the author used* as much sarcasm as he *used* in his fifth novel. [*Correct*]

The majority of tense errors will occur with the improper use of present and past tense in both simple and perfect forms. However, you would be wise to prepare for errors in future tense, and study the progressive forms as well.

Shift in Verb Tense

In a sentence with two events occurring at two different times, it is imperative to use two verb tenses to show the order in which the action takes place. However, in sentences with two events happening simultaneously, the verbs must share the same tense. The second most common verb tense error occurs when there is a shift in verb tense in a sentence with simultaneous events. Here is an example:

> While Paul Revere rode from Lexington to Concord on the last leg of his famous journey, John Hancock and Sam Adams, wanted for their treacherous comments against the British monarchy, had escaped Lexington by foot.   [*Incorrect*]

Two events are happening at the same time:
   1. Revere rode from Lexington to Concord
   2. Hancock and Adams escaped Lexington

However, there are two verb tenses present. *Rode* is in simple past tense, and *had escaped* is in past perfect tense, thus indicating that the escape took place before Revere rode from Lexington to Concord. The very first word of the sentence, *while*, reveals that this is not true. Both events occurred at the same time so they both need the same verb tense:

> While Paul Revere *rode* from Lexington to Concord on the last leg of his famous journey, John Hancock and Sam Adams, wanted for their treacherous comments against the British monarchy, *escaped* Lexington by foot.   [*Correct*]

In sentences with two events taking place, evaluate whether the events are simultaneous or separated by time. Then, check the verbs to make sure that the tenses convey the accurate sequence of events.

Verb Tense Problem Set

Please complete the problem set and review the answer key and explanations. *Answers on pages 342.*

1. Today, because of public education and government breeding programs, the state of Michigan reports three times <u>as many peregrine falcon nests than it has</u> in 1970.

    (A) as many peregrine falcon nests than it has
    (B) as many peregrine falcon nests than it had
    (C) as many peregrine falcon nests than it did
    (D) as many peregrine falcon nests than it had been reporting
    (E) as many peregrine falcon nests than it does

2. Scientists <u>believe that the great white shark has evolved</u> from the megalodon, a prehistoric shark measuring over 50 feet in length.

    (A) believe that the great white shark has evolved
    (B) believe that the great white shark evolved
    (C) believed that the great white shark has evolved
    (D) are believing that the great white shark has evolved
    (E) have believed that the great white shark has evolved

3. At the time of the Great Depression, the government <u>was more involved in the regulation of the economy than it ever was before</u>, which is why it is often blamed for the economic collapse.

    (A) was more involved in the regulation of the economy than it ever was before
    (B) was more involved in the regulation of the economy than it ever would have been before
    (C) having been more involved in the regulation of the economy than it ever was before
    (D) was more involved in the regulation of the economy than it ever had been before
    (E) was to be more involved in the regulation of the economy than it ever will have been before

Verb Tense Problem Set

4. Beginning as an NBC radio program in 1937, the soap opera *Guiding Light* <u>moved to CBS television in 1952 and is</u> currently the longest running drama in broadcast history.

   (A) moved to CBS television in 1952 and is
   (B) had moved to CBS television in 1952 and is
   (C) had been moved to CBS television in 1952 and is
   (D) moved to CBS television in 1952 and was
   (E) moved to CBS television in 1952 and will be

5. <u>The Goodyear Blimp will provide aerial footage of the car race</u>, which occurs just fifteen miles from its airbase in Ohio, for as long as the race is sponsored by the tire company.

   (A) The Goodyear Blimp will provide aerial footage of the car race
   (B) The Goodyear Blimp has provided aerial footage of the car race
   (C) The Goodyear Blimp will have been providing aerial footage of the car race
   (D) The Goodyear Blimp will have provided aerial footage of the car race
   (E) The Goodyear Blimp will be providing aerial footage of the car race

Verb Tense Problem Set Answer Key

Correct answers are in bold.

1. Today, because of public education and government breeding programs, the state of Michigan reports three times <u>as many peregrine falcon nests than it has</u> in 1970.

    (A)   as many peregrine falcon nests than it has
    (B)   as many peregrine falcon nests than it had
    (C)   **as many peregrine falcon nests than it did**
    (D   as many peregrine falcon nests than it had been reporting
    (E)   as many peregrine falcon nests than it does

This sentence not only has a verb tense error, but it has the wrong verb as well. Because Michigan made the report in 1970, the sentence needs a past tense verb in the underlined portion. *Has* is present tense. *Had* is past test, but we need a verb that mirrors *reports*: *reports three times as many as it <u>had</u>* or *reports three times as many as it <u>did</u>*. *Did* is the correct word choice. Choice (D) used the past perfect progressive, and Choice (E), although using the correct verb, uses the present tense.

2. Scientists <u>believe that the great white shark has evolved</u> from the megalodon, a prehistoric shark measuring over 50 feet in length.

    (A)   believe that the great white shark has evolved
    (B)   **believe that the great white shark evolved**
    (C)   believed that the great white shark has evolved
    (D)   are believing that the great white shark has evolved
    (E)   have believed that the great white shark has evolved

There are two events occurring in this sentence; *scientists believe*, which is occurring in the present, and *the great white shark evolved*, which happened in the past. Therefore, the verb in the past should be simple past, not past perfect as in Choice (A). Choice (B) is the only answer that offers the simple past tense of to evolve (*evolved*), and does not change the tense of *to believe*.

3. At the time of the Great Depression, the government <u>was more involved in the regulation of the economy than it ever was before</u>, which is why it is often blamed for the economic collapse.

    (A)   was more involved in the regulation of the economy than it ever was before
    (B)   was more involved in the regulation of the economy than it ever would have been before
    (C)   having been more involved in the regulation of the economy than it ever was before
    (D)   **was more involved in the regulation of the economy than it ever had been before**
    (E)   was to be more involved in the regulation of the economy than it ever will have been before

There are two events in the sentence: 1.) *the government's involvement at the time of the Great Depression*, and 2.) *the government's involvement prior to the Great Depression*. However, the same past tense verb, *was*, is used to convey the action for both events. The earlier action needs the past perfect form of the verb: *had been*. Answer (D) is the only choice to use *had been*.

4. Beginning as an NBC radio program in 1937, the soap opera *Guiding Light* <u>moved to CBS television in 1952 and is</u> currently the longest running drama in broadcast history.

    (A) moved to CBS television in 1952 and is
    (B) had moved to CBS television in 1952 and is
    (C) had been moved to CBS television in 1952 and is
    (D) moved to CBS television in 1952 and was
    (E) moved to CBS television in 1952 and will be

This sentence contains two actions: 1.) *the soap moved to CBS in 1952* and 2.) *the soap is the longest running show in the present*. Therefore, the verb tenses are correct. The past action receives the simple past verb moved, and the present action receives the simple present form of *to be*. Choice (B) uses the past perfect *had moved*, Choice (C) uses a past perfect form with another helping verb (*had been moved*), Choice (D) incorrectly uses the past tense (*was*) for the current action, and Choice (E) uses the future tense (*will be*) for a present action.

5. <u>The Goodyear Blimp will provide aerial footage of the car race</u>, which occurs just fifteen miles from its airbase in Ohio, for as long as the race is sponsored by the tire company.

    (A) The Goodyear Blimp will provide aerial footage of the car race
    (B) The Goodyear Blimp has provided aerial footage of the car race
    (C) The Goodyear Blimp will have been providing aerial footage of the car race
    (D) The Goodyear Blimp will have provided aerial footage of the car race
    (E) The Goodyear Blimp will be providing aerial footage of the car race

This sentence indicates that the aerial coverage will continue into the future until an unknown point. This sort of statement requires a future progressive verb (*will be providing*). Choice (B) uses a past tense. Choices (A), (C), and (D) use a future tense, but they are not simple progressive.

SC

Verbs that take a direct object are called **transitive verbs**. Examples include the verbs *set*, *commanded*, and *drives* in the following sentences:

$$\overset{\text{vb.}}{\underline{\text{set}}} \; \text{the} \; \overset{\text{do.}}{table}$$
I <u>set</u> the *table*.

$$\text{She} \; \overset{\text{vb.}}{\underline{\text{commanded}}} \; \text{the} \; \overset{\text{do.}}{army}$$
She <u>commanded</u> the *army*.

$$\text{He} \; \overset{\text{vb.}}{\underline{\text{drives}}} \; \text{a} \; \overset{\text{do.}}{tractor}$$
He <u>drives</u> a *tractor*.

Some verbs cannot take a direct object, such as *sleep* or *smile*. While you can *set* or *drive* something, you cannot *smile* or *sleep* something. Verbs that do not take a direct object are called **intransitive verbs**. They are often followed by an adverb or a phrase that acts as an adverb.

She smiles often.

I sleep on a futon.

Transitive verbs, those that take a direct object, can be constructed in the active or passive voice. In an **active voice**, the subject of the sentence completes the action of the verb:

<u>Joan of Arc</u> <u>commanded</u> the French army.

Joan of Arc, the subject, is responsible for the action of the sentence. She *commanded*.

In the **passive voice**, the subject does not perform the action of the sentence; rather, the action is done to the subject:

<u>Joan of Arc</u> <u>was burned</u> at the stake by *the Duke of Bedford*.

In this sentence, the Duke of Bedford completes the action, and Joan receives the action (ouch!). Sentences in the passive voice might not always identify who or what is responsible for the action:

<u>Joan of Arc</u> <u>was burned</u> at the stake.

Joan is still receiving the action, but whoever is burning her is unclear.

The active voice is almost always preferred in writing and on the GMAT. Not only is it more concise, but it gives sentences more snap and zing, and keeps paragraphs more lively. It also accepts responsibility for the action; you'll likely find the passive voice used by politicians, lawyers, schoolyard bullies, and those looking to blame someone else for their actions:

The <u>governor</u> <u>was forced</u> to increase taxes.

Who forced the governor to increase taxes? A sentence in the active voice puts the blame on the governor, where it should have been all along:

The <u>governor</u> <u>increased</u> taxes.

The passive voice is not incorrect or ungrammatical—it's just that the active voice is preferred most of the time. One instance in which the passive voice is favored is when *who* or *what* did the action is not as important as *to whom* or *to what* it was done, such as in describing processes or writing scientific reports:

The molten <u>steel</u> <u>is poured</u> into a cooling vat.

It is not important who pours the molten steel, but it is important to know that the steel is poured.

You can more easily recognize passive verbs by their use of a form of the verb *to be* with a past participle:

am pulled
is teased
was convicted
has been sighted
will be monitored

Look at the following sentence in the passive voice:

     subj.   vb.   object of the preposition
A <u>bald eagle</u> <u>has been sighted</u> by the *Department of Natural Resources*.

To make the verb active, simply flip the positions of the subject and the object of the preposition:

                subj.   vb.   do.
The <u>Department of Natural Resources</u> <u>sighted</u> a *bald eagle*.

The active voice is also favored for your Analytical Writing Assignment. To make your sentences more concise and effective, avoid the passive voice.

On the GMAT, the use of passive voice is typically a secondary error. For example, a sentence might be written in the passive voice, but it also has a blatant pronoun error. The correct answer choice will be the only answer with the acceptable correction of the pronoun error, but it might also change the verb to the active voice in the process. Consider the following example:

> By the time a way to stop the ozone layer from deteriorating is discovered by scientists, global temperatures will be rising for over two hundred years, causing the polar ice caps to gradually melt.

(A) By the time a way to stop the ozone layer from deteriorating is discovered by scientists, global temperatures will be rising

(B) By the time scientists discover a way to stop the ozone layer from deteriorating, global temperatures will be rising

(C) By the time a way to stop the ozone later from deteriorating is discovered by scientists, global temperatures would have been rising

(D) By the time scientists discover a way to stop the ozone layer from deteriorating, global temperatures will have been rising

(E) By the time a way to stop the ozone layer from deteriorating is discovered by scientists, global temperatures will rise

The sentence has a grammatically incorrect verb. *Will be rising* should be in the perfect progressive form: *will have been rising*. The only answer choice to make this correction also switches from passive voice to active voice. Since an active construction is always preferred, choice (D) is correct. Note that choice (B) also uses the active voice, but it fails to correct the verb error.

The use of active voice and passive voice should never be mixed in the same sentence, and this type of grammatically incorrect sentence is individually tested on the GMAT. Look at an example:

> After last month's Board of Directors' meeting, the airline released plans to revamp flight plans and the new policy concerning aircraft weight limits was approved. *[Incorrect]*

This sentence illegally switches from the active voice (*the airline released plans to revamp flight plans*) to the passive voice (*the new policy concerning aircraft weight limits was approved [by the airline]*).

The sentence must stay completely active or passive, and since the active voice is preferred, switch the passive portion of the sentence:

> After last month's Board of Directors' meeting, the airline released plans to revamp flight plans and *approved the new policy concerning aircraft weight limits*. *[Correct]*

Remember, choose answer choices that use the active voice while correcting grammatical errors.

SC

Verb Voice Problem Set

Please complete the problem set and review the answer key and explanations. *Answers on page 348.*

1. France's longest-ruling monarch, Louis XIV, <u>inherited the throne at the age of four and the country was ruled by him for 72 years</u>.

    (A) inherited the throne at the age of four and the country was ruled by him for 72 years
    (B) had inherited the throne at the age of four and the country was ruled by him for 72 years
    (C) inherited the throne at the age of four and ruled the country for 72 years
    (D) inherited the throne at the age of four and the country had been ruled by him for 72 years
    (E) had inherited the throne at the age of four and he ruled the country for 72 years

2. Al Pacino had already turned down the role of Han Solo <u>when Harrison Ford was casted by George Lucas in 1975</u>.

    (A) when Harrison Ford was casted by George Lucas in 1975
    (B) when George Lucas cast Harrison Ford in 1975
    (C) when Harrison Ford had been cast by George Lucas in 1975
    (D) when George Lucas casted Harrison Ford in 1975
    (E) when Harrison Ford would be cast by George Lucas in 1975

Verb Voice Problem Set Answer Key

Correct answers are in bold.

1. France's longest-ruling monarch, Louis XIV, <u>inherited the throne at the age of four and the country was ruled by him for 72 years</u>.

    (A) inherited the throne at the age of four and the country was ruled by him for 72 years
    (B) had inherited the throne at the age of four and the country was ruled by him for 72 years
    (C) inherited the throne at the age of four and ruled the country for 72 years
    (D) inherited the throne at the age of four and the country had been ruled by him for 72 years
    (E) had inherited the throne at the age of four and he ruled the country for 72 years

The sentence has two actions completed by Louis XIV, but one is in the active voice (*Louis inherited the throne*) and the other is in the passive voice (*the country was ruled by Louis*). A sentence cannot switch between active and passive voice. In order for the sentence to have matching construction, the passive portion must become active (*Louis ruled the country*). Choice (C) correctly fixes this problem.

2. Al Pacino had already turned down the role of Han Solo <u>when Harrison Ford was casted by George Lucas in 1975</u>.

    (A) when Harrison Ford was casted by George Lucas in 1975
    (B) when George Lucas cast Harrison Ford in 1975
    (C) when Harrison Ford had been cast by George Lucas in 1975
    (D) when George Lucas casted Harrison Ford in 1975
    (E) when Harrison Ford would be cast by George Lucas in 1975

The main error in this sentence is the incorrect form of the verb *to cast*. Because it is an irregular verb, the past tense is *cast,* not *casted*. The only answer choices that use the correct form are (B), (C), and (E). Choice (C) creates a tense problem in the dependent clause; Ford was offered the role after Pacino passed, but (C) makes these two actions simultaneous. Choice (E) uses a helping verb (*would*) that is reserved for conditional hypothetical statements. Choice (B) not only corrects the past tense of *to cast*, but it makes the passive clause an active construction.

CHAPTER SIXTEEN: ERRORS WITH NOUNS AND PRONOUNS

Noun Agreement

Nouns must agree in number to the nouns they are referencing. This means that singular nouns must be used to refer to singular nouns, and plural nouns must be used to refer to plural nouns. Errors often occur when the nouns are far apart in the sentence, causing the reader to forget that the second noun is referring to the first. Look at the faulty noun reference below:

> *Bill and Lissy* believed that if they were coached every day and dedicated themselves to practice, their dream of becoming *a professional skater* could someday be a reality.   [*Incorrect*]

How are Bill and Lissy, two people, going to combine together to be ONE professional skater? If they have a fantastic plastic surgeon, this sentence might be grammatically correct. But the GMAT does not deal with possibilities unless they are acknowledged in a conditional statement. *Bill and Lissy*, two people, dream of becoming two *skaters*. A plural noun is needed to agree with the subject it is referencing.

> *Bill and Lissy* believed that if they were coached every day and dedicated themselves to practice, their dream of becoming *professional skaters* could someday be a reality.   [*Correct*]

The nouns do not always have to be at opposite ends of the sentence, however, to trip up the unprepared test taker:

> *Hospitals* have always been thought of as a *place* for the sick and dying so many people avoid *them*, even for preventative medicine.   [*Incorrect*]

In this sentence, there are two shifts in number (*hospitals* to *place* and *place* to *them*), and the sentence needs to be consistent:

> *Hospitals* have always been thought of as *places* for the sick and dying so many people avoid *them*, even for preventative medicine.   [*Correct*]

Noun agreement errors occur in a small fraction of the questions in *The Official Guide to GMAT Review*, but are closely related to Pronoun and Antecedent errors, covered in the next section.

SC

Pronouns

As we discussed in the introduction, pronouns take the place of nouns and refer to people or things previously mentioned in the sentence or surrounding sentences. A list of the most common pronouns follows:

all	everything	its	nothing	something	we
another	few	itself	one	that	what
any	he	many	others	their	which
anybody	her	me	our	theirs	who
anyone	hers	mine	ours	them	whom
anything	herself	my	ourselves	themselves	whose
both	him	myself	several	these	you
each	himself	neither	she	they	your
either	his	nobody	some	this	yours
everybody	I	none	somebody	those	yourself
everyone	it	no one	someone	us	yourselves

An antecedent is the word a pronoun stands for in the sentence. In the following passage, <u>buttons</u> is an antecedent for *several*:

Do you need some extra <u>buttons</u>? I have *several* over here.

Some pronouns, like *several*, can serve as other parts of speech as well. Look at *several* in the next sentence:

I have *several* extra buttons over here.

In this sentence, *several* is an adjective, describing the number of buttons.

Personal pronouns are those that refer to particular people or things, such as *I, you, he, her, we, they, me*, and *yourself*.

Indefinite pronouns are just the opposite. They do not refer to any particular people or things, and include words such as *all, everyone, each, somebody*, and *something*.

Relative pronouns are used to introduce a clause and will be discussed in detail later in this section. They include words like *who, which*, and *that*.

While searching for errors on the GMAT, look for three specific pronoun errors—pronoun and antecedent agreement, unclear pronoun reference, and incorrect pronoun choice—all of which are covered on the following pages.

Pronoun and Antecedent Agreement

Like subjects that agree with verbs and nouns that agree with other nouns, pronouns must agree in gender, person, and number with their antecedent. Gender agreement (*the man lost his wallet*) and person agreement (*If one is hungry, one may eat*) are not tested on the GMAT, but number agreement is a common error, appearing in many questions in *The Official Guide to GMAT Review*.

A singular antecedent must employ a singular pronoun:

> The girl mailed her application.
> Owen thought he deserved a raise.
> The dog chases its tail.

A plural antecedent must use a plural pronoun:

> The girls won their game.
> The children wonder what they might be when they grow up.

Compound antecedents must also receive plural pronouns:

> Grace and Hakim are proud of themselves.
> Although Harry, Ron, and Hermione are fictional, they come to life in the book.

As with other areas of agreement, GMAC will put distance between the antecedent and the pronoun so that you might fail to notice that they don't agree. The test makers will also use singular and plural nouns in between, hoping you'll incorrectly choose one of them as the antecedent. Look at an example:

> While the definition of Generation X is hotly debated concerning the age ranges of its members, culturists generally agree that they describe a group of adults that are self-focused, cynical, and skeptical.   [*Incorrect*]

In this sentence, there are five nouns—*definition, Generation X, age ranges, members,* and *culturists*—preceding the word *they*, so it is hard to spot the real antecedent, which is *definition*. To paraphrase, the sentence states "*The definition is hotly debated but it describes a group.*" Since definition is singular, it needs the pronoun *it*, rather than *they*. Notice that the correction of the pronoun also means a correction to the verb *describe*, in order to achieve subject verb agreement with the new pronoun:

> While the *definition* of Generation X is hotly debated concerning the age ranges of its members, culturists generally agree that *it describes* a group of adults that are self-focused, cynical, and skeptical.   [*Correct*]

If you find a pronoun in a sentence, immediately identify the antecedent.

SC

The GMAT has two other pronoun agreement tricks up its computer-generated sleeve: indefinite pronouns and misleading words used as antecedents. These sentences will test your ability to determine what sounds correct versus what is correct.

Just as indefinite pronouns can cause havoc with subject and verb agreement, they also meddle with pronoun and antecedent agreement. The indefinite pronouns *anyone, anybody, each, everyone, everybody, one, someone, somebody, no one,* and *nobody* are always singular antecedents on the GMAT. This is often confusing to students who think of *everybody, everyone,* and *every one* as a large group of people. However, look at the roots of the words: *body* and *one.* They are singular. Look for errors with these words and a plural pronoun on the GMAT:

> Every one of the soldiers reported that they had completed the training exercise prior to the incident, although the lieutenant claimed several members of the squadron were not present.   [*Incorrect*]

In this sentence, *every one* is the antecedent, thus it is singular. However, the pronoun reference, *they*, is plural. Look at the correction:

> *Every one* of the soldiers reported that *he or she* had completed the training exercise prior to the incident, although the lieutenant claimed several members of the squadron were not present.   [*Correct*]

Similarly, *few, many,* and *several* are plural antecedents, so watch for singular pronouns which do not agree with them:

> A few of the nurses from the emergency room were disgruntled to learn that he or she had been moved to another area of the hospital due to the budget crisis.   [*Incorrect*]

The word *few* is always plural, so its pronoun stand-in must also be plural:

> A *few* of the nurses from the emergency room were disgruntled to learn that *they* had been moved to another area of the hospital due to the budget crisis.   [*Correct*]

The final pronoun agreement error occurs with the use of misleading words. The makers of the GMAT will use singular antecedents that sound plural, such as *army* or *citrus*, and plural antecedents that sound singular, such as *cacti* or *persons*. Combine one of these misleading words with an improper pronoun, and you have a perfect GMAT sentence:

> With the release of their fifth album, *Hotel California*, the band explored the pursuit of the American dream when accompanied by the loss of innocence and the presence of temptations.   [*Incorrect*]

This sentence might sound acceptable to you. However, *band* is a singular antecedent, so *their* is incorrectly used. The sentence can be amended two ways:

> With the release of *their* fifth album, *Hotel California*, the *members* of the band explored the pursuit of the American dream when accompanied by the loss of innocence and the presence of temptations.   [*Correct*]

Or:

> With the release of *its* fifth album, *Hotel California*, the *band* explored the pursuit of the American dream when accompanied by the loss of innocence and the presence of temptations.   [*Correct*]

On test day, if you are given a sentence containing a pronoun, immediately identify the antecedent and look for agreement between the two. If they are in agreement, look for another error in the sentence. However, if they disagree, begin searching for the answer choices that correct the error—this can save you valuable time!

SC

Noun Agreement and Pronoun and Antecedent Agreement Problem Set

Please complete the problem set and review the answer key and explanations. *Answers on page 356.*

1. Despite their cute and cuddly image, <u>hippopotamuses—Africa's most feared animal— account </u>for more human deaths than any other African creature.

   (A) hippopotamuses—Africa's most feared animal—account
   (B) hippopotamus—Africa's most feared animal—account
   (C) hippopotamus—Africa's most feared animal—accounts
   (D) hippopotamuses—Africa's most feared animals—account
   (E) hippopotamuses—Africa's most feared animals—accounts

2. The bank has offered so many convenient services, such as checking by phone and online banking, <u>that many of their customers no longer visit the bank itself</u>.

   (A) that many of their customers no longer visit the bank itself
   (B) that each of its customers no longer visit the bank itself
   (C) that many of their customers no longer visit the bank themselves
   (D) that many of its customers no longer visit the bank itself
   (E) that many of its customers no longer visit the bank him or herself.

Noun Agreement and Pronoun and Antecedent Agreement Problem Set

3. <u>For Romanian farmers, rain dances called *paparudas* are an important ritual</u>, used to invoke rain and guarantee a successful harvest.

    (A) For Romanian farmers, rain dances called *paparudas* are an important ritual
    (B) For Romanian farmers, a rain dance called *paparudas* are an important ritual
    (C) For a Romanian farmer, rain dances called *paparudas* are an important ritual
    (D) For Romanian farmers, a rain dance called *paparudas* are important rituals
    (E) For Romanian farmers, rain dances called *paparudas* are important rituals

4. Upon hearing of the chairman's illness, the committee motioned <u>to postpone their next meeting until after he was released</u> from the hospital.

    (A) to postpone their next meeting until after he was released
    (B) to postpone its next meeting until after he was released
    (C) to postpone their next meeting until after he or she was released
    (D) to postpone their next meeting until after they were released
    (E) to postpone its next meeting until after each was released

Noun Agreement and Pronoun and Antecedent Agreement Problem Set Answer Key

Correct answers are in bold.

1. Despite their cute and cuddly image, <u>hippopotamuses—Africa's most feared animal—account</u> for more human deaths than any other African creature.

   (A) hippopotamuses—Africa's most feared animal—account
   (B) hippopotamus—Africa's most feared animal—account
   (C) hippopotamus—Africa's most feared animal—accounts
   (D) hippopotamuses—Africa's most feared animals—account
   (E) hippopotamuses—Africa's most feared animals—accounts

The subject of the sentence, *hippopotamuses*, is plural, as is evidenced by the plural noun and the use of a plural pronoun (*their*). So *hippopotamuses* must be Africa's most feared *animals*, also plural. While Choice (E) also makes this correction, it ruins the subject verb agreement by using the singular *accounts*, rather than the plural *account*.

2. The bank has offered so many convenient services, such as checking by phone and online banking, <u>that many of their customers no longer visit the bank itself</u>.

   (A) that many of their customers no longer visit the bank itself
   (B) that each of its customers no longer visit the bank itself
   (C) that many of their customers no longer visit the bank themselves
   (D) that many of its customers no longer visit the bank itself
   (E) that many of its customers no longer visit the bank him or herself.

Bank is a misleading word. We think of the people working there, not the singular structure itself. However, it is singular, so it needs a singular pronoun. *Their* should be *its*. Choice (D) is the only one that makes this change without incorrectly changing another part of the sentence.

3. <u>For Romanian farmers, rain dances called *paparudas* are an important ritual,</u> used to invoke rain and guarantee a successful harvest.

    (A) For Romanian farmers, rain dances called *paparudas* are an important ritual
    (B) For Romanian farmers, a rain dance called *paparudas* are an important ritual
    (C) For a Romanian farmer, rain dances called *paparudas* are an important ritual
    (D) For Romanian farmers, a rain dance called *paparudas* are important rituals
    (E) For Romanian farmers, rain dances called *paparudas* are important rituals

The subject, *rain dances*, is plural, so all referring nouns should also be plural. The name of the dance is plural (*paparudas*), but the word *ritual* is singular. It must match the plural referents. Choice (D) makes this correction, but changes the subject to a singular noun, thus it is incorrect. Choice (E) is best.

4. Upon hearing of the chairman's illness, the committee motioned <u>to postpone their next meeting until after he was released</u> from the hospital.

    (A) to postpone their next meeting until after he was released
    (B) to postpone its next meeting until after he was released
    (C) to postpone their next meeting until after he or she was released
    (D) to postpone their next meeting until after they were released
    (E) to postpone its next meeting until after each was released

The word *committee* is misleading. It takes more than one person to make a committee, so you might think it is plural when in fact it is singular. Therefore, the pronoun *their* is incorrect—it should be *its*. Only Choice (B) makes this change without changing another part of the sentence.

Relative Pronouns

A clause
beginning with a
relative pronoun
should be
positioned as
close as possible
to the noun it
is modifying.
Look at how
a sentence's
meaning can be
changed when its
relative clause is
moved:

"The All Star
game determines
home field
advantage for
the World Series,
which is held
halfway through
the season."

Read more
about misplaced
modifiers in the
next chapter.

Relative pronouns are appropriately named because they *relate* groups of words to another noun or pronoun. Relative pronouns include *who, whom, that, which, whoever, whomever,* and *whichever.* Look at the following example:

> In Major League Baseball, the All-Star game, *which* is held halfway through the season, determines home field advantage for the World Series. [*Correct*]

In this sentence, the relative pronoun appears in a clause (*which is held halfway through the season*) and relates to the antecedent *game.* They may also appear in a phrase:

> The league *that* wins will play four of seven games at its championship team's home stadium.   [*Correct*]

The pronoun *that*, in the phrase *that wins*, relates to *league.*

It is easy to identify relative pronouns; you can remove them and their accompanying clauses or phrases and the sentence will still make sense. However, the meaning might be slightly altered:

> In Major League Baseball, the All-Star game determines home field advantage for the World Series.
>
> Removed: *which is held halfway through the season*

> The league will play four of seven games at its championship team's home stadium.
>
> Removed: *that wins*

When referring to people, use *who, whom, whoever,* and *whomever.* When referring to a place, a thing, or an idea, use *that, which,* and *whichever.* Failure to follow these rules is the most common relative pronoun error on the GMAT. Look at the example:

> The team who I follow just signed a multi-million dollar contract with the best home run hitter since Mark McGuire.   [*Incorrect*]

While the *team* is made up of people, the *team* itself is a thing. Therefore, *who* is an incorrect relative pronoun used to refer to it. The correct pronoun is *that*:

> The team *that* I follow just signed a multi-million dollar contract with the best home run hitter since Mark McGuire.   [*Correct*]

The most
common relative
pronoun errors on
the GMAT occur
when a pronoun
used to refer to
a person is used
to refer to a
thing, or when a
pronoun used to
refer to a thing is
used to refer to a
person.

SC

Be on the lookout for the reverse error, as well:

The obnoxious fan *that* threw the cup into left field was thrown out of the stadium.   [*Incorrect*]

If the sentence is referring to a fan that circulates air, than *that* is correct because it is referring to a thing. But the context of the sentence tells us that *fan* is referring to a person who roots for a team, so *that* must be replaced with *who*:

The obnoxious fan *who* threw the cup into left field was thrown out of the stadium.   [*Correct*]

There is good news and bad news about the remaining relative pronoun errors on the GMAT. The good news: you do not need to know when to use *which* and when to use *that*, a common grammatical error. The explanation is long and boring and littered with vocabulary terms. But now for the bad news: you do need to know when to use *who* and when to use *whom*. Fortunately, there are two easy tricks to help you keep the two words straight.

Trick #1: Use *whom* when it follows a preposition:

He threw the ball <u>at</u> *whom*?

Mr. Kobiyashi, <u>with</u> *whom* I am attending the game, is well-known for his stance on inter-league play.

Trick #2: Substitute *he* or *him* for *who* or *whom* in the clause or in the sentence. If *he* makes sense, the answer is *who*. If *him* makes sense, the answer is *whom*:

The manager yelled at the umpire, *whom* had called the pitch a strike, before throwing first base into the dugout.   [*Incorrect*]

To test if *whom* is correct in this sentence, begin by separating the clause it appears in from the rest of the sentence:

whom had called the pitch a strike

Then, substitute both *he* and *him* for *whom*. Which one makes sense?

he had called the pitch a strike   OR   *him* had called the pitch a strike

Because *he* makes sense, the correct relative pronoun should be *who*:

The manager yelled at the umpire, *who* had called the pitch a strike, before throwing first base into the dugout.   [*Correct*]

Sometimes you might have to rearrange the clause or the sentence in order for either one to make sense:

> With such a large score deficit, the game seems lost, no matter *who* they send in to relieve the pitcher.　　[*Incorrect*]

Begin by separating the clause containing the relative pronoun:

> no matter *who* they send in to relieve the pitcher

You may need to delete phrases while rearranging sentences. Notice how "no matter" was dropped here.

Substituting *he* or *him* for who does not make sense, so rearrange the sentence:

> they send *who* in to relieve the pitcher

Now substitute:

> they send *he* in　　OR　　they send *him* in

Him is correct, so *whom* is the correct relative pronoun:

> With such a large score deficit, the game seems lost, no matter *whom* they send in to relieve the pitcher.　　[*Correct*]

Relative pronoun errors such as these occur in a small percentage of the questions in *The Official Guide to GMAT Review*. However, as you'll see in the next section, relative pronouns are often ambiguous or implied, leading to an entirely different set of errors.

Relative Pronoun Problem Set

Please complete the problem set and review the answer key and explanations. *Answers on page 362.*

1. As a result of reality television shows such as American Idol, <u>many aspiring rock stars that would never have had the means to pursue their dreams</u> now have become major celebrities.

    (A) many aspiring rock stars that would never have had the means to pursue their dreams
    (B) many aspiring rock stars which would never have had the means to pursue their dreams
    (C) many aspiring rock stars whom would never have had the means to pursue their dreams
    (D) many aspiring rock stars who would never have had the means to pursue their dreams
    (E) many aspiring rock stars so that would never have had the means to pursue their dreams

2. <u>The distance between the two runners, which is over 50 meters,</u> cannot be made up with only three laps to go in the race.

    (A) The distance between the two runners, which is over 50 meters
    (B) The distance between the two runners, who is over 50 meters
    (C) The distance between the two runners, whom is over 50 meters
    (D) The distance between the two runners, that is over 50 meters
    (E) The distance between the two runners, whoever is over 50 meters

3. At the conclusion of the space shuttle launch, <u>everyone whom attended agreed that it was a spectacular sight</u>.

    (A) everyone whom attended agreed that it was a spectacular sight
    (B) everyone who attended agreed that it was a spectacular sight
    (C) everyone whom attended agreed whom it was a spectacular sight
    (D) everyone who attended agreed as to it being a spectacular sight
    (E) everyone whom attended agreed which it was a spectacular sight

Relative Pronoun Problem Set Answer Key

Correct answers are in bold.

1. As a result of reality television shows such as *American Idol*, <u>many aspiring rock stars that would never have had the means to pursue their dreams</u> now have become major celebrities.

    (A) many aspiring rock stars that would never have had the means to pursue their dreams
    (B) many aspiring rock stars which would never have had the means to pursue their dreams
    (C) many aspiring rock stars whom would never have had the means to pursue their dreams
    (D) many aspiring rock stars who would never have had the means to pursue their dreams
    (E) many aspiring rock stars so that would never have had the means to pursue their dreams

Rock stars are people, not things, so the correct relative pronoun is *who*. If you follow Trick #2 from the section, you would see that *whom* is incorrect when *him* is substituted into *him would never have had the means*.

2. <u>The distance between the two runners, which is over 50 meters</u>, cannot be made up with only three laps to go in the race.

    (A) The distance between the two runners, which is over 50 meters
    (B) The distance between the two runners, who is over 50 meters
    (C) The distance between the two runners, whom is over 50 meters
    (D) The distance between the two runners, that is over 50 meters
    (E) The distance between the two runners, whoever is over 50 meters

The sentence is correct as is. The relative pronoun *which* is referring to *the distance*, a thing. Some test takers might be thrown off by its placement in the sentence; thinking it is referring to *runners*, they might mistakenly select *who* or *whom*.

3. At the conclusion of the space shuttle launch, <u>everyone whom attended agreed that it was a spectacular sight</u>.

    (A) everyone whom attended agreed that it was a spectacular sight
    (B) everyone who attended agreed that it was a spectacular sight
    (C) everyone whom attended agreed whom it was a spectacular sight
    (D) everyone who attended agreed as to it being a spectacular sight
    (E) everyone whom attended agreed which it was a spectacular sight

To test the relative pronoun, *whom*, insert *he* and *him* into the clause *whom attended*: *he attended* or *him attended*? Since *he* is correct, *who* is the correct relative pronoun. Choices (B) and (D) both offer this correction. (D), however, changes *that* to *as to it being*, a wordy and awkward expression. (B) is correct.

Ambiguous and Implied Pronouns

The most common pronoun errors on the GMAT are ambiguous and implied pronouns, occurring in a large number of the questions in *The Official Guide to GMAT Review*.

Ambiguous pronoun errors occur when the proper antecedent is unclear, leaving the reader to wonder whom or what the pronoun is referencing. Ambiguous pronouns most often occur when the pronoun can refer to more than one antecedent:

> After Ryan called Seth, *he* went to visit Katina.

Who went to see Katina? Ryan or Seth? The sentence needs to be rewritten:

> Solution 1: After Ryan called Seth, Ryan went to visit Katina.

> Solution 2: Ryan went to visit Katina after he called Seth.

Sometimes you can replace the pronoun with a noun, as in the first example. In some instances, though, this solution can create an awkward sentence, and you must rearrange the sentence entirely, as was done in the second example.

Unfortunately, ambiguous pronouns might be harder to spot on the GMAT:

> Looking at written warnings, actual citations, and even arrest records, it is evident that releasing tagged fish is still a driving force behind the DNR's monitoring of the waterways, like that of other state agencies. [*Incorrect*]

This sentence lacks a clear antecedent for *that (of other state agencies)*. Do other state agencies have similar warnings, citations, and arrests? Or do they always release tagged fish? Or do they share the same driving force? Or do they monitor the water in the same fashion? The context of the sentence and our prior knowledge tell us that other state agencies have the same driving force, but this must be made clear in the sentence:

> Looking at written warnings, actual citations, and even arrest records, it is evident that releasing tagged fish is still a driving force behind the DNR's monitoring of the waterways, *as it is for* other state agencies. [*Correct*]

To correct the sentence, we added a conjunction and a verb and changed the pronoun and its antecedent. The new antecedent, *releasing tagged fish*, is the reference for *it*. Now the comparison is more clear; *X is a driving force for Y as X is for Z.*

SC

Similar to ambiguous pronouns, but much more prominent on the GMAT, are implied pronouns. These are pronouns that do not have an antecedent in the sentence; the antecedent is implied by the reader. They are used so often in speech that they are difficult to spot in sentences. Look at the following:

> Last night on the news, they said that pilot error caused the air show collision.   [*Incorrect*]

Who are *they*? We can infer that the writer meant the news anchor or the reporter made this statement. Because our speech is informal, we make similar statements every day. But because we are preparing for a test of standard English, we must provide an antecedent for every pronoun!

> Last night on the news, *the anchor* said that pilot error caused the air show collision.   [*Correct*]

Another implied pronoun error comes from possessive nouns. They can never be used as an antecedent, as they are acting as an adjective in the sentence:

> Although I own the band's album, I have never seen them in concert. [*Incorrect*]

> Although I own the band's album, I have never seen **the band** in concert. [*Correct*]

Of course, GMAC will attempt to hide implied pronouns in more complex sentences, often containing other pronouns:

> During World War II, the French strategy for protection was a wall of staggered forts and lookout points called the Maginot Line, but its weakest section ultimately led to their invasion.   [*Incorrect*]

This sentence has two pronouns but one of them lacks an antecedent. The antecedent for *its* is *wall*; this is correct. However, there is no logical noun referent for *their*. We know that *their* is referring to the French, but in the sentence, *French* is an adjective used to modify *strategy*. *France* does not appear as a noun in the sentence, and pronouns must refer to nouns or other pronouns. The sentence must be changed:

> During World War II, the French strategy for protection was a wall of staggered forts and lookout points called the Maginot Line, but its weakest section ultimately led to France's invasion.   [*Correct*]

One out of every ten or eleven questions in *The Official Guide to GMAT Review* contains an error involving a pronoun, and the majority of these errors are ambiguous and implied pronouns. You would be wise to locate and confirm the antecedent for any pronoun on the GMAT.

Ambiguous and Implied Pronoun Problem Set

Please complete the problem set and review the answer key and explanations. *Answers on page 366.*

1. Student admissions to medical school are not accepted solely based on their MCAT scores; other considerations include their undergraduate grade point averages and extracurricular activities.

   (A) Student admissions to medical school are not accepted solely based on their MCAT scores
   (B) Students seeking admission to medical school are not accepted solely based on their MCAT scores
   (C) Student admissions to medical school are not accepted solely based on the schools' MCAT scores
   (D) Student admissions to medical school are not accepted solely based on MCAT scores
   (E) Students seeking admission to medical school are not accepted solely based on its MCAT scores

2. Hippies, rebellious youth of the 1960s and 1970s, expressed their desire for pacifism and tolerance through peace movements, which included marches and protests.

   (A) their desire for pacifism and tolerance through peace movements, which included
   (B) its desire for pacifism and tolerance through peace movements, which included
   (C) their desire for pacifism and tolerance through peace movements, that were to include
   (D) such desire for pacifism and tolerance through peace movements, which included
   (E) its desire for pacifism and tolerance through peace movements, including

3. From 1995 to 1999, the posted speed limit on Montana's highways was "reasonable and prudent," meaning their drivers could travel at speeds in excess of 80 mph when road conditions were good.

   (A) meaning their drivers could travel
   (B) meaning its drivers could travel
   (C) meaning that their drivers could travel
   (D) meaning drivers could travel
   (E) which meant their drivers could travel

4. Marco Polo's travels are documented in his book, *Il Milione*, which took him over seventeen years.

   (A) travels are documented in his book, *Il Milione*, which took him over seventeen years
   (B) travels are documented in his book, *Il Milione*, which took over seventeen years to travel
   (C) travels, which took Polo over seventeen years to complete, are documented in his book, *Il Milione*
   (D) travels are documented in his book, *Il Milione*, which took the explorer over seventeen years
   (E) travels, which having taken him over seventeen years, are documented in the book, *Il Milione*

Ambiguous and Implied Pronoun Problem Set Answer Key

Correct answers are in bold.

1. <u>Student admissions to medical school are not accepted solely based on their MCAT scores</u>; other considerations include their undergraduate grade point averages and extracurricular activities.

    (A) Student admissions to medical school are not accepted solely based on their MCAT scores
    (B) Students seeking admission to medical school are not accepted solely based on their MCAT scores
    (C) Student admissions to medical school are not accepted solely based on the schools' MCAT scores
    (D) Student admissions to medical school are not accepted solely based on MCAT scores
    (E) Students seeking admission to medical school are not accepted solely based on its MCAT scores

This sentence has two implied pronouns, *their* and *their*, only one of which is in the underlined portion of the sentence. Therefore, the correction must create an antecedent for the second *their*. Begin by looking at the first *their*. It is implied that *their* refers to the *students*. However, *student* is used as an adjective to modify *admissions*, and is not in the noun form that is needed for an antecedent. Choice (B) corrects this error, and gives the second *their* a clear antecedent. Choice (C) states that medical schools take the MCAT. Choice (D) removes the first offending pronoun, but does not provide an antecedent for the second *their*. Choice (E), like (C), states that the medical school takes the MCAT.

2. Hippies, rebellious youth of the 1960s and 1970s, expressed <u>their desire for pacifism and tolerance through peace movements, which included</u> marches and protests.

    (A) their desire for pacifism and tolerance through peace movements, which included
    (B) its desire for pacifism and tolerance through peace movements, which included
    (C) their desire for pacifism and tolerance through peace movements, that were to include
    (D) such desire for pacifism and tolerance through peace movements, which included
    (E) its desire for pacifism and tolerance through peace movements, including

The two pronouns in the sentence, *their* and *which*, have clear antecedents: *hippies* and *movements*. The sentence is grammatically correct.

THE POWERSCORE GMAT VERBAL BIBLE

3. From 1995 to 1999, the posted speed limit on Montana's highways was "reasonable and prudent," <u>meaning their drivers could travel</u> at speeds in excess of 80 mph when road conditions were good.

    (A) meaning their drivers could travel
    (B) meaning its drivers could travel
    (C) meaning that their drivers could travel
    (D) meaning drivers could travel
    (E) which meant their drivers could travel

The sentence has an ambiguous pronoun: *their*. Is *their* referring to Montana or to highways? If it is referring to Montana, the possessive noun is functioning as an adjective. Therefore, replacing *their* with *its* in Choice (B) creates an agreement problem with *its* and the antecedent *highways*. Choices (C) and (E) still contain *their*. Choice (D) is correct.

4. Marco Polo's <u>travels are documented in his book, *Il Milione*, which took him over seventeen years</u>.

    (A) travels are documented in his book, *Il Milione*, which took him over seventeen years
    (B) travels are documented in his book, *Il Milione*, which took over seventeen years to travel
    (C) travels, which took Polo over seventeen years to complete, are documented in his book, *Il Milione*
    (D) travels are documented in his book, *Il Milione*, which took the explorer over seventeen years
    (E) travels, which having taken him over seventeen years, are documented in the book, *Il Milione*

The offending pronoun in this sentence is a relative pronoun: *which*. It is unclear whether *which* refers to *travels* or to *book*. Did his travels take 17 years to complete, or did the book take 17 years to complete? Currently, the pronoun is situated next to the name of the book, so it appears to be referencing the book. However, the infinitive *to complete* is needed on the end of the relative clause, and only Choice (C) makes this correction. It also corrects an implied pronoun and moves the relative clause to correctly refer to *travels*.

THE POWERSCORE GMAT VERBAL BIBLE

CHAPTER SEVENTEEN: ERRORS INVOLVING MODIFIERS

Adjectives Versus Adverbs

An adjective is a word that describes or modifies a noun or a pronoun. *Skinny* is an adjective. You can have a *skinny* <u>horse</u>, *skinny* <u>children</u>, and a *skinny* <u>file</u>. <u>She</u> can be *skinny*, <u>it</u> can be *skinny*, <u>they</u> can be *skinny*.

An adverb is a word that describes or modifies a verb, adjective, or other adverb. *Quickly* is an adverb used to modify a verb. You can <u>skip</u> *quickly*, <u>count</u> *quickly*, and <u>brush</u> *quickly*. *Extremely* is an adverb used to modify adjectives or other adverbs. You can be *extremely* <u>skinny</u> or lose weight *extremely* <u>quickly</u>.

The GMAT may test your knowledge of when to use an adjective versus when to use an adverb. Look at an example:

> The main tourist attraction in Dorchester-on-Thames, a rather tiny village west of London, is the surprising large abbey; built in the seventh century, it remains one of the largest churches in Oxfordshire.   [*Incorrect*]

The sentence contains several adjectives and adverbs. *Rather*, an adverb, correctly modifies the adjective *tiny*. However, look at *surprising*. Is the abbey surprising, or is the size of the abbey surprising? The second part of the sentence references the vast size, so *surprising*, an adjective, is not modifying *abbey*—it is modifying *large*, and thus must be made into an adverb. By adding an *–ly*, we can correct this error:

> The main tourist attraction in Dorchester-on-Thames, a rather tiny village west of London, is the *surprisingly* large abbey; built in the seventh century, it remains of one of the largest churches in Oxfordshire. [*Correct*]

The incorrect use of an adjective or an adverb occurs less frequently than errors with verbs and pronouns. If another error is not immediately apparent in a GMAT sentence, find the adjectives and adverbs. Check that each adjective modifies a noun or pronoun, and that each adverb modifies a verb, adjective, or other adverb.

Quantifiers

Nouns can be divided into two categories—count nouns and non-count nouns.

Count nouns are aptly named; they are objects that you can count:

> five *dogs*
> a million *ideas*
> two dozen *donuts*
> a *window*
> seven *students*

Non-count nouns, sometimes referred to as mass nouns, are not so easy to count:

> some *water* (five water?)
> a little *sunshine* (a million sunshine?)
> most of the *applause* (two dozen applause?)
> a good deal of *wood* (a wood?)
> no *harm* (seven harm?)

Quantifiers are the modifying words that come before the noun and tell how many or how much. They are underlined below:

> <u>five</u> dogs
> <u>some</u> water
> <u>two dozen</u> donuts
> <u>most of the</u> applause
> <u>no</u> harm

The following quantifiers can only be used with count nouns (such as *flowers*):

> <u>many</u> flowers
> <u>both</u> flowers
> <u>a few</u> flowers
> <u>few</u> flowers
> <u>several</u> flowers
> <u>a couple of</u> flowers
> <u>none of the</u> flowers
> <u>numerous</u> flowers
> <u>a number of</u> flowers

Some quantifiers can only be used with non-count nouns (such as *talking*):

much talking
a little talking
little talking
a bit of talking
a good deal of talking
no talking
an amount of talking

The biggest offenders on the GMAT are *many/ much* and *few/ little*.

And other quantifiers can be used with both count nouns and non-count nouns:

all of the flowers	all of the talking
some flowers	some talking
most flowers	most talking
a lot of flowers	a lot of talking
plenty of flowers	plenty of talking
a lack of flowers	a lack of talking

So if *much* cannot be used with *flowers*, doesn't it seem likely that GMAC will use this type of error on the GMAT? Absolutely! Unfortunately, it will not be as easy to spot as *Much of the flowers are blooming*. As in all other GMAT questions, there will likely be words or phrases between the offending quantifier and its noun:

The botanist was pleased to see that much of the recently planted and heavily fertilized flowers were in bloom.   [*Incorrect*]

Flowers are count nouns, and must be used with *many*:

The botanist was pleased to see that *many* of the recently planted and heavily fertilized flowers were in bloom.   [*Correct*]

The presence of a quantifier in a GMAT sentence should cause you to check that the correct quantifier is in use.

SC

Adjectives Versus Adverbs and Quantifiers Problem Set

Please complete the problem set and review the answer key and explanations. *Answers on page 374.*

1. Patrons reported that they would visit the restaurant more <u>frequent than they currently do, provided the management hired an efficient waitstaff and offered more nightly specials</u>.

    (A) frequent than they currently do, provided the management hired an efficient waitstaff and offered more nightly specials
    (B) frequent than they currently do, provided the management hired an efficient waitstaff and offered more night specials
    (C) frequent than they currently do, provided the management hired a more efficient waitstaff and offered more nightly specials
    (D) frequently than they currently do, provided the management hired an efficient waitstaff and offered more nightly specials
    (E) frequent than they current dine, provided the management hired an efficient waitstaff and offered more nightly specials

2. <u>Although the area had little traffic and pedestrians, the developers were convinced that</u> the restaurant should be opened in the district; it was only a matter of time before urban sprawl would bring residents and visitors alike.

    (A) Although the area had little traffic and pedestrians, the developers were convinced that
    (B) Although the area had few traffic and pedestrians, the developers were convinced that
    (C) Although the area had little traffic and few pedestrians, the developers were convinced that
    (D) Although the area had few traffic and little pedestrians, the developers were convinced that
    (E) Although the area had a little traffic and pedestrians, the developers were convinced that

Adjectives Versus Adverbs and Quantifiers Problem Set

3. Many celebrities, such as Britney Spears, Tom Cruise, and Jessica Simpson, <u>have secretly vacationed on Turtle Island in Fiji, an exclusively tropical resort known for its privacy and beauty</u>.

    (A) have secretly vacationed on Turtle Island in Fiji, an exclusively tropical resort known for its privacy and beauty
    (B) have secretly vacationed on Turtle Island in Fiji, an exclusive, tropical resort known for its privacy and beauty
    (C) have vacationed in secret on Turtle Island in Fiji, an exclusively tropical resort known for its privacy and beauty
    (D) have secretly vacationed on Turtle Island in Fiji, an tropically exclusive resort known for its privacy and beauty
    (E) have secretly vacationed on Turtle Island in Fiji, an exclusively tropical, private, beautiful resort

4. <u>The volume of the aquarium, when made with glass, is not as numerous as the volume of the plastic aquarium</u>.

    (A) The volume of the aquarium, when made with glass, is not as numerous as the volume of the plastic aquarium
    (B) The volume of the aquarium, which is made with glass, is not as numerous as the volume of the plastic aquarium
    (C) The volume of the aquarium, which is made with glass, is greater than the volume of the plastic aquarium
    (D) Made of glass, the volume of the aquarium is lesser than the volume of the plastic aquarium
    (E) When the aquarium is made of glass, the volume is less than the volume of the plastic aquarium

Adjectives Versus Adverbs and Quantifiers Problem Set
Answer Key

Correct answers are in bold.

1. Patrons reported that they would visit the restaurant more <u>frequent than they currently do, provided the management hired an efficient waitstaff and offered more nightly specials</u>.

    (A) frequent than they currently do, provided the management hired an efficient waitstaff and offered more nightly specials
    (B) frequent than they currently do, provided the management hired an efficient waitstaff and offered more night specials
    (C) frequent than they currently do, provided the management hired a more efficient waitstaff and offered more nightly specials
    (D) frequently than they currently do, provided the management hired an efficient waitstaff and offered more nightly specials
    (E) frequent than they current dine, provided the management hired an efficient waitstaff and offered more nightly specials

2. <u>Although the area had little traffic and pedestrians, the developers were convinced that</u> the restaurant should be opened in the district; it was only a matter of time before urban sprawl would bring residents and visitors alike.

    (A) Although the area had little traffic and pedestrians, the developers were convinced that
    (B) Although the area had few traffic and pedestrians, the developers were convinced that
    (C) Although the area had little traffic and few pedestrians, the developers were convinced that
    (D) Although the area had few traffic and little pedestrians, the developers were convinced that
    (E) Although the area had a little traffic and pedestrians, the developers were convinced that

As the sentence appears now, the quantifier *little* applies to both *traffic* and *pedestrians*; the area had *little traffic* and *little pedestrians*. *Little* should only be used with non-count nouns, so it is correctly placed with *traffic*. However, when placed with *pedestrians*, it appears as if the area has the presence of *small pedestrians*. *Few* should be placed with *pedestrians*, as in Choice (C).

3. The volume of the aquarium, when made with glass, is not as numerous as the volume of the plastic aquarium.

   (A) The volume of the aquarium, when made with glass, is not as numerous as the volume of the plastic aquarium
   (B) The volume of the aquarium, which is made with glass, is not as numerous as the volume of the plastic aquarium
   (C) The volume of the aquarium, which is made with glass, is greater than the volume of the plastic aquarium
   (D) Made of glass, the volume of the aquarium is lesser than the volume of the plastic aquarium
   (E) When the aquarium is made of glass, the volume is less than the volume of the plastic aquarium

This sentence pairs *numerous*, a quantifier for a count noun, with *volume*, a non-count noun. Only Choice (E) uses *less than*.

Frequent, an adjective, is modifying *visit*, a verb, therefore it must be changed into an adverb, *frequently*. Only Choice (D) makes this correction.

4. Many celebrities, such as Britney Spears, Tom Cruise, and Jessica Simpson, have secretly vacationed on Turtle Island in Fiji, an exclusively tropical resort known for its privacy and beauty.

   (A) have secretly vacationed on Turtle Island in Fiji , an exclusively tropical resort known for its privacy and beauty
   (B) have secretly vacationed on Turtle Island in Fiji , an exclusive, tropical resort known for its privacy and beauty
   (C) have vacationed in secret on Turtle Island in Fiji, an exclusively tropical resort known for its privacy and beauty
   (D) have secretly vacationed on Turtle Island in Fiji , an tropically exclusive resort known for its privacy and beauty
   (E) have secretly vacationed on Turtle Island in Fiji , an exclusively tropical, private, beautiful resort

The issue in this sentence is the adverb *exclusively*. Should it stay an adverb, and modify *tropical*, or should it become an adjective, and modify *resort*? The phrase *exclusively tropical* is redundant—a climate cannot be both tropical and arid or both tropical and polar. Plus, the context of the sentence indicates that the resort is exclusive; celebrities *secretly* stay there because it is *private*. Only Choice (B) makes this correction.

Adjective and adverbs are always modifiers, which are words or phrases used to tell something about another word or phrase in the sentence. The adjectives and adverbs in italics below modify the underlined words in the following sentences:

I want the *blue* necklace for my birthday.
He *barely* passed the test.
Your home is *very beautiful*.

Modifiers can be phrases and clauses, too:

Matt drove the go-cart *that wouldn't go over ten miles an hour*.
Unable to control her temper, the customer threw down her purse and demanded a refund.
My uncle, *who once played on the professional tour*, gives golf lessons on the weekend.

All of the modifiers above are adjective phrases; they each modify a noun or a pronoun. Similarly, adverb phrases often modify verbs:

Lynne made hamburgers *while I sliced vegetables*.
In the movie, the actor plays an innocent banker accused of stealing.
You must finish your dinner *before you are allowed to go outside*.

Modifiers, both as individual words and as phrases, are like leeches. They have the bad habit of attaching themselves to any words with which they come in contact, and some writers have the bad habit of putting modifiers next to the wrong word, creating a **misplaced modifier**. Look at the following example:

He *nearly* fell ten feet.

Nearly, an adverb, is the modifier in this sentence. It is in the correct location if the sentence means:

He almost fell but he didn't but it would have been a ten foot fall if he did.

In the original sentence, *nearly* is placed next to *fell*, so it has leeched on to modify that word. In this position in the sentence, it can only mean *almost fell*.

But what if the modifier changed positions and leeched onto the adjective *ten feet*?

He fell *nearly* ten feet.

SC

Now the sentence has a completely different meaning:

He did fall, and he fell almost ten feet before hitting the ground.

GMAC may test you on a single misplaced adjective or adverb, especially with *barely*, *nearly*, *only*, and *just* because they often leech on to the wrong word. A single-word misplaced modifier such as these will likely occur in a sentence containing a more blatant grammatical error. However, the most common modifier error occurs when a phrase or clause is misplaced in a sentence:

Short on money, <u>the action figure</u> was the best present Marsha could find. [*Incorrect*]

In this sentence, most readers will deduce that Marsha is short on money. However, because of the placement of the modifying phrase next to the wrong noun, the sentence is seriously flawed. As it reads now, the action figure was short on money (as if little GI Joes were out shopping at the mall). To correct these types of sentences, rearrange them and/or add words to convey the true meaning:

Short on money, <u>Marsha</u> felt that the action figure was the best present she could find.   [*Correct*]

Or:

The action figure was the best present Marsha could find based on the money she had left.   [*Correct*]

Many questions in *The Official Guide to GMAT Review* have a misplaced modifier in the introductory clause of the sentence. Look at another:

Produced in London, Alfred Hitchcock directed his first film, *The Pleasure Garden*, for Gainsborough Pictures.   [*Incorrect*]

While it is true that Hitchcock was born in London, the sentence currently reads that Hitchcock himself was produced in London. The sentence is attempting to convey that the film was produced in London. Rearrange the sentence:

The Pleasure Garden, Alfred Hitchcock's first film, was produced in London for Gainsborough Pictures.   [*Correct*]

Note that we have completely changed the modifier; *Alfred Hitchcock's first film* now modifies the title of the film, *The Pleasure Garden*.

When an introductory phrase or clause is a modifier, the word immediately after the phrase or clause must be the referent:

<u>Preparing for the picnic,</u> <u>Mom</u> made potato salad.

<u>Scavengers of the ocean,</u> <u>blue crabs</u> will feast on most anything on the sea floor.

A similar problem is the **dangling modifier**. A dangling modifier, which usually occurs in the introductory phrase or clause, does not have a logical connection to any word or phrase in the sentence:

> *Driving to Florida*, <u>the dog</u> needed to stop often.   [*Incorrect*]

In the sentence above, the dog is driving to Florida.

> *Driving to Florida*, <u>we</u> needed to stop often because of the dog. [*Correct*]

Try a more difficult version:

> Using the Fujita Scale, a tornado's intensity can be rated on a scale of zero to six in order to predict possible damage and warn people in its path. [*Incorrect*]

Who is using the Fujita Scale? The way the sentence stands now, the *intensity* is using the scale. The proper referent, be it *scientists* or *researchers* or *stormchasers*, is not identified, thus creating a dangling modifier:

> *Using the Fujita Scale*, <u>scientists</u> can rate a tornado's intensity on a scale of zero to six in order to predict possible damage and warn people in its path.   [*Correct*]

Misplaced modifiers often occur with relative clauses, which are clauses that begin with a relative pronoun such as *that* and *which*. Relative clauses should occur immediately after the word or phrase they are modifying:

> <u>Yogi Rock</u>, *which is a rock on Mars*, was named for its resemblance to Yogi Bear.
> <u>Applications</u> *that are incomplete* will be thrown away.
> The <u>biology professor</u>, *who is visiting from Harvard*, was honored at a banquet.

Look at how the meaning of the first sentence from the examples above is changed when the relative clause is moved:

> Yogi Rock was named for its resemblance to Yogi Bear, which is a rock on Mars. [*Incorrect*]

The sentence now reads that Yogi Bear is a rock on Mars. We know that this is wrong; Yogi Bear is a cartoon character, and Yogi Rock is the rock on Mars. The placement of modifiers is crucial to the meaning of the sentence.

Errors with modifiers, including misplace words, misplaced phrases and clauses, and dangling modifiers, occur on a large percentage of the questions in *The Official Guide to GMAT Review*. It is extremely important to have a firm understanding of their proper placement.

Modifier Placement Problem Set

Please complete the problem set and review the answer key and explanations. *Answers on page 380.*

1. Known for her compassion and commitment, <u>International Nurses' Day is celebrated each year on Florence Nightingale's date of birth to honor her career in nursing</u>.

   (A) International Nurses' Day is celebrated each year on Florence Nightingale's date of birth to honor her career in nursing

   (B) Florence Nightingale's date of birth to honor celebrated each year on International Nurse' Day to honor her career in nursing

   (C) Florence Nightingale's career in nursing is honored each year on International Nurses' Day, which is celebrated on the date of her birth

   (D) International Nurses' Day, celebrated each year on Florence Nightingale's date of birth, honors her career in nursing

   (E) Florence Nightingale is honored for her career in nursing each year on International Nurses' Day, which is celebrated on the date of her birth

2. Although the Wright Brothers' first <u>plane only flew 120 feet, it was an instrumental moment in aviation history</u>.

   (A) plane only flew 120 feet, it was an instrumental moment in aviation history

   (B) plane flew only 120 feet, the event was an instrumental moment in aviation history

   (C) plane only flew 120 feet, aviation history was an instrumental moment

   (D) plane flew only 120 feet, an instrumental moment in aviation history

   (E) plane only flew 120 feet, the plane was an instrumental moment in aviation history

3. <u>The schedule for the skate park's construction, which will serve</u> skateboarders, rollerbladers, and bikers, was detailed at the city council meeting.

   (A) The schedule for the skate park's construction, which will serve

   (B) The schedule for the skate park's construction, that which will serve

   (C) The schedule for the skate park's construction, planned to serve

   (D) The skate park's construction schedule, which will serve

   (E) The construction schedule for the skate park, which will serve

Modifier Placement Problem Set Answer Key

Correct answers are in bold.

1. Known for her compassion and commitment, <u>International Nurses' Day is celebrated each year on Florence Nightingale's date of birth to honor her career in nursing</u>.

   (A) International Nurses' Day is celebrated each year on Florence Nightingale's date of birth to honor her career in nursing
   (B) Florence Nightingale's date of birth to honor celebrated each year on International Nurses' Day to honor her career in nursing
   (C) Florence Nightingale's career in nursing is honored each year on International Nurses' Day, which is celebrated on the date of her birth
   (D) International Nurses' Day, celebrated each year on Florence Nightingale's date of birth, honors her career in nursing
   (E) Florence Nightingale is honored for her career in nursing each year on International Nurses' Day, which is celebrated on the date of her birth

Currently, the sentence states that International Nurses' Day, rather than Florence Nightingale, is known for its compassion and commitment. Since the introductory clause is not underlined, it cannot be moved; we know that the noun *Florence Nightingale* must be the first word to follow the clause. Only Choice (E) makes this correction. Choices (B) and (C) are not correct, because *Florence Nightingale* is used as an adjective (rather than a noun) to modify *date of birth* and *career in nursing*.

2. Although the Wright Brothers' first <u>plane only flew 120 feet, it was an instrumental moment in aviation history</u>.

   (A) plane only flew 120 feet, it was an instrumental moment in aviation history
   (B) plane flew only 120 feet, the event was an instrumental moment in aviation history
   (C) plane only flew 120 feet, aviation history was an instrumental moment
   (D) plane flew only 120 feet, an instrumental moment in aviation history
   (E) plane only flew 120 feet, the plane was an instrumental moment in aviation history

It is difficult to find the misplaced modifier in this sentence, and if you do not read all of the answer choices, you might incorrectly choose (A), thinking there is no error. However, Choices (B) and (D) should tip you off that the adverb *only* is in the wrong place. As it reads now, the plane *only* <u>flew</u> (as opposed to <u>swam</u>, <u>ran</u>, or <u>drove</u>). But it should read that it flew *only* <u>120 feet</u> (as opposed to <u>200 feet</u>, <u>1 mile</u>, or <u>cross country</u>). Choice (B) is also correct because it eliminates the ambiguous pronoun *it*.

3. <u>The schedule for the skate park's construction, which will serve</u> skateboarders, rollerbladers, and bikers, was detailed at the city council meeting.

   (A) The schedule for the skate park's construction, which will serve
   (B) The schedule for the skate park's construction, that which will serve
   (C) The schedule for the skate park's construction, planned to serve
   (D) The skate park's construction schedule, which will serve
   (E) The construction schedule for the skate park, which will serve

The relative clause is currently modifying construction: construction *which will serve skateboarders, rollerbladers, and bikers*. It is actually the *park* that that will serve these three groups of people.

Verb Forms as Modifiers

A verb **infinitive** is the word *to* combined with the root form of the verb:

to cook   to think   to be   to dance   to smile

Although infinitives look like verbs, they are actually noun phrases, adjective phrases, and adverb phrases:

As a noun: Maria <u>loves</u> *to cook*.

In the previous sentence, *to cook* is the direct object because it modifies the verb *loves*. Thus *to cook* is a noun. The next sentence shows how it can be used as an adjective:

As a adjective: Her dream *to cook* with Emeril <u>came</u> true.

The noun, *dream*, is being modified by *to cook with Emeril*, making *to cook* an adjective. Finally, look at *to cook* as an adverb:

As an adverb: She <u>was hired</u> *to cook* for the President.

In this sentence, to cook modifies the verb, *was hired*. It is acting as an adverb.

A present infinitive is used with another verb to describe a present situation:

I <u>like</u> *to cook*.
He <u>is waiting</u> for the hamburger *to cook*.

A perfect infinitive describes a time that occurred before the verb in the sentence:

She <u>was proud</u> *to have cooked* for Elvis.
I <u>would like</u> *to have cooked* for you before you left.

Similarly, participles are not verbs, either. They are also modifiers. Present participles work with the verb to describe the action:

I <u>am</u> *cooking*.
We <u>are</u> *cooking* a turkey for Thanksgiving dinner.

Past participles use a form of the helping verb *has* to describe past action:

I <u>had</u> *cooked* a casserole that day.
We <u>have</u> *cooked* a turkey every Thanksgiving.

Errors in verb form on the GMAT typically occur when an infinitive or participle is missing. Look at the following sentence:

> Although most Americans believe that the Emancipation Proclamation was enacted to end slavery, Abraham Lincoln truly intended for the document should preserve the Union.   [*Incorrect*]

The independent clause in this sentence (*Abraham Lincoln truly intended for the document should preserve the Union*) violates grammatical rules. It has two uncompounded verbs: *intended* and *should preserve*. Instead, *preserve* should be in its infinitive form as an adverb, modifying the real verb, *intended*:

> Although most Americans believe that the Emancipation Proclamation was enacted to end slavery, Abraham Lincoln truly <u>intended</u> for the document *to preserve* the Union.   [*Correct*]

You may also find an error in which the participle form of a verb can correct the sentence by acting as modifier:

> For the Stegosaurus, a dinosaur from the late Jurassic Period, the seventeen bony plates embedded in its back were necessary elements for survival, to regulate its temperature throughout its bus-sized body and to protect it from much larger carnivores.   [*Incorrect*]

In this sentence, the infinitives *to regulate* and *to protect* have nothing to modify. There are two ways to fix this sentence. One, we can add a verb such as *used* before the first infinitive. This gives *to regulate* and *to protect* a verb to modify:

> For the Stegosaurus, a dinosaur from the late Jurassic Period, the seventeen bony plates embedded in its back were necessary elements for survival, <u>used</u> *to regulate* its temperature throughout its bus-sized body and *to protect* it from much larger carnivores.   [*Correct*]

The other solution involves using the participle form of the verbs *to regulate* and *to protect*:

> For the Stegosaurus, a dinosaur from the late Jurassic Period, the seventeen bony plates embedded in its back were necessary elements for survival, *regulating* its temperature throughout its bus-sized body and *protecting* it from much larger carnivores.   [*Correct*]

By changing *to regulate* to *regulating* and *to protect* to *protecting*, the entire phrase now acts correctly as an adjective to modify *elements for survival*.

These modifier errors are less common than misplaced and dangling modifiers, and are often confused with verb errors.

Verb Forms as Modifiers Problem Set

Please complete the problem set and review the answer key and explanations. *Answers on page 384.*

1. Despite winning multiple Grammys for his jazz recordings, Harry Connick, Jr. decided to experiment with funk in the mid-nineties, before returning to jazz later that decade.

    (A) decided to experiment with funk in the mid-nineties, before returning to jazz
    (B) decided experimenting with funk in the mid-nineties, before returning to jazz
    (C) decided to experiment with funk in the mid-nineties, before to return to jazz
    (D) deciding to experiment with funk in the mid-nineties, before returning to jazz
    (E) decided that he would experiment with funk in the mid-nineties, before returning to jazz

2. During the Roman Republic, a slave's testimony in judicial hearings was admissible only if it was obtained by torture, as officials believed that slaves could not be trusted telling the truth otherwise.

    (A) as officials believed that slaves could not be trusted telling the truth otherwise
    (B) as officials believed that slaves could not be trusted having told the truth otherwise
    (C) as officials believed that slaves could not be trusted to tell the truth otherwise
    (D) as officials believing that slaves could not be trusted telling the truth otherwise
    (E) as officials had believed that slaves could not be trusted telling the truth otherwise

3. The most important piece of educational legislation to be enacted in the 1970's was the Individual Education Plan (IEP), to ensure that both gifted and learning disabled children receive instruction appropriate to their level and abilities.

    (A) to ensure that
    (B) having ensured that
    (C) to ensuring that
    (D) having been ensured that
    (E) implemented to ensure that

Verb Forms as Modifiers Problem Set Answer Key

Correct answers are in bold.

1. Despite winning multiple Grammys for his jazz recordings, Harry Connick, Jr. <u>decided to experiment with funk in the mid-nineties, before returning to jazz</u> later that decade.

    (A) decided to experiment with funk in the mid-nineties, before returning to jazz
    (B) decided experimenting with funk in the mid-nineties, before returning to jazz
    (C) decided to experiment with funk in the mid-nineties, before to return to jazz
    (D) deciding to experiment with funk in the mid-nineties, before returning to jazz
    (E) decided that he would experiment with funk in the mid-nineties, before returning to jazz

This sentence is grammatically correct. The infinitive *to experiment* correctly modifies *decided*, and *returning to jazz*, a participle form of *to return*, modifies *Harry Connick, Jr.* The other answer choices incorrectly modify *decided* and *Harry Connick, Jr.* or they use an actual verb as a modifier.

2. During the Roman Republic, a slave's testimony in judicial hearings was admissible only if it was obtained by torture, <u>as officials believed that slaves could not be trusted telling the truth otherwise</u>.

    (A) as officials believed that slaves could not be trusted telling the truth otherwise
    (B) as officials believed that slaves could not be trusted having told the truth otherwise
    (C) as officials believed that slaves could not be trusted to tell the truth otherwise
    (D) as officials believing that slaves could not be trusted telling the truth otherwise
    (E) as officials had believed that slaves could not be trusted telling the truth otherwise

The sentence incorrectly uses a participle form (*telling*) of the verb *to tell*, when the infinitive is needed to modify the verb *trusted*.

3. The most important piece of educational legislation to be enacted in the 1970's was the Individual Education Plan (IEP), <u>to ensure that</u> both gifted and learning disabled children receive instruction appropriate to their level and abilities.

    (A) to ensure that
    (B) having ensured that
    (C) to ensuring that
    (D) having been ensured that
    (E) implemented to ensure that

The sentence has an infinitive, *to ensure*, that does not modify anything. It needs the verb, *implemented*, to serve its purpose. Choice (E) is best.

SC

CHAPTER EIGHTEEN: ERRORS INVOLVING CONJUNCTIONS

Coordinating Conjunctions

Coordinating conjunctions are used to join nouns, pronouns, verbs, prepositional phrases, adjectives, and even adverbs. There are seven coordinating conjunctions:

and	but	or	yet	for	nor	so

An infrequent error occurs when the incorrect coordinating conjunction is used to join two parts of speech. However, a larger number of questions test your knowledge of correlating conjunctions, which are pairs of coordinating conjunctions:

either..or	neither..nor	both..and	not only..but also
not..but	whether..or	as..as	

GMAC seems to think they can trip you up by using a correlative conjunction without its proper partner:

> The flying buttresses on Notre Dame de Paris not only serve to add embellishment to the cathedral, which many argue is the most beautiful in France, and also to support and protect the structure.   [*Incorrect*]

As you can see, *not only* is partnered with *and also*. The correct correlation is *not only..but also*:

> The flying buttresses on Notre Dame de Paris *not only* serve to add embellishment to the cathedral, which many argue is the most beautiful in France, *but also* to support and protect the structure.   [*Correct*]

Coordinating conjunctions and correlative conjunctions are also used to link items in a series:

> Neapolitan ice cream has <u>chocolate</u>, <u>vanilla</u>, *and* <u>strawberry</u> sections.
> <u>Saunders</u>, <u>Peterson</u>, *or* <u>Goldsmith</u> will be promoted to the vacant position.

"Either..or" and "neither..nor" create common errors on the GMAT. Watch for "either" incorrectly being partnered with "and" and "neither" illegally matched with "or."

If you spot one half of a correlating conjunction on the exam, verify that the other half is present. Otherwise the sentence must be corrected.

SC

Conjunctions are fairly straightforward when used in series like these. However, the GMAT might present you with a compound predicate (two verbs) that contains a series; both situations should receive a conjunction, but only one is given, creating a perfect test question:

> Since the teacher introduced the reward system, students have begun paying closer attention, completing homework, following directions, and have stopped causing disruptions during lessons.   [*Incorrect*]

This sentence is missing a conjunction, causing confusion and a grammatical error. Begin by looking at the compound predicate:

> Students have begun X *and* have stopped Y.

Diagramming sentences is a grammatical technique used to map out the subject and predicate and their parts of speech. The concept is not really needed to help you prepare for the GMAT, but in this instance, it might allow you see that the two verbs in the predicate both connect to the subject:

```
                       pred.
       subj.        have begun X
     Students  ||      and
                    have stopped Y
```

Now, notice that X, *what was begun*, is a series. All series must be joined by a conjunction:

> Students have begun paying closer attention, completing homework, *and* following directions

When diagrammed, the solution becomes clearer:

```
                            pred.
                    have begun paying closer attention, completing homework, and
       subj.        following directions
     Students  ||      and
                    have stopped causing disruptions during lessons
```

Put them together in sentence form. There should be two conjunctions in the sentence: one to separate the series, and one to create the compound predicate:

> Since the teacher introduced the reward system, students have begun paying closer attention, completing homework, *and* following directions, *and* have stopped causing disruptions during lessons.   [*Correct*]

If you encounter a coordinating or correlating conjunction on the GMAT, check first to see if it is used in a comparison. Since comparison errors are more common, look for errors in parallel structure or illogical or incomplete comparisons. If the comparison is correct, then examine the conjunction for proper usage and grammar.

Subordinating Conjunctions

Subordinating conjunctions connect a dependent clause to an independent clause, while stating the relationship between the two clauses. In the following sentences, the independent clause is underlined, the dependent clause is in italics, and the subordination conjunction is in bold:

> I took my umbrella **because** *it was raining*.
> ***Despite*** *all of the drama*, <u>my office is a great place to work</u>.
> <u>I was shocked</u> **when** *I won the award*.
> ***After*** *hearing all of the testimony*, <u>the judge ruled in favor of the plaintiff</u>.

The most common subordinating conjunctions are:

after	because	if	so that	till	whenever
although	before	now that	than	unless	where
as	even if	provided	that	until	wherever
as if	even though	since	though	when	while
as though	how				

Errors with subordinating conjunctions can occur when an inappropriate conjunction is used, thus confusing the relationship of the two clauses. Take a simple sentence as an example:

> <u>I cried</u> ***although*** *I was sad*.   [*Incorrect*]

In this sentence, *although* does not create an effective relationship between the dependent clause and the independent clause. Because is a much better conjunction:

> <u>I cried</u> ***because*** *I was sad*.   [*Correct*]

You may also have to add a subordinating conjunction to correct a comma splice. A **comma splice** occurs when two complete sentences are only separated by a comma:

> I was sad, I cried.   [*Incorrect*]

This sentence can be corrected several ways, and the most obvious is to remove the comma and add a period in its place. However, you will never have a two sentence solution in the GMAT Sentence Correction questions. The easiest way to correct the sentence is to add a subordinating conjunction, making the first sentence a dependent clause:

> ***Because*** *I was sad*, <u>I cried</u>.   [*Correct*]

On the GMAT, comma splices are never corrected with a two sentence solution.

SC

This is called **subordination** because we have made one of the sentences subordinate to the main clause. The new dependent clause can no longer stand on its own as a sentence.

Be sure to read every answer choice in case you don't notice a secondary error right away. The answer choices will often clue you in to other errors in the sentence.

Watch for subordinating conjunction errors as secondary errors in sentences. The main errors will likely be much more blatant, such as subject and verb agreement or verb tense. Choosing the right conjunction or adding a conjunction will be an auxiliary correction. Look at an example:

1. <u>Global warming has already made the Hudson River a seeming fragile ecosystem</u>, the introduction of invasive species has the potential to destroy nearly all of the aquatic plants and animals that inhabit the river.

   (A) Global warming has already made the Hudson River a seeming fragile ecosystem
   (B) Global warming has already made the Hudson River a seemingly fragile ecosystem
   (C) While global warming has already made the Hudson River a seemingly fragile ecosystem
   (D) Because global warming has already made the Hudson River a seeming fragile ecosystem;
   (E) Global warming has made the Hudson River a seemingly fragile ecosystem

One error in this sentence is the use of the adjective *seeming*. It is modifying *fragile*, another adjective, so it should be in the form of the adverb *seemingly*. Choices (B), (C), and (E) make this correction. But only Choice (C) addresses the issue of the comma splice. By adding the subordinating conjunction *while*, the relationship between the two clauses is defined and a comma splice is avoided.

A specific conjunction error that is tested on the GMAT is the use of the subordinating conjunction *as* versus the use of the preposition *like*.

When *like* is used as a preposition, it must be followed by a noun or pronoun and it must be used to compare two things:

<u>I</u> look *like* my <u>sister</u>.   I = sister
Like <u>a detective</u>, <u>Andrea</u> solved the puzzle.   Andrea = detective
The <u>fountain</u> sounds *like* a bubbling <u>brook</u>.   fountain = brook

As, on the other hand, is a subordinating conjunction. Subordinating conjunctions are used to introduce dependent clauses. *As* should never be used to compare two things:

As I mentioned earlier, the test date has been moved up.
It appears *as* if the St. Louis Cardinals are going to lose again.
My dog is very skittish, *as* you might expect a rescued animal to be.

Problems occur when writers start using *like* for *as* and *as* for *like*, which is easy to do. Just substitute *like* for the word *as* in the three sentences above:

INCORRECT:
Like I mentioned earlier, the test date has been moved up.
It appears *like* the St. Louis Cardinals are going to lose again.
My dog is very skittish, *like* you might expect a rescued animal to be.

Most of us are guilty of making this mistake. Unfortunately, the GMAT is unforgiving and does not allow for error. The test will also make your job more difficult by putting this error in a longer sentence:

The developers of Wembley Stadium claim that the new sliding roof will attract future Olympic Games, provide more comfortable seating for spectators, and close as a retractable dome does to protect players and fans from the elements.   [*Incorrect*]

In this sentence, *as* is used in a subordinate clause: *as a retractable dome does*. However, *as* is used to make a comparison between the new sliding roof and a retractable dome. All comparisons should use the preposition *like*. This also means adding an object of the preposition:

The developers of Wembley Stadium claim that the new sliding roof will attract future Olympic Games, provide more comfortable seating for spectators, and close *like a retractable dome* to protect players and fans from the elements.   [*Correct*]

SC

You must also know the difference between *like* and *such as*. *Like*, as we noted, is a preposition used to compare. *Such as* is a conjunction used to introduce examples:

> *Like* residents of Wisconsin and Ohio, many native Midwesterners have their own unique accent.   [*Correct*]

> Native residents of many Midwestern states, *such as* Wisconsin and Ohio, have their own unique accent.   [*Correct*]

The best rule to remember is that when the word *like* is used as a preposition, it must be used to make a comparison.

Conjunctions Problem Set

Please complete the problem set and review the answer key and explanations. *Answers on page 392.*

1. In *The Matrix*, Neo can choose either the blue pill, which will allow him to forget all that he has learned <u>and return to life as he knew it, and the red pill, which will keep him in reality</u>.

    (A) and return to life as he knew it, and the red pill, which will keep him in reality
    (B) and return to life as he knew it, or the red pill, which will keep him in reality
    (C) or return to life as he knew it, and the red pill, which will keep him in reality
    (D) but also return to life as he knew it, and the red pill, which will keep him in reality
    (E) and return to life as he knew it, for the red pill, which will keep him in reality

2. While a supernova originally causes a star to increase in brilliance, it will eventually cause the star's light to gradually <u>decline and disappear, as a flashlight fading from weakening batteries</u>.

    (A) decline and disappear, as a flashlight fading from weakening batteries
    (B) decline and disappear, like a flashlight fading from weakening batteries
    (C) decline or disappear, as a flashlight fading from weakening batteries
    (D) either decline or disappear, as a flashlight fading from weakening batteries
    (E) decline and disappear, just as a flashlight fading from weakening batteries

3. Edgar Allan Poe attended the University of Virginia and West Point Military Academy <u>and was expelled from both of them; he incurred gambling debts at Virginia and</u> intentionally neglected his duties at West Point.

    (A) and was expelled from both of them; he incurred gambling debts at Virginia and
    (B) as he was expelled from both of them; he incurred gambling debts at Virginia and so
    (C) but was expelled from both of them; he incurred gambling debts at Virginia but also
    (D) and was expelled from both of them; he incurred gambling debts at Virginia but
    (E) but was expelled from both of them; he incurred gambling debts at Virginia and

Conjunctions Problem Set Answer Key

Correct answers are in bold.

1. In *The Matrix*, Neo can choose either the blue pill, which will allow him to forget all that he has learned <u>and return to life as he knew it, and the red pill, which will keep him in reality</u>.

    (A) and return to life as he knew it, and the red pill, which will keep him in reality
    (B) and return to life as he knew it, or the red pill, which will keep him in reality
    (C) or return to life as he knew it, and the red pill, which will keep him in reality
    (D) but also return to life as he knew it, and the red pill, which will keep him in reality
    (E) and return to life as he knew it, for the red pill, which will keep him in reality

Either must always be used with *or*. The confusion might occur in deciding which *and* to replace with *or*. The clause following *the blue pill* tells two things that the pill can do: forget *and* return. *And* is correctly used here. It is incorrectly used to describe Neo's choice: *either* the blue pill *or* the red pill. Choice (B) makes this correction.

2. While a supernova originally causes a star to increase in brilliance, it will eventually cause the star's light to gradually <u>decline and disappear, as a flashlight fading from weakening batteries</u>.

    (A) decline and disappear, as a flashlight fading from weakening batteries
    (B) decline and disappear, like a flashlight fading from weakening batteries
    (C) decline or disappear, as a flashlight fading from weakening batteries
    (D) either decline or disappear, as a flashlight fading from weakening batteries
    (E) decline and disappear, just as a flashlight fading from weakening batteries

The conjunction *and* correctly compounds the verb, so Choices (C) and (D) are eliminated. The error occurs when *as* is used to make a comparison in a simile; the star's light to a flashlight's light. *Like* must be used in comparisons, and (B) makes this correction.

3. Edgar Allan Poe attended the University of Virginia and West Point Military Academy <u>and was expelled from both of them; he incurred gambling debts at Virginia and</u> intentionally neglected his duties at West Point.

    (A) and was expelled from both of them; he incurred gambling debts at Virginia and
    (B) as he was expelled from both of them; he incurred gambling debts at Virginia and so
    (C) but was expelled from both of them; he incurred gambling debts at Virginia but also
    (D) and was expelled from both of them; he incurred gambling debts at Virginia but
    (E) but was expelled from both of them; he incurred gambling debts at Virginia and

This sentence has two coordinating conjunctions underlined. The first *and* comes after an independent clause that states that Poe attended two colleges. Which conjunction fits best to then say that he was expelled from both of those colleges? *But*. Only Choices (C) and (E) make this correction. Then look at the second *and*. It compounds the verb; *he incurred and neglected*. It is correct, so Choice (C) is eliminated.

392

CHAPTER NINETEEN: ERRORS IN CONSTRUCTION

Comparisons

Opinions. Everybody has one. There are opinion polls, opinion pages, opinion reports. We seek expert opinions, the majority opinion, and dissenting opinions. With all of the opinions we hear everyday, it is no wonder that comparisons are so common in our speech and prose:

> I cheered for Magic Johnson more than I cheered for Larry Bird.
> *The Green Mile* is Stephen King's most allegorical book.
> I'd prefer a hamburger over a chicken sandwich.

Written comparisons follow specific rules of Standard English, so they are often tested on the GMAT. You will be asked to identify and correct three types of comparison errors: faulty comparative degree, illogical comparisons, and incomplete comparisons.

Faulty comparisons are common errors in the Sentence Correction section of the GMAT.

Comparative Degree

Comparative degree refers to the three separate degrees of intensity conveyed by adjectives and adverbs. These three levels are called the positive (describes one object), comparative (evaluates two objects), and superlative (ranks three or more objects). Consider the following chart.

	Positive (One Object)	Comparative (Two Objects)	Superlative (Three or More Objects)
adj.	warm	warmer	warmest
adj.	dark	darker	darkest
adj.	dry	drier	driest
adj	sunny	more sunny or sunnier	most sunny or sunniest
adv.	steadily	more steadily	most steadily
adv.	wildly	more wildly	most wildly
adj.	ferocious	more ferocious	most ferocious
adv.	ferociously	more ferociously	most ferociously

In the positive level, adjectives and adverbs appear in their base form. For the comparative degree, we add *–er* to the end of the word or use *more* or *less* before the word. Superlative comparisons need *–est* at the end or *most* or *least* before the word. Most adjectives and adverbs will always follow this pattern. As a general rule, add *–ed* and *–est* to one syllable words, and *more/less* and *most/least* to words with two or more syllables. However, like *sunny* in the chart above, some words can use either form, so trust your ear.

The use of an incorrect degree occurs when the comparative level is used to rank three or more objects, or when the superlative degree is used to rank two objects.

> Mary is the wealthier of the three musicians.   [*Incorrect*]

Wealthier implies that there are only two musicians being compared, but the sentence states that there are three. The sentence should use the superlative degree:

> Mary is the *wealthiest* of the three musicians.   [*Correct*]

Sentences will, of course, be more complex on the GMAT:

> In many respects, George Bush and George W. Bush had the same political agenda, but the younger Bush, who was able to pass more legislation, had the most cooperative Congress.   [*Incorrect*]

Two Presidents and their Congresses are being compared so the comparative degree should be used:

> In many respects, George Bush and George W. Bush had the same political agenda, but the younger Bush, who was able to pass more legislation, had the *more cooperative* Congress.   [*Correct*]

There are several sentences like this one in *The Official Guide to GMAT Review*.

Illogical and Incomplete Comparisons

Illogical comparisons are the most common comparison error on the GMAT.

The most common comparison error is the illogical comparison. When presented with a comparison, be sure that the two objects being compared are alike. For example, you cannot compare a truck to a town, a novel to a thumb tack, or a flashlight to a closet. However, it would be acceptable to compare a truck to a car, a novel to a movie, or a flashlight to a candle. Illogical comparisons often occur as the result of an introductory phrase or clause:

> Like most desks at work, Spence has his laden with pictures of his family.   [*Incorrect*]

At first glance, it may look and sound correct, but it is completely illogical. Because of the introductory phrase (*like most desks at work*), *desks* are being compared to *Spence*. Instead, Spence's desk needs to be compared to all of the other desks:

> Spence's desk, like most desks at work, is laden with pictures of his family.   [*Correct*]

SC

Or Spence needs to be compared to his coworkers:

> Spence, like most of the employees at work, has his desk laden with pictures of his family.   [*Correct*]

Now try a sentence with more complicated subject matter. Can you spot the illogical comparison?

> Completed sometime between 480 and 450 B.C., the play *Oedipus Rex* by Sophocles is much more foreboding than fourteenth-century William Shakespeare.   [*Incorrect*]

This sentence is comparing a *play* to *William Shakespeare*. It needs to compare Sophocles' *play* to William Shakespeare's *plays*:

> Completed sometime between 480 and 450 B.C., the play *Oedipus Rex* by Sophocles is much more foreboding than the fourteenth-century plays by William Shakespeare.   [*Correct*]

Sometimes a comparison is not parallel, creating an illogical statement:

> While the company insists that its starting salary for a man working in the executive branch of the organization is the same as a woman in equal capacity, the watchdog group found a significant gender wage gap. [*Incorrect*]

The comparison, when broken down and extraneous phrases are removed, *should* be:

> X is the same *for* Y as *for* Z

In other words:

> Salary is the same *for* a man as *for* a woman

Notice that the comparison must be parallel; both parts start with *for*. Without the pronoun *for*, the original sentence is not parallel and is comparing *salary* to *a woman*. To correct the sentence, add the second *for* to create parallelism:

> While the company insists that its starting salary *for* a man working in the executive branch of the organization is the same as *for* a woman in equal capacity, the watchdog group found a significant gender wage gap. [*Correct*]

Parallel structure is discussed further in this chapter.

Keywords that should alert you to a comparison include *more, most, less, least, rather than, like,* and *unlike*. If you find these key words in a GMAT sentence, verify that the comparison is logical and complete.

It is not enough to make sure that all comparisons are made using like objects—sometimes you have to make sure that there are two objects present! Without two objects, you end up with an incomplete comparison, which is less common on the GMAT, but still tested nevertheless. Look at an example:

> The grand champion bulldog, owned by Mrs. Seifert, had a stockier build and more even gait than Mr. Murphy's.   [*Incorrect*]

It does not take a Best of Show judge to figure out that Mrs. Seifert's bulldog is being compared to Mr. Murphy's bulldog, but it must be stated in the sentence. Currently, the sentence is comparing a bulldog's build and gait to something owned by Mr. Murphy, but the something is not stated. Many people would read this sentence and believe the bulldog's build and gait is being compared to Mr. Murphy's build and gait. Add the referent to the sentence to correct this error:

> The grand champion bulldog, owned by Mrs. Seifert, had a stockier build and more even gait than Mr. Murphy's *bulldog.*   [*Correct*]

Comparison errors are responsible for a large portion of the questions in *The Official Guide to GMAT Review*.

Remember, comparison errors are common! Watch for faulty comparative degree, illogical comparisons, and incomplete comparisons.

Comparisons Problem Set

Please complete the problem set and review the answer key and explanations. *Answers on page 398.*

1. <u>Like Mozart's first concerts, Frederic Chopin began performing at age six</u>, both for private parties and public charity events.

    (A) Like Mozart's first concerts, Frederic Chopin began performing at age six
    (B) Like Mozart's young age, Frederic Chopin began performing at age six
    (C) Like Mozart and his first concerts, Frederic Chopin began performing at age six
    (D) Like Mozart, Frederic Chopin began performing at age six
    (E) Like Mozart's first concerts, Frederic Chopin's concerts began performing at age six

2. <u>Of all the celestial bodies in our solar system, Pluto will likely be the more difficult to explore</u>, due to its icy surface and distance from Earth.

    (A) Of all the celestial bodies in our solar system, Pluto will likely be the more difficult to explore
    (B) Of most the celestial bodies in our solar system, Pluto will likely be the more difficult to explore
    (C) Of all the celestial bodies in our solar system, Pluto will likely be the most difficult to explore
    (D) Of all the celestial bodies in our solar system, Pluto will likely be the difficultest to explore
    (E) Of all the celestial bodies in our solar system, Pluto will likely be the more difficult to explore of all

3. Americans have a difficult time understanding the inability to improve one's status under a feudal society, but feudalism's hierarchal system is much more rigid <u>than</u> a democracy.

    (A) than
    (B) than that of
    (C) than is so of
    (D) compared to
    (E) compared to that of

Comparisons Problem Set Answer Key

Correct answers are in bold.

1. <u>Like Mozart's first concerts, Frederic Chopin began performing at age six</u>, both for private parties and public charity events.

    (A) Like Mozart's first concerts, Frederic Chopin began performing at age six
    (B) Like Mozart's young age, Frederic Chopin began performing at age six
    (C) Like Mozart and his first concerts, Frederic Chopin began performing at age six
    (D) Like Mozart, Frederic Chopin began performing at age six
    (E) Like Mozart's first concerts, Frederic Chopin's concerts began performing at age six

In the current sentence, *concerts* are being illogically compared to *Chopin*. Mozart must be compared to Chopin, as they are both people and both classical musicians. Only (D) makes this comparison.

2. <u>Of all the celestial bodies in our solar system, Pluto will likely be the more difficult to explore</u>, due to its icy surface and distance from Earth.

    (A) Of all the celestial bodies in our solar system, Pluto will likely be the more difficult to explore
    (B) Of most the celestial bodies in our solar system, Pluto will likely be the more difficult to explore
    (C) Of all the celestial bodies in our solar system, Pluto will likely be the most difficult to explore
    (D) Of all the celestial bodies in our solar system, Pluto will likely be the difficultest to explore
    (E) Of all the celestial bodies in our solar system, Pluto will likely be the more difficult to explore of all

This is an error of comparative degree. There are more than two celestial bodies being referenced, so the superlative form of *difficult* must be used. Pluto is the *most* difficult to explore, Choice (C).

3. Americans have a difficult time understanding the inability to improve one's status under a feudal society, but feudalism's hierarchal system is much more rigid <u>than</u> a democracy.

    (A) than
    (B) than that of
    (C) than is so of
    (D) compared to
    (E) compared to that of

The illogical comparison in this sentence is a *hierarchal system* to a *democracy*, or *rigid* to a *democracy*. It is evident that the author intends to compare feudalism's hierarchal system to democracy's hierarchal system. Choice (B) presents the pronoun, *that*, to go in place of *democracy's hierarchal system*. Many might question why Choice (E) is not correct. It is because of the word *more*. When used in a comparison, it should be coupled with *than*: *more...than* vs. *more...compared to*.

398

Parallel Structure

Look around you. Most everything in your office or living room or kitchen is symmetrical, meaning that if we cut an object in half along an imaginary plane, both sides of the object would look exactly the same. People like symmetry; we like symmetrical lamps on symmetrical tables with symmetrical picture frames. Scientists have even proven that we like symmetrical mates— subconsciously, we are more attracted to people with symmetrical faces than those who might have a dimple or freckle on just one side!

The developers of Standard English were no different. They liked symmetrical sentences, meaning that if a sentence had two similar parts linked by a conjunction, the two parts had to be identical in form. They called these properly constructed sentences "parallel." Look at the following parallel sentence:

> The donation might be used *to fund the new playground* or *to replace the old bus*.

Examine the two italicized verb phrases in the sentence, and note that their parts of speech match:

infinitive   n.
to fund the new playground

infinitive   n.
to replace the old bus

The pattern is symmetrical: an infinitive verb followed by a noun. This sentence is parallel.

The GMAT will test your ability to recognize this pattern using a sentence such as the following:

> The donation might be used *to fund the new playground* or *replacing the old bus*. [*Incorrect*]

There are two things the donation may be used to do:

infinitive   n.
to fund the new playground

prog. verb   n.
replacing the old bus

The patterns no longer match. The second phrase uses a progressive form of the verb instead of the infinitive form. The sentence now violates parallel structure.

Sometimes sentences have three or more similar parts linked by a conjunction. In these cases, all of the items in the series must follow the same pattern:

The new employee will be responsible for *filing paperwork*, *answering phones*, and *taking new orders*. [*Correct*]

Look at the three things the new employee will be responsible for:

prog. vb.   n.
filing paperwork

prog. vb.   n.
answering phones

prog. vb.   n.
taking new orders

All three jobs follow the same form: a verb in the progressive form, followed by a noun.

If one of the verbs has a different form than the other two, the sentence is no longer parallel:

The new employee will be responsible for *filing paperwork*, *answering phones*, and *will take new orders*. [*Incorrect*]

The last phrase does not match the first two:

prog. vb.   n.
filing paperwork

prog. vb.   n.
answering phones

future vb.   n.
will take new orders

It contains a simple future tense form of a verb, which does not match the progressive pattern established by the first two.

Errors in parallel structure occur in dozens of questions in *The Official Guide to GMAT Review*. They may occur with almost any part of speech, including verbs, nouns, and adjectives.

Unparallel construction is a prevalent error on the GMAT because it can occur with almost any part of speech.

SC

Parallel Verbs

Errors in verb form, which we just studied in the two previous examples, are the most common parallelism errors on the test. And why shouldn't they be? Every sentence has to have a verb.

It is sentences with more than one verb that cause problems. Two or more verbs can appear in:

> A compound sentence:
> I *drove* the entire trip, **but** Bryan *claimed* to be more tired.

> A compound predicate:
> The car *rolled* down the hill **and** *crashed* into the fence.

> And a relative clause:
> The class *that sold the most cookies* **and** *won the prize* had a party after school.

If you encounter a GMAT sentence with two verbs separated by a conjunction, check to ensure that the verbs are parallel in form.

Let's look at an example in a more complex sentence:

> The Department of Motor Vehicles is considering a new paging system that would alleviate lines for walk-in customers renewing their licenses and if employees are overwhelmed they would be assisted.   [*Incorrect*]

This sentence contains two verbs in a relative clause that tells what the new system would do:

> *alleviate lines for walk-in customers renewing their licenses* and
> *if employees are overwhelmed they would be assisted*

The verbs in the clause are unparallel in form and tense. The two effects of the paging system are *(it) would alleviate X and (would) assist Y.* The helping verb *would* before *assist* can be omitted, but the main verbs must be parallel:

> *alleviate lines for walk-in customers renewing their licenses* and
> *assist employees who are overwhelmed*

Rewrite the sentence in this form to create a parallel sentence:

> The Department of Motor Vehicles is considering a new paging system that would alleviate lines for walk-in customers renewing their licenses and assist employees who are overwhelmed.   [*Correct*]

Parallel Nouns

Nearly all nouns are naturally parallel. Problems arise, however, with gerunds, which are verb forms that end in *–ing* and act as a noun. Look at the following verb:

I <u>am running</u> in circles.

In this sentence, *running* is in the present progressive form of the verb, and is coupled with *am*. It is properly functioning as a verb. But look at *running* in another sentence:

Running is my least favorite form of exercise.

In this sentence, *running* is a noun. Verbs that end in *-ing* and act like nouns are gerunds, and when they are used on the GMAT in a compound subject or in a sequence, they must all act as nouns. Examine the following sentence:

Opened in 1869, the Transcontinental Railroad had immediate and far-reaching effects on America, including a population explosion in the West, the decline of Native Americans, joining of East Coast culture and Western convention, and cultivation of thousands of acres of new farm land. [*Incorrect*]

The sentence lists a series of results due to the railroad, all in noun form: *explosion, decline, joining,* and *cultivation*. However, look at the gerund *joining*. Without an article to precede it, a reader may mistake the noun for a verb. To correct the error, use *the*:

Opened in 1869, the Transcontinental Railroad had immediate and far-reaching effects on America, including a population explosion in the West, the decline of Native Americans, *the joining* of East Coast culture and Western convention, and cultivation of thousands of acres of new farm land. [*Correct*]

Occasionally, a verb will masquerade as a gerund, and thus need to be changed. Here is an example:

Symptoms of a severe allergic reaction to a bee sting may include dizziness, hives or rashes, swelling of the wound, difficulty breathing, intense itching, and losing consciousness. [*Incorrect*]

This sentence has many gerunds ending in *-ing* and one verb pretending to be a gerund. Look at the short list of symptoms of an allergic reaction: *dizziness, hives, swelling, difficulty, itching,* and *losing*. All but the last one are nouns. In order for *losing* to be a noun, it would have to refer to not coming in first, as in *Losing is difficult to swallow*. In the bee sting sentence, *losing* is a verb; it describes an action.

Because the sentence is not parallel, we must change *losing* to a noun:

> Symptoms of a severe allergic reaction to a bee sting may include dizziness, hives or rashes, swelling of the wound, difficulty breathing, intense itching, and *loss of* consciousness.

Remember, gerunds are the only types of noun parallelism tested; if you find a sentence with a verb ending in *–ing*, check to see if that verb is really a noun. If so, immediately check that it is parallel with the other nouns in the sentence.

Parallel Prepositions

The use of prepositions in a series must also be parallel. A preposition must either be used by all members of a series or by only the first member of the series. Both of the following sentences are correct:

> You can succeed on the GMAT *by* reading, *by* studying, and *by* taking a prep class.   [*Correct*]

> You can succeed on the GMAT *by* reading, studying, and taking a prep class.   [*Correct*]

However, this sentence is incorrect:

> You can succeed on the GMAT *by* reading, *by* studying, and taking a prep class.   [*Incorrect*]

Only two of the items in the series use the preposition *by*, making the sentence ungrammatical.

A series using prepositions does not have to repeat the same preposition:

> We have a government *of* the people, *by* the people, and *for* the people.

Just ensure that all of the objects receive a preposition. This sentence is incorrect:

> You can travel to the town *on* a plane, *in* a car, or boat.   [*Incorrect*]

The nouns *plane* and *car* are the objects of the prepositions *on* and *in*. Because the noun *boat* is in the same series, it must also be the object of a preposition:

> You can travel to the town *on* a plane, *in* a car, or *by* a boat.   [*Correct*]

Also check prepositions to ensure that their objects are parallel. Look at an example:

> Critics of the current Bowl Championship Series feel that moving from a computer-ranking format to creating a playoff system will improve the integrity of the competition.   [*Incorrect*]

This sentence employs the common expression *moving from X to Y*. The object of *from* (*X*) should be in the same form as the object of *to* (*Y*). Currently, it looks like *moving from a format to creating*. *From* is followed by a noun, but *to* is followed by a verb. Correct the sentence by giving each preposition a noun object:

> Critics of the current Bowl Championship Series feel that moving *from* a computer-ranking <u>format</u> *to* a playoff <u>system</u> will improve the integrity of the competition.   [*Correct*]

Now the sentence is parallel.

Parallel Conjunctions

The presence of a correlating conjunction should warn you to verify first the correct use of partnered conjuctions and then the parallel structure.

Like nouns, conjunctions themselves are naturally parallel. The words or phrases that follow a conjunction can cause unparallel sentences, though, so you would be wise to watch for them on the GMAT. Correlative conjunctions, such as *either..or* and *not only..but also*, are the biggest culprits. As we learned in the previous chapter, correlative conjunctions include:

either..or	neither..nor	both..and	not only..but also
	not..but	whether..or	as..as

The words immediately following each conjunction need to be in a similar, parallel format:

either X *or* Y: We accept *either* <u>cash</u> or <u>money order</u>.
                                                 n.   n.

both X *and* Y: She is *both* <u>artistically gifted</u> *and* <u>academically inclined</u>.
                                  adv.   adj.   adv.   adj.

whether X *or* Y: I am deciding *whether* <u>to eat pizza</u> *or* <u>to eat spaghetti</u>.
                                     infinitive n.   infinitive n.

Notice that each word or phrase after the first conjunction matches the format of the word or phrase after the second conjunction. Look at an example of how the GMAT might attempt to trick you with correlative conjunctions:

> Aloe is used not only to soothe burns but also it also heals fungal infections such as ringworm.   [*Incorrect*]

An infinitive verb and a noun (*to soothe burns*) follow *not only*, but a pronoun, simple present verb, and noun (*it heals infections*) follow *but also*. The format, *not only X but also Y*, insists that the X and Y are parallel:

> Aloe is used *not only* <u>to soothe burns</u> *but also* <u>to heal fungal infections</u> such as ringworm.   [*Correct*]

Finally, watch for the use of a conjunction in unparallel clauses. This can occur when one of the clauses is missing a conjunction:

> Behaviorists agree that how a teenage boy dresses and his performance in athletics contribute to his degree of popularity.   [*Incorrect*]

This sentence has two clauses, X and Y, which must be parallel. Currently, X begins with the conjunction *how*: *how a teenage boy dresses*. Y begins with a pronoun: *his performance in athletics*. To make them parallel, they must both begin with a preposition:

> Behaviorists agree that *how* <u>a teenage boy dresses</u> and *how* <u>he performs in athletics</u> contribute to his degree of popularity.

Note that the phrases following the conjunctions are also parallel; they both contain a subject and a present tense verb.

Parallel Comparisons

As discussed in the previous section, comparisons are the source of many errors in the Sentence Correction portion of the GMAT. They cause further problems when they violate parallel structure. Look at the offending sentence below:

> Jim Thorpe, the legendary multi-sport star, enjoyed playing football more than he ran track and field, but it was winning the gold medal at the 1912 Olympic pentathlon that shot him to fame.   [*Incorrect*]

The comparison in this sentence is *enjoyed X more than Y*. Again, the X and the Y must be parallel, but they are not. *Playing football* and *he ran track and field* are not in equivalent format. The first uses a progressive verb followed by a noun. The second adds a subject, past tense verb, and a noun. To correct the sentence, model the second part of the comparison after the first:

> Jim Thorpe, the legendary multi-sport star, enjoyed *playing* <u>football</u> more than *running* <u>track and field</u>, but it was winning the gold medal at the 1912 Olympic pentathlon that shot him to fame.   [*Correct*]

A comparison is a parallel trap, because you must always compare two or more things, setting the stage for an error in one half of the sentence.

Remember to be on the lookout for *more, most, less, least, rather than, like,* and *unlike* to signal a comparison.

Parallel Structure Problem Set

Please complete the problem set and review the answer key and explanations. *Answers on page 408.*

1. By the time Robert Clark Young was fourteen years old, he was reading a second language, authoring a novel, <u>and had published newspaper articles</u>.

    (A) and had published newspaper articles
    (B) and published newspaper articles
    (C) and would publish newspaper articles
    (D) and publishing newspaper articles
    (E) and was publishing newspaper articles

2. A school teacher is no longer responsible for just imparting knowledge; he or she must now take on multiple roles, such as counseling a troubled child, <u>disciplining an unruly student, and to entertain a generation which lacks an attention span</u>.

    (A) disciplining an unruly student, and to entertain a generation which lacks an attention span
    (B) to discipline an unruly student, and to entertain a generation which lacks an attention span
    (C) disciplining an unruly student, and entertaining a generation which lacks an attention span
    (D) disciplining an unruly student, and to entertain a generation lacking an attention span
    (E) as disciplining an unruly student, and to entertaining a generation which lacks an attention span

3. Samoset, the first Native American to make contact with the Pilgrims, assisted the colonists <u>by teaching proper planting techniques, revealing the best fishing locations, and translating</u> native languages.

    (A) by teaching proper planting techniques, revealing the best fishing locations, and translating
    (B) by teaching proper planting techniques, by revealing the best fishing locations, and translating
    (C) by teaching proper planting techniques, revealing the best fishing locations, and to translate
    (D) by teaching proper planting techniques, revealing the best fishing locations, and he translated
    (E) by teaching proper planting techniques, revealing the best fishing locations, and that he translated

Parallel Structure Problem Set

4. In order to qualify for the PGA Tour, aspiring golfers are required to place in the top 30 at Qualifying School, <u>win three events on the Nationwide Tour, or to finish in the top 20</u> of the Nationwide Tour's earnings list.

   (A) win three events on the Nationwide Tour, or to finish in the top 20
   (B) win three events on the Nationwide Tour, or finishing in the top 20
   (C) to win three events on the Nationwide Tour, or finishing in the top 20
   (D) to win three events on the Nationwide Tour, finishing in the top 20
   (E) to win three events on the Nationwide Tour, or to finish in the top 20

5. Children at the daycare spend their time either engaging in educational activities, such as math games and reading circles, or <u>they play with their</u> peers in a supervised setting.

   (A) they play with their
   (B) they will play with their
   (C) they are playing with their
   (D) to play with their
   (E) playing with their

6. The human resource department looked at an insurance program that would cover all vision-related procedures, including laser surgery, and <u>if employees paid out-of-pocket expenses they would be reimbursed</u>.

   (A) if employees paid out-of-pocket expenses they would be reimbursed
   (B) paying out-of-pocket expenses would be reimbursed
   (C) reimburse employees who paid out-of-pocket expenses
   (D) reimbursing employees paying out-of-pocket expenses
   (E) employees to be reimbursed for paying out-of-pocket expenses

Parallel Structure Problem Set Answer Key

Correct answers are in bold.

1. By the time Robert Clark Young was fourteen years old, he was reading a second language, authoring a novel, <u>and had published newspaper articles</u>.

    (A) and had published newspaper articles
    (B) and published newspaper articles
    (C) and would publish newspaper articles
    (D) and publishing newspaper articles
    (E) and was publishing newspaper articles

The sentence has a series of two past progressive verbs (*was reading, authoring*) followed by a past perfect verb (*had published*). The third item in the series must use another past progressive verb (*publishing*). Since the first verb uses the helping verb *was* but the second verb does not use it, the third verb should not have a helping verb either. Therefore, Choice (E) is incorrect. Only Choice (D) makes the correction.

2. A school teacher is no longer responsible for just imparting knowledge; he or she must now take on multiple roles, such as counseling a troubled child, <u>disciplining an unruly student, and to entertain a generation which lacks an attention span</u>.

    (A) disciplining an unruly student, and to entertain a generation which lacks an attention span
    (B) to discipline an unruly student, and to entertain a generation which lacks an attention span
    (C) disciplining an unruly student, and entertaining a generation which lacks an attention span
    (D) disciplining an unruly student, and to entertain a generation lacking an attention span
    (E) as disciplining an unruly student, and entertaining a generation which lacks an attention span

The verb phrases should be in the present progressive form to match *counseling*; *counseling, disciplining,* and *entertaining*. Both (C) and (E) make this correction, but (E) unnecessarily adds *as*. Only (C) is correct.

3. Samoset, the first Native American to make contact with the Pilgrims, assisted the colonists <u>by teaching proper planting techniques, revealing the best fishing locations, and translating</u> native languages.

    (A) by teaching proper planting techniques, revealing the best fishing locations, and translating
    (B) by teaching proper planting techniques, by revealing the best fishing locations, and translating
    (C) by teaching proper planting techniques, revealing the best fishing locations, and to translate
    (D) by teaching proper planting techniques, revealing the best fishing locations, and he translated
    (E) by teaching proper planting techniques, revealing the best fishing locations, and that he translated

This original sentence is parallel making Choice (A) correct. The three verbs are in progressive form; *teaching, revealing,* and *translating* and only the first item uses a preposition.

4. In order to qualify for the PGA Tour, aspiring golfers are required to place in the top 30 at Qualifying School, <u>win three events on the Nationwide Tour, or to finish in the top 20 </u>of the Nationwide Tour's earnings list.

(A) win three events on the Nationwide Tour, or to finish in the top 20
(B) win three events on the Nationwide Tour, or finishing in the top 20
(C) to win three events on the Nationwide Tour, or finishing in the top 20
(D) to win three events on the Nationwide Tour, finishing in the top 20
(E) to win three events on the Nationwide Tour, or to finish in the top 20

The sentence lists three requirements; *to place, win,* and *to finish.* Two of the verbs are in the infinitive form and one is in simple present. The use of *to* for a list of infinitives must be used with *all* the verbs in the series or with *only the first* verb. So the requirements must be *to place, to win,* and *to finish,* OR *to place, win,* and *finish.* Only Choice (E) makes one of these corrections.

5. Children at the daycare spend their time either engaging in educational activities, such as math games and reading circles, or <u>they play with their</u> peers in a supervised setting.

(A) they play with their
(B) they will play with their
(C) they are playing with their
(D) to play with their
(E) playing with their

This sentence uses the coordinating conjunction *either..or.* Phrases following both *either* and *or* must be parallel. *Either* is followed by a present progressive verb and prepositional phrase (*engaging in educational activities*). *Or* is followed by a pronoun, simple present tense verb, and prepositional phrase (*they play with their peers*). It must be changed to a present progressive verb and prepositional phrase to match *either.* Choice (E) is correct.

6. The human resource department looked at an insurance program that would cover all vision-related procedures, including laser surgery, and <u>if employees paid out-of-pocket expenses they would be reimbursed</u>.

(A) if employees paid out-of-pocket expenses they would be reimbursed
(B) paying out-of-pocket expenses would be reimbursed
(C) reimburse employees who paid out-of-pocket expenses
(D) reimbursing employees paying out-of-pocket expenses
(E) employees to be reimbursed for paying out-of-pocket expenses

This sentence contains a clause with unparallel verbs. The correct form is *that X and Y.* The X (*would cover*) and Y (*if employees paid out-of-pocket expenses they would be reimbursed*) should be parallel, but the Y goes in a completely different direction. It can be corrected two ways: *would reimburse,* or just *reimburse.* Only (C) makes the correction.

Semicolons

A semicolon is used to join two closely-related independent clauses:

> The night before the SAT, Ken stayed up until midnight; he suspected this was the reason he did so poorly on the test.   [*Correct*]

Remember, an independent clause can stand alone as a sentence. Therefore, the clause on either side of the semicolon must be a complete sentence:

> The night before the SAT, Ken stayed up until midnight.
> He suspected this was the reason he did so poorly on the test.

Never use a semicolon with a dependent clause, as in the following:

> The night before the SAT, Ken stayed up until midnight; which is why he did so poorly on the test.   [*Incorrect*]

If the clause on either side of the semicolon cannot stand alone as a sentence, you cannot use a semicolon. *Which is why he did so poorly on the test* is a dependent clause, so the sentence is structurally flawed.

Semicolon errors on the GMAT occur when the one side of the semicolon is a dependent clause. To correct the error, you may be required to change the dependent clause into an independent clause, or you may remove the semicolon and use a subordinating conjunction instead.

> The worst pandemic in history, the bubonic plague swept through Eurasia during the 1300s and killed over 200 million; nearly one in three people. [*Incorrect*]

The portion after the semicolon (*nearly one in three people*) is not an independent clause and cannot stand alone as a sentence, as it is completely missing a verb. To correct the sentence, create an independent clause:

> The worst pandemic in history, the bubonic plague swept through Eurasia during the 1300s and killed over 200 million; *nearly one in three people died.*   [*Correct*]

Or, remove the semicolon by using a relative clause:

> The worst pandemic in history, the bubonic plague swept through Eurasia during the 1300s and killed over 200 million, *which was nearly one in three people.*   [*Correct*]

These errors are easy to spot; if you see a semicolon in a question on the GMAT, immediately check that the clauses on both sides of the semicolon are independent clauses.

Semicolons are the only punctuation tested on the GMAT.

Semicolon Problem Set

Please complete the problem set and review the answer key and explanations. *Answers on page 412.*

1. Despite the fact that it has a duck-shaped bill and lays eggs, the platypus is not a <u>bird; rather</u> the most unique mammal in Australia and quite possibly the world.

   (A) bird; rather
   (B) bird, but rather
   (C) bird; rather that of
   (D) bird; it is that of
   (E) bird, but that of

2. Barbra Steisand, whose career spans four decades, has received ten Grammy awards, including three for Best Female <u>Vocal; in 1964, 1965, and 1966</u>.

   (A) Vocal; in 1964, 1965, and 1966
   (B) Vocal, winning in 1964, 1965, and 1966
   (C) Vocal; occurring in 1964, 1965, and 1966
   (D) Vocal; a win in 1964, 1965, and 1966
   (E) Vocal; having won in 1964, 1965, and 1966

Semicolon Problem Set Answer Key

Correct answers are in bold.

1. Despite the fact that it has a duck-shaped bill and lays eggs, the platypus is not a <u>bird; rather</u> the most unique mammal in Australia and quite possibly the world.

    (A) bird; rather
    (B) bird, but rather
    (C) bird; rather that of
    (D) bird; it is that of
    (E) bird, but that of

The portion behind the semicolon is a dependent clause; it is completely lacking a verb (*rather the most unique mammal in Australia and quite possibly the world*). Only Choice (B) correctly joins the two clauses by subordinating the dependent clause with the subordinating conjunction *but*.

2. Barbra Steisand, whose career spans four decades, has received ten Grammy awards, including three for Best Female <u>Vocal; in 1964, 1965, and 1966</u>.

    (A) Vocal; in 1964, 1965, and 1966
    (B) Vocal, winning in 1964, 1965, and 1966
    (C) Vocal; occurring in 1964, 1965, and 1966
    (D) Vocal; a win in 1964, 1965, and 1966
    (E) Vocal; having won in 1964, 1965, and 1966

The portion behind the semicolon (*in 1964, 1965, and 1966*) is a prepositional phrase and cannot stand alone as a sentence. Choices (C), (D), and (E) all place a dependent clause after the semicolon. Only (B) creates a verb phrase that correctly modifies the subject.

Idioms

Traditionally, an idiom is an expression that does not make literal sense. To native speakers of American English, idioms are as natural as baseball and apple pie. To non-native speakers, however, idioms can sometimes pose problems. Look at the following idiom as an example.

Make up your mind!

Most people know that this means "*Decide!*," but for many foreign-born speakers of English, the expression can mean one of two things:

1. Put together your brain!
2. Apply cosmetics to your brain!

Idioms are everywhere:

Hold your horses; I'll be ready in a minute!
That comment was *below the belt* and you should apologize.
The toddler screamed *at the top of her lungs*.
The news of their engagement *came out of left field*.

Imagine what a person might picture when hearing the idioms above if he or she is unfamiliar with American idiom! Of course, America is not the only English-speaking country to create idioms. In New Zealand, you can be *off your oats* (meaning you've lost your appetite); in Australia, you can be *up a gum-tree* (meaning you're puzzled); and in Great Britain, you can be *in bulk* (meaning you're laughing).

Our language has all kind of quirks. *Slim* and *fat* are opposites, but *slim chance* and *fat chance* mean the same thing. You can fill *in* the blank while you fill *out* a form. Barns burn *down*, newspaper burns *up*, fog burns *off*, fires burn *out*, and meatloaf just burns. These idioms, however silly when broken down and analyzed, are Standard American English.

If *true* idioms such as these were used on the GMAT, the test might be a bit easier. But the term "idiom" has become a catch-all on standardized tests, used to refer to any expression or word combination that is accepted as Standard American English. So it should be no surprise, then, that a quarter of the sentences in *The Official Guide to GMAT Review* are guilty of idiom violations.

On the GMAT, faulty idiom can occur in all parts of speech. Smaller words, such as prepositions and conjunctions, are more prone to fall victim to faulty idiom, because the makers of the test are hoping you won't notice such a small mistake, especially when they put more difficult words in between.

One of the biggest Sentence Correction culprits—the erroneous idiom—often occurs because of the smallest words.

SC

Look at an example:

> During the Civil War, a fierce disagreement in Kentucky took place among those residents who supported the election of Abraham Lincoln with those who wanted to secede with Jefferson Davis.   [*Incorrect*]

The choice of *among* or *between* is often tested on the GMAT.

This sentence contains two idiom errors. The first is the use of *among. Among* is a preposition used to refer to relationships with three or more objects. The correct preposition is *between*, which cites a relationship between two objects. There are two groups of residents in the sentence, so *between* is a better preposition:

> During the Civil War, a fierce disagreement in Kentucky took place *between* those residents who supported the election of Abraham Lincoln with those who wanted to secede with Jefferson Davis.   [*Incorrect*]

One little preposition still causes this entire sentence to be ungrammatical, but you might not notice the error due to the words surrounding the idiom. When the modifiers are removed, the correct idiom is:

> *a disagreement between X <u>and</u> Y*

The conjunction *and* should be used to link the two nouns in disagreement. However, the current sentence uses the preposition *with* in the idiom*: a disagreement between X <u>with</u> Y*. To correct the sentence, substitute *and* for *with*:

> During the Civil War, a fierce disagreement in Kentucky took place *between* those residents who supported the election of Abraham Lincoln <u>*and*</u> those who wanted to secede with Jefferson Davis.   [*Correct*]

The faulty idiom might also occur in phrases:

> The number of volunteers at the Relay for Life increased by more than twice from 2002 to 2005.   [*Incorrect*]

The error should be easier to spot in this sentence. The idiom violation, *increased by more than twice*, should be replaced by *more than doubled*:

> The number of volunteers at the Relay for Life <u>*more than doubled*</u> from 2002 to 2005.   [*Correct*]

PowerScore has compiled a list of the most common idiom errors found in *The Official Guide to GMAT Review*. These errors and their corrections are presented in the chart on the following two pages.

SC

Unidiomatic Expression:	Correction:	Correct Idiom Form:
The problem developed *after when* the meeting was over.	The problem developed *after* the meeting was over.	verb + *after*
The teachers want a discipline plan *as strong or stronger than* the present policy.	The teachers want a discipline plan *as strong as* the present policy.	*X as strong as Y*
The students are *better served by* discipline *instead of by* leniency.	The students are *better served by* discipline *than by* leniency.	*better served by X than by Y*
There is an argument *between* those who want red *with* those who want blue.	There is an argument *between* those who want red *and* those who want blue.	*between X and Y*
It is best to train a dog *by* reward, *but not* punishment.	It is best to train a dog *by* reward, *rather than* punishment.	*by X rather than Y*
The *connection of* height *and* weight influences weight loss.	The *connection between* height *and* weight influences weight loss.	*connection between X and Y*
Adam *considers* education *to be* a part of the problem.	Adam *considers* education a part of the problem.	*considers X Y* (when considers means "regard as")
The doctor is *credited as* having cured polio.	The doctor is *credited with* having cured polio.	*credited with*
The newly-hatched butterfly's survival *depends on if* it can dry its wings by nightfall.	The newly-hatched butterfly's survival *depends on whether* it can dry its wings by nightfall.	*depends on whether*
The teams were *determined from* a random drawing.	The teams were *determined by* a random drawing.	*determined by* (when expressing cause)
Brett has *double as many* candy bars as Rob.	Brett has *twice as many* candy bars as Rob.	*twice as many*
I fell asleep *due to the fact that* I was tired.	I fell asleep *because* I was tired.	*because* (due to means attributable to)
Internal Affairs was created *for monitoring* conduct.	Internal Affairs was created *to monitor* conduct.	*to monitor* + noun
The number of volunteers *increased by more than twice*.	The number of volunteers *more than doubled*.	*more than doubled*
Heidi decided to eat *instead of* starving.	Heidi decided to eat *rather than* starve.	*rather than* (more formal)
The fight was caused by the *interaction where* two personalities collide.	The fight was caused by the *interaction of* two colliding personalities.	*interaction of*
The flower will continue <u>its growth</u> *into the coming* months.	The flower will continue <u>to grow</u> *in the coming* months.	*in the coming* + noun.
The final decision *is if* Jud deserves a raise.	The final decision *is whether* Jud deserves a raise.	*is whether*
School supplies, *like* paper and pencils, are provided.	School supplies, *such as* paper and pencils, are provided.	*such as* (to list examples)
Tasha is *maybe* the tallest person in our office.	Tasha is *probably* the tallest person in our office.	verb + *probably*
He *mistook* the Honda *as* a Toyota.	He *mistook* the Honda *for* a Toyota.	*mistook X for Y*
Hip problems are much *more common among* large dogs *than* smaller breeds.	Hip problems are much *more common among* large dogs *than among* smaller breeds.	*more common among X than among y*
Miranda spoke *more* openly *than never before*.	Miranda spoke *more* openly *than ever before*.	*more X than ever before*
The sweater is *not* made of wool; *rather* cotton.	The sweater is made *not* of wool, *but rather* of cotton.	*not X but rather Y*
Her guess *of there being* 112 marbles in the jar was wrong.	Her guess *that* 112 marbles were in the jar was wrong.	*that* (to begin relative clause)
Jupiter cannot be explored by man *on account of* it being made of gas.	Jupiter cannot be explored by man *because* it is made of gas.	*because X is Y*
Jupiter cannot be explored by man *because of* it being made of gas.	Jupiter cannot be explored by man *because* it is made of gas.	*because X is Y*
I *question if* Chris is telling the truth.	I *question whether* Chris is telling the truth.	*question whether*
The *raising of costs* of automobile ownership has convinced me to continue riding my bike.	The *rising cost* of automobile ownership has convinced me to continue riding my bike.	*rising cost*
Dave's music ranges from classical sounds that belong to another era *and* modern beats heard in nightclubs.	Dave's music ranges from classical sounds that belong to another era *to* modern beats heard in nightclubs.	*ranges from X to Y*

Unidiomatic Expression:	Correction:	Correct Idiom Form:
The camp has passed a rule *requiring* the uncertified counselors *should* complete CPR training.	The camp has passed a rule *requiring* the uncertified counselors *to* complete CPR training.	*requiring X to Y* OR *requiring that X Y*
The *rivalry between* the Boston Red Sox *with* the New York Yankees is most prominent in October.	The *rivalry between* the Boston Red Sox *and* the New York Yankees is most prominent in October.	*rivalry between X and Y*
The power is *shifting from* the employer *with* the employee.	The power is *shifting from* the employer *to* the employee.	*shifting from X to Y*
The more you practice typing, your skill becomes *greater*.	*The more* you practice typing, *the greater* your skill becomes.	*the more X, the greater Y*
I do not *think of* the tomato *to be* a fruit.	I do not *think of* the tomato *as* a fruit.	*think of X as Y*
The teacher *was influential on* James.	The teacher *was an influence on* James.	*was an influence on*
While being a medical student, she performed her first surgery.	As a medical student, she performed her first surgery.	*as* (to introduce a phrase)
The bar *requires that* patrons *are* over eighteen years of age.	The bar *requires that* patrons *be* over eighteen years of age.	*requires that X be Y*
Dr. Watts is *worried over* the cat's recovery.	Dr. Watts is *worried about* the cat's recovery.	*worried about*
The object floated when we *expected for* it to sink.	The object floated when we *expected* it to sink.	*X is expected to Y*
The company *prohibits* sales representatives *to* make unsolicited calls.	The company *prohibits* sales representatives *from* making unsolicited calls.	*X prohibits Y from doing Z*

This chart represents the idiom errors that occur most frequently in *The Official Guide to GMAT Review*. Please see the appendix for an additional list of other idiomatic expressions.

Remember, idiom errors are in a quarter of the questions from the book. It is imperative to memorize the correct idiom formats from the previous chart, as well as look for additional idiom error in each question on the GMAT.

Idiom Problem Set

Please complete the problem set and review the answer key and explanations. *Answers on page 418.*

1. <u>Perched atop</u> a high mountain ridge in the Andes, the Incan city of Machu Picchu is believed to have served as a country retreat for Incan nobility.

   (A) Perched atop
   (B) Perched high atop
   (C) Perched on top
   (D) Perched on
   (E) Perched above

2. Jacobs Field, completed in Cleveland in 1994, did much <u>to raise the energy and revive</u> a worn-down city formally referred to as "the mistake by the lake."

   (A) to raise the energy and revive
   (B) to raise the energy of a worn down city and revive
   (C) to raise the energy and to revive
   (D) in reviving and raising the energy of
   (E) to revive and raise the energy of

3. During a divorce, children are often <u>viewed like bargaining chips; it is important</u> for parents to remember that a child's well-being must be considered separately from the division of property.

   (A) viewed like bargaining chips; it is important
   (B) viewed as bargaining chips; it is important
   (C) viewed to be bargaining chips; it is important
   (D) viewed like bargaining chips, and it is important
   (E) viewed like bargaining chips, so it is important

4. Upon his death, it was discovered that Secretariat's heart <u>was bigger by three times the size of an average horse</u>, which many believe to be the reason for the stallion's stunning speed.

   (A) was bigger by three times the size of an average horse
   (B) was three times the size bigger of an average horse
   (C) was three times the size larger of an average horse's heart
   (D) was three times the size of an average horse's heart
   (E) was three times as large as an average horse

5. A recent study indicates that more and more college graduates are opting <u>to rent a home or apartment instead of</u> to buy real estate—a trend fueled by rising market costs and new spending habits.

   (A) to rent a home or apartment instead of
   (B) to rent a home or apartment rather than
   (C) to rent a home or apartment opposed to
   (D) renting a home or apartment instead of
   (E) renting a home or apartment instead of choosing

6. Spam, the unsolicited e-mails that litter inboxes across the world, <u>is estimated at 90% of all internet traffic</u> in the United States today.

   (A) is estimated at 90% of all internet traffic
   (B) is estimated for 90% of all internet traffic
   (C) is estimated to be 90% of all internet traffic
   (D) is estimated at 90% in all internet traffic
   (E) is estimated as 90% of all internet traffic

Idiom Problem Set Answer Key

Correct answers are in bold.

1. <u>Perched atop</u> a high mountain ridge in the Andes, the Incan city of Machu Picchu is believed to have served as a country retreat for Incan nobility.

    (A) Perched atop
    (B) Perched high atop
    (C) Perched on top
    (D) Perched on
    (E) Perched above

Perched atop is correct idiom. Choice (A) is correct. While Choice (B) also uses *atop*, it adds a second *high* to the introductory phrase which changes the meaning of the original sentence.

2. Jacobs Field, completed in Cleveland in 1994, did much <u>to raise the energy and revive</u> a worn-down city formally referred to as "the mistake by the lake."

    (A) to raise the energy and revive
    (B) to raise the energy of a word down city and revive
    (C) to raise the energy and to revive
    (D) in reviving and raising the energy of
    (E) to revive and raise the energy of

The correct idiom is *to raise the X of Y*. Without the preposition *of*, the idiom no longer makes sense. Choice (E) correctly states *to raise the energy of*, and puts the phrase closer to the object of the preposition so that it does not get lost in a lengthy sentence.

3. During a divorce, children are often <u>viewed like bargaining chips; it is important</u> for parents to remember that a child's well-being must be considered separately from the division of property.

    (A) viewed like bargaining chips; it is important
    (B) viewed as bargaining chips; it is important
    (C) viewed to be bargaining chips; it is important
    (D) viewed like bargaining chips, and it is important
    (E) viewed like bargaining chips, so it is important

The correct idiom is *viewed as*. The current sentence incorrectly uses *viewed like*. Choice (B) uses the correct idiom. The semicolon is correctly used in the sentence, so Choices (D) and (E) are incorrect.

4. Upon his death, it was discovered that Secretariat's heart <u>was bigger by three times the size of an average horse</u>, which many believe to be the reason for the stallion's stunning speed.

    (A) was bigger by three times the size of an average horse
    (B) was three times the size bigger of an average horse
    (C) was three times the size larger of an average horse's heart
    (D) was three times the size of an average horse's heart
    (E) was three times as large as an average horse

The correct idiom is *X is three times the size of Y* or *X is three times as large as Y*. Both (B) and (C) can be eliminated as they do not follow this format. Choice (E) is incorrect due to an illogical comparison; it compares Secretariat's heart to the average horse, rather than to the average horse's heart. Choice (D) is correct.

5. A recent study indicates that more and more college graduates are opting <u>to rent a home or apartment instead of</u> to buy real estate—a trend fueled by rising market costs and new spending habits.

    (A) to rent a home or apartment instead of
    (B) to rent a home or apartment rather than
    (C) to rent a home or apartment opposed to
    (D) renting a home or apartment instead of
    (E) renting a home or apartment instead of choosing

The preferred idiom when discussing choice is *to X rather than to Y*. The current sentence incorrectly uses *instead of*: *to X instead of to Y*. Choices (D) and (E) incorrectly change verb forms, and Choice (C) uses the faulty idiom *to X opposed to Y*.

6. Spam, the unsolicited e-mails that litter inboxes across the world, <u>is estimated at 90% of all internet traffic</u> in the United States today.

    (A) is estimated at 90% of all internet traffic
    (B) is estimated for 90% of all internet traffic
    (C) is estimated to be 90% of all internet traffic
    (D) is estimated at 90% in all internet traffic
    (E) is estimated as 90% of all internet traffic

The correct idiom is *estimated to be*. Only (C) makes this correction. All other answer choices contain incorrect idiom.

SC

420

CHAPTER TWENTY: ERRORS INVOLVING STYLE

Wordy Language ▊▊▊▊▊▊▊▊▊▊▊▊▊▊

There is a common misconception among many students and even some professionals that a longer, more verbose sentence creates a more formal, eloquent essay. But long-winded sentences lead to overworked readers, who often lose the meaning of the sentence in the sea of meaningless words. Sentences such as these are dismissed by English teachers as "wordy." Concise sentences are preferred, meaning that much is expressed in few words. On the GMAT, you will encounter wordy sentences in which you must choose a concise correction.

There are two types of wordiness to avoid on the GMAT. The first type is wordy expressions, which are common in everyday speech. Look at an example:

> Regardless of the fact that Jay Gatsby had become a millionaire, it is obvious that his sense of accomplishment was not fulfilled until the day that he was able to win Daisy's heart.   [*Incorrect*]

There are three very wordy expressions in this sentence; *regardless of the fact, it is obvious that,* and *until the day he was able to win*. These phrases can be removed or shortened in order to create a more concise sentence:

> <u>Although</u> Jay Gatsby had become a millionaire, his sense of accomplishment was not fulfilled <u>until</u> he <u>won</u> Daisy's heart.   [*Correct*]

Although shorter, this sentence is stronger, more vivid, and more direct than its wordy predecessor.

Examine some examples of common wordy expressions and their concise corrections. A much more detailed list of wordy expressions is available in the appendix.

Wordy Expression	*Concise Correction*
after the conclusion of	after
at this point in time	now
despite the fact that	although, even though, despite
due to the fact that	because, because of, since, for, as
excessive number of	too many
in order to	to
in the event that	if
is in a position to	can
regardless of the fact that	although, despite

Your analytical writing assignment must also avoid wordiness and redundancy.

SC

While the wordy expressions in the chart are common errors in everyday speech, some wordiness is created by the context of the sentence. The author may use a pronoun and a second verb when a compound verb would have sufficed. Or there may be a prepositional phrase modifying a noun, when a one-word adjective might have accomplished the same feat. Try an example:

Many border collies, intelligent working dogs used on ranches, have been known to herd cattle without their being trained.   [*Incorrect*]

This sentence adds an unnecessary pronoun: *their*. In fact, the pronoun adds ambiguity and awkwardness, causing the reader to briefly wonder if the *cattle* were untrained. But upon a second reading, it is evident that the prepositional phrases at the end of the sentence refer to border collies. Remove the wordy *their* and the sentence is less awkward and more concise:

Many border collies, intelligent working dogs used on ranches, have been known to herd cattle without being trained.   [*Correct*]

Be wary of an unnecessary repeated subject on a Sentence Correction question. A subject need only appear one time in a clause:

Upon reaching the crocodile-filled river, the gazelles, which are a type of antelope, they swim across in a large herd to increase their group survival rate.   [*Incorrect*]

The subject of this sentence is *gazelles*, which is stated just after the introductory phrase (*upon reaching the crocodile-filled river*). A relative clause (*which are a type of antelope*) follows the subject. Remember, relative clauses add modifying information, but can be removed without ruining the sentence. If we take this relative clause away, the error is much more obvious:

Upon reaching the crocodile-filled river, the *gazelles they* swim across in a large herd to increase their group survival rate.

This sentence has unnecessarily repeated the subject after a relative clause.

To correct the sentence, simply remove the second subject, *they*:

Upon reaching the crocodile-filled river, the gazelles, which are a type of antelope, swim across in a large herd to increase their group survival rate. [*Correct*]

Because wordiness is often more of an offense in style rather than an outright error in grammar, it is commonly a secondary correction on the GMAT. A sentence will likely contain a blatant error in grammar, such as in subject verb agreement or verb tense, with two answer choices that correct the major error. However, only one of those answer choices will present a concise correction for the bout of wordiness.

SC

Look at an example:

Researchers have proven that eating broccoli helps <u>in the prevention of cancer due to the fact that they contain</u> multiple cancer-fighting chemicals.

(A) in the prevention of cancer due to the fact that they contain
(B) in the prevention of cancer since they contain
(C) prevent cancer due to the fact that they are containing
(D) in the prevention of cancer due to the fact that it contains
(E) prevent cancer because it contains

The main error in this sentence is that the pronoun _they_ does not agree with its antecedent _broccoli_. Choices (D) and (E) change _they_ to _it_, correcting the most prominent error. However, the sentence contains two secondary errors involving wordiness; _in the prevention of_ can be economically written as _prevent_, and _due to the fact that_ is a wordy expression that can be replaced with _because_. Only choice (E) corrects the main pronoun antecedent agreement error while also correcting the wordy language.

Expect to see wordiness errors in a large number of the questions in _The Official Guide to GMAT Review_.

Redundant Expressions

A subcategory of wordiness is redundancy, in which unnecessary repetition detracts from a sentence. One type of redundant phrase occurs when a word is used to modify another word that is defined by the first word. Take the example "terrible disaster." Isn't a disaster by definition _terrible_? You don't hear of fantastic disasters, or pretty good disasters, or even mediocre disasters. They are all terrible! So it would be a terrible mistake to allow this redundant expression to go uncorrected on the GMAT. Beware of these other redundant expressions:

advance planning	meet together
all year round	necessary requirement
annually each year	new breakthrough
biography of his life	past history
close proximity	postpone until later
customary habit	protest against
end result	reduced down
essential requirement	repeat again
exactly identical	reverse back
forward progress	rising increase
free gift	sharing the same
group together	temporary loan
honest truth	usual habit
joint cooperation	wealthy millionaire

Unfortunately, redundant expressions will not always be situated next to each other in a GMAT sentence:

The plummeting attendance figures have fallen so low that the owner closed the speedway.   [*Incorrect*]

In this sentence, the word *plummeting* has already established that the figures have *fallen* and are *low*, so it is redundant to mention this again. The sentence must be edited:

The plummeting attendance figures caused the owner to close the speedway.   [*Correct*]

Finally, beware of conjunctions becoming redundant. Certain conjunctions correlate and are meant to work together, like *not only..but also* and *both..and*. However, when these are not correctly matched and they are used with another conjunction, such as *and, as well as*, and *and also*, it creates a redundant expression:

Studies of several successful entrepreneurs have shown that they all share two common characteristics; they are both motivated by an overwhelming need for achievement as well as driven by desire for independence. [*Incorrect*]

As a coordinating conjunction, *both* should always be accompanied by *and*. However, in this sentence, *as well as* takes the place of *and*, and the conjunctions become redundant. A sentence does not need *both* and *as well as* to express the presence of two items. Correct the sentence with *and*:

Studies of several successful entrepreneurs have shown that they all share two common characteristics; they are *both* motivated by an overwhelming need for achievement *and* driven by desire for independence.   [*Correct*]

Redundancy occurs a small portion of the sentences in *The Official Guide to GMAT Review*.

Wordy Language and Redundant Expressions Problem Set

Please complete the problem set and review the answer key and explanations. *Answers on page 426.*

1. With the advent of MP3 players, researchers believe that the Compact Disc <u>may in the very near future face the same fate as the long-playing record</u>.

    (A) may in the very near future face the same fate as the long-playing record
    (B) might face in the very near future the same fate as the long-playing record
    (C) might in the very near future face the same fate as the long-playing record
    (D) may soon face the same fate as the long-playing record
    (E) in near future may face the same fate as the long-playing record

2. <u>As history has revealed, a sudden irrational panic among stockholders has caused the Dow Jones Industrial Average to plummet in the past.</u>

    (A) As history has revealed, a sudden irrational panic among stockholders has caused the Dow Jones Industrial Average to plummet in the past
    (B) A sudden irrational panic among stockholders has caused the Dow Jones Industrial Average to plummet in the past, as revealed by history
    (C) A sudden irrational panic among stockholders can cause the Dow Jones Industrial Average to plummet in the past
    (D) As history has revealed, a sudden irrational panic can cause the Dow Jones Industrial Average stockholders to plummet in the past
    (E) As history has revealed, a sudden irrational panic among stockholders can cause the Dow Jones Industrial Average to plummet

3. The Coast Guard believes that the crew of the Edmund Fitzgerald was unaware that the boat was taking on water, not only because of their last radio transmission, but also <u>because of the lack of a distress signal, too</u>.

    (A) because of the lack of a distress signal, too
    (B) because of the lack of a distress signal
    (C) because the distress signal was lacking, too
    (D) the lack of a distress signal, too
    (E) due to the lack of a distress signal, too

Wordy Language and Redundant Expressions Problem Set Answer Key

Correct answers are in bold.

1. With the advent of MP3 players, researchers believe that the Compact Disc <u>may in the very near future face the same fate as the long playing record</u>.

   (A) may in the very near future face the same fate as the long-playing record
   (B) might face in the very near future the same fate as the long-playing record
   (C) might in the very near future face the same fate as the long-playing record
   (D) may soon face the same fate as the long-playing record
   (E) in near future may face the same fate as the long-playing record

The wordy expression in this sentence is *in the very near future*. The most economical version of this phrase is *soon*, as seen in Choice (D).

2. <u>As history has revealed, a sudden irrational panic among stockholders has caused the Dow Jones Industrial Average to plummet in the past</u>.

   (A) As history has revealed, a sudden irrational panic among stockholders has caused the Dow Jones Industrial Average to plummet in the past
   (B) A sudden irrational panic among stockholders has caused the Dow Jones Industrial Average to plummet in the past, as revealed by history
   (C) A sudden irrational panic among stockholders can cause the Dow Jones Industrial Average to plummet in the past
   (D) As history has revealed, a sudden irrational panic can cause the Dow Jones Industrial Average stockholders to plummet in the past
   (E) As history has revealed, a sudden irrational panic among stockholders can cause the Dow Jones Industrial Average to plummet

The sentence has a redundancy issue. The introductory clause, *as history has revealed*, shows that the event took place in the past. Therefore, *in the past* is redundant anywhere else in the sentence. This eliminates Choices (A), (B), and (D). Choice (C) has a verb tense problem. *Can cause* does not agree with *in the past*. However, the same verb in the correct answer choice, (E) shows that the panic has happened in the past and can happen again in the future.

3. The Coast Guard believes that the crew of the Edmund Fitzgerald was unaware that the boat was taking on water, not only because of their last radio transmission, but also <u>because of the lack of a distress signal, too</u>.

   (A) because of the lack of a distress signal, too
   (B) because of the lack of a distress signal
   (C) because the distress signal was lacking, too
   (D) the lack of a distress signal, too
   (E) due to the lack of a distress signal, too

This sentence also has a redundant expression. Because it is already using *also*, *too* is redundant. Only Choice (B) removes *too*, making it the correct answer choice. Choice (C) is awkward and unparallel. Choice (D) is unparallel without *because*. Choice (E) is wordy.

Chapter Twenty-one: Multiple Errors

Double and Triple Errors

There are often multiple errors in a sentence on the GMAT. Sentences with two errors occur in nearly one-third of the questions in *The Official Guide to GMAT Review*. Triple error sentences occur less frequently, but you are still likely to encounter one or two on your test.

As we saw in the sections on passive voice and wordiness, sentences with multiple errors often have a blatant main error that is easily identified and a secondary error that might be much harder to spot. It is extremely important to read all of the answer choices; Choice (B) or (C) might correct the main error, but fail to address the secondary issue. You might not even realize that there is a second error until you read Choices (D) and (E). Let's look at an example:

> During the charity walk-a-thon, the number of miles walked by the fifteen volunteers were combined to total 110 miles, a distance that is about Long Island's length.

(A) were combined to total 110 miles, a distance that is about Long Island's length
(B) were combined to total 110 miles, a distance about the length of Long Island
(C) was combined to total 110 miles, a distance that is about Long Island's length
(D) was combined to total 110 miles, about Long Island's length
(E) was combined to total 110 miles, a distance about the length of Long Island

The major error in this sentence involves subject verb agreement. The subject, *number*, is singular, but the verb, *were*, is plural. We can eliminate Choices (A) and (B) because they do not correct this major error. Choice (C) changes the plural *were* to the singular *was*, and leaves the rest of the sentence as is. Many hasty test takers would choose (C) and move on to the next sentence. You must approach the GMAT much more cautiously! Choice (D) and (E) also change *were* to *was*, so you should examine each of these answers to see if any other corrections are made to the sentence. Choice (D) removed *a distance*, causing the sentence to become less clear and leaving *about* without a definite noun to modify. You can eliminate (D). Choice (E) has removed the wordy relative clause *that is* without ruining the meaning of the sentence. Choice (C) failed to do this. Choice (E) also uses a noun and prepositional phrase to discuss the length of Long Island, and this removes the bit of awkwardness that existed with the possessive formation *Long Island's length*. Choice (E) is best.

Although we eliminated choice (B) immediately, notice that it removed the wordy *that is* and reworded the awkward possessive. It corrected the minor errors, but ignored the main error. Choice (C) corrected the blatant error, but did not fix the flaw in style. Again, it is imperative to read each answer choice before making your selection!

Sentences with two or more errors appear in nearly one-third of Sentence Completion questions.

After Choice (A), be sure to read all of the remaining answer choices! In sentences with multiple errors, some choices will trick test takers by only correcting one of the errors.

SC

Other sentences will have double or triple errors that are equally destructive in their grammatical downfalls. For example, a sentence might have an obvious error in pronoun agreement coupled with an equally blatant error in parallel structure. Whether a sentence has multiple secondary mistakes or multiple obvious errors, it will likely have misleading answer choices that only correct one of the errors rather than both. This is why it is imperative to read each answer choice before moving on; you may find one selection further down the list that has the same correction you just chose for one error, but goes one step further to correct another problem with the sentence.

The following practice set will not only test your ability to find multiple errors, but also your knowledge of all of the grammatical errors and usage flaws discussed in this portion of the book. Good luck!

Double and Triple Errors Problem Set

Please complete the problem set and review the answer key and explanations. *Answers on page 431.*

1. After the announcement that London would host the 2012 Olympics, the Olympic Committee revealed that Paris had <u>been in competition with London much longer than Madrid</u>.

   (A) been in competition with London much longer than Madrid
   (B) competed with London much longer than Madrid
   (C) been in competition with London much longer than had Madrid
   (D) competed with London much longer than had Madrid
   (E) been in competition much longer with London than Madrid

2. The manager believed that the sales contest was responsible for a reduction in absenteeism, <u>increase in customer satisfaction as well as an increase in employee morale</u>, and a boost in profits.

   (A) increase in customer satisfaction as well as an increase in employee morale
   (B) an increase in customer satisfaction and in employee morale
   (C) an increase in customer satisfaction along with employee morale
   (D) customer satisfaction increasing, along with employee morale
   (E) customer satisfaction and employee morale being increased

3. In ancient Greece, a male member of the Spartan society did not become a full citizen <u>until when the age of thirty was reached</u>, at which point he had already given ten years of military service.

   (A) until when the age of thirty was reached
   (B) until the age of thirty was reached
   (C) until he reached the age of thirty
   (D) when the age of thirty was reached
   (E) until when he reached the age of thirty

4. In Aztec society, childbirth was compared to warfare, and women <u>who died in labor were honored in the same way as men who died in battle</u>.

   (A) who died in labor were honored in the same way as men who died in battle
   (B) whom died in labor were honored just as men whom died in battle
   (C) whom died in labor were honored in the same way as men whom died in battle
   (D) who died in labor were honored just as men who died in battle
   (E) in labor who died were honored in the same way as men in battle who died

5. Of all the musicians who attended Juilliard School, Yo-Yo Ma <u>is maybe the more prolific and definitely the most celebrated cellist, in large part due to his wide-ranging</u> repertoire.

   (A) is maybe the more prolific and definitely the most celebrated cellist, in large part due to his wide-ranging
   (B) is maybe the most prolific and definitely the most celebrated cellist, in large part due to his wide-ranging
   (C) is probably the most prolific and definitely the most celebrated cellist, in large part due to his wide-ranging
   (D) is probably the more prolific and definitely the most celebrated cellist, in large part because of his wide-ranging
   (E) is maybe the most prolific and definitely the most celebrated cellist, in large part because of his wide-ranging

6. Unlike most other crustaceans, such as lobsters, crabs, and barnacles, <u>dry land provides a terrestrial habitat for the woodlouse</u>.

   (A) dry land provides a terrestrial habitat for the woodlouse
   (B) a terrestrial habitat is the home of a woodlouse
   (C) woodlice live in a terrestrial habitat
   (D) dry land provides a terrestrial habitat for woodlice
   (E) the woodlouse lives in a dry, terrestrial habitat

Double and Triple Errors Problem Set

Please complete the problem set and review the answer key and explanations. *Answers on page 217-224.*

7. Since 2000, the number of registered lobbyists in Washington, D.C. <u>have grown by more than twice, due to the government growing rapidly</u> and the single party control of the executive and legislative branches.

   (A) have grown by more than twice, due to the government growing rapidly
   (B) has more than doubled, due to the government growing rapidly
   (C) has grown by more than twice, due to the rapid growth of government
   (D) have increased by twice as much, due to the government rapidly growing
   (E) has more than doubled, due to the rapidly growing government

8. Published in 1892, <u>Charlotte Gilman Perkins tells the story of a woman's descent in madness when she is confined to a room</u> by her dictatorial husband in *The Yellow Wallpaper*.

   (A) Charlotte Gilman Perkins tells the story of a woman's descent in madness when she is confined to a room by her dictatorial husband in *The Yellow Wallpaper*
   (B) *The Yellow Wallpaper*, by Charlotte Gilman Perkins, describes a woman's descent into madness when she is confined to a room by her dictatorial husband
   (C) Charlotte Gilman Perkins' *The Yellow Wallpaper* tells the story of a woman's descent in madness when she is confined to a room by her dictatorial husband
   (D) a woman's descent in madness when she is confined to a room by her dictatorial husband is told by Charlotte Gilman Perkins in *The Yellow Wallpaper*
   (E) *The Yellow Wallpaper* tells of a woman's descent into madness when she is confined to a room by her dictatorial husband, a story by Charlotte Gilman Perkins.

9. By a vote of 98 to 1, the United States Senate enacted the USA Patriot Act, <u>which grants law enforcement officials greater authority in investigating suspected terrorists</u>.

   (A) which grants law enforcement officials greater authority in investigating suspected terrorists
   (B) that grants law enforcement officials greater authority to investigate suspected terrorists
   (C) granting law enforcement officials greater authority with investigating suspected terrorists
   (D) which will grant law enforcement officials greater authority for suspected terrorists investigations
   (E) having granted law enforcement officials greater authority for investigating suspected terrorists

10. Of the dozen hybrid automobiles tested, three of the models that used battery power <u>for the conservation of gasoline went over 250 miles per gallon.</u>

   (A) for the conservation of gasoline went over 250 miles per gallon
   (B) for the conservation of gasoline had 250 miles per gallon
   (C) to conserve gasoline got over 250 miles per gallon
   (D) to conserve gasoline went at 250 miles per gallon
   (E) for conserving gasoline went over 250 miles per gallon

Double and Triple Errors Problem Set Answer Key

Correct answers are in bold.

1. After the announcement that London would host the 2012 Olympics, the Olympic Committee revealed that Paris had <u>been in competition with London much longer than Madrid</u>.

    (A) been in competition with London much longer than Madrid
    (B) competed with London much longer than Madrid
    (C) been in competition with London much longer than had Madrid
    (D) competed with London much longer than had Madrid
    (E) been in competition much longer with London than Madrid

The comparison in the sentence is incomplete. Right now, both *with* and *had* can follow *longer than*, so the comparison is incomplete. You do not know whether Paris had competed with London much longer than Paris had competed with Madrid, or whether Paris had competed with London longer than Madrid had completed with London. Choices (A), (B), and (E) are therefore wrong. Choices (C) and (D) let us know that it is the latter (Paris had competed with London longer than Madrid had competed with London), but Choice (D) corrects the wordy phrase *been in competition with*. Choice (D) is correct.

2. The manager believed that the sales contest was responsible for a reduction in absenteeism, <u>increase in customer satisfaction as well as an increase in employee morale</u>, and a boost in profits.

    (A) increase in customer satisfaction as well as an increase in employee morale
    (B) an increase in customer satisfaction and in employee morale
    (C) an increase in customer satisfaction along with employee morale
    (D) customer satisfaction increasing, along with employee morale
    (E) customer satisfaction and employee morale being increased

The main error is a lack of parallelism between three noun phrases in a series *(a reduction in, increase in, and a boost in). An* must be added before the second noun phrase (*increase in*) not only to make the series parallel, but also to signify that *increase* is a noun rather than a verb. We can eliminate choices (A), (D), and (E) based on this analysis. The secondary error is one of wordiness and redundancy. *As well as* is wordy, and the use of *increase* twice is redundant. Choice (C) uses *along with*, which is wordy and unidiomatic. Choice (B) is best.

3. In ancient Greece, a male member of the Spartan society did not become a full citizen <u>until when the age of thirty was reached</u>, at which point he had already given ten years of military service.

    (A) until when the age of thirty was reached
    (B) until the age of thirty was reached
    (C) until he reached the age of thirty
    (D) when the age of thirty was reached
    (E) until when he reached the age of thirty

The most blatant error in the sentence is the unidiomatic phrase *until when*. It should strictly be *until*, eliminating (D) and (E). The other error in the sentence is the use of the passive voice—*the age of thirty was reached [by him]*. The active voice—*he reached the age of thirty*—must be used to match the active voice in the final clause (*he had already given*). Choice (C) makes this second correction.

4. In Aztec society, childbirth was compared to warfare, and women <u>who died in labor were honored in the same way as men who died in battle</u>.

    (A) who died in labor were honored in the same way as men who died in battle
    (B) whom died in labor were honored just as men whom died in battle
    (C) whom died in labor were honored in the same way as men whom died in battle
    (D) who died in labor were honored just as men who died in battle
    (E) in labor who died were honored in the same way as men in battle who died

The sentence is grammatically correct. Choices (B) and (C) incorrectly use *whom*. Choices (B) and (D) incorrectly use *just*—an incomplete comparison is created without *in the same way as*. And Choice (E) is an awkward nightmare.

5. Of all the musicians who attended Juilliard School, Yo-Yo Ma <u>is maybe the more prolific and definitely the most celebrated cellist, in large part due to his wide-ranging</u> repertoire.

    (A) is maybe the more prolific and definitely the most celebrated cellist, in large part due to his wide-ranging
    (B) is maybe the most prolific and definitely the most celebrated cellist, in large part due to his wide-ranging
    (C) is probably the most prolific and definitely the most celebrated cellist, in large part due to his wide-ranging
    (D) is probably the more prolific and definitely the most celebrated cellist, in large part because of his wide-ranging
    (E) is maybe the most prolific and definitely the most celebrated cellist, in large part because of his wide-ranging

The most flagrant error is the incorrect use of comparative degree. Yo-Yo Ma is being compared to all of the musicians who attended Juilliard, and the use of the word *all* indicates that more than two attended. This is verified by the use of *most* in the second part of the phrase. Therefore, *more prolific* must be *most prolific*. Choices (A) and (D) are eliminated. The other error is the unidiomatic use of *maybe*. The correct word is *probably*. This eliminates (B) and (E), leaving (C) as the best choice.

6. Unlike most other crustaceans, such as lobsters, crabs, and barnacles, <u>dry land provides a terrestrial habitat for the woodlouse</u>.

    (A) dry land provides a terrestrial habitat for the woodlouse
    (B) a terrestrial habitat is the home of a woodlouse
    (C) woodlice live in a terrestrial habitat
    (D) dry land provides a terrestrial habitat for woodlice
    (E) the woodlouse lives in a dry, terrestrial habitat

This sentence contains three errors. The most prominent error is the misplaced modifier in the introductory clause. Currently, *crustaceans* are compared to *dry land*. In order for the woodlouse to be compared to crustaceans, it must appear after the clause. Choices (A), (B), and (D) can be removed. The sentence also has a noun agreement error. *Crustaceans* is plural, but *woodlouse* is singular. The correct noun is *woodlice*. Finally, *dry land* and *terrestrial habitat* are redundant. Only one is needed. Choice (C) makes all three corrections.

7. Since 2000, the number of registered lobbyists in Washington, D.C. <u>have grown by more than twice,</u> <u>due to the government growing rapidly</u> and the single party control of the executive and legislative branches.

    (A) have grown by more than twice, due to the government growing rapidly
    (B) has more than doubled, due to the government growing rapidly
    (C) has grown by more than twice, due to the rapid growth of government
    (D) have increased by twice as much, due to the government rapidly growing
    (E) has more than doubled, due to the rapidly growing government

This sentence has three errors. The first is an error of subject verb agreement. The subject is *number* (not *lobbyists*), so the verb *have* does not agree. The correct verb is *has*, eliminating Choices (A) and (D). The second error is an unidiomatic expression. *Grown by more that twice* is incorrect idiom. The correct phrase is *more than doubled*. This eliminates Choice (C). The final error is in parallel structure. The correct format is *due to X and Y*, where X and Y are parallel. In the current sentence, the X consists of a noun and verb, while the Y consists of just a noun. Only Choice (E) takes care of the prior issues and makes X and Y parallel with two nouns (*government* and *control*).

8. Published in 1892, <u>Charlotte Gilman Perkins tells the story of a woman's descent in madness when</u> <u>she is confined to a room by her dictatorial husband in *The Yellow Wallpaper*.</u>

    (A) Charlotte Gilman Perkins tells the story of a woman's descent in madness when she is confined to a room by her dictatorial husband in *The Yellow Wallpaper*
    (B) *The Yellow Wallpaper*, by Charlotte Gilman Perkins, describes a woman's descent into madness when she is confined to a room by her dictatorial husband
    (C) Charlotte Gilman Perkins' *The Yellow Wallpaper* tells the story of a woman's descent in madness when she is confined to a room by her dictatorial husband
    (D) a woman's descent in madness when she is confined to a room by her dictatorial husband is told by Charlotte Gilman Perkins in *The Yellow Wallpaper*
    (E) *The Yellow Wallpaper* tells of a woman's descent into madness when she is confined to a room by her dictatorial husband, a story by Charlotte Gilman Perkins.

As the sentence is written now, *published in 1892* incorrectly modifies *Charlotte Gilman Perkins*, and people are not published! Choices (B), (C), and (E) make a correction that modifies the story, rather than the person, thus eliminating (A) and (D). Also, there is an idiom error with *descent*; the correct form is *descent into X*. Choices (B) and (E) make this correction. However, Choice (E) is awkward and has misplaced the modifying phrase *a story by Charlotte Gilman Perkins*. Choice (B) is best.

9. By a vote of 98 to 1, the United States Senate enacted the USA Patriot Act, <u>which grants law enforcement officials greater authority in investigating suspected terrorists</u>.

(A) **which grants law enforcement officials greater authority in investigating suspected terrorists**

(B) that grants law enforcement officials greater authority to investigate suspected terrorists

(C) granting law enforcement officials greater authority with investigating suspected terrorists

(D) which will grant law enforcement officials greater authority for suspected terrorists investigations

(E) having granted law enforcement officials greater authority for investigating suspected terrorists

The sentence is correct. Choice (B) incorrectly uses *that* to introduce a clause. Choice (C) used the unidiomatic *authority with*. Choice (D) is awkward and unidiomatic, and uses a future tense verb for something that is occurring in the present. Choice (E) improperly uses a progressive form of *to grant* and is unidiomatic.

10. Of the dozen hybrid automobiles tested, three of the models that used battery power <u>for the conservation of gasoline went over 250 miles per gallon.</u>

(A) for the conservation of gasoline went over 250 miles per gallon

(B) for the conservation of gasoline had 250 miles per gallon

(C) **to conserve gasoline got over 250 miles per gallon**

(D) to conserve gasoline went at 250 miles per gallon

(E) for conserving gasoline went over 250 miles per gallon

The sentence is wordy and unidiomatic. The infinitive form of the verb *to conserve* is much more concise and less awkward than the wordy *for the conservation of gasoline. Went over* would be correct idiom if we were measuring how far the cars traveled (*went over 250 miles*), but is incorrect when used with gas mileage. The correct idiom is *got over 250 miles per gallon*. Only Choice (C) makes these two corrections.

CHAPTER TWENTY-TWO: SENTENCE CORRECTION STRATEGIES

Now that you are armed with the grammatical concepts covered on the GMAT, it is time to learn some strategies for attacking Sentence Correction questions. Your new knowledge of grammar may help you quickly locate sentence errors, but the following strategies can add to your problem-solving ability, as well as assist you with errors that are not immediately evident.

Look for Error Indicators

Throughout the Sentence Correction portion of this book, PowerScore has featured certain words, phrases, or grammatical patterns that are prevalent on the GMAT. These words and patterns are indicators of specific errors, and should act as "warning signs" when you encounter them on the test. If your Sentence Completion question has an error indicator, you should check that word, phrase, or pattern for the specific error that often accompanies it. For example, if the smart test taker found the word *like* in a sentence, he would immediately verify that *like* is being correctly used to make a comparison, rather than incorrectly used in the place of *as*.

In the following list, you'll find all of the indicators and the characteristic errors that often occur with the word or phrase. We've also listed the chapter in which the error was discussed.

Error Indicator:	**Long phrase between the subject and the verb**
Common Error(s):	Faulty subject verb agreement
Reviewed in:	Chapter Four

Error Indicator:	**The subject comes after the verb (inverted sentence)**
Common Error(s):	Faulty subject verb agreement
Reviewed in:	Chapter Four

Error Indicator:	***The number of***
Common Error(s):	Faulty subject verb agreement
Reviewed in:	Chapter Four
Notes:	Remember that *number* is a singular subject. However, the object of the preposition *of* will often be plural, such as *the number of applicants*. This will lead many test takers to use a plural verb, when a singular verb is required.

Error Indicator:	*Each* or *every*
Common Error(s):	Faulty subject verb agreement
	Faulty pronoun antecedent agreement
Reviewed in:	Chapter Four and Chapter Five
Notes:	*Each* and *every* are always singular, but are often assigned plural verbs or pronouns on the GMAT

Error Indicator:	**The use of *had* with a main verb**
Common Error(s):	Incorrect verb tense
Reviewed in:	Chapter Four

Error Indicator:	**Dates or time periods mentioned in the sentence**
Common Error(s):	Incorrect verb tense
Reviewed in:	Chapter Four
Notes:	Dates and time periods are often the contextual clues for the placement of the verb in the past, present, or future tense.

Error Indicator:	*If*
Common Error(s):	Incorrect verb tense in a conditional clause
Reviewed in:	Chapter Four
Notes:	The word *if* may signify a conditional clause, which is often involved in illegal verb tense errors.

Error Indicator:	**Past participle verb with *to be* as a helping verb (such as *was selected*, *will be driven*, etc.)**
Common Error(s):	Passive voice
Reviewed in:	Chapter Four

Error Indicator:	*They* and *their*
Common Error(s):	Faulty pronoun antecedent agreement
Reviewed in:	Chapter Five
Notes:	The plural personal pronouns *they* and *their* are often used incorrectly with singular antecedents.

Error Indicator:	**Quantifiers, such as *many*, *few*, and *some***
Common Error(s):	Incorrectly matched with count nouns or mass nouns
Reviewed in:	Chapter Six

Error Indicator:	**Introductory modifying clause**
Common Error(s):	Misplaced modifier
Reviewed in:	Chapter Six
Notes:	If a sentence begins with a modifying clause, the subject being modified should immediately follow the clause

SC

Error Indicator:	*Like* or *as*
Common Error(s):	Incorrect word choice
Reviewed in:	Chapter Seven
Notes:	The preposition *like* is used incorrectly for the conjunction *as*.

Error Indicator:	*And* and *or*
Common Error(s):	Incorrect conjunction choice
	Faulty parallelism
Reviewed in:	Chapter Seven and Chapter Eight
Notes:	The coordinating conjunctions *and* and *or* are not interchangeable, so GMAC may use *and* when *or* is more appropriate, and vice versa. More commonly, though, *and* and *or* signify faulty parallelism between the verbs they are connecting.

Error Indicator:	**Correlating conjunctions such as *not only..but also* and *either..or***
Common Error(s):	Incorrect conjunction choice
	Faulty parallelism
Reviewed in:	Chapter Seven
Notes:	Correlative conjunctions must be properly matched with their partner. *Neither* must always be with *nor*, rather than *or*. The GMAT will match these conjunctions with a different ending. Also, the nouns or verbs that follow each part of a correlative conjunction must be parallel. In *not only X, but also Y*, the nouns or verbs that take the place of X and Y must have the same grammatical pattern.

Error Indicator:	*Like, unlike, more, most, less, least, better,* **and** *worse*
Common Error(s):	Incomplete or illogical comparisons
	Faulty parallelism in a comparison
Reviewed in:	Chapter Eight

Error Indicator:	**A semicolon (;)**
Common Error(s):	A dependent clause on either side of the semicolon
Reviewed in:	Chapter Eight
Notes:	A semicolon must separate two independent clauses

You should study this list prior to the test. The more familiar you are with these error indicators, the more likely you are to spot them on the actual GMAT.

Even the most experienced test taker is bound to be faced with a sentence in which an error is not immediately present. The sentence might be grammatically correct, making answer choice (A) the best option. However, before choosing (A) and moving on, read each answer choice and compare it to the original sentence. What was changed? Was it changed for a legitimate reason? If not, you can eliminate the answer choice. But if the change does correct an error, you know that answer choice (A) is no longer correct.

You might also spot a major error immediately and select an answer choice that corrects your error. But do not move on yet! What if there is a minor error in the sentence which you have not noticed? You should always read all of the answer choices and compare them to the original sentence. If there is a minor error, it will be corrected in an answer choice which also corrects the major error. Failing to read all four answer choices can cause you to miss important questions on the test.

Reading the four new answer choices can help you find errors you might otherwise overlook.

Let's look at an example to explore how to use the answer choices:

<u>Several of the canvases that were singed and incinerated in yesterday's museum fire were</u> painted by a famous Russian artist.

   (A)   Several of the canvases that were singed and incinerated in yesterday's museum fire were

   (B)   In yesterday's museum fire, several of the canvases that had been singed and incinerated were

   (C)   Yesterday several of the canvases that were singed or incinerated in the museum fire were

   (D)   Several of the canvases that were singed and incinerated in yesterday's museum fire had been

   (E)   Several of the canvases that were singed or incinerated in yesterday's museum fire had been

Test takers might read this sentence and miss the two errors. The novice test taker would select Choice (A) and move on to the next question, but he would be wrong. The master test taker would start with Choice (B), and compare it to the original sentence:

Original:
<u>Several of the canvases that were singed and incinerated in yesterday's museum fire were</u> painted by a famous Russian artist.

Choice (B):
In yesterday's museum fire, several of the canvases that had been singed and incinerated were painted by a famous Russian artist.

First, Choice (B) moved the modifier *in yesterday's museum fire* to the front of the sentence. Did this modifier need to be moved? No. Is it incorrectly placed in this new location? No, but the sentence structure is changed. It's not an error, but was an unnecessary change. So look at the other difference between

SC

the original and (B). The first simple past tense *were* was changed to the past perfect *had been*. Remember, the past perfect is used to show the first event to take place in the past when there are two events from the past in the same sentence. Which happened first to the canvases? The singeing and incinerating or the painting? The painting occurred first, so *had been* should be attached to the second *were* in the sentence:

> Several of the canvases that were singed and incinerated in yesterday's museum fire *had been* painted by a famous Russian artist.

So we have found one error by looking at what was changed in Choice (B). Which answer choices use *had been* in place of the second *were*? Choices (D) and (E). We can eliminate Choices (A), (B), and (C).

Now compare the original sentence to Choice (D):

> *Original:*
> Several of the canvases that were singed and incinerated in yesterday's museum fire were painted by a famous Russian artist.

> *Choice (D):*
> Several of the canvases that were singed and incinerated in yesterday's museum fire had been painted by a famous Russian artist.

The only difference between these two sentences is the correction of the second *were* to *had been*. Some test takers might hastily choose (D) and move on, but the master test taker would check the final answer choice before making a decision:

> *Original:*
> Several of the canvases that were singed and incinerated in yesterday's museum fire were painted by a famous Russian artist.

> *Choice (E):*
> Several of the canvases that were singed or incinerated in yesterday's museum fire had been painted by a famous Russian artist.

Choice (E) also uses *had been*, but makes a second change that is so small it is often missed. *Singed and incinerated* became *singed or incinerated*. Can something be both *singed* and *incinerated* at the same time? No. It would be one *or* the other, making *or* the correct preposition. Choice (E) is the best answer.

We used the answer choices to find the errors in this sentence. This is an invaluable tool on the Sentence Correction portion of the GMAT. You do not have the time or the ability to record the original sentence and the answer choice on paper; you must make your comparisons by looking at the computer screen. Still, a quick study of each of the words in the original sentence compared to each of the words in the answer choices should alert you to possible errors in the sentence.

SC

Eliminate Answer Choices

An important test-taking skill is the ability to eliminate answer choices. By disregarding certain answers, you save time and increase your chances of selecting correctly when forced to make an educated guess. As we saw in the previous example on analyzing answer choices, we were able to eliminate Choices (A), (B), and (C) after comparing Choice (B) to the original sentence. On a paper and pencil format test, we simply cross off these corresponding letters in the test booklet, but as discussed in Chapter One, the GMAT CAT format can present a challenge to students not used to finding test questions on a computer screen. Instead, we must use our scratch paper or personal whiteboard to create an answer chart, placing *X*s next to the rows for (A), (B), and (C).

While eliminating answer choices, do not mull over one choice too long. Because the test is timed, you cannot spend a lot of time on each answer choice. If you are not sure about the answer choice, leave it as a "contender" and move on. You might find an answer choice further down the list which will clearly eliminate the one you were pondering.

If you find that have eliminated all four of the possible corrections, choose Choice (A), representing no error in the sentence. On occasion you may eliminate all five answer choices. If this occurs, go back to the sentence and reevaluate each answer choice.

Substitute New Words and Phrases

Substitution is a key to the quantitative portion of the GMAT. We substitute numbers for variables and symbols for words. By turning the unfamiliar into the familiar, we are able to grasp concepts and problems which might have appeared unsolvable at first glance.

Substitution also works in the verbal sections of the GMAT. Taking unfamiliar words or language patterns and substituting more familiar forms can help you conquer the toughest test questions. We have highlighted several methods for substitution throughout this book, such as the use of *he* and *him* for *who* and *whom* when determining the correct pronoun choice. But you can also use substitution to test agreement, idiom, and other grammatical rules.

Take, for example, the following sentence with an idiom error:

> The newly enacted term limits prohibited the popular city council chairperson to run for office during the next election.

The idiom occurs in *prohibited the popular city council chairperson to run.*

SC

If the GMAT sentence is too lengthy or confusing, substitute words or variables into the entire phrase to shorten or clarify the expression:

> *prohibited the popular city council chairperson to run*
> prohibited X to Y
> prohibited me to work

Then substitute other words *for prohibited* and *to work*, to make sure that they are correct idiom:

> prohibited me to work
> kept me to work
> prevent me to work
> forbid me to work ✓

> prohibited me to work
> prohibited me of working
> prohibited me in working
> prohibited me from working ✓

At this point, you should realize that the infinitive *to work* belongs with *forbid*, but not *prohibited*. *Prohibited* needs a noun, followed by the preposition *from* and a gerund, such as *working*:

> prohibited X from Y
> prohibited me from working
> *prohibited the popular city council chairperson from running*

The correct sentence reads:

> The newly enacted term limits *prohibited the popular city council chairperson from running* for office during the next election.

This type of substitution can work in several grammatical areas on the GMAT. You can use it to check subject-verb agreement and pronoun-antecedent agreement, substituting a pronoun for a noun or a noun for pronoun:

> In South America and Southern Mexico, a colony of Driver ants, known for their fiercely defensive behavior, have been known to kill immobile livestock, such as tethered cows or corralled horses.   [*Incorrect*]

By removing the prepositional phrase with the subject and the modifying phrase in the center of the sentence, we can isolate the subject and verb:

> a colony have been known

SC

Now, substitute a pronoun for the subject:

it have been known

This is obviously incorrect. The verb should be the singular *has*:

it *has* been known

Now you can correct the original sentence:

In South America and Southern Mexico, a colony of Driver ants, known for their fiercely defensive behavior, *has* been known to kill immobile livestock, such as tethered cows or corralled horses.   [*Correct*]

When presented with a pronoun, substitute the noun antecedent in its place to verify agreement:

During the charity auction, the organization collected over two hundred thousand dollars, nearly twice as much as they expected.

The pronoun in this sentence is *they*. Find its antecedent, and substitute it in the pronoun's place:

During the charity auction, the organization collected over two hundred thousand dollars, nearly twice as much as *the organization* expected.

they = the organization

Can the plural pronoun *they* refer to the singular subject *organization*? No. The correct pronoun must be singular:

During the charity auction, the organization collected over two hundred thousand dollars, nearly twice as much as *it* expected.

You may find other ways to use substitution as you practice for the GMAT. There are not any specific rules for its use; as long as you retain the same sentence structure, you are free to use other words or phrases to make the unfamiliar a little more familiar.

Rearrange the Phrase, Clause, or Sentence ████████

Some sentences are easier to understand or analyze when they are rearranged. We have seen this while working with inverted subjects and verbs and sentences constructed in the passive voice. It is also an important skill in choosing between *who* or *whom*. Look at an example:

> NASA has agreed to send one American astronaut to the International Space Station for a six month experiment, although who it will send has yet to be determined.   [*Incorrect*]

The first step in determining the appropriate pronoun is to separate the clause containing *who* from the rest of the sentence:

> although *who* it will send has yet to be determined

You can even eliminate the excess modifiers and concentrate on the specific phrase with the pronoun:

> *who* it will send

We cannot clearly substitute *he* or *him* while the sentence is in the current arrangement:

> *he* it will send
> *him* it will send

Rearrange the phrase to find the clear pronoun:

> it will send *who*
> it will send *he*
> it will send *him* ✓

Because *him* works in the rearranged phrase, the correct pronoun is *whom*:

> it will send *whom*

Insert *whom* into the original sentence:

> NASA has agreed to send one American astronaut to the International Space Station for a six month experiment, although *whom* it will send has yet to be determined.   [*Correct*]

As in the example above, and covered extensively in Chapter Four, you can remove extraneous words, phrases, and clauses to isolate the offending error. Remember that subjects are never in prepositional phrases and that agreement errors can also occur in clauses.

Use Miscellaneous Strategies

We discussed Choice (A) in Chapter Two, but it bears mentioning again: Do not read answer choice (A). The first answer choice is an exact replica of the underlined portion of the original sentence. If you read Choice (A), you waste valuable time that can be spent on other answer choices or sentences.

If you know that the original sentence contains an error, but are unable to determine the proper correction, pick the shortest answer choice. This is particularly true for questions that have a wordy or awkward underlined portion. GMAC often tests for concise sentences—those that express the intended meaning in as few words as possible—thus the shortest answer is often correct.

Finally, after choosing an answer choice, read the entire sentence again, only this time with your correction in place of the underlined portion. Make sure that the sentence looks and sounds grammatically correct. If your answer choice meets these qualifications, choose it and move on to the next problem.

Practice

Here at PowerScore, we cannot adequately stress the importance of completing as many practice questions as possible. By working through real GMAT questions, you'll be able to implement strategies and concepts you've learned in this book, as well as discover patterns that tend to repeat throughout the test. It is extremely important to use real test questions during your study session; simulated questions do not always reflect the proper sentence structure or content that is used on the GMAT. Real sentence correction questions are available in two books produced by GMAC: *The Official Guide for GMAT Review* and *The Official Guide for the GMAT Verbal Review*. They also publish a guide for quantitative review. All three books are available on our website at www.powerscore.com, or by calling our offices at (800) 545-1750. We have provided you with twenty more practice questions in the following problem set, but we highly recommend that you complete all of the real questions in GMAC's two official guides.

SC

Sentence Completion Strategies Problem Set

Please complete the problem set and review the answer key and explanations. *Answers on page 447.*

1. Although he had proposed funding cuts to the CIA <u>while being a senator</u>, John Kerry sought to bolster military spending after the American terrorist attacks.

   (A) while being a senator
   (B) while in Senate
   (C) at the time of him being a senator
   (D) as being a senator
   (E) as a senator

2. <u>An article about the "Seinfeld Curse," which was published just before *The New Adventure's of Old Christine* were cast</u>, predicted that Julia Louis-Dreyfus would be the only former Seinfeld cast member to succeed in another sitcom.

   (A) An article about the "Seinfeld Curse," which was published just before *The New Adventure's of Old Christine* were cast
   (B) An article about the "Seinfeld Curse," which was published just before *The New Adventure's of Old Christine* was cast
   (C) An article about the "Seinfeld Curse," published just before *The New Adventure's of Old Christine* were cast
   (D) *The New Adventure's of Old Christine* was cast just before an article about the "Seinfeld Curse" was published,
   (E) *The New Adventure's of Old Christine,* cast just before an article about the "Seinfeld Curse" was published

3. Due to the decrease in active lifestyles and the increase in high-fat diets, the adult obesity rate in the United Kingdom <u>increased by more than threefold</u> from 1980 to 2006.

   (A) increased by more than threefold
   (B) increased by more than triple
   (C) increased more than three times
   (D) more than tripled
   (E) had more than tripled

4. While some propose to improve bus transportation and timing for the school district's students by changing bus routes, others <u>by suggesting fining the bus company to increase the incentive for on-time pick-ups, and still others by demanding</u> the district use a different transportation company.

   (A) by suggesting fining the bus company to increase the incentive for on-time pick-ups, and still others by demanding
   (B) suggest fining the bus company to increase the incentive for on-time pick-ups, and still others demand
   (C) suggest the fine of the bus company to increase the incentive for on-time pick-ups, and still others by demanding
   (D) suggest the fining of the bus company to increase the incentive for on-time pick-ups, and still others are demanding
   (E) by suggesting the fining of the bus company and increasing the incentive for on-time pick-ups, and still others demand

5. According to the latest education report, <u>the number of teachers working without valid certificates has increased</u> by thirteen percent in the last ten years.

   (A) the number of teachers working without valid certificates has increased
   (B) teachers working without valid certificates have been increasing
   (C) the number of teachers working without valid certificates have increased
   (D) there have been increases in the number of teachers working without valid certificates
   (E) an increasing number of teachers have been working without valid certificates

SC

Sentence Completion Strategies Problem Set

6. <u>A vault was so securely constructed and reinforced in the San Francisco bank that</u> even a magnitude seven earthquake did not disturb the vault's contents.

    (A) A vault was so securely constructed and reinforced in the San Francisco bank that
    (B) So securely was a vault construction and reinforcement in the San Francisco bank
    (C) It was so secure that a vault was constructed and reinforced in the San Francisco bank
    (D) A vault that was so securely constructed and reinforced in the San Francisco bank
    (E) Constructed and reinforced so securely in the San Francisco bank was a vault that

7. Representatives from the college, <u>one who</u> is a member of the admissions board, will be available to talk to potential students about applications, personal statements, and standardized test scores.

    (A) one who
    (B) one of whom
    (C) one of which
    (D) one of them whom
    (E) with one of them who

8. The sex of baby alligators and many other reptiles—such as crocodiles and snapping turtles—<u>are determined from the temperature of the nest; above</u> ninety degrees yields males, while lower temperatures yield females.

    (A) are determined from the temperature of the nest; above
    (B) is determined from the temperature of the nest; temperatures above
    (C) is determined by the temperature of the nest; temperatures above
    (D) are determined by the temperature of the nest; those above
    (E) is determined from nest temperature; rising above

9. Unlike an interest-bearing checking account, which requires a minimum deposit and monthly balance, <u>a customer who opens a free checking account is not required to maintain</u> a specific balance.

    (A) a customer who opens a free checking account is not required to maintain
    (B) with a free checking account there is no requirement of
    (C) a free checking account does not require the customer to maintain
    (D) free checking account customers are not required to maintain
    (E) for the free checking account customer there is no requirement of

10. <u>Each of the Pacific Northwest states—Washington, Oregon, Montana, and Idaho—were admitted in the Union</u> in the nineteenth century, following the Lewis and Clark Expedition.

    (A) Each of the Pacific Northwest states—Washington, Oregon, Montana, and Idaho—were admitted in the Union
    (B) Washington, Oregon, Montana, and Idaho—each of the Pacific Northwest states—was admitted in the Union
    (C) Admitted to the Union, each of the Pacific Northwest states—Washington, Oregon, Montana, and Idaho—were
    (D) Washington, Oregon, Montana, and Idaho—the Pacific Northwest states—each one was admitted to the Union
    (E) Each of the Pacific Northwest states—Washington, Oregon, Montana, and Idaho—was admitted to the Union

Sentence Completion Strategies Problem Set Answer Key

Correct answers are in bold.

1. Although he had proposed funding cuts to the CIA <u>while being a senator</u>, John Kerry sought to bolster military spending after the American terrorist attacks.

    (A) while being a senator
    (B) while in Senate
    (C) at the time of him being a senator
    (D) as being a senator
    (E) as a senator

Being is rarely used correctly on the GMAT. In this sentence, it is wordy and unidiomatic. Choices (C) and (D) repeat this wordiness. Choice (B) causes some ambiguity in determining who or what was in the Senate. Choice (E) concisely corrects the error.

2. <u>An article about the "Seinfeld Curse," which was published just before *The New Adventures of Old Christine* were cast</u>, predicted that Julia Louis-Dreyfus would be the only former *Seinfeld* cast member to succeed in another sitcom.

    (A) An article about the "Seinfeld Curse," which was published just before *The New Adventures of Old Christine* were cast
    (B) An article about the "Seinfeld Curse," which was published just before *The New Adventures of Old Christine* **was cast**
    (C) An article about the "Seinfeld Curse," published just before *The New Adventures of Old Christine* were cast
    (D) *The New Adventures of Old Christine* was cast just before an article about the "Seinfeld Curse" was published
    (E) *The New Adventures of Old Christine,* cast just before an article about the "Seinfeld Curse" was published

The title of the television show, *The New Adventures of Old Christine*, might trick test takers into choosing a plural verb (*were*), but there is only one television show, thus requiring a singular verb (*was*). Choice (B) makes this correction.

3. Due to the decrease in active lifestyles and the increase in high-fat diets, the adult obesity rate in the United Kingdom <u>increased by more than threefold</u> from 1980 to 2006.

    (A) increased by more than threefold
    (B) increased by more than triple
    (C) increased more than three times
    (D) more than tripled
    (E) had more than tripled

Choice (A) uses the preposition *by*, but does not provide a noun object for the preposition, since *threefold* is an adjective. Choice (B) makes the same error, but uses the adjective *triple*. Choice (C) changes the meaning of the sentence, indicating that adult obesity rates increased on three separate occasions. Choice (D) is correct because it is concise and it uses proper idiom. Choice (E) also uses correct idiom, but it incorrectly uses the past perfect tense (*had*), since there is only one past tense verb in the sentence.

4. While some propose to improve bus transportation and timing for the school district's students by changing bus routes, others <u>by suggesting fining the bus company to increase the incentive for on-time pick-ups, and still others by demanding</u> the district use a different transportation company.

(A) by suggesting fining the bus company to increase the incentive for on-time pick-ups, and still others by demanding

(B) suggest fining the bus company to increase the incentive for on-time pick-ups, and still others demand

(C) suggest the fine of the bus company to increase the incentive for on-time pick-ups, and still others by demanding

(D) suggest the fining of the bus company to increase the incentive for on-time pick-ups, and still others are demanding

(E) by suggesting the fining of the bus company and increasing the incentive for on-time pick-ups, and still others demand

The correct answer choice, Choice (B), creates a parallel construction with *some propose, others suggest, and still others demand*. Choices (A) and (E) lose parallelism with *by suggesting*. Choice (C) uses the wordy *the fine of the bus company* and loses parallelism with *by demanding*. Choice (D) also uses a wordy expression, *the fining of*. It also loses paralellism with *are demanding*.

5. According to the latest education report, <u>the number of teachers working without valid certificates has increased</u> by thirteen percent in the last ten years.

(A) the number of teachers working without valid certificates has increased

(B) teachers working without valid certificates have been increasing

(C) the number of teachers working without valid certificates have increased

(D) there have been increases in the number of teachers working without valid certificates

(E) an increasing number of teachers have been working without valid certificates

The sentence is correct. Because the subject is *number*, Choice (A) correctly uses the singular *has*. Choices (C), (D), and (E) violate subject and verb agreement by using *the number..have*. The verb in Choice (B) suggests that the thirteen point increase has occurred every year, rather than cumulatively over ten years.

6. <u>A vault was so securely constructed and reinforced in the San Francisco bank that</u> even a magnitude seven earthquake did not disturb the vault's contents.

(A) A vault was so securely constructed and reinforced in the San Francisco bank that

(B) So securely was a vault construction and reinforcement in the San Francisco bank

(C) It was so secure that a vault was constructed and reinforced in the San Francisco bank

(D) A vault that was so securely constructed and reinforced in the San Francisco bank

(E) Constructed and reinforced so securely in the San Francisco bank was a vault that

The correct idiom is *so X that Y*, which is used in the original sentence: *so securely contracted and reinforced that even an earthquake did not disturb its contents*. Choice (A) is correct.

7. Representatives from the college, <u>one who</u> is a member of the admissions board, will be available to talk to potential students about applications, personal statements, and standardized test scores.

   (A) one who
   (B) one of whom
   (C) one of which
   (D) one of them whom
   (E) with one of them who

The *one* is referring to one of the representatives, so we must use *who* or *whom* to refer to a person. This eliminates Choice (C). Just as we say *one of the representatives*, we must say *one of who* or *one of whom*. Since the pronoun is following the preposition *of*, it must be *whom*. *One of whom* in Choice (B) is the correct.

8. The sex of baby alligators and many other reptiles—such as crocodiles and snapping turtles—<u>are determined from the temperature of the nest; above</u> ninety degrees yields males, while lower temperatures yield females.

   (A) are determined from the temperature of the nest; above
   (B) is determined from the temperature of the nest; temperatures above
   (C) is determined by the temperature of the nest; temperatures above
   (D) are determined by the temperature of the nest; those above
   (E) is determined by nest temperature; rising above

This sentence has errors in several areas: subject and verb agreement, idiom, and semicolons. Begin with subject and verb agreement. The subject is *sex*, a singular noun, rather than *alligators*. The correct verb, then, is *is*, rather than *are*. This eliminates Choices (A) and (D). The next error is idiom. The correct idiom is *determined by* (not *determined from*), which eliminates choice (B). Finally, we must put an independent clause on each side of the semicolon. Choice (E) does not have a subject for *rising above* (what is rising above?), so it is a fragment. Only Choice (C) makes all three corrections.

9. Unlike an interest-bearing checking account, which requires a minimum deposit and monthly balance, <u>a customer who opens a free checking account is not required to maintain</u> a specific balance.

   (A) a customer who opens a free checking account is not required to maintain
   (B) with a free checking account there is no requirement of
   (C) a free checking account does not require the customer to maintain
   (D) free checking account customers are not required to maintain
   (E) for the free checking account customer there is no requirement of

This sentence contains an illogical comparison; *the interest-bearing checking account* is compared to *a customer*. It must compare the *an interest-bearing checking account* to *a free checking account*. Only Choice (C) makes this logical comparison (note that *free checking account* is an adjective in Choices (D) and (E)).

10. <u>Each of the Pacific Northwest states—Washington, Oregon, Montana, and Idaho—were admitted in the Union</u> in the nineteenth century, following the Lewis and Clark Expedition.

   (A) Each of the Pacific Northwest states—Washington, Oregon, Montana, and Idaho—were admitted in the Union

   (B) Washington, Oregon, Montana, and Idaho—each of the Pacific Northwest states—was admitted in the Union

   (C) Admitted to the Union, each of the Pacific Northwest states—Washington, Oregon, Montana, and Idaho—were

   (D) Washington, Oregon, Montana, and Idaho—the Pacific Northwest states—each one was admitted to the Union

   (E) Each of the Pacific Northwest states—Washington, Oregon, Montana, and Idaho—was admitted to the Union

Remember that *each* and *every* are always singular subjects. *States* is not the subject because it is in a prepositional phrase. Similarly, the names of the states are not a compound subject, because they are in a phrase separated by dashes. *Each* is the subject and should be paired with the singular *was*, rather than the plural *were*. Only Choice (E) makes this correction. Choice (B) incorrectly uses a compound subject with *was*. Choice (C) makes the same error as (A), and Choice (D) creates a fragment with the names of the states.

CHAPTER TWENTY-THREE: TEST READINESS

The day before the test

On the day before your GMAT appointment, we recommend that you study very little, if at all. The best approach for most students is to simply relax as much as possible. Read a book, see a movie, or play a round of golf. If you feel you must study, we recommend that you only briefly review each of the concepts covered in this book.

If you are not familiar with the location of your test center, drive by the test center and survey the parking situation. This will alleviate anxiety or confusion on the day of the test.

Eat only bland or neutral foods the night before the test and try to get the best sleep possible.

The morning of the test

Attempt to follow your normal routine on the morning of the test. For example, if you read the paper every morning, do so on the day of the test. If you do not regularly drink coffee, do not start on test day. Constancy in your routine will allow you to focus on your primary objective: performing well on the test.

Dress in layers, so you will be warm if the test center is cold, but also able to shed clothes if the test center is hot.

You must arrive at the test center approximately 30 minutes before your scheduled appointment time.

We strongly believe that performing well requires confidence and a belief that you can perform well. As you prepare to leave for the test, run though the test in your head, visualizing an exceptional performance. Imagine how you will react to each math problem, essay question, and verbal problem. Many athletes use this same visualization technique to achieve optimal performance.

The following pages contain general notes on preparing for the day of the GMAT.

Do not study hard the day before the test. If you haven't learned the material by then, that final day won't make much difference.

At the test center

Upon check-in, test supervisors will ask you for acceptable personal identification (typically a driver's license or a passport). Supervisors are instructed to deny admission to anyone who does not present a photo ID containing a signature. They may also take a thumbprint, photograph you, or videotape you.

The test supervisors will assign each examinee a work station. You are not permitted to choose your own station.

Once you are seated, testing will begin promptly.

Food and drink are not allowed in the testing room.

You may not leave your work station during the timed portions of the test.

Yes, you read that correctly. You may be thumbprinted or photographed at the test center. This is done for test security purposes.

If you engage in any misconduct or irregularity during the test, you may be dismissed from the test center and may be subject to other penalties for misconduct or irregularity. Actions that could warrant such consequences include creating a disturbance, giving or receiving help, removing scratch paper or notes from the testing room, eating or drinking during the test, taking part in an act of impersonation or other forms of cheating, or using books, calculators, ear plugs, headsets, rulers, or other aids. The penalties for misconduct are high: you may be precluded from attending business school.

If you encounter a problem with the test or test center itself, report it to a test administrator. Reportable problems include power outages, computer malfunctions, and any unusual disturbances caused by an individual.

If you feel anxious or panicked for any reason before or during the test, close your eyes for a few seconds and relax. Think of other situations where you performed with confidence and skill.

After the test

At the end of the test you will be presented with the option of cancelling your score. This is the only opportunity you have to cancel your score, and you must make the decision without the benefit of knowing how you scored. Once a score is cancelled, it cannot be reinstated and you do not receive a refund of your test fee.

If you choose to accept your score, you will immediately see your unofficial scores from the multiple choice sections, and you can print out a copy of your results. Official test results will be mailed to you approximately two weeks after the test.

Thank you for choosing to purchase the *PowerScore GMAT Verbal Bible*. We hope you have found this book useful and enjoyable, but most importantly we hope this book helps raise your GMAT score.

In all of our publications we strive to present the material in the clearest and most informative manner. If you have any questions, comments, or suggestions, please do not hesitate to e-mail us at *gvbible@powerscore.com*. We love to receive feedback, and we do read every e-mail that comes in!

Also, if you have not done so already, we strongly suggest you visit the website for this book at:

www.powerscore.com/gvbible

This free online resource area contains supplements to the book material, provides updates as needed, and answers questions posed by students. There is also an official evaluation form that we encourage you to use.

If we can assist you in any way in your GMAT preparation or in the business school admissions process, please do not hesitate to contact us. We would be happy to help.

Thank you and best of luck on the GMAT!

COMPLETE CHAPTER ANSWER KEY

The chapter-by-chapter answer key lists every problem in this book in chronological order and identifies the classification of the question. You can use this answer key as a quick reference when you are solving problems. Each problem is explained in more detail in the text of the chapter.

Critical Reasoning Section Answer Key ■■■■■■■■■■■■■■■■■■■■■■■■■■

Chapter 2: Logical Reasoning Basics Chapter Text

1. Must	(B)	Page 16

Chapter 4: Must Be True Chapter Text

1. Must	(D)	Page 71
2. Must	(E)	Page 73
3. Must	(B)	Page 79
4. Must	(B)	Page 80
5. Must	(B)	Page 82

Chapter 4: Must Be True Problem Set

1. Must	(A)	Page 86
2. Must	(B)	Page 86
3. Must	(E)	Page 87
4. Must	(C)	Page 87
5. Must	(C)	Page 87
6. Must	(C)	Page 87

Chapter 5: Weaken Chapter Text

1. Weaken	(A)	Page 98
2. Weaken	(B)	Page 100

Chapter 5: Weaken Problem Set

1. Weaken	(B)	Page 104
2. Weaken	(D)	Page 104
3. Weaken	(B)	Page 105
4. Weaken	(A)	Page 105
5. Weaken	(A)	Page 106
6. Weaken	(E)	Page 106

Chapter-by-Chapter Answer Key

Chapter 6: Cause and Effect Chapter Text

1. Flaw-CE	(D)	Page 119

Chapter 6: Cause and Effect Problem Set

1. Weaken-CE	(D)	Page 123
2. Must-CE	(C)	Page 123
3. Weaken-CE	(C)	Page 124
4. Weaken-CE	(B)	Page 124

Chapter 7: Strengthen and Assumption Chapter—Strengthen Text

1. Strengthen	(E)	Page 134
2. StrengthenX	(E)	Page 136
3. StrengthenX-CE	(E)	Page 139

Chapter 7: Strengthen and Assumption Chapter—Strengthen Problem Set

1. Strengthen	(A)	Page 142
2. Strengthen	(B)	Page 142
3. StrengthenX-CE	(B)	Page 143
4. Strengthen-CE	(D)	Page 143

Chapter 7: Strengthen and Assumption Chapter—Assumption Text

1. Assumption	(D)	Page 152
2. Assumption	(A)	Page 154
3. Assumption-CE	(E)	Page 162

Chapter 7: Strengthen and Assumption Chapter—Assumption Problem Set

1. Assumption	(C)	Page 167
2. Assumption	(B)	Page 167
3. Assumption	(D)	Page 168
4. Assumption	(A)	Page 168

Chapter-by-Chapter Answer Key

Chapter 8: Resolve Chapter Text

1. Resolve	(C)	Page 175
2. Resolve	(B)	Page 177

Chapter 8: Resolve Problem Set

1. Resolve	(B)	Page 180
2. Resolve	(A)	Page 180
3. Resolve	(B)	Page 181
4. Resolve	(D)	Page 181

Chapter 9: Numbers and Percentages Chapter Text

1. Must-#%	(C)	Page 188
2. Must-#%	(C)	Page 191
3. Flaw-#%	(B)	Page 195

Chapter 9: Numbers and Percentages Problem Set

1. Flaw-#%	(D)	Page 199
2. Must-#%	(E)	Page 199
3. Assumption-#%	(D)	Page 200

Reading Comprehension Section Answer Key ▐▬▬▬▬▬▬▬▬▬▬▬▬

Chapter 13: Putting It All Together

Practice Passage I   Page 304
  1. C   2. D   3. E   4. E

Practice Passage II   Page 305
  1. B   2. A   3. D   4. E

Chapter 15: Errors Involving Verbs

Subject and Verb Agreement Problem Set

1.	D	Page 328
2.	B	Page 328
3.	E	Page 328
4.	E	Page 328
5.	C	Page 329
6.	E	Page 329

Verb Tense Problem Set

1.	C	Page 340
2.	B	Page 340
3.	D	Page 340
4.	A	Page 340
5.	E	Page 340

Verb Voice Problem Set

1.	C	Page 347
2.	B	Page 347

Chapter 16: Errors with Nouns and Pronouns

Noun Agreement and Pronoun and Antecedent Agreement Problem Set

1.	D	Page 354
2.	D	Page 354
3.	E	Page 355
4.	B	Page 355

Relative Pronouns Problem Set

1.	D	Page 361
2.	A	Page 361
3.	B	Page 361

Ambiguous and Implied Pronouns Problem Set

1.	B	Page 365
2.	A	Page 365
3.	D	Page 365
4.	C	Page 365

Chapter 17: Errors Involving Modifiers

Adjective Versus Adverbs and Quantifiers Problem Set

1.	D	Page 372
2.	C	Page 372
3.	E	Page 373
4.	B	Page 373

Modifier Placement Problem Set

1.	E	Page 379
2.	B	Page 379
3.	E	Page 379

Verb Forms as Modifiers Problem Set

1.	A	Page 383
2.	C	Page 383
3.	E	Page 383

Chapter 18: Errors Involving Conjunctions

Conjunctions Problem Set

1.	B	Page 391
2.	B	Page 391
3.	E	Page 391

Chapter 19: Errors in Construction

Comparisons Problem Set

1.	D	Page 397
2.	C	Page 397
3.	B	Page 397

Parallel Structure Problem Set

1.	D	Page 406
2.	C	Page 406
3.	A	Page 406
4.	E	Page 407
5.	E	Page 407
6.	C	Page 407

Chapter-by-Chapter Answer Key

Semicolons Problem Set

1.	B	Page 411
2.	B	Page 411

Idiom Problem Set

1.	A	Page 417
2.	E	Page 417
3.	B	Page 417
4.	D	Page 417
5.	B	Page 417
6.	C	Page 417

Chapter 20: Errors Involving Style

Wordy Language and Redundancy Problem Set

1.	D	Page 425
2.	E	Page 425
3.	B	Page 425

Chapter 21: Multiple Errors

Double and Triple Errors Problem Set

1.	D	Page 429
2.	B	Page 429
3.	C	Page 429
4.	A	Page 429
5.	C	Page 429
6.	C	Page 429
7.	E	Page 430
8.	B	Page 430
9.	A	Page 430
10.	C	Page 430

Chapter 22: Sentence Correction Strategies

Sentence Correction Strategies Problem Set

1.	E	Page 445
2.	B	Page 445
3.	D	Page 445
4.	B	Page 445
5.	A	Page 445
6.	A	Page 446
7.	B	Page 446
8.	C	Page 446
9.	C	Page 446
10.	E	Page 446

CONTACTING POWERSCORE

POWERSCORE GMAT VERBAL BIBLE INFORMATION:

Student Web Section: www.powerscore.com/gvbible
E-mail: gvbible@powerscore.com

POWERSCORE GMAT COURSE INFORMATION:

Effective GMAT Preparation
Full and Weekend Courses
99th Percentile Instructors
Real GMAT Questions

Web: www.powerscore.com/gmat

POWERSCORE GMAT TUTORING INFORMATION:

One-on-one meetings with a PowerScore GMAT expert.

Web: www.powerscore.com/gmat/content_tutoring.cfm

POWERSCORE BUSINESS SCHOOL ADMISSIONS CONSULTING INFORMATION:

Personalized application and admission assistance.

Web: www.powerscore.com/gmat/content_admissions.cfm

POWERSCORE INTERNATIONAL HEADQUARTERS:

PowerScore
57 Hasell Street
Charleston, SC 29401

Toll-free information number: (800) 545-1750
Facsimile: (843) 414-6998
Website: www.powerscore.com
E-mail: gmat@powerscore.com